ADVANCES IN THE SOCIOLOGY OF LANGUAGE – I

Contributions to the Sociology of Language

1

Edited by
Joshua A. Fishman
Yeshiva University

MOUTON · THE HAGUE · PARIS

Advances in the Sociology of Language

Volume I
Basic Concepts, Theories and Problems:
Alternative Approaches

Edited by
Joshua A. Fishman
Yeshiva University

MOUTON · THE HAGUE · PARIS

2nd edition, 1976

ISBN: 90-279-7732-1 (clothbound)

Jacket design by Jurriaan Schrofer

© 1971, Mouton & Co, The Hague

Printed in the Netherlands by Mouton & Co, Printers, The Hague

Dedicated to the
memory of Max Weinreich,
peerless sociologist
of language, mentor
and friend.

Preface

Joshua A. Fishman

ADVANCES IN THE SOCIOLOGY OF LANGUAGE

In many fields of inquiry books of readings have recently proliferated to such an extent that it has become necessary to consider whether or not they contribute to scholarship (Onuf 1969). The sociology of language, I believe, is not yet overburdened with such collections and it is my hope that the present two-volume collection may be as well received and as much utilized by colleagues and students as was the one that it attempts to update (Fishman 1968).

A FORMATIVE HALF-DECADE

Much has happened to the sociology of language in the six years that have elapsed since the summer of 1964 when the Committee on Sociolinguistics of the Social Science Research Council convened a group of linguists and social scientists for eight weeks of joint study (Ferguson 1965). Not the least of these has been the alacrity with which the co-existence of *the sociology of language* and *sociolinguistics* has been accepted by various segments of the scholarly community. Writing in 1964 (when the first *Readings* were actually completed, only to be delayed for four years on the publisher's assembly line) it seemed clear to me that *sociology of language* implied a broader field of interest, and one that was less linguacentric, than did *sociolinguistics*. In the last few years I have found linguists more willing to grant this point and sociologists more insistent in connection with it than I had ever dreamt would be the case. Therefore, after having succumbed briefly to the more exotic appellation (e.g. Fishman 1970), I have subsequently returned whole-heartedly to my original usage and to the one which is in closer agreement with my own interests and sympathies (Fishman 1971). I believe that many of those who still refer to "sociolinguistics" in the current collection will also come to prefer "the sociology of language" in the years to come, particularly as the differing implications of these two names and the approaches they signify become more widely recognized.

SOCIOLINGUISTICS

After all is said and done, the differences between these two areas or emphases of specialization may well be far less significant than their similarities. Both are concerned with the interpenetration between societally patterned variation in language usage and variation in other societally patterned behavior, whether viewed in intra-communal or in inter-communal perspective. However, the adherents of *sociolinguistics* tend to stress the first part of this definition ("societally patterned variation in language usage"), finding in such emphasis a welcome expansion of the more traditional approaches to the underlying regularity of language. Sociolinguistics has been viewed, very largely, as a means of widening the contextual horizons of linguistics, beyond the phrase, beyond the sentence, beyond the utterance, to the speech act, the speech event and the speech occasion. Social units such as the latter (and other units by means of which they are ethnographically detailed) can be demonstrated to regulate, predict or generate systematic phonological, syntactic, morphological and sema:.:ic patterns where only free variation or weak. structure would be evident without their aid.

Essentially then, sociolinguistics has normally accepted the linguistic pursuit of system-in-language, although it has usually derived such system from the data of natural speaking (or natural writing) per se, rather than from more artificial corpuses elicited from informants. As a result, in the space of half a decade, erstwhile sociolinguists have come to claim or admit that what they were doing was "really linguistics" – perhaps of a somewhat broader, newer kind, a kind that recognized social-contextual units as well as the more traditional intra-code units – and that the term sociolinguistics might ultimately no longer be needed once most linguists came to recognize and accept the newer approaches and goals with which the broader contextualization of language structures was associated. Thus, the leading advocates and adherents of *sociolinguistics* are also commonly the ones that prophesy its earliest demise, not for lack of success but, on the contrary, as a result of hopefully carrying the day within the fold of linguistics proper.

SOCIOLOGY OF LANGUAGE

No such self-liquidating prophecy characterizes the sociology of language. It does not seek to capture or replace sociology as a whole or any of its specializations. Nor does it merely seek to relate communicative content or whole-code designations to social categories or social structures. Certainly it seeks whatever level of linguistic sophistication may be necessary in focusing upon micro-level or macro-level social processes and social problems. Rather than emphasize the ethnography of communication as an end in and of itself *the sociology of language* would hope to utilize the ethnography of communication, as it would utilize sociolinguistics and social science more generally, in order to more fully explain variation in societally patterned behaviors pertaining to language maintenance and language shift, language nationalism and language planning, etc. However, not only are supportive and adversary behaviors toward particular languages or language varieties close to the heart of the sociology of language but so are group self-identification behaviors, group formation and dissolution processes, network permeability differentials, referential membership behaviors, language attitudes and beliefs, etc. All in all then, the *sociology of language* is concerned with language varieties as targets, as obstacles and as facilitators, and with the users and uses of language varieties as aspects of *more encompassing social patterns or processes*.

The relationship between the sociology of language and sociolinguistics is thus a part-whole relationship, with the whole not only being greater than any of the parts but also greater than the sum of all of the parts taken separately. While continuing to use the adjectival and adverbial modifier *sociolinguistic* it is now clearer to me than it was in the past that the sociology of language has a path of its own to follow. Those colleagues who joined and encouraged me in the organization of committees on the sociology of language in the International Sociological Association and in the American Sociological Association have in many instances seen this path more quickly and more clearly than I and have increasingly clarified the differences between the sociology of language and sociolinguistics which I initially recognized largely on an intuitive level in 1964.

SEVERAL RECENT DEVELOPMENTS

The current two volume collection reflects the increased sophistication, subtlety and interdisciplinary grasp of specialists in the sociology of language in comparison to that which obtained half a decade
earlier. In comparison to the collection that preceded the present
one the sociology of language currently appears to be:

(a) substantially more *integrated* around systematic questions
rather than merely descriptive, fragmentary or accidental in focus.

(b) substantially more *data oriented,* as distinct from merely
programmatic or argumentative.

(c) substantially more *quantitative,* as distinct from ethnographic,
anecdotal or observational in so far as data analysis is concerned, and

(d) substantially more *interdisciplinary,* combining both linguistic
and social science skills at an advanced level, rather than referring to
one parent discipline or the other in a purely passive or ceremonial vein.

All four of the above mentioned characteristics or trends of more
recent sociology of language strike the compiler of this collection
not only as being essentially praiseworthy but also as further justifying
and solidifying the designation of the field itself. The movement from
bias to theory and from theory to data (and, by and large, to pub-
licly verifiable data) should not only make possible better theory
in the future but should also make possible a stronger movement
from data to application. The tendency to quantify is not only a tendency toward greater precision and rigor but also makes possible
more difficult questions as well as more complex models than would
otherwise be feasible. The genuinely interdisciplinary nature of the
work indicates that one who is merely a "linguistics appreciator" in
the sociology of language will soon be as dated and as limited as one
who is merely a "music appreciator" in the field of musicology. Hopefully, "sociology appreciators" will also become increasingly rare
among linguists who claim to have serious interests in language and
society. There is much evidence of such a trend too in many of the
papers included in this collection.

A final indication of the greater maturation and stabilization of this
field relative to its position half a decade ago is the fact that most of
those whose work is sampled in this collection are fully identified
with the sociology of language or an allied field, are continuing to
revise and advance their work in this connection, and may be expected to remain active in it for many years to come.

SPECIALIZED AND GENERAL INTEREST

In order to fully reflect tendencies (a) and (d), above, volume I of this 2 volume collection has been specifically devoted to *Basic Concepts, Theories and Problems: Alternative Approaches*. In order to fully reflect tendencies (b) and (c), above, volume II has been particularly devoted to *Selected Studies and Applications*. Although there is undoubtedly a direct relationship between these four matters the separation into two volumes should permit students and instructors to more intensively utilize one *or* the other, if that is in accord with their preference, and to do so with greater ease (and at lower cost) than would be the case with a doubly large one-volume collection. Instructors eager to stress theoretical issues and to illustrate them via their own favorite choice of up-to-date as well as "classical" readings may well prefer to require volume I, leaving volume II for less intensive library use in conjunction with journal articles of a varied nature. However, in those settings (academic and applied) in which a balanced variety of recent empirical studies and applied considerations is more difficult to come by than is personally pleasing integrative approach, volume II may well represent required reading, while volume I may be consulted less intensively. Finally, the current and prospective specialist or devotee, for whom the sociology of language as a whole is a field of wide-ranging and rather permanent interest and concern, may well find both volumes to be essential in his study and research. Such, at least, is my hope and expectation.

INTERNATIONAL SOCIOLOGY OF LANGUAGE

The truly international nature of the sociology of language as a field of inquiry is somewhat masked in this collection by the monolingual nature of its contents. Nevertheless, the uniformity of language of publication is of far less significance with respect to the richness of this field than is the great and welcome diversity in the backgrounds of the scholars involved in it and the even greater diversity in the societies and social settings that these scholars have examined.

THANKS

Obviously, a rather large group of students, colleagues and friends deserves to be thanked for helping with the selection of papers and with the preparation of this collection more generally. In this connection I would like to particularly thank not only those authors (and publishers) who gladly granted the permissions without which this volume could not have appeared, but also those authors who helped persuade various publishers to permit republication, and even those authors who sought to influence their publishers along similar lines but who were not successful in doing so. To all of them go my heartfelt thanks for their implied complement, both to me and to the sociology of language.

Jerusalem, 1970

REFERENCES

Ferguson, Charles A.,
  1965 "Directions in sociolinguistics; report on an interdisciplinary seminar", *SSRC Items,* 19, no. 1, 1-4.
Fishman, Joshua A.,
  1968 *Readings in the Sociology of Language* (The Hague, Mouton).
  1970 *Sociolinguistics; A Brief Introduction* (Rowley, Mass., Newbury House).
  1971 "The sociology of language; an interdisciplinary social science approach to language in society", Volume I, this collection (Also in *Current Trends in Linguistics,* 19ʳ¹ ¹, 12, 1629-1784, and as a volume published by Newbury House, Rowley, Mass.)
Onuf, Nicholas G.,
  1969 "Do books of readings contribute to scholarship?" *International Organization,* 23, 98-114.

Contents

Susan M. Ervin-Tripp

SOCIOLINGUISTICS*

I. INTRODUCTION

Group therapy session:
Joe: Ken face it, you're a poor little rich kid.
Ken: Yes, Mommy. Thank you.

Class notes No. 11 of Harvey Sacks

Classroom scene:
Mrs. Tripp: Miss Hayashijima?
Student: Yes, sir.

The possibility of insult and of humor based on linguistic choices means that members agree on the underlying rules of speech and on the social meaning of linguistic features. Linguistic selection is deeply enmeshed in the structure of society; members can readily recognize and interpret socially codified deviations from the norms.

During the past few years, the systematic study of the relation of linguistic forms and social meaning has greatly accelerated. The formal recognition of a field of sociolinguistics has been marked in the United States by courses, programs, seminars, and textbooks (Bright, 1966; Fishman, 1968; Hymes, 1964b; Gumperz and Hymes, 1964, in press; Lieberson, 1966). In two respects, the recent history of the field seems different from that of psycholinguistics. Psychologists

* From: *Advances in Experimental Social Psychology* 4 (1969), 91-165 (Leonard Berkowitz, ed.). New York, Academic Press. Reprinted with permission.

were largely consumers in the interaction between the fields of psychology and linguistics. Out of concerns that arose from theoretical questions indigenous to psychology, they found that linguistic methods and concepts could provide entirely new ways of accounting for phenomena they had already observed and raise new questions of great interest to them as psychologists. In contrast, many of the central figures in the development of sociolinguistics are regarded as linguists and have developed their sociolinguistic concepts because they found social features continually central to linguistic descriptions. A second difference lies in the disciplinary diversity of social scientists; it is not clear just what the 'socio-' implies in the new field. It will be obvious in this article that anthropologists, sociologists, social psychologists, and psychotherapists all have trodden on the terrain we shall define as sociolinguistic, without being much aware of each other.

This article is confined to micro-sociolinguistics, though some references to larger social phenomena are unavoidable. Sociolinguistics in this context will include studies of the components of face-to-face interaction as they bear on, or are affected by, the formal structure of speech. These components may include the personnel, the situation, the function of the interaction, the topic and message, and the channel. As Fishman has pointed out, sociolinguistics is thus distinct from "communication". "It is concerned with *characteristics of the code* and their relationship to characteristics of the communicators or the communication situation, rather than with message or communication functions and processes alone" 1967, p. 590.

During the past decade, psycholinguistics has been profoundly affected by the impact of structural linguistics. Psychologists have come to recognize that verbal output and comprehension are guided by 'rules',[1] so that unique sentences can be produced and understood by speakers in the same speech community. Currently, performance models are beginning to be developed which can account for speech, imitation, comprehension, and other forms of performance, and studies are being made of the development of these abilities in children and of the interpretation of deviant utterances (Chapman, 1967; Ervin-Tripp and Slobin, 1966; Slobin and Welsh, 1967).

In this article, evidence will be assembled to show that the rules of verbal output and comprehension must be organized to specify social features. We can assume that the next step will be the development of sociolinguistic performance models, studies of socialization and the development of sociolinguistic competence (Slama-Cazacu,

---

[1] 'Rules' in this article are not prescriptive but descriptive. They may not be in conscious awareness. Unlike habits, they may include complex structures inferred from the occurrence of interpretable and appropriate novel behavior.

1960; Slobin, 1967), and research on the interpretation of sociolinguistically deviant behavior.

This article has three main sections. The first will provide some detailed examples of what kinds of sociolinguistic rules we can expect to find, the second will define specific features which may be the components of sociolinguistic rules, and the third will examine examples of research on differences in rules between different speech communities.

II. SOCIOLINGUISTIC RULES

A. Alternation Rules

1. American Rules of Address

A scene on a public street in contemporary U.S.:
"What's your name, boy?" the policeman asked ....
"Dr. Poussaint. I'm a physician ...."
"What's your first name, boy? ..."
"Alvin."

Poussaint (1967, p. 53)

Anybody familiar with American address rules (see footnote 1) can tell us the feelings reported by Dr. Poussaint: "As my heart palpitated, I muttered in profound humiliation .... For the moment, my manhood had been ripped from me .... No amount of self-love could have salvaged my pride or preserved my integrity ... [I felt] self-hate." It is possible to specify quite precisely the rule employed by the policeman. Dr. Poussaint's overt, though coerced, acquiescence in a public insult through widely recognized rules of address is the source of his extreme emotion.

Brown and Ford (Hymes, 1964b) have done pioneering and ingenious research on forms of address in American English, using as corpora American plays, observed usage in a Boston business firm, and reported usage of business executives. They found primarily first name (FN) reciprocation or title plus last name (TLN) reciprocation. However, asymmetrical exchanges were found where there was age difference or occupational rank difference. Intimacy was related to the use of multiple names.

Expanding their analysis from my own rules of address. I have found the structure expressed in the diagram in Fig. 1. The advantage of formal diagraming is that it offers precision greater than that of discursive description (Hymes, 1967). The type of diagram presented here, following Geoghegan (in press), is to be read like a computer flow

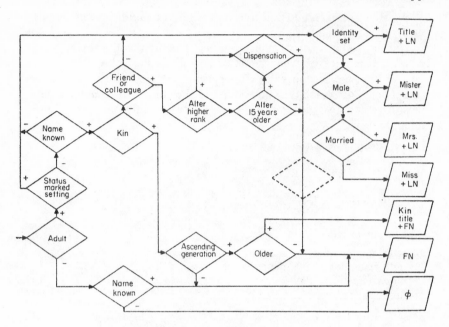

Fig. 1. An American address system.

chart. The entrance point is on the left, and from left to right there is a series of selectors, usually binary. Each path through the diagram leads to a possible outcome, that is, one of the possible alternative forms of address.

Note that the set of paths, or the rule, is like a formal grammar in that it is a way of representing a logical model. The diagram is not intended as a model of a process of the actual decision sequence by which a speaker chooses a form of address or a listener interprets one. The two structures may or may not correspond. In any case, the task of determining the structure implicit in people's knowledge of what forms of address are possible and appropriate is clearly distinct from the task of studying how people, in real situations and in real time, make choices. The criteria and methods of the two kinds of study are quite different. Just as two individuals who share the same grammar might not share the same performance rules, so two individuals might have different decision or interpretation procedures for sociolinguistic alternatives, but still might have an identical logical structure to their behavior.

The person whose knowledge of address is represented in Fig. 1 is assumed to be a competent adult member of a western American academic community. The address forms which are the 'outcomes' to be accounted for might fit in frames like "Look, – – – –, it's time to leave". The outcomes themselves are formal sets, with alternative realizations. For example, first names may alternate with nicknames, as will be indicated in a later section. One possible outcome is no-naming, indicated in Fig. 1 by the linguistic symbol for zero [Ø].

The diamonds indicate selectors. They are points where the social categories allow different paths. At first glance, some selectors look like simple external features, but the social determinants vary accor-ding to the system, and the specific nature of the categories must be discovered by ethnographic means. For example, 'older' implies know-ledge of the range of age defined as contemporary. In some southeast Asian systems, even one day makes a person socially older.

The first selector checks whether the addressee is a child or not. In face-to-face address, if the addressee is a child, all of the other dis-tinctions can be ignored. What is the dividing line between adult and child? In my own system, it seems to be school-leaving age, at around age 18. An employed 16-year-old might be classified as an adult.

Status-marked situations are settings such as the courtroom, the large faculty meeting, or Congress, where status is clearly specified, speech style is rigidly prescribed, and the form of address of each person is derived from his social identity, for example, "Your honor", "Mr. Chairman". The test for establishing the list of such settings is whether personal friendships are apparent in the address forms or whether they are neutralized (or masked) by the formal requirements of the set-ting. There are, of course, other channels by which personal relations might be revealed, but here we are concerned only with address alter-nations, not with tone of voice, connotations of lexicon, and so on.

Among nonkin, the dominant selector of first-naming is whether alter is classified as having the status of a colleague or social acquain-tance. When introducing social acquaintances or new work colleagues, it is necessary to employ first names so that the new acquaintances can first-name each other immediately. Familiarity is not a factor within dyads of the same age and rank, and there are no options. For an American assistant professor to call a new colleague of the same rank and age "Professor Watkins" or "Mr. Watkins" would be considered strange, at least on the West Coast.

Rank here refers to a hierarchy within a working group, or to ranked statuses like teacher–pupil. In the American system, no dis-tinction in address is made to equals or subordinates since both receive FN. The distinction may be made elswhere in the linguistic system, for example, in the style of requests used. We have found that subor-dinates outside the family receive direct commands in the form of imperatives more often than equals, to whom requests are phrased in other ways at least in some settings (see below).

A senior alter has the option of dispensing the speaker from offering TLN by suggesting that he use a first name or by tacitly accepting first name. Brown and Ford (Hymes, 1964a) have discussed the ambiguity that arises because it is not clear whether the superior, for instance, a professor addressing a doctoral candidate or younger instructor, wishes to receive back the FN he gives. This problem is mentioned by Emily Post: "It is also effrontery for a younger person to call an older by her or his first name, without being asked to do so. Only a very underbred, thickskinned person would attempt it" (Post, 1922, p. 54). In the American system described in Fig. 1, age difference is not significant until it is nearly the size of a generation, which suggests its origin in the family. The presence of options, or dispensation, creates a locus for the expression of individual and situational nuances. The form of address can reveal dispensation, and therefore be a matter for display or concealment of third parties. No-naming or Ø is an outcome of uncertainty among these options.[2]

The *identity* set refers to a list of occupational titles or courtesy titles accorded people in certain statuses. Examples are Judge, Doctor, and Professor. A priest, physician, dentist, or judge may be addressed by title alone, but a plain citizen or an academic person may not. In the latter cases, if the name is unknown, there is no address form (or zero, Ø) available and we simple no-name the addressee. The parentheses below refer to optional elements, the bracketed elements to social selectional categories.

[Cardinal]:	Your excellency
[U.S. President]:	Mr. President
[Priest]:	Father (+ LN)
[Nun]:	Sister (+ religious name)
[Physician]:	Doctor (+ LN)
[Ph.D., Ed.D.], etc.:	(Doctor + LN)
[Professor]:	(Professor + LN)
[Adult], etc.:	(Mister + LN)
	(Mrs. + LN)
	(Miss + LN)

Wherever the parenthetical items cannot be fully realized, as when last name (LN) is unknown, and there is no lone title, the addressee is

---

[2] In the system in Fig. 1, it is possible to create asymmetrical address by using FN to a familiar addressee who cannot reciprocate because of rank or age difference, and his unwillingness or lack of dispensation, e.g., a domestic servant. E. Hughes has noted a shift from TLN to FN by physicians whose patients move from private fees to Medicare. This usage does not fit into the rule in Fig. 1.

no-named by a set of rules of the form as follows: Father $+ \emptyset \rightarrow$ Father, Professor $+ \emptyset \rightarrow \emptyset$, Mister $+ \emptyset \rightarrow \emptyset$, etc. An older male addressee may be called "sir" if deference is intended, as an optional extra marking.

These are my rules, and seem to apply fairly narrowly within the academic circle I know. Nonacademic university personnel can be heard saying "Professor" or "Doctor" without LN, as can school teachers. These delicate differences in sociolinguistic rules are sensitive indicators of the communication net.

The zero forms imply that often no address form is available to follow routines like "yes", "no", "pardon me", and "thank you". Speakers of languages or dialects where all such routines must contain an address form are likely in English either to use full name or to adopt forms like "sir" and "ma'am", which are either not used or used only to elderly addressees in this system.

One might expect to be able to collapse the rule system by treating kin terms as a form of title, but it appears that the selectors are not identical for kin and nonkin. A rule which specifies that *ascending generation* only receives title implies that a first cousin would not be called "cousin" but merely FN, whereas an aunt of the same age would receive a kin title, as would a parent's cousin. If a title is normally used in direct address and there are several members of the kin category, a first name may also be given (e.g., Aunt Louise). Frequently there are additional features marked within a given family such as patrilineal vs. matrilineal, and near vs. distant. Whenever the address forms for an individual person's relatives are studied, this proves to be the case, in my experience.

Presumably, the individual set of rules or the regional dialect of a reader of this article may differ in some details from that reported in Fig. 1. Perhaps sociolinguists will begin to use a favorite frame of linguists: "In my dialect we say . . ." to illustrate such differences in sociolinguistic rules. For example, I have been told that in some American communities there may be a specific status of familiarity beyond first-naming, where a variant of the middle name is optional among intimates. This form then becomes the normal or unmarked address form to the addressee.

"What's your name, boy?"
"Dr. Poussaint. I'm a physician."
"What's your first name, boy?"
"Alvin."

The policeman insulted Dr. Poussaint three times. First, he employed a social selector for race in addressing him as "boy", which neutralizes identity set, rank, and even adult status. If addressed to a white, "boy" presumably would be used only for a child, youth, or menial regarded as a nonperson.

Dr. Poussaint's reply supplied only TLN and its justification. He made clear that he wanted the officer to suppress the race selector, yielding a rule like that in Fig. 1. This is clearly a nondeferential reply, since it does not contain the FN required by the policeman's address rule. The officer next treated TLN as failure to answer his demand, as a non-name, and demanded FN; third, he repeated the term "boy" which would be appropriate to unknown addressees.

According to Figure 1, under no circumstances should a stranger address a physician by his first name. Indeed, the prestige of physicians even exempts them from first-naming (but not from "Doc") by used-car salesmen, and physicians' wives can be heard so identifying themselves in public in order to claim more deference than "Mrs." brings. Thus the policeman's message is quite precise: "Blacks are wrong to claim adult status or occupational rank. You are children." Dr. Poussaint was stripped of all deference due his age and rank.

Communication has been perfect in this interchange. Both were familiar with an address system which contained a selector for race available to both black and white for insult, condescension, or deference, as needed. Only because they shared these norms could the policeman's act have its unequivocal impact.

2. *Comparative Rule Studies*

The formulation of rules in this fashion can allow us to contrast one sociolinguistic system with another in a systematic way. A shared language does not necessarily mean a shared set of sociolinguistic rules. For instance, rules in educated circles in England vary. In upper class boarding schools, boys and some girls address each other by LN instead of FN. In some universities and other milieux affected by the public school usage, solidary address between male acquaintances and colleagues is LN rather than FN. To women it may be Mrs. or Miss + LN by men (not title + LN) or FN. Women usually do not use LN. Thus sex of both speaker and addressee is important.

In other university circles, the difference from the American rule is less; prior to dispensation by seniors with whom one is acquainted, one may use Mister or Mrs. rather than occupational title as an acceptably solidary but deferential form. Note that this is the solidary usage to women by some male addressees in other system. The two English systems contrast with the American one in allowing basically three, rather than two classes of alternatives for nonkin: occupational title + LN, M + LN, and FN/LN. The intermediate class is used for the familiar person who must be deferred to or treated with courtesy.

Two Asian systems of address have been described recently. The pioneering work of William Geohegan (in press) described the naming system of a speaker of Bisayan, a Philippine language. Geohegan's formal presentation of the system in a talk some years ago was the model for the rules used in the figures in this article. As in most systems, children routinely receive the familiar address form. The Bisayan system, like the American and English, chooses on the basis of relative rank, relative age, and friendship. But there are important differences. In the United States, all adult strangers are treated with deference; in the Bisayan system, social inferiors do not receive titled address. In the American system for nonkin, added age, like higher rank, merely increases distance or delays familiar address; in the Bisayan system, inferiors or friends who are older receive a special term of address uniting informality and deference.

The Korean system is even less like the American (Howell, 1967). In Korea, relative rank must first be assessed. If rank is equal, relative age within two years is assessed, and if that is equal, solidarity (e.g., classmates) will differentiate familiar from polite speech. This system differs both in its components and its order from the American and Bisayan rules. Both inferiors and superiors are addressed differently from equals. Many kinds of dyads differ in authority – husband-wife, customer-tradesman, teacher-pupil, employer-employee – and in each case, asymmetrical address is used. Adressees more than two years older or younger than the speaker are differentially addressed, so that close friendship is rigidly age-graded. Solidary relations arise from status, just as they do between equal colleagues in the American system, regardless of personal ties. There are more familiar address forms yet to signal intimacy within solidary dyads. If the English system has three levels, there are even more in the Korean system. Since the criteria were multiple in the Howell study, instead of a single frame, the comparison is not quite exact.

As Howell pointed out, the Korean system illustrates that the dimension of approach that Brown and Gilman (1960) called solidarity may in fact have several forms in one society. In the Korean system intimacy is separably from solidarity. This separation may also exist in the American system, but in a different way. One is required to first-name colleagues even though they are disliked. On the other hand, as Brown and Ford (Hymes, 1964b) showed, nicknames may indicate friendship more intimate than the solidarity requiring FN. They found that various criteria of intimacy, such as self-disclosure, were related to the *number* of FN alternates, such as nicknames and sometimes LN, which were used to an addressee, and they suggested that intimacy creates more complex and varied dyadic relations which speakers may signal by address variants. Thus, in the American system two points of major option for speakers exist: the ambiguous address relation between solidary speakers of unequal age or status and intimacy. Systems can be expected to vary in the points where address is prescribed or where options exist; Brown and Ford suggested a universal feature, on the other hand, in saying that in all systems frequent and intimate interaction should be related to address variation.[3] This, they suggest is related to a semantic principle of greater differentiation of important domains.

3. Two-Choice Systems
The brilliant work of Brown and Gilman (1960) which initiated the recent wave of studies of address systems was based on a study of T and V, the second person verbs and pronouns in European languages. In English, the same alternation existed before "thou" was lost.

One might expect two-choice systems to be somewhat simpler than a system like Bisayan, which in Geohegan's description gives 19 output categories. But the number of outcomes can be few although the number of selectors is many or the kinds of rules relating them complex. Figure 2 gives a description of the nineteenth century rules of the Russian gentry, as I derive them from the excellent analysis by Friedrich (1966), which gives sufficiently full detail to permit resolution of priorities. *Special statuses* refers to the tsar and God, who seem not to fit on any status continuum. *Status marked settings* mentioned by Friedrich were the court, parliament, public occasions, duels, and examinations. *Rank* inferiors might be lower in social class, army rank, or ethnic group, or be servants. *Familiarity* applied to classmates, fellow students, fellow revolutionaries, lovers, and intimate friends. There does not seem to be the prescription in the Korean and American solidary relation. A feature of the system which Friedrich's literary examples illustrate vividly is its sensitivity to situational features. Thus T means 'the right to use Ty', but not the obligation to do so. Within the kin group, households is of considerable importance because of the large households separated by distance in traditional Russia.

A slightly later Eastern European system described by Slobin (1963) is given in Figure 3. The Yiddish system is somewhat more like the American than like the Russian system in that deference is

---

[3] William Geohegan has privately suggested that in his Philippine studies the extremely high intimacy in families resulted in use of paralinguistic rather than lexical alternatives for "address variation" of the type Brown and Ford discuss.

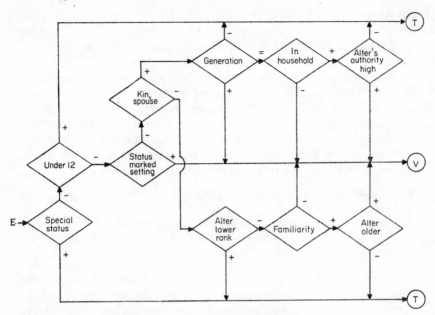

Fig. 2. Nineteenth century Russian address.

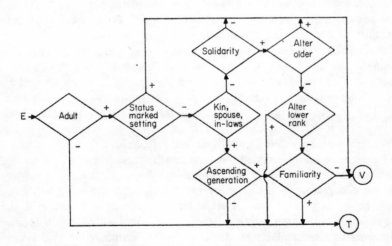

Fig. 3. Yiddish address system.

always given adult strangers regardless of rank. However, an older person receives deference, despite familiarity, unless he is a member of the kin group. In the American system, familiarity can neutralize age.

How have these systems changed? We have some evidence from the Soviet Union. The Russian revolutionaries, unlike the French, decreed V, implying that they wanted respect more than solidarity. The current system is identical to the old with one exception: Within the family, asymmetry has given way to reciprocal T, as it has in most of western Europe, at least in urbanized groups. For nonkin in ranked systems like factories, superiors receive Vy and give Ty:

When a new employee is addressed as Ty, she says: "Why do I call you 'vy' while you call me 'ty'?"
Kormilitzyn gleefully shoots back a ready answer: "If I were to call everyone 'vy' I'd never get my plan fulfilled. You don't fulfill plans by using 'vy' " (Kantorovich, 1966, p. 30).

Evidently the upperclass habit of using "vy" until familiarity was established (a system reflecting the fact that the T/V contrast itself came in from above as a borrowing from French) has seeped downward. "A half-century ago even upon first meeting two workers of the same generation would immediately use 'ty'. Today things are different. Middle-aged workers maintain 'vy' for a long time, or else adopt the intermediate form which is very widespread among people within a given profession: 'ty' combined with first name and patronymic" (Kantorovich, 1966, p. 81).

Kantorovich, true to the 1917 decree, complains about three features of the current system: ty to inferiors regardless of age, ty to older kin, and first names alone among young acquaintances. Thus he favors the more deferential alternative in each case. Social change in Russia has been relatively slow in sociolinguistic rules, has affected family life more than public life, and has spread the practices of the gentry among the workers.

The Puerto Rican two-choice system in Figure 4 is quite simple since it is a system of children. The data were generously supplied by Wallace Lambert and his collaborators from a large-scale study of comparative address systems in several cultures. Elementary and high school students filled in questionnaires about the forms of address given and received. In this chart, interlocale and intersubject differences have been suppressed. The striking feature of this system is that it requires only three discriminations. It is likely, of course, that adult informants would elaborate further details. Intimacy, in this system, refers to close ties of friendship, which can occur with others of widely

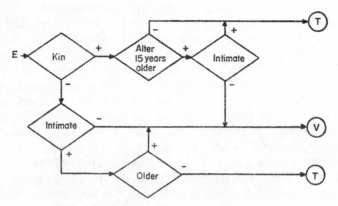

Fig. 4. Puerto Rican address system (children).

varying age, e.g., with godparents, and is quite distinct from solidarity, which arises from status alone. Adolescent girls, for example, do not give "tu" to a classmate unless she is a friend.

Lambert and his collaborators have collected slightly less detailed data from samples of schoolchildren in Montreal, from a small town in Quebec, from Mayenne, France, and from St. Pierre et Michelon, an island colony with close ties to France, much closer than to nearby Canada.

The system of kin address varies considerably. In both Mayenne and St. Pierre, all kin and godparents receive "tu". In Quebec, the urban middle class is moving in this direction, but the lower class and the rural regions from which it derives retain an address system like Puerto Rico's in which distance (including age) within the family is important. In some families, even older siblings receive "vous". If changes in kin address arise during social change, one would expect between-family differences to be greater than in nonkin address, since sanctions are intrafamily. Generally, "intimate" means parents, then aunts, uncles, and godparents, then grandparents. Some interfamily differences might be accounted for by finding which family members live in the household, which nearby, and which far away.

Lambert and Tucker (in press) have referred to a study of the social connotations of this changing system for urban school children in Montreal. Children were asked to judge taped family interaction varying in "tu" or "vous" to parents, and in the outcome of the inter-action – giving or not giving the child a requested bicycle. In addition to the class differences (*tu* users richer, more educated families), the judges drew from the pronoun usage a set of expectations about family values, resulting in favorable judgments when the interaction outcome was congruent. For instance, *tu*-using families sound modern and tolerant, the mothers more active, the fathers more tolerant than *vous*-using families, if they prove child-centered. However, it is *vous*-using families that sound religious, with a good family spirit, an active mother and tolerant father when the decision goes against the child.

Sex of addressee appears to be a feature of adult systems, or may influence the probabilities of intimacy where there is a selector. In Quebec, adults generally give "tu" to children and young men, regardless of familiarity. In St. Pierre, except to upper class girls, who are less likely to receive "tu" under any conditions, acquaintance legitimizes "tu" and is necessary even in addressing children. In Mayenne, middle class little boys said they received "tu" from everyone (and reported often reciprocating to strangers), but otherwise familiarity seems to be required, as in Puerto Rico, in the Mayenne system. Boys generally receive T from employers, and in the country and the urban lower class they receive T from service personnel. It should be noted that the analysis from the children's standpoint of what they receive is an interesting reflection of the fact that people know what they should say themselves, and they also expect some standard form from others. In analyzing the adult rule systems, however, the children's data are not the best; the adults of rural or lower class background may have different rules (e.g., service personnel, perhaps) than others.

The compressed presentation here of Lambert's work has indicated several directions for research on social criteria of address selection. Lambert has shown that these rules are sensitive indicators of differences between social groups and of social change. One must look beyond the address system for independent social features correlated with address systems of a defined type. In order to do such studies, a clear-cut formal system for typing properties of address systems (like language typologies) is necessary.

Lambert (1967b) has discussed the development of address rules with age. There are several interesting problems in the learning of these systems, one being the visibility of the various social selectors. One can assume that rank graduations in an adult system might be learned late (at least in terms of generalizability to new addressees), as would generation differentiations not highly related to age. A second problem emphasized by Lambert is the system of alternation itself. Children in most language communities learn fairly early to employ the asymmetry of first and second person (for a case study see McNeill, 1963). Thus if they always received T and gave V, there might be less difficulty; however, they see others exchanging reciprocal V and T as well as asymmetrical address, and they give T to some alters. These problems could be studied in natural language communities where the language structure provides different category systems and social selectors (Slobin, 1967).

4. Socialization

Adults entering a new system because of geographical or occupational mobility may have to learn new sociolinguistic rules. A contrastive analysis of formal rules, in combination with a theory of social learning, would allow specification of what will happen.

First, we can predict what the speaker will do. We can expect, on the basis of research on bilinguals (Ervin-Tripp, in press; Haugen, 1956), that the linguistic alternatives will at first be assimilated to familiar forms, to "diamorphs". Thus a Frenchman in the United States might start out by assuming that Monsieur = Mister, Madame = Mrs., and so on.

However, the rules for occurrence of these forms are different in France. In the polite discourse of many speakers, routines like "merci", "au revoir", "bonjour", "pardon" do not occur without an address form in France, although they may in the United States. One always says "Au revoir, Madame" or some alternative address form. "Madame" differs from "Mrs." in at least two ways. Unknown female addressees of a certain age are normally called "Madame" regardless of marital status. Further, Mrs. $+ \emptyset = \emptyset$; Madame $+ \emptyset =$ Madame. As a matter of fact, the rule requiring address with routines implies that when LN is not known, there cannot be a 'zero alternate' – some form of address must be used anyway, like the English "sir". As a result of these differences in rules, we can expect to hear elderly spinsters addressed as "Pardon me, Mrs."

How do listeners account for errors? I suggested earlier that shifting at certain points in sociolinguistic rules is regularly available as an option. Normally, it is interpreted as changing the listener's perceived identity or his relation to the speaker. The result may be complementary, as "sir" to an unknown working class male, or insulting, as "Mommy" to an adolescent male. If the learner of a sociolinguistic system makes an error that falls within this range of interpretable shifts, he may constantly convey predictably faulty social meanings. Suppose the speaker, but not the listener, has a system in which familiarity, not merely solidarity, is required for use of a first name. He will use TLN in the United States to his new colleagues and be regarded as aloof or excessively formal. He will feel that first-name usage from his colleagues is brash and intrusive. In the same way, encounters across social groups may lead to misunderstandings within the United States. Suppose a used-car salesman regards his relation to his customers as solidary, or a physician so regards his relation to old patients. The American using the rule in Fig. 1 might regard such speakers as intrusive, having made a false claim to a solidary status. In this way, one can pinpoint abrasive features of interaction across groups.

Another possible outcome is that the alternative selected is completely outside the system. This would be the case with "Excuse me, Mrs." which cannot be used under any circumstances by rule 1. This behavior is then interpreted with the help of any additional cues available, such as the face, dress, or accent of a foreigner. In such cases, if sociolinguistic rules are imperfectly learned, there may be social utility in retaining an accent wherever the attitude toward the group of foreigners is sufficiently benign; it is better to be designated a foreigner than to risk insulting or offending addressees.

5. Integrated Sociolinguistic Rules

The rules given above are fractional. They are selective regarding the linguistic alternations accounted for. They define only specific linguistic entries as the universe of outcomes to be predicted. If one starts from social variables, a different set of rules might emerge. This is the outlook of William Geohegan (in press) and Ward Goodenough (1965), as well as Dell Hymes (1964a), who suggested taking "a specific or universal function, such as the distinguishing of the status or role of man and woman, derogation, respect, or the like, and . . . investigating the diverse means so organized within the language habits of the community, . . . [rather than] looking for function as a correlative of structure already established" (p. 44).

Using such an approach, Goodenough examined behavior toward a range of statuses, and found that it was possible to rank both the statuses and the forms of behavior into Guttman scales and equivalent classes, grouped at the same scale point (1965). In this way, various kinds of verbal and nonverbal behavior can be shown to be outcomes of the same social selectors.

Deference, the feature studied by Goodenough, may be indicated by pronoun alternations, names or titles, tone of voice, grammatical forms, vocabulary, and so on (Capell, 1966, pp. 104ff; Martin, in Hymes, 1964b). Deferential behavior in some systems may be realized only in special situations such as in introductions or in making requests. If one compares an isolated segment of two sociolinguistic systems, he cannot legitimately conclude that a given social variable is more important in one system than in the other. It may simply be realized through a different form of behavior.

It is not clear how the different realizations of social selectors might be important. Address, pronominal selection, or consistent verb suffixing (as in Japanese) can be consciously controlled more readily, perhaps, than intonation contours or syntactic complexity. Frenchmen report "trying to use 'tu' " with friends. Such forms can be taught by rule specification to children or newcomers. Forms which allow specific exceptions, or which have options so that too great or too little frequency might be conspicuous, cannot be taught so easily. Such rules can be acquired by newcomers only by long and intense exposure rather than by formal teaching.

Some alternations are common and required, others can be avoided. Howell reported that in Knoxville, Tennessee, Negroes uncertain of whether or not to reciprocate FN simply avoided address forms to colleagues (Howell, 1967, pp. 81–83), an approach that Brown and Ford also observed in the academic rank system. In a pronominal rank system like French or Russian such avoidance is impossible. Among bilinguals, language switching may be employed to avoid rank signaling (Howell, 1967; Tanner, 1967). The avoidable selector can be considered a special case of the presence of options in the system. Tyler (1965) has noticed that morphological deference features (like the Japanese) are more common in societies of particular kinship types, such as lineage organization.

This description was primarily drawn from the standpoint of predicting a speaker's choice of alternatives in some frame. It is also possible to examine these rules from the standpoint of comprehension or interpretation, as have Blom and Gumperz (in press) in their discussion of *social meaning*. Just as one can comprehend a language without speaking it, as actors we can interpret the social meaning of the acts of others without necessarily using rules identical to our own. The relation between production and comprehension rules remains to be studied.

B. Sequencing Rules

1. Leave-Taking

After an introduction, when you have talked for some time to a stranger whom you have found agreeable, and you then take leave, you say, "Goodby, I am very glad to have met you," or "Good-by, I hope I shall see you again soon' – or 'some time." The other person answers, "Thank you," or perhaps adds, "I hope so, too."

Emily Post (1922, p. 9)

The sequential events mentioned in this description are Introduction + Conversation + Leave-taking. Leaving aside the components of the first two, elsewhere specified, leave-taking (LT) has two parts, for the two actors.

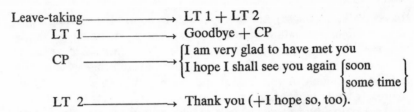

Leave-taking ⟶ LT 1 + LT 2

LT 1 ⟶ Goodbye + CP

CP ⟶ { I am very glad to have met you
I hope I shall see you again { soon
some time } }

LT 2 ⟶ Thank you (+I hope so, too).

This is a notation, borrowed from grammars, illustrating a phrase structure rule. The plus marks indicate sequential events, the arrows expansions or replacements in the "derivation tree" to be read as "rewrite leave-taking as LT 1 + LT 2", the braces alternatives, and the parentheses optional elements. The more general rule states that introduction always precedes the other two events. Presumably the rules will indicate that while introduction and leave-taking are relatively fixed routines, conversation can be expanded to hours. We can regard these routines as transition markers between speech events.

2. Summons Sequence

A phone rings in Jim's home:

Jim: Hello.
George: Hi, how are you?
Jim: O.K., but listen, I'm in a phone booth and this is my last dime. Barbara's phone is busy and I won't be able to meet her at seven. Could you keep trying to get her for me and tell her?
George: What the hell are you talking about?

> Adapted from Schegloff (in press)

Jim was a sociology student who was trying to violate rules of telephone conversation. The rules derived by Schegloff from a large sample of phone conversations can be characterized as follows:

Summons Sequence ⟶ Summons + Answer + Continuation + Response

Summons ⟶ { Courtesy Phrase [to stranger]
Attention-call [nonstranger]
Telephone bell ... }

Answer [phone] ⟶ Greeting 1 (+ Identification [office])

Continuation ⟶ (Greeting 2) + (Identification) + Message

Response ⟶ (Deferral +) Reply to message

Following every summons, there are three phases to complete the cycle. The omission of any part, if a second party is present, is unusual and must be accounted for. The summons can be realized in a variety of ways, depending on whether alter is physically present, known, and so on. To a stranger one might say "pardon me!" or "hey!" Attention-calls include "waiter!" "Dr. Conant!" "Joe!" Their selection rules would be close to Figure 1.

Alter must answer a summons. Lecturers may find it hard to ignore waving hands in the audience. If there is nonresponse, the summons is repeated. On the phone: "Hello . . . Hello . . . Hello? . . . . Hello!" There are definite limits (longer for children) for such repetitions of summonses.

The next major step is that following the limited routines of exchanging greetings, the caller gives a message, explaining his reason for calling. In the example, Jim tried to play the role of caller rather than called. He did this by not giving George a chance to give a message and by giving a message itself semantically deviant and appropriate only to George's status as caller.

If the caller did not intend a summons, or if his need has vanished, he fills the continuation position with an account: "Never mind." "I was just saying hello." "I was just checking the phone." If he states a request, alter must respond.

We have not stated the rule in its full detail. The realizations of Greeting 1 vary, according to circumstance. Thus the alternatives might be "Yes", on an intercom, "Good morning, Macy's", for a receptionist on an institutional telephone, "Hello", on other outside phones. Greeting 2 has different alternation sets than Greeting 1, for example "Hi", to a friend, "How are you", to a friend, "Hello", to others. Thus the realizations of particular units in the sequencing rules may involve alternations which are dependent on social features. Also, some of the optional positions may be selected or omitted by social criteria.

The selection of certain alternates may entail an expansion at that position in the sequence. For example, if "How are you?" occurs as the Greeting 2 realization, the addressee must reply. The result may be an embedded interchange about his health. The called person at this point, like anyone asked this question, has two options. He can either give a routine response to nonintimate alters, such as "Okay", or "Fine", or, if the alter is a friend, he has the option of describing the real state of his health. Indeed, he may be obligated to do so since a close friend might be insulted at not being informed of his broken leg at the time of the conversation rather than later. Sacks has described the routine response as an obligation to lie, but formally it is a neutralization of the semantic selection feature – simply a briefer route.

If Greeting 2 establishes that the caller is a friend, the addressee has the option of providing a new greeting which is for a friend, as Greeting 1 was not:

"Hello."

"Hi, Joe. How are you?"

"Oh, hi. I'm okay . . ."

Note that by this system, "hi" is more intimate than "hello". Not so in 1922, when Emily Post said that "hello" is "never used except between intimate friends who call each other by the first name" (1922, p. 19).

In the conversation just cited, *identification* is through the channel of voice recognition. Between strangers, identification is required, according to Sacks' evidence (in press). Sacks has pointed out that self-identifications, introductions, and third-party categorizations are important social devices. Since everyone has many statuses, the selection in each case where a status (other than a proper name) is given follows certain fixed rules, among them consistency with other choices. In a series of such events in the same situation, the categories tend to be members of the same contrast set, e.g., occupations.

3. Invitation Sets

Slots in sequences such as the summons sequence are not necessarily recognized by the speakers or labeled by them. Sacks, for example, has cited in lectures the observation that many encounters include an optional sequence at a time when a newcomer enters a group or a dyad begins conversation. These he called "pre-invitation", "pre-invitation/rejection", "invitation", and "rejection".

　a. Pre-invitation.

"Hello? Hello. What are you doing?"

"Nothing."

The person called interprets the question as a preliminary to an invitation. If the reply is "nothing" the caller might suggest coming over, might launch into a long conversation, and so on. The person called does not talk about the things he is doing that are irrelevant to the supposed invitation.

　b. Pre-invitation/rejection.

"Can I see you for a moment?"

"What do you want?"

The question is designed to gather information suitable for deciding about offering an invitation or a rejection. So too, according to Sacks' analysis, the sequence in Pittenger, Hockett, and Danehy's *The First Five Minutes:*

Therapist: What brings you here . . .?
Patient: I don't feel like talking.

Sacks observes that the patient knows that her acceptability for therapy depends on her answer, also that she must reveal her private concerns to someone who is not yet defined as her regular physician, appropriate to such disclosures. Here the open-ended question underlines the ambiguity of the new relationship.

    c. Rejection. When a wife greets her husband by announcing that her visiting friends are discussing nursery schools or the sewing circle, she implies his absence would be welcome. In this act, the wife asserts that the activity of the group is bound to a category of which he is not a member.

    d. Invitation. Sacks cited the late arrival of a member to a group therapy session:

"Hi. We were having an automobile discussion."
". . . discussing the psychological motives for . . ."
"drag racing in the streets."

Here the latecomer was invited into the conversation by three members in one sentence.

    Emily Post referred to such practices as "including someone in conversation", and suggested that it can be done without an introduction, for example, by saying to a friend who arrives during a conversation with a gardener, "[Hello, Gladys,] Mr. Smith is suggesting that I dig up these cannas and put in delphiniums." This is evidently a semi-introduction, since it allows the superior to address the inferior, but without the implication of equality lying in a full introduction.

    These four slots are not recognized by speakers as such. They enter into complex sequencing rules which have not yet been analyzed sufficiently; it is clear, for example, that the first two occupy different positions, one being uttered by the summoner, the other by the respondent. Rejection/invitation are alternatives in the same rule. The function of and sequence rules for these speech acts can be checked not only from natural conversations but by experimental omission or alteration of the temporal location in the sequence of acts.

4. Narratives

Labov and Waletzky (1967) recently presented a framework for the analysis of informal narratives or oral versions of personal experience. Narratives, whether formal or casual, involve problems of sequencing *par excellence*, since it is inherent in the problem of narration that the hearer must understand the sequence in the *referent* events. The article defined a series of clause types in terms of their permutation properties. The preservation of causal relations implied by narrative sequence is evident as early as age 6, according to Brent and Katz, in very simple tasks (1967). A basic contrast in the analysis of Labov and Waletzky is between free clauses, which could occur anywhere in the narration (e.g., descriptions of character of hero), and clauses which must occur before, after, or between certain others, which define their displacement range.

By utilizing the units of this formal analysis to characterize the whole narrative sequence, Labov and Waletzky were able to identify five portions in the maximally expanded narrative, which they call orientation, complication, evaluation, resolution, and coda. The minimum possible narrative has only complication. While they noted that the amount of narrative structure used beyond the minimum was related to the verbal skill of the speaker, it was also apparent that differences of group styles, age, and so on could be profitably examined through such formal means.

5. Tying Rules

In his class lectures, Sacks has discussed many details of sequencing within conversations. One problem has to do with the sequence of speakers. In a dyadic conversation, he has found that the rule is alternation of adequate complete utterances between the two speakers. But in larger groups, more complex patterns obtain. The next speaker may be indicated by asking a question. Then the addressee has the right to the floor whenever he chooses to talk, and the asker has the right after the responder. The rule is such that other material can intervene between question and response. "When I've asked a question, then the pause between my talk and yours is your silence," according to Sacks. Thus a question is a "first speaker form", since it implies that a second speaker is called on. So, in the groups he has studied, is an insult.

Second speaker forms include pronouns tying back to earlier utterances, and pro-verbs. Some forms are even more complex, such as "I still say, though ..." which implies a third activity of which some prior one was done by the same person.

The result of using the sequence features Sacks has discussed is that a great deal of information can be obtained from single utterances. In the example, "Ken, face it, you're a poor little rich kid," he points out that we know that Ken is the addressee, that Ken now has the right to speak, that he has the right to give an insult to the speaker, and that some categorization device (e.g., Mommy) in a contrast set with "kid" is likely.

6. Speech Event Analysis

Sequence rules are appropriate for the description of what may be called "speech events", which, in turn, may be parts of or coterminous with *focused interaction* (Goffman, 1963). Traditionally, anthropologists were aware of such organized units only in the case of ceremonies and tales, where preservation of the same thematic sequences, or even the same wording, was highly valued. These repeated routines were, of course, obvious even to the most casual observer. *The Book of Common Prayer,* for example, clearly labels each speech event, its components, and the alternatives at each point.

Even so simple a sequence as a short telephone conversation, as Schegloff has shown, has underlying structural rules. These rules refer to abstract categories not evident on the surface of behavior. Since multi-party interactions must be even more complex, we can assume that the rules for such encounters will not be simple. At least, one cannot expect that the rules of speech events are any simpler than the grammar of sentences.

Frake (1964) identified segments of the speech event as *discourse stages.* Components of the stages or coterminous with them are *exchanges,* which Frake defined as "sets of utterances with a common topic focus", probably similar to Watson and Potter's (1962) *episodes.* *Speech acts* are utterances or utterance sets with an interpretable function. Examples might be the routines that can mark the boundaries of episodes such as "That reminds me . . .", promises, jokes, apologies, greetings, requests, or insults. Speech acts, unlike functions, are cultural units, and must be discovered by ethnological methods.

Some of the features of order between these units have been considered in the context of narration by Labov and Waletzky (1967) and others. The displacement sets and other categories they have defined for clauses can also apply to other units such as speech acts. Where displacement occurs, of self-identification, for instance, it may be marked by special routines, "By the way, my name is – – – –" which would not be used except for the deviation.

The categories which Schegloff and Sacks discussed are sufficiently general in many cases so that one can expect them to be found universally. The summons sequence is a good candidate. Schegloff showed, with respect to telephone conversations, that the basic rules he gave, with called answering first, caller providing initial topic, and so on, are required by the distribution of information at the start. On the other hand, the specific selections available within each formal category in this case are likely to be highly culture- or group-specific. The strategy for the discovery of alternations and of sequencing rules is similar. In the latter case, one tests the response of members to omissions or permutations, rather than to substitutions.

C. Co-occurrence Rules

1. Types of Rules

"How's it going, Your Eminence? Centrifuging okay? Also, have you been analyzin' whatch'unnertook t'achieve?"

The bizarreness of this hypothetical episode arises from the oscillations between different varieties of speech. It violates the co-occurrence rules that we assume English to have.

In the preceding section, we were concerned with the selection of lexical items, pronouns, or inflectional alternatives. We conceived of each instance as involving social selectors. Once a selection has been made, however, later occurrences within the same utterance, conversation, or even between the same dyad may be predictable. Whenever there is predictability between two linguistic forms, we can speak of co-occurrence rules.

Co-occurrence rules could be of two kinds. Predictability through time might be called horizontal, since it specifies relations between items sequentially in the discourse. Another type might be called vertical, specifying the realization of an item at each of the levels of structure of a language. For instance, given a syntactical form, only certain lexicon may normally be employed, and a particular set of phonetic values may realize the lexicon. If one learned political terms in New York and gardening terms in Virginia, the phonetic coloring of the lexicon might reflect their provenance in the individual's history. The most striking case lies in the well-practiced bilingual who uses French syntax and pronunciation for French vocabulary and English syntax and pronunciation for English vocabulary.

In the example, the following are violations of vertical co-occurrence:

(1) "How's it going" is a phrase from casual speech, but the suffix "-ing" is used, rather than "-in" which is normal for casual speech.

(2) An elliptical construction is used in the second utterance, which contains only a participle, but the formal "-ing" appears again.

(3) A technical word, "centrifuge" is used in the elliptical construction.

(4) The "-in" suffix is used with the formal "analyze".

(5) Rapid informal articulation is used for the pedantic phrase "undertook to achieve".

Horizontal co-occurrence rules refer to the same level of structure, and might be lexical or structural. The vocabulary in the example oscillates between slang and technical terms, the syntax between ellipsis and parallel nonellipsis. In bilingual speech, one may find structural predictability independent of lexicon, as in an example of Pennsylvania German:

Di kau ist over di fens jumpt.

Here the syntax and grammatical morphemes are German, the lexicon English. Horizontal co-occurrence rules governing selection of morphemes are common with lexical switching and phrase switching allowed. Diebold (1963) also gave examples in which Greek-Americans who can speak both languages with 'perfect' co-occurence rules, if they employ English loanwords in the Greek discourse, realize them in the Greek phonological system. This would suggest that for these speakers, horizontal phonological rules override vertical realization rules.

One of the startling aberrations in the example is the use of slang to a cardinal. We would expect to find that deferential address forms would be co-occurrent with formal style. One pictures a cardinal in a microbiology laboratory addressed by a janitor who knows technical terms but cannot fully control formal syntax and phonology. Like ungrammatical sentences, sociolinguistically deviant utterances become normal if one can define setting and personnel to locate them. This is of course the point. Wherever there are regular co-occurrences, deviant behavior is marked and may carry social meaning.

The most extreme forms of co-occurrence restrictions are likely to be found in ritualized religious speech in traditional societies. Here it would be blasphemous to utter the wrong speech. Indeed, Gumperz has suggested that linguistics first began with the Sanskrit scholars' efforts to identify the formal features of religious texts and transmit them unchanged. It is co-occurrence restrictions which allow the recognition of language in multilingual societies.

At the opposite extreme are the conditions in American college lecturing, where technical terms, slang, and informal and formal syntax may alternate to some extent. Friedrich also gives examples (1966) of delicate communication of changing relationships by shifts within conversations.

2. Style

a. Formal style. Style is the term normally used to refer to the co-occurrent changes at various levels of linguistic structure within one language. Hymes (1964) has commented that probably every society has at least three style levels: formal or polite, colloquial, and slang or vulgar.

If Hymes is right about a polite style which contrasts with the un-marked (or "normal") colloquial, it might be proposed that this is the style preferred in public, serious, ceremonial occasions. Co-occurrence restrictions are particularly likely because of the seriousness of such situations. The style becomes a formal marker for occasions of societal importance where the personal relationship is minimized. We would expect that the distant or superior form of address and pronoun is universally employed in public high style. In Figures 1 and 2 "status-marked situations" which call for titles and V may also call for polite style. Thus speakers who exchange colloquial style normally might change to this style in certain public occasions such as funerals or graduation ceremonies.

It might generally be the case in English that in otherwise identical situations, an alter addressed with TLN receives polite style more than one addressed with FN. Howell (1967, p. 99) reported such corre-lations in Korean. Formal lexicon and "-ing" should be related. Fischer (Hymes, 1964b) found that "criticizing, visiting, interesting, reading, correcting" and "flubbin, punchin, swimmin, chewin, hittin" occurred in a single speaker's usage. It is not clear here whether it is lexical style or topic that is at issue, since there were no examples of denotative synonyms with different vocabulary. Examples of the sort given in Newman (Hymes, 1964b), and found plentifully in English lexicon for body functions (e.g., urinate vs. weewee), provide clearer evidence for co-occurrence restrictions between lexicon and structure.

Labov (1966) did include "-ing" vs. "-in" in his study of style con-trasts in different social strata, and he found that it worked precisely as the phonological variables did. Polite style in a speaker might require a certain higher frequency of [r], of [ð] rather than [d] in, e.g., "this", and of "-ing" (see Figures 5 and 6). While the variables differentiating polite

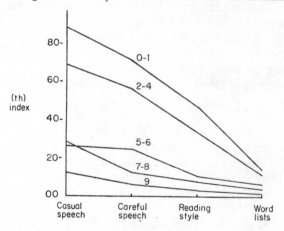

Fig. 5. Class and style stratification of [th] in thing, three, etc., for adult native New York City speakers (Labov, 1966).

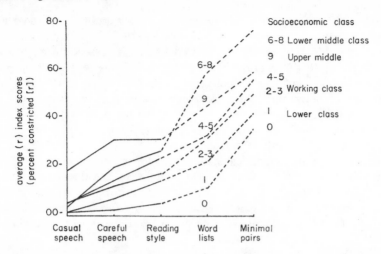

Fig. 6. Class stratification of [r] in guard, car, beer, beard, etc., for native New York City adults (Labov, 1966).

from casual style tended to be the same in different classes, the precise frequency reached for each variable varied (Labov, 1966). Thus his evidence suggests co-occurrence rules for grammatical morphemes and phonology. Labov (1966) and Klima (1964) considered the formal description of phonological and syntactic style features, respectively.

b. Informal style. In trying to sample different styles while interviewing, Labov made the assumption that speakers would use a more formal style during the interview questioning than at other times. He used several devices for locating such shifts contextually: speech outside the interview situation; speech to others, usually in the family; rambling asides; role-playing (specifically, getting adults to recite childhood rhymes); and answers to a question about a dangerous experience. He found that when "channel cues" (changes in tempo, pitch range, volume, or rate of breathing) indicated a change to casual or spontaneous speech within a speech episode, the phonological features changed. In the examples illustrating the shifts, lexicon and syntax changed too.

It is commonly the case that as one moves from the least deferent speech to the most, from the informal to the ceremonial, there is more elaboration and less abbreviation. Probably this difference is a universal, for two reasons. One is that elaboration is a cost, and is therefore most likely to occur in culturally valued situations or relationships (Homans, 1958). The other is that a high degree of abbreviation is only possible in in-group communication. While ceremonials may be confined to a sacred few, wherever they have a public function and must communicate content, we can assume that this principle of elaboration holds. Elaboration could be defined with respect to a surface structure, or to the complexity of embedded forms in the syntax, or some such criteria. A very brief poem might be, in fact, more complex in terms of rules and 'effort' of compression more complex than a discursive report of the 'same' content. Some forms are unambiguous: suffixed vs. unsuffixed forms, as in Japanese honorifics or polite verb suffixes, titles vs. nontitles, and so on.

From a formal grammatical standpoint, ellipsis is more complex than nonellipsis, since the grammar must contain an additional rule. It is not clear how ellipsis might be handled in a performance model. However, ellipsis in the syntactical sense is clearly more common in informal speech. Some examples can be given from questions and answers:

"Do (you(want(more cake?"
"I would like more cake."
"I'd like more cake."
"I would."
"Me."

From Soskin and John's text of (1963) of a married couple; we find the following:

Bet you didn't learn it there. . . .
Your name? (from attendant) . . .
Want me to take it . . .
Wanna take your shoes off? . . .
Getting seasick, dear? . . .
Think I can catch up with them? . . .
Not that way! . . .
Directly into it. . . .

The formal rules for sentence contractions and ellipsis are readily written.

Another form of ellipsis is that used in conversational episodes in second-speaker forms or to complete one's own earlier utterances. From Soskin and John (1963):

That fish, Honey. . . .
But I have a handicap. . . .
Like this? . . .
Which? This? Down here? . . .
You should be able to. . . .
Undulating! . . .
Yeah, if you want to. . . .

Rowed! . . .
With both of them! . . .
Well, you wanted to. . . .
You sure are. . . .
Well, I could. . . .

These forms of ellipsis are learned. Brent and Katz (1967) found that pronominalization is rare in young children; it is obligatory in second speaker rules. Bellugi (1967) found also that contractions occur later than uncontracted forms in the speech of children.

Semantic compression is also available in casual speech among intimates as will be evident later.

Phonetically, a form which occurs in casual speech more than in polite styles is rapid speech, which entails horizontal restrictions.

"What are you doing?"
"Whaddya doin?"
"Whach doon?"

There are regular phonetic alternations related to rate, e.g.:

(1) Retention of syllable of major stress and peak pitch.
(2) As degree of speeding increases, loss of segments with weakest stress.
(3) Loss or assimilation of semivowels.
        [r] in postvocalic position lost.
        [d] + [y] → [j], e.g., "Whadja do?"
        [t] + [y] → [č], e.g., "Whacha doin?"[4]
(4) Marginal phonological distinctions like /hw/ vs. /w/ may be lost, perhaps part of casual speech style.
(5) Unstressed vowels centralized.

There is a *reverse* set of rules available to speakers used to the above alternations. The extra-slow style may be employed in sounding-out for a dictionary or over the telephone. Thus normal "school" may become slow [sɨkuwɨl].

3. Registers and Occupational Argots

Husband: Whaddya say you just *quit* . . .

    Wife: I can't simply *quit* the airlines because *notice must* be *given*, but I'll certainly take what you *say* into *consideration*, and *report* it to my *superiors* . . .

---

[4] Alert readers will note these 'rules' will not account for non-voicing of [č] in ellipsis of underlying "what are" but not of "what did", suggesting the rules cannot use merely surface phonetic segments.

Husband: I don't *know* you. I don't feel *close* to you.
   Wife: Well, I'm *awfully sorry*. There's *nothing* I can do right now because I *am* preparing a *meal*, but *if* you'll *wait* until *after* I've made the *beverage*, perhaps —
Husband: I can't *stand* it. I want *out,* I want a *divorce!*
   Wife: Well, all I can *say* is, it's been nice having you *aboard* —

Nichols and May (1959)

The register of airlines or tourist businesses is revealed here in lexical choices like meal, beverage, and aboard, and "preparing in meal" rather than "getting breakfast". Register is reflected primarily in lexicon, since different topics are required in different milieux. However, in this case the paralinguistic features also change, including stress on words like "must", "am", "if", "after", "do", "about", "will", "back", which would usually not be stressed. In the register of psychologists are both professional lexicon like "interaction" and syntactic structures like the passive "It was felt that".

Slang is similar to register variation in that the alternates are primarily lexical. As Newman (Hymes, 1964b) has pointed out, the actual forms used are not necessarily different, but in sacred or slang contexts they take on a different meaning, so that in speaking of slang vocabulary one must include both form and semantic features. Since slang is highly transitory by definition, it will be understood in a given sense only within the group or network where it developed or to which it has moved at a given time. Thus one might predict that the selection rules for slang should restrict it to addressees to whom one claims a solidary relation. By this interpretation, a college lecture laced with slang is a claim on the identification of the audience. The nature of no-occurrence restrictions with slang needs investigation.

4. Linguistic Repertoire

Co-occurrence restrictions refer to the selection of alternates within the repertoire of a speaker in terms of previous or concomitant selections. The range of alternates should be known in a study of restriction. In an American monolingual, the range is likely to include informal style, slang, perhaps an occupational register, and some formal style. Labov (1964) has pointed out, however, that it is rare to control a very wide stylistic range unless one is a speech specialist, and that upwardly mobile persons usually lose the "ability to switch 'downwards' to their original vernacular" (p. 92).

In many parts of the world, a code that is relatively distinct from the casual vernacular is used in formal situations. This condition, called "diglossia" in Ferguson's (Hymes, 1964b) classic article, may, because of the greater code difference, be accompanied by more co-occurrence restriction than is style shifting, where the common features of the styles may outweigh their differences. Examples where the codes are related are Greece, German Switzerland, Haiti, and Arab countries. Standard languages coexisting with local dialects are somewhat less distinguished, and historically the dialect does not usually maintain itself except phonetically, though there may be ideological resistance to borrowing from the standard (Blom and Gumperz, in press).

Where diglossia takes the form of bilingualism (Fishman, 1967), one might at first assume that the co-occurrence restrictions would primarily govern the high form. Such a condition exists in many American bilingual communities with English as the high form. However, these are not usually pure cases, since English is the vernacular if there are casual contacts outside the immigrant community. Under these conditions, there can be considerable interpenetration (Gumperz, 1967; Ervin-Tripp, 1969).

Co-occurrence restrictions in common-sense terms refer to "language-mixing". Some bilingual communities have strong attitudinal opposition to switching (usually they mean lexical co-occurrence). Blom and Gumperz (in press) found that in a Norwegian village, speakers were unconscious of the use of standard forms and were very upset to hear tapes showing lack of co-occurrence restrictions in behavior. In practice, the maintenance of coordinate or segregated systems depends upon social factors. Coordinate bilingualism is possible if there is a complete range of equivalent lexicon in both systems, and social support for the bilingualism. If this is not the case, some topics cannot be discussed, some emotions cannot be conveyed, and borrowing, perhaps surrounded by a routine disclaimer frame, will occur. The other social conditions permitting such segregation in diglossia are the closed network circumstances reported by Blom and Gumperz (in press), where certain topics and transactional types simply would not occur in casual discourse. Thus American researchers can find rich grounds for the study of behavioral support or loss of co-occurrence rules, in either English style, registers, or multilingualism.

III. SWITCHING

If a given speaker is observed during his daily round, all the features of his speech may show some systematic changes. The total repertoire of some speakers is far greater than others. Some are bilinguals, and some are community leaders with a wide range of styles reflecting their varying relationships and activities. In this section, we shall bring together evidence on some of the major classes of variables affecting variation within individual speakers.

A. Personnel

In any act of communication, there is a "sender" and one or more "receivers" who together may be called "interlocutors" (Hymes, 1962). In addition, there may be present an audience which is not the primary addressee of the message. The distribution of these roles has been discussed elsewhere (Ervin-Tripp, 1964). The role of sender, or speaker, is rarely distributed in equal time to all participants. There appear to be four factors which affect the amount of talking each participant may do. One factor is the situation. In informal small-group conversation, the roles of sender and receiver may alternate. In a sermon, the sender role is available to only one participant; in choral responses in a ritual, or in a question period following a lecture, the role of sender is allocated at specific times. The allocation of the role of sender is specified by sequencing rules for each type of speech event, and a sender may select his successor by a question or a gaze. A second, related, determinant of the amount of talking is the role the participant has in the group and his social and physical centrality. He may be a therapy patient, chairman, teacher, or switchboard operator, so that his formal status requires communication with great frequency; he may informally select such a role, as in the case of a raconteur or expert on the topic at hand. Third there is a personal constant carried from group to group. The net effect of the second and third factors is that the sending frequency of participants in a group is almost always unequal, and it has been shown to have regular mathematical properties in *ad hoc* discussion groups (Stephan and Mishler, 1952; Bales and Borgatta, 1955). Because relative frequency of speaking is steeply graded, not evenly distributed, in a large group the least frequent speaker may get almost no chance to speak. Knutson (1960) was able to produce radical alterations in participation rates by forming homogeneous groups on the basis of participation frequency. He found that talkative persons were generally regarded as better contributors, so there was great surprise when the homogeneously quiet group produced better work, by objective outside ratings.

The receiver role is also unequally distributed, even in face-to-face groups, being allocated in work talk to the most central, the most powerful, those with highest status, the most frequent speakers, and in highly valued groups, to the most deviant. In social conversation, proximity may be important (Hare, 1962, p. 289; Schachter, 1951).

In addition to their roles within the interaction situation, the personnel bring with them other statuses. These are, according to Goodenough (1965), "rights, duties, privileges, powers, liabilities, and immunities". I have mentioned that one of the functions of identity marking in speech is to indicate precisely what is required in the relationship. In any particular interaction, of course, not all the statuses of all participants are relevant. Obviously, the specific relations tying participants are most salient, e.g., a husband and his wife or an employer and his employee.

In addition to determining the forms that interaction might take, the identity of alter, and his relation to ego, will establish whether interaction is possible or obligatory. For example, following a death in the family, there is a specific sequence of persons who must be informed (Sacks' example).

Personnel include the audience as well as the receiver. The presence of others can, wherever there are options, weigh the selectors differently, according to whether one wants to conceal or display them to others. Thus, in a medical laboratory, technicians employ more formal and deferential speech to doctors when the supervisor or patients are present. In public the relation doctor-technician takes precedence over familiarity, so that, "Hey, Len, shoot the chart to me, will ya?" becomes, "Do you want the chart, Doctor?" Note the co-occurrence of formal structure and formal address.

I indicated in Section II that there are formal constraints on address. The rules for reference to third parties are more complex, for they are related both to the third party and to the addressee. In the American system, where the adult personnel present exchange FN they may regularly omit T in reference to third parties whom they normally address with TFN or TLN. If an addressee is lower in age or rank, e.g., a child or employee, and uses T to the referent, then T is used by both parties in reference. Thus "Daddy" might be used in addressing a child. Emily Post recommended that women refer to their husbands as TLN to inferiors in rank or age, "my husband" to strangers, and FN to friends "on the dinner list" (1922, p. 54). The friend, however, could not necessarily address the husband by FN (presumably some familiarity criterion was in use). "It is bad form to go about saying 'Edith Worldly' or 'Ethel Norman' to those who do not call them Edith or Ethel, and to speak thus familiarly of one whom you do not call by her first name, is unforgivable."

When the addressee is equal or slightly superior in rank, and thus eligible for receiving confidences (Slobin *et al.*, in press), when they share statuses which exclude the referent party, emotion toward the referent may be revealed. These constraints apply in particular to pejorative or affectionate nicknames toward persons addressed with TLN.

To the extent that the referent and addressee are alike, there is an implication of deference to the addressee in the form of reference selected. In the Japanese system of honorifics and "stylemes" (Martin, in Hymes, 1964b) both the terms for the referent and the verb suffixes are altered by deference, i.e., by selectors of relative rank, age, sex, and solidarity. In the most polite style, dialect forms are absent and the suffixes are employed. Children of ages 8 or 9 first learn control over reference, but still employ dialect forms freely and do not differentiate age of addressees by the "stylemes" (i.e., linguistic markers) of polite speech (Horikawa *et al.*, 1956). Possibly there is in Japanese, as in English, a rule by which reference employs honorifics when a child is addressed; thus it becomes the normal name for the referent.

Deference is undoubtedly a social feature present in all sociolinguistic systems to some degree. The most elaborate structural forms are evidently those found in the Far East. Geertz' description of the Javanese system is of general importance; he contrasted "stylemes", including affixes and function morphemes governed by co-occurrence restrictions, as in our formal style, with honorific vocabulary which is more sporadic. It seems, like the American "sir", to be governed by a rule of frequency (Martin, in Hymes, 1964b), rather than required presence or absence (Geertz, 1960).

Language choice itself, rather than stylistic alternatives, may be governed by addressee features of rank, age, and solidarity. Rubin's (1962) characterization of the alternation between Spanish and Guarani in Paraguay, according to addressee, nearly matches Figure 2, with V = Spanish, and T = Guarani.

Familiarity entered into several of the address rules in Section II. Familiarity increases the probability that an addressee will be talked to, and for this reason familiar interaction is likely to be marked by many forms of ellipsis at all levels, unless some setting or deference constraints interfere. Omissions of subject and modal follow this pattern in English, as a form of syntactic ellipsis. In-group slang frequently is situationally selected by familiarity of addressee.

When a friend is addressed in the Two Person Communication game, in which separated parties communicate solely by verbal messages, the selections among nonsense forms or colors are coded more efficiently, even though there is no feedback. In studies of sorority girls, comparison of speech to friend and nonfriend addressees repeatedly revealed a contrast in the *time* to describe objects when the speaker saw one and the hearer an array. The friends were both more succinct and more successful. Only in part was this difference because of reference to obviously private experience; e.g., "It's the color of Jan's new sweater". Most conspicuous was the contrast between technical descriptions to nonfriends and metaphorical description to friends; e.g., "It's an elephant doing the push-ups". The striking feature of these metaphorical descriptions is that they are very successful even when a nonfriend encounters them; thus, the question arises, Why not use metaphor to strangers? Two explanations need testing: possibly the use of metaphor seems self-revealing; our formal educational system clearly downgrades metaphorical forms of description. The contrast between Brent and Katz' (1967) college students and Job Corps Negroes illustrates the latter fact; given geometrical forms, descriptions much like college students' familiar speech were given by the less educated subjects.

How does the similarity of speech between friends arise? It is a common feature of interaction between two persons that if the parameters of speech are different they become more similar during the interaction. Thus, a given person's speech may vary depending on the speech features of the addressee. This phenomenon has been noted in the production features of rate, durations, and silence (e.g., Matarazzo *et al.* 1965), and is clearly the case for such features as lexical selection and syntax in addressing children. Ramanujan has commented that Brahmins adopt stereotyped non-Brahmin speech when addressing non-Brahmins; the same comparison needs to be made across social classes in this country. Address to children, i.e., baby talk, is also likely to be stereotyped. If in fact the similarity is an effect of the speech of alter, it should increase during the course of a long interaction; if it arises purely from stereotypes, it may remain unchanged.

In multilingual communities there must be some regularities in the control over the code to be used if both are to speak in the same code (Barker, 1947; Herman, 1961). Perhaps the more powerful controls the code choice, if setting and topic permit an option. Deference might be realized either by the adaptation of the lower ranked person to the preference of the higher, or by respectful avoidance of imitation – "keeping one's place". Cross-cultural research is needed to locate systematic features of social systems which may predict which party in a dyad changes more, and in which linguistic features. Further speculations are given in Grimshaw's survey paper (in press).

The most dramatic example of language shift affected by addressee is baby talk. This is a speech style occurring in many societies (Ferguson, 1964) for address to infants, and often to pets and lovers. In English, baby talk affects all levels of structure.

Most speakers are likely to be conscious of baby-talk lexicon, as they often are of the lexical features of styles. Baby-talk lexicon includes words like "potty", "weewee", "bunny", "night-night", "mommy", and "daddy". Many other words in adult speech become appropriate for speaking to infants when the suffix "-ie" is added. Work in progress by Kerry Drach and Ben Kobashigawa suggests that speech to children may be dramatically different in syntax, being simpler, and containing fewer errors, fewer subordinate clauses, more repetitions, and more imperatives and questions requiring feedback.

Phonological effects and paralinguistic features are especially conspicuous. Samples of talk to infants show certain general phonetic changes such as palatalization. Most striking is the use of a higher pitch and a sing-song, wide-ranging intonation. The younger the infant, the higher the pitch. Observations of the social distribution of this style show it to be more common in addressing other people's children than one's own. For instance, nurses use the paralinguistic features, at least, in persuading children, and in cooperative nurseries comparison of own-child and other-child addressees shows a distinct shift to more age attribution to own child.

Children themselves use many of the features of adult baby talk very early. In addressing younger siblings they may adopt lexical and paralinguistic features of the adult baby talk as early as age 2. In role-play, they use phrases and address terms from baby talk, e.g.; "Goo-goo, little baby", and freely employ the sing-song intonation in addressing "babies". In other respects, their role play is stereotyped rather than strictly imitative, for example, in the frequent use of role-names. It may be that the intonational and lexical features of baby talk may function simply as role markers in their play.

B. *Situation*

A situation refers to any constellation of statuses and setting which constrains the interaction that should or may occur – what Barker and Wright (1954) called the "standing behavior patterns". A situation, like a status, is a cultural unit, so that ethnological study is necessary to determine classes of situations.

At the university, a class is a situation. From the standpoint of the authorities, the criteria include the presence of an authorized instructor, students, and an approved time and place. From the standpoint of the instructor and students, there are strong constraints on function and on topical relevance.

Recently a student and faculty strike at the University of California brought these criteria to light. Instructors varied in which features of the definition they suspended in their effort to meet their obligations to the students but not to the university administration. Some met at a different time, others at a different place. Some used the same setting but discussed strike issues or public affairs. When the administration threatened to fire instructors who "failed to meet their obligations", it was not at all clear whether they used a minimal or maximal set of criteria.

Situation is most clearly defined when there are jointly dependent statuses and locales: church and priest, school and teacher, store and salesgirl, bus and driver, restaurant and waitress, plane and stewardess, clinic and physician. If the same personnel encounter each other elsewhere, for instance, at a baseball game, address terms (as distinct from attention-getting terms) may remain the same, but everything else about the interaction is likely to change.

If we examine these clear cases, we see that there are constraints on expected activities, rights, and obligations, and that there are, in several cases, clearly defined speech events such as the church service, the classroom lecture, the order to the waitress, the welcome, oxygen lecture of the stewardess, and the medical history in the clinic. Both the activities and the speech events are likely to be specific to the locale, though we might conceive of asking some information questions of the teacher or physician when he is off duty.

Because the activities and speech events have sequencing rules, they may be demarcated into discourse stages. The boundaries may be marked by routines or by code changes. After a church service, priest and parishioner may exchange personal greetings as friends, the priest using a radically different style than in his sermon. After a formal lecture, the opening of the floor to questions in cases of diglossia is signaled by a switch to the "lower" code, e.g. colloquial Arabic or Guarani (Ferguson, in Hymes 1964b; Rubin, in press). These are predictable discourse stages, and in this respect they differ from shifts which are at the option of the participants. Blom and Gumperz (in press) mentioned that local residents of Hemnisberget might use standard Norwegian when enacting their roles as buyer and seller, but if one wished to initiate a private conversation on personal matters, he would shift to the local dialect.

Analogous style switches occur here between colloquial speech and occupational argots, according to personnel present or situation. In some academic communities, it is considered a breach of etiquette to use occupational argot or discuss occupational topics at a dinner party or other "social situation"; others define these rules solely by personnel. Thus, the topic and register may change when wives are listening or when there is occupational diversity among the participants.

One strategy in identifying situations, is to look for folk terminology for them, such as church service, party, interview, picnic, lunch break, conversation, chat, class, and discussion. The status-oriented interaction between customers and sales personnel or waitresses has no name, and the interaction arising from statuses in work organizations has no folk name in English. If there is some independent and reliable way of identifying situational categories, then the difference between the named and the unnamed is important, for it suggests that the named situations enter into members' accounts.

Restricted languages illustrate situational constraints vividly. In hamburger stands and short-order cafes in the United States, abbreviated forms of speech appear. In these settings, there is a premium on speed in transmission of orders from the waitress to the cook. The number of alternatives is semantically limited, with certain high probabilities. In the ordering, one can see evidence that the code has been reduced almost to the minimum required for efficiency, within the structure of English syntax, by radical ellipsis. In studies by Brian Stross (1964) and by Marion Williams (1964), corpora were collected in a range of local settings:

one	one hamburger
two sweets	two sweet rolls
barbeef	barbecued beef sandwich
boil five	5-minute boiled egg
burger without	one hamburger without onions
beeny up	bacon and eggs, sunny side up
bacon and	bacon and eggs (differs with locale)
one M. O.	one hamburger, mustard only
L. T. plain	lettuce and tomato salad
ham and over rye	ham and eggs over, on rye
five squirt three	five coffees, three with cream

Stross pointed out that the underlying rule for all of these instances, except the last, is (number) + (name) + (describer). This kind of syntax appears in normal English in phrases like "five hamburgers without onions". The odd appearance of the restricted syntax arises from the optional omission of *any* of these elements, and from the appearance in the describer class of items like "and" and "without" which normally do not appear alone. It is hard to think of any way of omitting the function word rather than the noun in "without onions", but in the case of "ham and eggs" it seems possible that the form could be "ham eggs". This would violate the general rule that the last item be a describer and obviously subordinate. Note that when there is an adjective-noun phrase in the gloss, the two can be compressed into one word by making the adjective a prefix, as in "barbeef".

The abbreviation devices summarized by Stross include loss of segments (burger), use of initials (especially to replace conjoined nouns), loss of name (of most probable item), container for contents (cup for spaghetti), and preparation unique to an item (boil for egg).

The last item on the list does not follow the structural rule. It comes from a trucker's cafe, in which the corpus was kitchen talk rather than waitress ordering. This corpus was distinguished by a lot of colorful slang, much of it from vintage army usage and pejorative in tone. The efficiency pressure did not take priority here, and the structural rules were therefore different. Single word examples are "wop" for spaghetti, "pig" for hot dogs, "rabbit" for salad, and "grease" for fries. Longer units of the slang type are "burn a cow" for two well-done hamburgers, "bowl a slop" for a bowl of the soup of the day, "cap'ns galley" for pancakes topped by egg. That abbreviation did not dominate is suggested in cases which the other rule would reduce: "one order grease", "one wop with balls". In the last case humor wins out over brevity, which would yield "one wop with" or even "wop with". "One green bitch with T.I." for green goddess salad with thousand island dressing could have been reduced to "green T.I." or "bitch T.I."

Restaurants in Switzerland and London were observed, and similar forms of restricted language were found only in London's "Wimpy bars". Here the forms are so similar to American hamburger stands that one can guess that some of the language traveled with the product. In the interchanges in other restaurants, no evidence of radical ellipsis was found. One reason may be that observations were made within kitchens and, as we have seen in regard to the trucker's cafe, kitchen talk evidently is not constrained by the same brevity pressures as orders to the kitchen.

The mere cataloging of cultural units is not likely to bear much fruit unless the features of the situations which effect sociolinguistic rules can be identified. Moscovici (1967) has cleverly manipulated situational features in the Two Person Communication game. It is common to speak of "formal" situations, but it is not clear what makes a situation formal. Labov has suggested that degree of self-monitoring constitutes a dimension permitting alignment of situations on a continuum. Work- or status-oriented situations vs. person-oriented situations provides another contrast. In the first case, there is likely to be some criterion of achievement in an activity; in the second, the focus of attention can be turned to selves and to expressions of personal emotions. Watson (1958) distinguished work, family, and sociable interaction. But these differences are essentially differences in function.

C. Speech Acts, Topic, and Message

"What are you talking about?" "We were just saying hello." "We were telling jokes". "I was introducing Joe." Subordinate to organized exchanges like parties and work situations are classes we have called "speech acts." In the above examples, their identity is suggested by the folk classification. Here the informants can label segments of interaction.

There also must be unlabeled interaction. "Hello. Where is the post office?" addressed to a passerby, or, "My name is George Landers. What time is it?" to a stranger, violate, according to Labov, sequencing rules. If this is the case, the conjoined segments must have identifiable properties by which the rules can be characterized abstractly. In bilingual interaction, the segments may entail language shift.

There is no reason to assume that speech acts are the same everywhere. Certain special forms of discourse like poetry and speech-making may have components known only to specialists. Whether and why there are labels used in the teaching of these performances is itself a sociolinguistic problem.

Speech acts in English include greetings, self-identification, invitations, rejections, apologies, and so on. The ones identified so far tend to be routines, but we can expect to find other more abstract units as research proceeds.

When conversations have an explicit message with informational content, they can be said to have a *topic*. "What are you talking about?" "Nothing". "Gossip". "Shop talk". "The weather". "The war". "We were having an automobile discussion about the psychological motives for drag-racing in the streets." In everyday discourse, the question of topic is most likely to occur in invitations or rejections so that the answers serve either to exclude a new arrival or to give him enough information to participate. Besides selecting personnel for participation, topics may be governed by a continuity rule. In a formal lecture in a university, there is a constraint on continuity and relevance, just as there is in technical writing, where editing can enforce the constraint. Evidences of constraint are apologies for deviation: "That reminds me . . ." "Oh, by the way . . ." "To get back to the question . . ." "To change the subject . . ." Cultural rules regarding speech events may include constraints as to the grounds for relevance.

Kjolseth (1967) has found in analysis of some group interaction that topical episodes are key factors in speakers' tactics:

A performer's tactic may be to direct his episode as a probe into the preceding episode. In contrast, in another situation his tactic may be to extend and elaborate some antecedent episode. On still another occasion his tactic may be to close off and limit a previous episode . . . . These tactical types are based on, or defined in terms of, two qualities abstracted from the performances: (a) the episodic locus of relevances drawn from the existent conversation resource, and (b) the purpose of the episode with respect to surrounding episodes.

Lennard and Bernstein (in press) have examined topical continuity in therapeutic sessions, and found the amount of continuity to be related to satisfaction. The three examples given by Kjolseth would involve topical continuation, recycling, or change, respectively. These general features of speech events require that members be able to identify relevance but not necessarily label topics.

There is yet a third form of evidence that topic may be a cultural unit.

Bilinguals can frequently give reliable accounts of topical code-switching, and their behavior often corresponds, in general, to their accounts (Ervin-Tripp, 1964).

We can thus argue that *topic* must be a basic variable in interaction, on the grounds that speakers can identify topical change as generating code-shift, that speakers can sometimes report what they are talking about, and that topical continuity, recycling, and change may be normative features of speech events, or at least relevant to values regarding good conversations.

The analysis of *messages* refers to two-term relationships, whereas *topic* is a single term allowing for simple taxonomies. Here I intend to refer only to the manifest or explicit message. The reason for the distinction is that latent content categories typically refer to intent (e.g., Dollard and Auld, 1959; Katz, 1966; Leary, 1957; Marsden, 1965). My position here is that intent or function is part of the constellation of social features out of which interaction is generated. It can be realized in a variety of ways, of which verbal interaction is only one. We seek regular rules by which one can relate underlying categories with their formal realizations or the formal features of interaction with their social meanings. Failure to discover such rules has led to considerable discouragement with the evident arbitrariness of content classifications in studies of natural discourse.

The manifest message, on the other hand, is the product of the social features of the situation as well as of intent, and is therefore inseparable from the interaction product. All the selections made in realization of the functions of communication can carry some kind of information, whether about the speaker, the situation, the hearer, or the topic. In detail, given alternations cannot do all at once, though they may be ambiguous as to which is intended. In this case, the *message* is intended to refer only to what is said or implied about the topic. There have been numerous summaries of ways of classifying messages (e.g., Pool, 1959). A recent innovation is logical analysis (Véron *et al.*, 1965). The underlying structure of logical linkages between terms in utterances is analyzed, and semantic relations are then described in terms of logical relations between pairs of units (e.g., equivalence, inference, conjunction, specification of conditions, sequential relations, explanation, and opposition, causes). A Markov semantic analysis revealed very large and consistent differences between subject groups, which were, in the study reported, clinical categories.

The same speaker information potentially can be realized through different means, for example, through explicit message content and through paralinguists features. The conflict between these messages creates an interesting question about which is dominant. According to

Mehrabian and Wiener (1967), who used controlled stimulus materials, regardless of the instructions to the listeners, the tone of voice is the dominant signal for judging affect. What is called the "double bind" must be a consequence of more than conflicting messages; for instance, it could be a requirement of overt response to the overt message on one occasion and to the paralinguistic cue on another, with no signal as to which is required.

The definition of appropriate units for analysis is important in comparing results of different studies. Watson and Potter (1962) discussed a macro-unit, the episode, which is defined by the stability of component features: the role system of the participants, the major participants, the focus of attention, and the relationship toward the focus of attention. The unit thus may be less than an utterance in length or may include the contributions of many speakers. In Lennard's research, one might say that satisfaction is related to the length of episodes. Watson and Potter chose the term "focus of attention" in order to differentiate cases where the topic is a person's experience, an ongoing activity, or an abstract referential category as in a "discussion."

In thematic analyses, it is common to use either episodic (Katz, 1966) or sentence units (Auld and White, 1956). However, the sentence is not, strictly speaking, a unit in oral discourse. One can see texts in which long sequences of clauses linked by "and then . . ." occur. Are these separate sentences or one sentence? There have been four criteria used separately with different results: message criteria, structural or linguistic units (e.g., any segment containing a verb or naming phrases in isolation; John and Berney, 1967), pauses, and intonational contours (Dittman and Llewellyn, 1967).

D. Functions of Interaction

1. Criteria
Firth (Hymes, 1964b) was among many who sought to identify the functions of speech. He included phatic communion (solidarity); pragmatic efficiency (accompanying work); planning and guidance; address; greetings, farewells, adjustment of relations, and so on; and speech as a commitment (courts, promises). Primarily, his view of function was the social value of the act.

To a psychologist, function is likely to be viewed from the standpoint of the interacting parties, either the sender or the receiver. Soskin has played tapes to listeners and asked them to report what they would *say* and what they would *think*. This method assumes that function is effect. It is close to Blom and Gumperz' (in press) criterion of social meaning.

A second method is to analyze actual instances of acts and to infer whether the receiver's response satisfied the speaker, either from his overt behavior or by questioning him. This method includes action, response, and reaction. It is derived from Skinner's (1957) theory that speech is operant behavior which affects the speaker through the mediation of a hearer. Feedback and audience consistency presumably "shape" effective speech in the normal person. In this method, function is identified by classes of satisfactory listener responses.

If intent, conscious or unconscious, is imputed to a speaker on the basis of some features of the content or form of his speech, a third form of functional analysis appears. This, of course, is the method of latent content analysis (e.g., Katz, 1966; Watson, 1958).

A set of function categories was devised to account for the initiation of dyadic interaction on the basis of a corpus of instances of action, response, and reaction (Ervin-Tripp, 1964): The list includes explicit requests for goods, services, and information; implicit requests for social responses; offering of information or interpretations; expressive monologues; routines; and speech to avoid alternative activities.

Soskin and John (1963) devised a category system based on a combination of structural and semantic features. We can use their system to subclassify each of the above functional categories. For example, the following might all be requests for the loan of a coat:

"It's cold today." (structone)
"Lend me your coat." (regnone)
"I'm cold." (signone)
"That looks like a warm coat you have." (metrone)
"Br-r-r." (expressive)
"I wonder if I brought a coat." (excogitative)

One simple way to examine requests is to compare regnones, in which the request function is explicit, with all other categories, in terms of social distribution. In a term paper, Bessie Dikeman and Patricia Parker (1964) found that within families indirect request forms dominated between equals, almost half were regnones when seniors addressed juniors, and from juniors, regnones dominated. Examples from their paper are these:

"Where's the coffee. Dremsel?" (it is visible).
(to wife) [gloss: bring me the coffee]
"Is that enough bacon for you and Thelma?" (to husband)
[gloss: save some for Thelma]
"It's 7:5." (to daughter)
[gloss: hurry up]
"Mother, you know I don't have a robe. Well, we're
having a slumber party tomorrow night."

"Oh, dear I wish I were taller." (to adult brother)
[gloss: get down the dishes]

In factory settings, by contrast, requests to subordinates were more
often regnones and often direct imperatives.

In a sample of requests offered during 80 hours of observation in a
university office, Carol Pfuderer (1968) found that the major selector
was familiarity and rank.

(1) Whatever their status, familiar peers used direct imperatives.

(2) When the peer was farther away, the imperative was followed by
tag questions, "please", address forms, with rising pitch, e.g., "ask Mar-
cy, why don't you?"

(3) Requests within the addressee's territory were deferential, even
to familiar peers.   ·

(4) Requests to addressees of either higher or lower rank took the
form of modal questions ("Would you get me some coffee, Jeanie?"),
pragmatic neutralizations, or displacement of addressee. Neutralization
refers to cases where two different functions could be realized by identical speech acts, which are therefore ambiguous, in intent.

(5) Pragmatic neutralizations included information questions ("Has
anyone gone to Accounting this week?" "Whose turn is it to make
coffee this week, Ruby?") and structones ("It's stuffy in here"; "Someone
has to see Dean Smith").

(6) Where there was a large rank difference upward, the request
might be displaced to an addressee nearer in rank. For example, a
request for a stapler by a seated secretary was given not to the senior
professor standing next to it but to a peer standing equidistant from it,
and the deferential form was used: "Joan, would you please get the
stapler for me?"

Request and persuasion require action on the part of alter so that the
obligations and privileges inherent in the social relations of the personnel are likely to be realized in differences in linguistic expression. We
might expect pragmatic neutralization when the requestor is deferent
or reluctant to ask at all, or in situations where requests are highly
frequent and familiarity produces high mutual nurturance and assurance
of interpretability. In the restaurant studies, "please" was used for
requested acts extraneous to the addressee's duties, perhaps a version of
the territoriality feature in Miss Pfuderer's findings.

We can expect that where variant address forms exist, they might alternate in request situations. Milla Ayoub (1962), in a discussion of
bipolar kin terms in Arabic, pointed out that in addition to proper
names, a mother could call her son by either of two terms that can also
mean "my mother". When a parent wishes to cajole or placate a child,

but not command him, he uses these bipolar terms. This is particularly the case with sons. These terms are never heard in direct commands.

In discussing current address practices in the Soviet Union, Kantorovich (1966) mentioned that friends might switch from "*ty*" to "*vy*" with first name and patronymic when help was asked.

2. *Approval-Seeking*

In human communication, as among lower primates (Diebold, 1967), many of the signals for what we have called "requests for social responses" are gestural or paralinguistic. Rosenfeld (1966) found that among American males, liking was related to the following factors in the speaker's behavior: long sentences, few self-words, and high reinforcement of the speech of alter through head nods and verbal routines; among women, frequent initiation of utterances, many sentences per speech, many speech disturbances and false starts, many questions and many words referring to alter, and reinforcement by nods produced greater liking by strangers. Rosenfeld also found which of these features were subject to conscious manipulation under instructions and role-playing: volubility, frequency of speaking and length of sentences, and more speech disturbances, as well as verbal reinforcing routines. The major omission is the semantic component (the kind Dale Carnegie discusses) of orienting the *content* of the interaction to alter rather than self. Probably address forms change also, among friends, when affiliative functions are primary. Tyler (1965), for example, suggested that certain address alternatives in the Koya kin system are employed when cross-cousins engage in the joking relationship which is their privilege. It was noted earlier that such alternates might even be used in deferential address with familiar addressees, for example, "Dr. S." rather than "Dr. Smith" from technician to physician when outsiders were absent.

There may prove to be classes of functionally equivalent responses by alter, such as head nods and brief verbal routines both occuring as options in response to the same stimuli. The identification of these response classes in turn can provide a criterion for recognizing the speech variables which elicit them from alter, and thus provide grounds for classifying "approval-seeking behavior", more objective than the intuition of judges. Of course whether or not there is any empirical value in these categories depends on whether or not they enter into speech rules consistently.

3. *Effects of Function Shifts*

Functions can enter into rules for the selection of settings by participants, the selection of addressees, and formal changes within the interaction.

"Oh my back, it's killing me today. I can hardly move."
"Yeah, it must be the weather. My leg's been aching all day."
"I was supposed to get a shot of cortisone today, but my husband couldn't take me to the doctor's."
"I hurt my leg in the army . . ." (long description).
"Oh. Well, I must get back to work."

Something went wrong in this interaction. The woman did not, in effect, respond to the man's story of woe and terminated the conversation.

The collection of large corpora of natural sequences might not yield enough such instances for analysis by classification; a role-playing method might be one approximation. We might find that responses to statements of physical distress take the form of inquiries of cause, routine sympathy expressions, or offers of help. In this case, none of these happened. Instead, the addressee himself made a statement of physical distress and preempted the floor. Watson and Potter (1962) stated that when the focus of attention of conversation is tied to self, "interaction is governed by rules of tact." Presumably these include certain obligations of response and limitations on inquiry topics. Only a method which allows gathering data on appropriate responses and testing the consequences of inappropriate responses can identify what these rules might be.

In the course of any given discourse segment, we can expect to find changes in the functions, which, in turn, affect form. These episodes arise from:

(1) Sequencing rules within the speech event.

(2) Changes in the activity, if any, accompanying the interaction (e.g., a ball game, dinner preparation).

(3) Disruptive events such as the arrival of new personnel, accidents like bumps, sneezes, and phone calls, which require routines to correct the situation.

(4) Shifts arising from unexpected responses of alter, leading to changes in tactics or a change in function.

(5) Function satiation. Functions presumably oscillate in patterned ways in stable groups.

(6) Topic-evoked shifts in functions. Under the impact of instructions or of associative dynamics, the topic may change in the course of the conversation. These changes can alter the available resources for the participants and thereby change their intent. If the topic shifts from childrearing to economics, for example, a bachelor may find he has greater resources for displaying knowledge and receiving recognition. He may speak more and use more technical vocabulary, perhaps even to the point that listeners do not understand. Many such instances have

been observed in the speech of bilinguals when topic and language were controlled by instructions (Ervin, 1964; Ervin-Tripp, 1964, 1967).

Blom and Gumperz (in press) found that among university-trained villagers, many features of standard Norwegian appeared when topics shifted from local to nonlocal. But they found that the change depended on the message. In the offering of information, speakers with a large repertoire of speech alternatives can maximize credibility by adopting the most suitable role. Thus, discussion of university structure might elicit use of more standard Norwegian forms than would gossip about instructors, where student speech features would be adopted, especially those shared with addressees.

Gumperz has noted that among Puerto Ricans in Jersey City, in situations where Spanish is spoken, English is an attention getter. In Trukese and Ponapean (Fischer, 1965), a phonotactic feature of the other language is a marker for function shifting of specific kinds that fit the stereotypes of the groups, just as a dialect feature might be here.

As functions change, address too may change through a conversation. David Day has described changes when an argument occurred in a class regarding an instructor's views of the student's beliefs. Address progressed from FN to Dr. LN to Professor LN. In comments with other students as addressee, LN was used in reference to the instructor in front of him. Concurrently, slang decreased.

When there is agreement about the normal, unmarked address form to alters of specified statuses, then any shift is a message. Friedrich (Hymes, 1964b) gave convincing cases of momentary shifts at times of personal crises. He pointed out that in a public setting, friends would mask their intimacy with V; in talking of personal topics they could invoke their friendship with "ty" and remove it for impersonal topics with "vy".

Kantorovich (1966, p. 43) gave similar examples in current practice: "I say 'ty' to my subordinates, but I certainly don't do this in order to belittle them. I know that they'll answer me with 'vy', but this isn't grovelling – it's a mark of respect . . . . Somebody I call 'ty' is somehow closer to me than someone I have to call 'vy' . . . . If I get mad at one of my workers, and he needs a bawling out, I frequently switch to 'vy' . . . ."

" . . . When cursing, many people who customarily use 'ty' suddenly switch to 'vy', and many who are on a mutual 'vy' basis switch to 'ty' " (Kostomarov, 1967).

In systems with age or rank asymmetries of address, the use of the more deferential form to an equal or subordinate can mean either that they are receiving respect or are being put off at a distance. Brown and Gilman (1960) found that conservatives use V more than radicals. To account fully for the interpretation of such actions by the receivers, we need to know the other signals, such as tone of voice and other address features, and the available ambiguities of the relationship. In the case of courtship, for example, the important dimension is closeness or distance, and address changes would be so interpreted.

E. Rules for Switching

I have emphasized throughout this article that linguistic interaction is a system of behavior in which underlying functions are realized through an organized set of output rules within a social situation. If the function requires conveying an explicit message with informational content, some semantic information is presented in the alternatives selected. Other alternatives require the representation of social information.

In addressee-dominated rules like those in Section II, the effects of function switching can be represented as transformations upon the outputs of the addressee rules. They may take the form of simple replacements, e.g., if familiarity exists, different names may be employed as a direct representation of varied functions. Thus a mode or selector for familiarity and for function is added to the branching rules. Similarly, Tyler (1966) has formal rules for selection of kin reference according to situation, after other semantic selectors.

Blom and Gumperz (in press) have suggested that metaphorical switching simply consists of treating the addressee as though his social features were different. In this case, the rule acts upon the selection points. In the case of Dr. Poussaint, hostile intent was represented in the selection of Child – rather than Adult – at the first selection point. Presumably this possibility suggested itself by the existence of a traditional southern system of address to Negroes in which all but the very old (aunty) were addressed as children. When Sacks asked his students to play the role of boarders with their families during vacation, their silence, politeness of address and request, and withdrawal from gossip and semantic ellipsis in conversation were interpreted by their families as evidence of sickness or hostility.

The Russian example implies that a simple transformation upon the output forms can express hostility; on the other hand, the inversion may be a consequence of transformation of selection features, making the friend a nonfriend and the formal associate an inferior. Such general rules are a necessity if familiarity is absent, since they permit the interpretation of new instances on the basis of the hearer's general knowledge of the system of sociolinguistic rules.

'Rules' could refer to structures for generating or interpreting speech, to reports of beliefs about practices, or to standards of correctness. We have given examples of all three kinds of rules, not always clearly distinguishing them. Labov's Index of Linguistic Insecurity (1966) compared the last two.

Behavioral rules and reports about behavior are likely to be systematically different. If the norms contain a probability or frequency factor, a speaker's beliefs are, instead, categorical (Labov, 1966). Beliefs about the social selectors in sociolinguistic rules are more likely to include features of personnel (since categorization devices realize these features) than to note functional variation. Syntactical variables are not remembered (Sachs, 1967) beyond the time needed for decoding, unless they are markers that help us classify the speaker.

In multilingual communities, phonological, syntactic, and semantic shifting is not observed (Gumperz, 1964, 1967). Even borrowed vocabulary is unnoticed by members if values oppose borrowing (Blom and Gumperz, in press). Some speakers cannot remember the language in which they just spoke, let alone report it to an interviewer. These phenomena are not merely grounds for distrusting members' reports. Just as reference to a relative (Tyler, 1966) is affected by more than the semantic dimensions of reference, so the act of describing even to one's self, is a product which could realize a variety of functions. Members' reports are likely to be as sensitive to social variation as any speech act mentioned in this article, and therefore prove as amenable to study.

IV. LINGUISTIC DIVERSITY

A. The Fundamentals of Communication

The fundamental fact about language is its obvious diversity. Moving from country to country, region to region, class to class, and caste to caste, we find changes in language. Linguistic diversity apparently is related to social interaction.

Linguistic similarity must be explained, for it is clear that separated sets of speakers will develop different languages. Two quite different bases for similarity can be examined: the fundamental requirement of mutual intelligibility among people who belong to the same social community, and the consequences of variability in overt behavior in terms of social values.

A test for mutual intelligibility might be the Two Person Communication game. First used by Carroll (1958) several decades ago, it has recently been revived (Maclay, 1962; Krauss and Weinheimer, 1964; Brent and Katz, 1967). A hearer out of sight of a speaker selects, constructs, or in some way responds to instructions from a speaker regarding a set of materials. Feedback may or may not be allowed. The advantage of this method is that one can examine the relation between success in the objective task and various speech features, and that the social relation of speaker and hearer can be controlled. For our question about the degree of similarity required for intelligibility, we shall assume optimal social attitudes (Wolff, in Hymes, 1964b) and simply concern ourselves with features of linguistic structure. No feedback is allowed, and we shall ask what the bare minimum of linguistic similarity might be that would allow successful transmission of messages about referents.

(1) There must be shared categories of meaning so that speakers will attend to the same features of the referent materials.

(2) There must be shared lexicon identifying the significant referents, attributes, relationships, and actions, and shared central meanings for this lexicon. Languages which are related and have many cognates are instances.

(3) The shared lexicon must be recognizable. Thus its morphophonemic realizations must be similar, and the phonological and phonetic systems must be sufficiently alike to allow recognition of the similar items. Precisely what these limitations entail is not clear. Wurm and Laycock (1961) have shown that both phonetic and phonemic differences can lead to asymmetrical intelligibility of cognates among related dialects. They have found instances where A understood B but not vice versa. They suggested use of a phonetic hierarchy of rank to account for such cases. For instance, they found that the speaker using a stop could understand a speaker using a homologous fricative, but not the reverse. This suggestion is important and needs further testing. I would have predicted the reverse, on the grounds that a speaker's repertoire in comprehension includes child variants, which tend to be of 'higher rank' phonetically than their adult models.

A second point they make is that the phonological system relationships, i.e., those found in contrastive analysis, may allow predictions. We can suppose that one-to-one high frequency substitutions might be easy to recognize where the phonetic realization, but not the phonological system, is affected. Comprehension of foreign accents is easiest in such cases. O'Neil (in press) found that Faroese could understand Icelanders, but not vice versa, because of many-to-one conversion rules.

Further, there must be some similarities in phonotactic rules so that the lexical forms can be related. In instances of children's renditions of adult words, we often find that adults cannot comprehend because of the radical alteration in the word formation. Thus [mana] and [ŋən] are unlikely to be recognized as "banana" and "gun", and [me] and [ni] in another child are even less likely to be recognized as "blanket" and "candy", although each arises from regular replacement rules (Ervin-Tripp, 1966). In each case, the initial consonant is nasal if a nasal occurs anyplace in the adult word, and it is homologous with the initial consonant of the model word. Other word length and syllable-forming canons differ for two children.

(4) There must be shared order rules for the basic grammatical relations. By basic relations (McNeill, 1966), we mean subject-verb, verb-object, and modifier-head. Unless these minimal structures can be identified, the communication of messages is not possible, although topics or labels could be listed. Of course, these order constraints do not apply where the lexical items could only express one of these relations, as often is the case.

There has been, to my knowledge, no research raising precisely the above structural questions and using the Two Person Communication game. Esper (1966) studied the transmission of linguistic forms through a series of speakers experimentally, employing referents and artificial languages, but in a different procedure. He found surprisingly rapid morphological regularization, which suggests that this is the "natural" tendency historically, within socially isolated groups.

Stewart (1967) has commented on two natural instances of cross-language communication where precisely these factors might impair intelligibility. He cited two examples in which the dialect might impair intelligibility: "Ah 'own know wey 'ey lib", he argued, contains sufficient changes in phonetic realizations, word-formation rules, and so on, to seriously impair recognition of "I don't know where they live". "Dey ain't like dat" is likely to be misunderstood as "They aren't like that" rather than "They didn't like that." The dialect translation of the first would be "Dey not like dat" or "Dey don't be like dat," depending on a semantic contrast, not realized in standard English, between momentary and repeated conditions. This second example indicates that the basic grammatical relations may be the same, but misunderstanding still remains possible. Of course, Stewart was not discussing the highly restricted referential situation of our experiment.

The fascinating permutations on this experimental procedure would permit testing many analogs of natural language change and language contact. We have predicted that when speaker A addresses listener B, under optimal social conditions, the success of the intial communication depends on structural relations between languages *a* and *b*. If B has had earlier experience with other speakers of *a*, we might expect him to have learned to translate features of *a* into *b*, to some extent. It must take some frequency of instances to recognize structural similarities. We already know that A will provide better instructions, even without any feedback, with time (if he is old enough) (Krauss and Weinheimer, 1964). Where exchange is always unidirectional, B learns to understand language *a* to some degree, and becomes a 'passive bilingual'. Note that B is not just listening but is required by the task to perform actions;

thus, he is not like a television watcher.

If give-and-take can occur, it is conceivable that a third language, c, might develop, with shared properties drawn from a and b. Such a development would be like the growth of a pidgin between two mono-linguals under the press of trade or other limited encounters (Reinecke, in Hymes, 1964b). One test of the degree to which c is actually inter-mediate between the other two, or a composite, is to test whether when c is the code, A can communicate more successfully with B than he first did with B. That is, we assume that if c is closer to b than was a, it should be a more efficient means of communication, even to a neophyte listener.

The encounter of speakers from different language communities has had a variety of outcomes in natural conditions, including mutual bilin-gualism, the evolution of a pidgin, and one-way bilingualism (Reinecke, in Hymes, 1964b; Weinreich, 1953). It might be possible to explore the social conditions yielding these varied results by controlled manipulation of conditions.

An important feature of this procedure is that it can allow separate assessment of *comprehension* and *speech similarity*. If system a is un-derstood or perhaps translated into b by the listener, there is no impli-cation that B necessarily can speak language a. It is quite a separate issue whether features of a enter into the speech of B; under some social conditions, features could perhaps be transmitted without comprehen-sion.

Several recent studies of intergroup 'comprehension' make the issue of objective measurement of intelligibility important. Peisach (1965) has studied replacement of omitted items (the Cloze procedure) in passages of children's speech. She found that middle class children do better than lower class children in replacing every nth word verbatim in the middle class samples of speech, and on the lower class speech they do as well as the lower class children. When similarity of grammatical category alone is considered, she found Negro speech replaceable equally by all, but white speech easier for the middle class children (and for white children). The Cloze procedure requires actual emission of the appropriate response. It can be considered a form of comprehension test only if one believes in the "analysis-by-synthesis" theory of com-prehension; it is not, on its face, a comprehension measure. Another way of stating the results is that middle class children can predict and imitate lower class and Negro speech, but lower class and Negro children are unwilling (or unable) to produce middle class and white speech by the fifth grade. Harms (1961) found the opposite among adults, who "understood" speakers of high social rank best, or of their own level when using Cloze.

Labov and Cohen (1967) have some striking evidence suggesting that many Negro children, also in New York, can comprehend but not produce standard English. Many of the children highly motivated to imitate sentences gave back "I asked Alvin if he knows how to play basketball" as "I asks Alvin do he know how to play basketball." These translations are regarded by the children as accurate imitations. Likewise "Nobody ever saw that game" would become "Nobody never saw that game". For the deep grammatical differences not arising by deletion rules out of the standard grammar, the children frequently *understood* but were not able to produce the standard forms. Nor did they notice the difference, going directly to the meaning (Jacqueline Sacks, 1967).

Two groups can communicate extremely well, indeed perfectly, though they speak different languages. Multilingual conversations are an everyday occurence in many social milieux. There may be interspersed lexical borrowings in both languages, but if there is a common semantic core, mutual communication can survive very different realization rules.

If it is the case that the social life of a community could be carried on without speech similarity, then we cannot explain language similarity solely by the demands of basic communication. A more profound account is needed.

B. Communicative Frequency

A common explanation for the evidence of linguistic similarity and its distribution is the frequency of communication between speakers. The most obvious determinants of frequency are proximity, work, power, and liking. If one undertakes to write a rule predicting who will speak to whom, with a given intent, proximity always enters into the rule. Thus in housing projects, people at positions near high-traffic points are talked with more; in classrooms, neighbors become acquainted; and in small groups, seating controls interchange frequency (Hare and Bales, 1963).

Some selection factors may make proximity secondary, except as a cost component, so that we find people commuting hours to a place of work or flying six thousand miles to a conference. In small groups, resources or status, assigned or assumed, may increase frequency of interchange (Bales *et al.*, 1951). Considerable research suggests that people select "similar" addressees for social interaction, which, in turn, increases their liking. Homans, in fact, pointed out that the interaction arising from sheer proximity could create "sentiments" (1950) and thereby increase liking. All of these features which measurably increase interaction in studies of face-to-face groups have cumulative effects that are visible sociologically.

These features of face-to-face interaction compounded over many individuals should be evident in the geographical distribution of linguistic features. One of the oldest forms of sociolinguistics is dialect geography. The distribution of particular speech features is mapped, the boundaries being isoglosses. Normally these are not identical for different speech features. Extensive studies have been made of such distributions in Europe and in the United States – for instance, of bag vs. sack, grea/s/y vs. grea/z/y. In general, linguistic features reveal the patterns of migration, intermarriage, and transportation routes. If there are natural barriers or social barriers to marriage or friendship, isoglosses may appear. Thus, McDavid (1951) noted that the rise of the large northern ghettoes in the past 40 years has led to an increase in the linguistic distance between northern whites and Negroes. Individual lexical items may follow the salesman: 'tonic' is used in the Boston marketing area for soft drinks, and 'chesterfield' for couch or sofa in the San Francisco wholesale region.

The political boundaries between communities are sharp but may not seriously affect interaction frequency over time. This we can infer from the fact that isoglosses do not match political boundaries. Isoglosses often do not even correspond with each other; that is, individual features may not diffuse at the same time or in the same way. Changes, as one would expect on a frequency model, are gradual. Gumperz (1958), in a study of phonemic isoglosses, found that changes were gradual even within the isoglosses. The functional load or practical importance of the contrast gradually decreased until it disappeared, and the phonetic distinctiveness also decreased.

The most extreme test of the argument that frequency of communication reduces speech diversity occurs in bilingual contacts. Gumpertz (1967) located a border region between Indo-Aryan and Dravidian speaking sectors of India in which speakers were bilingual, using Marathi and Kannada in different settings. These border dialects have become increasingly similar in centuries of bilingualism. They have the same semantic features, syntax, and phonology, and differ only in the phonemic shape of morphemes, what we might call the vocabulary and function words. Each dialect is essentially a morpheme-by-morpheme translation of the other. However, other speakers of Kannada still identify this dialect as a form of Kannada because they recognize its morphemes – it is simply a deviant form, as Jamaican Creole is a deviant form of English.

This example illustrates both convergence of speech with high interaction frequency, and the maintenance of contrast. The convergence occurs at those levels of language we believe are least conscious and least criterial for the identification of the language. Speakers tend to identify languages by the shape of the morphemes, by the vocabulary, but even more by its function words and inflectional and derivational morphemes. The Kannada-Marathi example demonstrates that in spite of high contact frequency, speakers may insist on maintaining linguistic diversity, and that they may, in fact, believe it to be greater than it is.

There are many instances, to be discussed later, where frequency is high but speech distinctiveness is maintained. Castes in India interact with high frequency; Negro servants in the United States interact with employers; lower class pupils interact with teachers; and monolingual Spanish-speaking grandmothers interact with monolingual English-speaking grandsons – yet diversity persists.

High frequency of communication is a necessary but not a sufficient condition for increased linguistic similarity. High frequency of communication must result, at a minimum, in passive bilingualism of both parties, active bilingualism of one party, or a lingua franca. The only necessity is that each understand the speech of the other.

We do not yet know what the consequences of passive control of two systems must be. Active control typically leads to convergence at certain levels, starting with semantic boundaries and frequency of syntactic options (Earle, 1967; Ervin, 1961; McNeill, 1966; Ervin-Tripp, in press). We have argued that there are cognitive reasons for such fusions and that they tend to take place when social conditions, such as contact with monolinguals, reading, and strong values about co-occurrence restrictions, do not provide strong support for system separation. Presumably, passive control of a second language has less impact.

Only one study has directly related the communication frequency of individual persons who all communicate to speech similarity. Hammer *et al.* (1965) measured the observed centrality of individuals, and also the person-to-person frequency for every pair in a New York coffee shop with a regular clientele. They obtained speech samples and used the Cloze procedure. Central persons were most predictable, and each person most successfully predicted the omitted items from the speech of persons with whom he interacted most.

It is not quite clear what is measured in Cloze. All phonological features are missing. What is included are semantic factors that influence collocations, vocabulary, and perhaps some aspects of grammar. This study at first seems to support frequency as a critical variable in similarity, but it may not actually meet the critical limitations. The study was done in a social setting, interaction was social, and the members were parts of friendship networks. That is, some third variable may have determined both interaction frequency and similarity on Cloze. The hidden variable seems to be cohesiveness.

C. *Cohesiveness and Linguistic Diversity*

It seems that people talk like those with whom they have the closest social ties. We do not know precisely why this is the case; it may be that the features of social relationships which bring about this result are not the same for all types of speech similarity. In social networks and groups, there is a high frequency of interaction. The high attraction of others in the group or network means that they not only serve as models but can also act as reinforcing agents in their responses to speech, affecting attitudes toward features in the community repertoire. In addition, there might be secondary reinforcement in sounding like a valued person.

All levels of speech appear to be affected. With respect to the phonetic realization of phonemes, age may constrain changes in the system. Even under optimal conditions, many persons over 12 years old seem to have difficulty changing their phonetic realization rules except under careful monitoring.

Labov (1966) has argued that the everyday vernacular is stabilized by puberty on the basis of the peer model. Cultures where peer ties are weaker (if any exist) would provide a valuable comparison.

The *functions* of communication in cohesive networks necessarily include a high frequency of requests for social reinforcement, and of expressive speech. The social group may or may not be concerned with information and opinion exchange for its own sake. Davis (1961), in a study of the maintenance or dissolution of 'great books' discussion groups, found that if there were many members of a social network in such a group, its durability was enhanced for college-educated members and decreased for noncollege-educated. He suggested that for the latter there might be a conflict between interaction practices in the network and the constraints of the discussion group. Bossard (1945) commented on large differences between families in the extent of information-exchange in dinner table conversation.

The most ingenious work on interfamily differences in communication has been conducted by Basil Bernstein. He has pointed out (in press a,b) that communicative patterns and socialization methods within families are related to occupational roles and to the character of a family's social network. Empirical support was found in mothers' reports of use of appeals to children, emphasis on different functions of language, and encouragement of interaction. In turn, London five-year-olds differed by social class (and by mothers' reports) in the variety of nouns and adjectives, use of relative clauses, use of pronouns with extraverbal referents, and in ability to switch style with task. That some of these differences may reflect performance customs rather than capacity is suggested by the report of Cowan (1967) that American working class children, though less successful than middle class children on the Two Person Communication game, learned fast when paired with middle class partners.

Hess and Shipman (1965), who observed actual mother-child interaction in Negro preschool families, found considerable social class variation and between-family variation in the extent to which mothers used the situation to elicit labeling and informational communication from the children. The measures correlated two years later with oral comprehension. Schatzmann and Strauss (1955) found social class differences in oral narratives that may be related to Bernstein's distinction. See also Lawton (1964).

There has been too little study of natural interaction *within* social groups to extricate what the important difference are – whether they lie in the amount of interaction of children with adults vs. peers and siblings, whether there are differences in encounters with strangers and training of children in competence with outsiders, or whether there are differences in emphasis in intragroup speech functions.

Because evidence about the verbal skills of lower class Negroes came from formal testing situations and classrooms, there have been widespread misconceptions about "verbal deprivation" in American society, with expensive educational consequences. Recent investigators such as Labov and Cohen (1967) in Harlem and Eddington and Claudia Mitchell in San Francisco and Oakland have recorded natural interaction. All have found that Negro lower class speakers are highly verbal in terms of speech frequency. Both adolescents and children engage with great skill in verbal games for which they have complex traditions. "Controlled situations" may, in fact, obscure the very skills which have been most developed within a particular group.

"General verbal deprivation" could conceivably exist. It most probably would be found in unusual social isolation, or in cases of social marginality, particularly where a language has been lost but there has not been full access to a range of functions in a second language. For further detailed discussion of research on this point and some new data, see Cazden (1966, 1967).

Topics of discourse are likely to be different in cohesive networks as a result of differing values and interests. This produces considerable impact on the semantic structure and lexicon.

One way of studying differences in messages arising from communication is to examine content shifts, under acculturation, where there may be radical changes in social allegiances. A study of this phenomenon in Japanese women married to Americans showed that there was considerable difference between women who gave messages typical of their agemates in Tokyo and those who were more like American women, even when speaking Japanese (Ervin-Tripp, 1967). Word associations, sentence completions, TATs, story completions, and semantic differentials were all used in both languages. In general, the women who remained more Japanese in response content would rather be Japanese than American, preserve more Japanese customs, and keep up strong ties to Japan. The chief characteristics of the women who shifted to American responses were that they identified with American women, had close American friends, read American magazines, and met somewhat less opposition to their marriage from Japanese friends and family. The last point implies that in Japan they may have been less conservative. Though both sets of women would seem, on the surface, to have had a cohesive tie to an American partner, the interviews revealed striking differences. Marriages in Japan involve far more social separation of husband and wife than here; for example, there is little joint socializing with nonkin. Many of the Japanese women in this country do not regard their husbands as confidants in trouble, and may, indeed, seldom see them. When either the husband or an American friend was regarded as a close confidant, the messages were more American. It is, in fact, not easy to give 'typically American' responses on many of these tests, so their ability to do so represents a considerable degree of subtle learning.

Semantic innovation is one of the striking features of cohesive groups. There may be new activities requiring new names; there may be finer discriminations required along continua; and there may be new conceptual categories. These are realized by lexical innovations which spread within the network. Examples are "she's in high drag" in the homosexual network, referring to a male homosexual in women's clothing (Cory, 1952); "prat", "breech", "insider", "tail pit", and "fob", pickpocket jargon for pockets (Conwell, 1937); "cooling the mark out" by the confidence man (Goffman, 1952); and "trivial", "motivated", and "reflexive", terms used among transformationalists and ethnomethodologists respectively, with special meanings. Many examples can be found in Mauer (1962).

A glimpse of the working of this process can be seen in the Two Person Communication game.

Krauss and Weinheimer (1964) found that reference phrases became abbreviated with practice. Given the limitation on necessary referential distinctions, abbreviated coding is efficient. The result is not merely a change in the external shape of the form but a semantic shift, since the simplest term comes to have the specific meaning of the highly qualified phrase. The authors mention analogies like "hypo" among photographers and "comps" among graduate students.

Brent and Katz (1967) made comparisons of types of coding of drawings by middle class whites and by Negro Job Corps teen-agers. Unfortunately, they used geometric shapes, which gives a distinct advantage to subjects who are formally educated. They found that the Negro subjects were relatively successful although they used nontechnical names like "sharp-pointed piece", "a square wiggling", and "the funny looking piece". It would be an advantage to use materials equally strange or equally familiar to both groups and to control network features of the speaker and listener. We have strong evidence that members of the same social group prefer nontechnical communication. Where materials are neutral (e.g., nonsense forms), nontechnical, highly metaphorical communication is most efficient in terms of both brevity and success in a nonfeedback condition.

Even though the semantic distinctions made are not new, group *jargon* or new morphophonemic realizations for lexical categories are common in cohesive groups. Occasionally, such terminology arises to allow secrecy before outsiders (though Conwell and Mauer commented that secrecy is better served by semantic shift employing conventional morphemes). New morphemes are the most apparent mark of an ingroup, whether or not they realize novel semantic distinctions. In fact, the best test for the symbolic value of the marker is whether it has referential meaning and, if so, whether it is translatable. Conwell (1937) pointed out that the pickpocket's terminology is not used before outsiders, but it is used to test the trustworthiness of a member of the network and to find how much he knows. In simple terms, the use of such terms can symbolize membership if the group is large or boundary maintenance is important; if the group is small, like a family, and its members known, the terms are used to indicate solidarity. Bossard (1945) cited examples of family words; many baby words or nicknames survive with such social meanings.

Where the incidence of social or regional dialect difference coincides with density of friendship network, the *structural* dialect features, including syntax and phonology, may come to be markers of cohesiveness. Blom and Gumperz (in press) found that the local dialect of Hemnisberget, Norway, had this significance to its residents.

Labov (1963) observed that the rate of dialect change was different in Martha's Vineyard among young men, depending upon their social loyalties. There was a change in progress very markedly differentiating young men from their grandparents. The men who went along in this direction were those who had the strongest local ties and did not want to move off-island. It is not clear whether or not interaction frequencies were also affected by the different values. The effects showed up in articulation.

Strong social ties affect all aspects of linguistic systems; our evidence suggests that the most quickly affected are the semantic system and lexicon – in short, the vocabulary. The structural morphemes evidently are not as sensitive to the forces of cohesion as are other morphemes.

D. *Identity Marking*

Every society is differentiated by age and sex; in addition, rank, occupational identities, and other categories will be found. Since the rights and duties of its members are a function of these identities, it is of great social importance to establish high visibility for them. Sometimes this has been done by legislation controlling permissible clothing, house type, and so on. Everywhere it seems to be the case that information about social identity is contained in speech variables. In urban societies, the social function of such marking is greater, since it may be the only information available; on the other hand, the social sanctions for violation may be reduced. McCormack (1960) has noted the spread of upper caste dialect features in urban lower caste speakers in India.

In some cases, there may be more frequent communication within, rather than between, categories. Clearly, this is not always the case; within the western family, communication occurs with high frequency across both sex and age categories. Therefore, something other than frequency of communication or group cohesion must account for the preservation of speech diversity which marks social identity.

It is not precisely clear what features of speech mark *sex* in the United States. In some languages (Haas, in Hymes, 1964b; Martin, in Hymes, 1964b) lexicon, function words, and phonological rules are different for males and females. The study of the training of boys by women in such societies would be enlightening. There are clearly topical differences arising from occupational and family status and, therefore, possibly semantic differences and differences in lexical repertoire. Masculinity-femininity tests have leaned heavily on differences in lexicon, particularly in the meanings realized, or in collocations. Sociolinguistic rules are probably not the same; e.g., speech etiquette concerning taboo words. Men and women do not use terms of address in quite the same way, and young women, at least, use more deferential request forms than young men. In fact, it is commonly the case in many languages that women employ more deferential speech, but one can expect that such differences are related to other indicators of relative rank. For example, in jury deliberations (Strodtbeck *et al.*, 1957), women are several steps lower in social class, in terms of their speech frequency and evaluation by fellow jurors. Labov (1966) and Levine and Crockett (1966) found more situational style shifting by women; Fischer (Hymes,

1964b) recorded the formal "-ing" suffix relatively more often from girls than boys.

Age differences in speech arise both through language change and age-grading. Though grandparent and grandchild may communicate, they are unlikely to have the same system. Labov (1963, 1966) related several such changes to current distributions. For instance, he points out the spread of "r" in New York City. In the top social class, in casual speech, "r" was used by only 43 % of the respondents over 40 years old but by twice as many of the younger respondents. Changes like ice box-refrigerator (for the latter object), and victrola-phonograph-record player-stereo are apparent to all of us.

In addition, certain lexicon or structures may be considered inappropriate at a particular age. Newman (Hymes, 1964b) remarked that slang is for the young Zunis. Children over a certain age are expected to stop using nursery terms like "bunny", "piggy", "potty", and "horsie", except in addressing infants. Pig Latin and other playful transforms (Conklin, in Hymes, 1964b) may be age-restricted. Stewart has claimed that a form he calls "basilect" is learned among Washington, D.C. Negroes from their peers in early childhood and begins to disappear, under negative sanctions, around age 7 or 8. Adolescents studied in New York (Labov and Cohen, 1947) had forms similar to the adolescent speech of some Washington D.C. speakers, including two features absent in standard English: a completive or intensive-perfective "I done seen it" or "I done forgot it" (semantically contrasted with the simple past or perfect); and a distinction with *be* analogous to the distinction between habitual use and momentary or ongoing action (a distinction made in the standard language only for other action verbs): "He be with us all the time", vs. "He with us right now" (He walks every day vs. He's walking right now).

Many statuses entail the learning of specialized languages or superposed varieties. The Brahmin, for example, is likely to have studied English and to have many more borrowings in his speech than the non-Brahmin. Brahmins can sometimes be identified by such borrowed forms or by literary vocabulary (McCormack, 1960), just as psychologists' occupational register can identify them. In addition, the functions and topics imposed by occupations can alter the speech of parents in the home, and in "anticipatory socialization" the children from different occupational milieux may be affected.

One way to differentiate similarity arising from cohesion from difference arising from identity marking is the presence of negative sanctions. Ramanujan pointed out (1967) that Brahmin parents specifically reject non-Brahmin items or use them with pejorative connotations. The Brahmins show, in several respects, that they·value the preservation of markers of their identity. They consciously borrow more foreign forms and preserve their phonological deviance so that their phonological repertoire is very large. They have maintained more morphological irregularities (like our strong verbs) in their development of various inflectional paradigms, even though the evidence suggests that the earlier language (now written) was more regular. The evidence from the Esper experiment (1966) and the evolution of the non-Brahmin dialects is that regularization is the more normal destiny unless some factor interferes. In cases of phonological difference from the non-Brahmin dialects, in the realization of cognates, they have, in morphemes where the realizations fall together in the two dialects and would thus be indistinguishable, innovated a distinction. The semantic space is far more differentiated, as is the lexicon. The learning of a language full of irregularities is obviously more difficult – every child spontaneously regularizes. Like the Mandarin learning Chinese characters, the Brahmin puts additional effort into the maintenance of an elite dialect because the reward is its distinctive marking of his identity.

One might assume that lower castes would adopt prestige speech, and there is, as cited earlier, some evidence of such tendencies in urban milieux. One way of prev;·nting such spread is the use of a non-Brahmin style when addressing non-Brahmins which, of course, reduces frequency of exposure. In addition, there are sanctions against such emulation.

American Negro speech may provide an example of identity marking although the evidence is ambiguous. Stewart has argued (1967) that Negro speech is based on creoles used in the early slave period, and that this history accounts for some of the basic semantic and syntactical differences Labov and Cohen (1967) have recently cited, which appear in various black communities all over the country. Labov has suggested that working class casual speech features connote solidarity, reducing the impact of standard English heard in school on casual style.

Certainly the clearest evidence of the identity-marking function of language is language maintenance during contact. Fishman (1967) has extensively discussed various features of language maintenance programs. Although the dominant groups in the United States have strongly favored language shift by immigrants, to the point of legislating against vernacular education, some groups continued to resist the loss of their language. Those who succeeded best, according to Kloss (in Fishman, 1967), did so either by total isolation (like the Canadian Dukhobors) or by living in sufficiently dense concentrations to allow a high frequency of ingroup communication and the use of their language for the widest range of social functions. In particular, many maintained their own educational facilities, e.g., Chinese, Japanese, and Russians, promoting in-group cohesion among the children. A critical turning point lies in the speech practices of teen-agers. Where they are forced to mix with outsiders in large urban schools or consolidated rural school districts, the group language tends to disappear.

In parts of the world where there is a stabilized condition of great language diversity, as in Africa and Asia, it is quite normal to retain the group vernacular as a home language but to be bilingual for wider communication. Probably the degree of language distance in these cases is relatively small, as Gumperz has pointed out (1967). In these instances, the shape of morphemes is an important identity marker; shifting between co-occurrent sets of morphemes by such bilinguals is merely a more extreme instance of the small group vocabulary of the family, stabilized through time by endogamy and by the high value placed on group identity markers.

An extreme case in the opposite direction occurs in initial invention of pidgins. Here values of identity may be unimportant, and the practical need to communicate dominates. In fact, pidgins tend to develop when the norms which sustain co-occurrence rules are missing. Thus they appear in the transitory encounters of traders away from home, in the fortuitous combination of diverse speakers in the setting of work – in plantations, mines, and harbor cities. In this respect, African urbanization and slavery shared a feature, and we may guess that earlier circumstances of urbanization in Europe also gave rise to pidgins. Pidgins are characterized structurally by morphological simplification and regularization, and by use of material from more than one language. At first, they are spoken with the phonetic features of the respective mother tongues. Of course, with time the pidgin can come to symbolize the subordinate-employer relation. Temporary communication systems much like pidgins occur widely in contact conditions in the United States. These situations have never been given the serious study they deserve.

When a pidgin becomes the mother tongue of its speakers (and thereby technically a creole), it may acquire all the values of group identity of other vernaculars. Meredith (1964) quoted a speaker of Hawaiian Pidgin (a creole language) who was subjected to a university requirement of mastery of standard English: "Why you try change me? I no want to speak like damn haole!" Meredith reported "hostility, disinterest, and resistance to change" in the remedial class.

E. *Attitudes toward Speech Diversity*

In studying phonological diversity in New York City speech, Labov (1966) identified three different categories of social phenomena arising from diversity. These he called "indicators", "markers", and "stereotypes".

Indicators are features which are noted only by the trained observer. For example, few people are aware that "cot" and "caught" are distinguished in some areas and not in others. Indicators are features which are functions of social indices like class or region but neither vary with style in a given speaker nor enter into beliefs about language.

Markers, in Labov's system, vary with both group membership and style of the speaker, and can be used in role-switching. In the New York City system, he found that "r", "oh", and "eh" were very powerful markers, in that they changed radically according to the self-monitoring of the speaker. In Fig. 5, the use of less [t] and more [th] with increased selfmonitoring is shown by the slopes. A speaker who in rapid excited speech might say, "It wasn't a good day but a bid one", or "Ian saw tree cahs goin by", might in reading say "bad", and "Ann saw three cars going by".

Stereotypes, like their social counterparts, may or may not conform to social reality, and tend to be categorical. Thus, although a working class man might use [t] or [d] only 40 % to 50 % of the time, he will be heard as always saying "dis", "dat", and "ting". Evidence suggests that children like "bath" vs. "baf", and "window" vs. "winda", though they may ignore simple phonetic shifts.

Hypercorrection involves the spread of a speech feature from a higher prestige group to another, with overgeneralization of the feature based on a categorical stereotype. In Fig. 6, the upper middle class used "r" considerably less in self-conscious speech than did the lower middle class, who believed it to be characteristic of the best speech. A more common example can be seen in the contrast between standard English "He and I came" and nonstandard "Him and me came". Hypercorrect versions can be found which yield "She wrote to him and I" or "She wrote to he and I". Lexical examples were given by Ian Ross (1956) and even by Emily Post (1922); usually these are instances of the extension of formal, literary, or commercial vocabulary into casual speech. Labov (1966) has shown that hypercorrection is greatest among speakers who score high on a Linguistic Insecurity Index, derived from comparison of what they report they say and what they select as correct in pairs which, in fact, are not markers. Levine and Crockett (1966) also found that the second highest group shifted most with style.

Blau (1956) has observed a very similar phenomenon among upwardly mobile persons in quite different measures of insecurity: These people report more nervousness, are more likely to discriminate against Negro neighbors than any other types, and in these respects the members of high and low social classes are more alike than the intermediate people, provided they are mobile.

Labov (1966) has suggested that there may be "unconscious" stereotypes which acount for borrowings which are not from prestige groups. He suggested that the masculinity connotation of working class casual speech might be such an instance. His measure of subjective reaction to speech samples required subjects to rank the speaker occupationally, thus, clearly asking for social class indicators rather than features implying some other social meaning.

The richest variety of work along this line is that of Lambert (1963, 1967) and his collaborators, who have had the same speaker use "guises" to produce samples. These then are rated for a great range of features like personality, intelligence, and physical traits. French Canadians, he found, rated a "French guise" as less intelligent and less a leader than the English-Canadian guise. In a study in Israel (Lambert *et al.*, 1965), on the other hand, it was found that Arabic-speaking and Hebrew-speaking subjects had mutually hostile stereotypes when judging the guises. Tucker and Lambert (in press) found that evaluation by northern white and southern Negro college students differed in that Mississippi Negro college speech was least favored by the whites, and southern educated white speech least favored by the Negroes. Top-valued forms were the same for both groups.

Harms (1961) recorded speech from different social classes and found that 10–15 second samples could be differentiated by listeners. Regardless of their own class, they rated high-ranked speakers as more credible. This method, like that of Lambert's, does not allow isolation of the critical linguistic features. Lambert, on the other hand, has been able to identify a far wider range of social meanings in the speech variations than did the single scales of Labov and of Harms.

Triandis *et al.* (1966) tried to balance various sources of judgment by counterbalancing race, messages (on discrimination legislation), and standard vs. nonstandard grammar. Slides were shown while a tape was played. College students who were uninfluenced by race as "liberals" were still much influenced by grammar, even more than by the message, in their judgment of the man's character, ideas, value, and social acceptability. Three-fourths of the variance on admiration and evaluation is carried by the linguistic contrast. A new test for liberals might be this: "Would you want your daughter to marry a man who says ain't?"

Some consequences of these stereotypes about language can be seen in Rosenthal and Jackson's (1965) finding that IQ rose 15 points when teachers were told arbitrary children were "fast gainers". Linguistic variables may convey the same message.

F. *Rules for Diversity*

William Labov has begun to use his large collection of material on speech of different New York City groups to discover rules accounting both for stylistic and intergroup diversity quantitatively. He has been able to use quantitative functions because he has been measuring articulation ranges and frequencies of occurrence as speech variables, as well as using quantitative measures of social variables. Thus the rules he can find are not categorical in structure like those in Section II.

Figure 5 shows that a phonetic feature is a linear function both of social class and of style. Because of the apparently regular change with style, Labov hypothesized that there is a single dimension he called "self-monitoring" underlying the style differences. Obviously, the relationship can be expressed by a linear equation in which the phonetic variable $= a$ (class) $+ b$ (style) $+ c$.

In the case of hypercorrection of the kind shown in Fig. 6, the measure of linguistic insecurity can be used as a function of style, increasing its slope. For such phonetic variables, the function is a (class) $+ b$ (style) (Linguistic Insecurity Index) $+ c$. Some adjustments are made for age as well, since there is an interaction of age, class, and norms.

These rules are important innovations. They treat linguistic phenomena as continuous variables. Whether the use of continuous measures is possible except at the phonetic and semantic edge of linguistics is not clear; frequencies certainly are quantifiable for discrete categories too. The rules, like those in Section II, introduce social features as integral components. Normally, social features are mentioned in linguistic descriptions as a last resort, such as in a few style variations like those in Japanese where morphological rules must consider addressee. Finally, they include, in a single formal description, the differences *between* speakers and the differences *within* speakers. The fact that this is possible is impressive evidence of the existence of an over-all sociolinguistic system larger than the cognitive structure of members individually. As Labov has pointed out, a single member sees the system only along the coordinates of his own position in it; he only witnesses the full style variation of his own social peers. In fact, the possibility of writing rules which transcend class suggests a new criterion for a speech community.

What do sociolinguistic rules, the major emphasis of this article, imply for the social psychologist? Most narrowly, they provide him with new and far more sensitive indices of class or group identification, socialization, and role-shifting than interviewing alone can supply. The great precision with which linguistic features can be specified makes them technically ripe both for measurement and for deeper and richer study of the process of interaction. Linguistic interaction is deeply embedded in nearly all our social processes, in socialization in the family, into new occupations, and into a new community.

Sociolinguistic rules are central to, even if they do not totally compose the organized structure which generates our social acts and through
which we interpret others. Just as the study of linguistic structure is
seen by many as a penetrating route to cognitive structure in the
individual, so may sociolinguistic rules lead to rules for social action.

APPENDIX. TAPE RECORDING

Several social psychologists have had severe disappointments when
they found that the taped material they had made at great expense was
useless because of poor recording method or storage. For details of
method see Samarin (1967) and Slobin (1967).

1. Equipment
First, make sure that the recording machine itself has a wide enough
frequency range for good voice recordings by testing *at the speed
needed*. If a battery machine is required, the Nagra, the Sony, or the
Uher are available, with new products appearing monthly. Videotapes
may require better quality sound receiving equipment as a supplement.

An additional investment in microphones and earphones other than
those supplied with the machine usually is worthwhile. Lavalier (neck)
microphones are desirable if a separate channel is available for each
person, and if scraping of clothing or handling of the microphone can
be avoided. In groups, stereo arrangements can both provide a wider
range of close recording and give binaural cues for identifying speakers
while minimizing background noise. Wireless microphones for children's groups, or figure-eight microphones for lined-up speakers and the
filtering out of noise at the sides may be appropriate. If several microphones are used simultaneously, it is necessary to provide occasional
synchronizing cues by voice or other device except on stereo.

2. Tape
Tape print-through can create blurred recordings by the transfer of
magnetic patterns from one layer of tape to another. It can be minimized
by the use of "low print-through" tape. Reducing the recording level
will also decrease print-through, which is usually not serious if the
original recording is very clear.

At the time of purchase, leaders should be spliced to tapes lacking
them. A leader spliced at both ends of a tape allows one to label it
before it is used, minimizing accidental erasures. Box labeling or reel
labeling is untrustworthy. Tape labeling is related to a log or index file.

3. Recording Techniques

Reverberation and other background noise is the chief enemy. If there is one wall, face the microphone away from it to deaden its input. If there is more than one, or metal cabinet, or floor reverberations, use curtains, coats, or any means of deadening the sound reflection. Open the windows if the outside is quiet. The microphone should be removed from the noisy machine, and placed equidistant from speakers – if possible, about a foot from them. Point the tail of the microphone at noise sources or too noisy personnel, to deaden their input.

Take the time to learn to record well, to train field workers under realistic conditions, and to test with as much care as one checks a team of coders. Good recordings should allow discrimination of Ruth and roof, boot and boots, mutts and much, sin and sing.

4. Storage

If recordings are made in a hot climate, mail them out and have them copied on a high-quality machine immediately for storage on low print-through tape. While Mylar tapes last relatively well, temperatures should be constant around 60°–70°C, and humidity kept low, if necessary with silica gel. Store on edge, far from sources of magnetism such as electric outlets and appliances. Language laboratories in large universities often have suitable storage room. Rewind tapes annually to reduce print-through and warping.

ACKNOWLEDGEMENTS

I am deeply indebted to John Gumperz and to William Labov for detailed commentary on a draft of this article, and to Dell Hymes and other members of the Sociolinguistics Committee of the Social Science Research Council, as well as to our work group in Berkeley, for discussions which have radically altered my view of this field. This article was written with the support of the Institute of Human Development and some aid from the Laboratory for Language Behaviour Research of the University of California. Elizabeth Closs-Traugott provided some address data. Student work contributing to generalizations in the text included studies by Renée Ackerman, Lou Bilter, Camille Chamberlain, Judith Horner, Andrea Kaciff, Terrence Keeney, Jane Logan, Dana Meyer, Paula Palmquist, Elaine Rogers, Joan von Schlegell, Elisabeth Selkirk, and Billi Wooley. Papers cited more fully can be obtained from the ERIC (Educational Resources Information Center) Clearinghouse for Linguistics at the Center for Applied Linguistics, 1717 Massachusetts Avenue, N. W., Washington, D.C. Soviet material was provided by Dan Slobin.

Sociolinguistics 83

BIBLIOGRAPHY

Auld, F., Jr., and Alice M. White,
1956 "Rules for dividing interviews into sentences", *Journal of Psychology* 42, 273-281.
Ayoub, Milla,
1962 "Bi-polarity in Arabic kinship terms", in H. G. Lunt (ed.), *Proceedings of the Ninth International Congress of Linguists* (The Hague: Mouton), pp. 1100-1106.
Bales, R. F. and E. F. Borgatta,
1955 "Size of groups as a factor in the interaction profile", in A. Hare, E. F. Borgatta, and R. F. Bales (eds.), *Small Groups* (New York: Wiley), pp. 396-413.
Bales, R. F., F. Strodtbeck, T. Mills, and Mary E. Roseborough,
1951 "Channels of communication in small groups", *American Sociological Review* 6, 461-468.
Barker, G. C.,
1947 "Social functions of language in a Mexican-American community", *Acta Americana* 5, 185-202.
Barker, R., and H. F. Wright,
1954 *Midwest and Its Children* (Evanston, Ill.: Row Peterson).
Bellugi, Ursula,
1967 "The acquisition of negation", Ph.D. dissertation, Harvard Graduate School of Education.
Bernstein, B. (ed.),
in press a *Language, Primary Socialisation and Education* (London: Routledge and Kegan Paul).
in press b "A socio-linguistic approach to socialisation: with some references to educability", in J. J. Gumperz and D. Hymes (eds.), *Directions in Sociolinguistics* (New York: Holt, Rinehart and Winston).
Blau, P.,
1956 "Social mobility and interpersonal relations", *American Sociological Review* 21, 290-295.
Blom, J. P., and J. J. Gumperz,
in press "Some social determinants of verbal behavior", in J. J. Gumperz and D. Hymes (eds.), *Directions in Sociolinguistics* (New York: Holt, Rinehart and Winston).
Boomer, D. S., and A. T. Dittman,
1965 "Hesitation pauses and juncture pauses in speech", *Language and Speech* 8, 215-220.
Bossard, J. H. S.,
1945 "Family modes of expression", *American Sociological Review* 10, 226-237.
Brent, S. B., and Evelyn W. Katz,
1967 "A study of language deviations and cognitive processes", OEO-Job Corps Project 1209, Progress Report No. 3 (Wayne State University).
Bright, W. (ed.),
1966 *Sociolinguistics* (The Hague: Mouton).
Brown, R. W., and A. Gilman,
1960 "The pronouns of power and solidarity", in T. Sebeok (ed.), *Style in Language* (Cambridge, Mass.: MIT Press), pp. 253-276.
Capell, A.,
1966 *Studies in socio-linguistics* (The Hague: Mouton).

84   *Susan M. Ervin-Tripp*

Carroll, J. B.,
  1958 "Process and content in psycholinguistics", in R. Glaser (ed.), *Current Trends in the Description and Analysis of Behavior* (Pittsburgh, Penn.: University of Pittsburgh Press), pp. 175-200.
Cazden, Courtney B.,
  1966 "Subcultural differences in child language: An inter-disciplinary review", *Merrill-Palmer Quarterly* 12, 185-219.
  1967 "On individual differences in language competence and performance", *Journal of Special Education* 1, 135-150.
Chapman, Robin S.,
  1967 "The interpretation of deviant sentences", Ph.D. Dissertation, University of California, Berkeley.
Conwell, C.,
  1937 *The Professional Thief* (Chicago, Ill.: University of Chicago Press).
Cory, D. W.,
  1952 *The Homosexual in America* (New York: Greenberg).
Cowan, P.,
  1967 "The link between cognitive structure and social structure in two-child verbal interaction", Symposium presented at the Society for Research on Child Development meeting.
Davis, J. A.,
  1961 "Compositional effects, systems, and the survival of small discussion groups", *Public Opinion Quarterly* 25, 574-584.
Diebold, A. R.,
  1963 "Code-switching in Greek-English bilingual speech", *Georgetown University Monograph* 15.
Diebold, A. R.,
  1967 "Anthropology and the comparative psychology of communicative behavior", in T. Sebeok (ed.), *Animal Communication: Techniques of Study and Results of Research* (Bloomington, Ind.: Indiana University Press).
Dikeman, Bessie, and Patricia Parker,
  1964 "Request forms", Term paper for Speech 160B, University of California, Berkeley.
Dittman, A., and Lynn G. Llewellyn,
  1967 "The phonemic clause as a unit of speech decoding", *J. of Personality and Social Psychology* 6, 341-348.
Dollard, J., and F. Auld Jr.,
  1959 *Scoring Human Motives: A Manual* (New Haven: Conn.: Yale University Press).
Drach, K., B. Kobashigawa, C. Pfuderer, and D. Slobin,
  1968 "The structure of linguistic input to children", Language Behavior Research Laboratory Working Paper No. 14, Berkeley, California.
Earle, Margaret J.,
  1967 "Bilingual semantic merging and an aspect of acculturation", *Journal of Personality and Social Psychology* 6, 304-312.
Ervin, Susan M.,
  1961 "Semantic shift in bilingualism", *American Journal of Psychology* 74, 233-241.
  1964 "Language and TAT content in bilinguals", *J. of Abnormal and Social Psychology* 68, 500-507.

Ervin-Tripp, Susan M.,
  1964 "An analysis of the interaction of language, topic, and listener", *American Anthropologist* 66, No. 6, Part 2, 86-102.
  1966 "Language development", in Lois and Martin Hoffman (eds.), *Review of Child Development Research*, Vol. 2 (New York: Russell Sage Foundation), pp. 55-106.
  1967 "An Issei learns English", *Journal of Social Issues* 23, No. 2, 78-90.
  1969 "Becoming a bilingual", in L. G. Kelly (ed.), *The Description and Measurement of Bilingualism"* (Toronto: Univ. of Toronto Press, pp. 26-35).

Ervin-Tripp, Susan M., and D. I. Slobin,
  1966 "Psycholinguistics", *Annual Review of Psychology* 18, 435-474.

Esper, E. A.,
  1966 "Social transmission of an artificial language", *Language* 42, 575-580.

Ferguson, C.A.,
  1964 "Baby talk in six languages", *American Anthropologist* 66, No. 6, Part 2, 103-114.

Fischer, J. L.,
  1965 "The stylistic significance of consonantal sandhi in Trukese and Ponapean", *American Anthropologist* 67, 1495-1502.

Fishman, J. A.,
  1966 *Language Loyalty in the United States* (The Hague: Mouton).
  1967a "Bilingualism with and without diglossia; diglossia with and without bilingualism", *Journal of Social Issues* 23, No. 2, 29-38.
  1967b Review of J. Hertzler: "A sociology of language", *Language* 43, 586-604.
  1968 *Readings in the Sociology of Language* (The Hague: Mouton).

Frake, C. O.,
  1964 "How to ask for a drink in Subanun", *American Anthropologist* 66, No. 6, Part 2, 127-132.

Friedrich, P.,
  1966 "Structural implications of Russian pronominal usage", in W. Bright (ed.), *Sociolinguistics* (The Hague: Mouton), pp. 214-253.

Geertz, C.,
  1960 *The Religion of Java* (Glencoe, Ill.: Free Press).

Geohegan, W.,
  in press "Information processing systems in culture", in P. Kay (ed.), *Explorations in Mathematical Anthropology* (Cambridge, Mass.: MIT Press).

Goffman, E.,
  1952 "Cooling the mark out", *Psychiatry* 15, 451-463.
  1957 "Alienation from interaction", *Human Relations* 10, 47-60.
  1963 *Behavior in Public Places* (Glencoe, Ill.: Free Press).

Goodenough, W. H.,
  1965 "Rethinking 'status' and 'role': toward a general model of the cultural organization of social relationships", in M. Banton (ed.), *The Relevance of Models for Social Anthropology* (London: Tavistock), pp. 1-24.

Grimshaw, A. D.,
  in press "Sociolinguistics", in N. Maccoby (ed.), *Handbook of Communication*.

Gumperz, J. J.,
  1958 "Phonological differences in three Hindi dialects", *Language* 34, 212-224.

1964   "Hindi-Punjabi code-switching in Delhi", in H. G. Lunt (ed.), *Proceedings of the Ninth International Congress of Linguists* (The Hague: Mouton), pp. 1115-1124.
1967   "On the linguistic markers of bilingual communication", *Journal of Social Issues* 23, No. 2, 48-57.
Gumperz, J. J., and D. Hymes (eds.),
1964   *The Ethnology of Communication. American Anthropologist* 66, No. 6.
in press   *Directions in Sociolinguistics* (New York: Holt, Rinehart, and Winston).
Hammel, E. A. (ed.),
1965   *Formal Semantic Analysis. American Anthropologist* 67, No. 5, Part 2.
Hammer, Muriel, Sylvia Polgar, and K. Salzinger,
1965   "Comparison of data-sources in a sociolinguistic study", Paper presented at American Anthropological Association meeting, Denver, Colorado.
Hare, A. P.,
1962   *Handbook of Small Group Research* (Glencoe, Ill.: Free Press).
Hare, A. P., and R. F. Bales,
1963   "Seating position and small group interaction", *Sociometry* 26, 480-486.
Harms, L. S.,
1961   "Listener comprehension of speakers of three status groups", *Language and Speech* 4, 109-112.
Haugen, E.,
1956   "Bilingualism in the Americas: A bibliography and research guide", *American Dialect Society* 26.
Herman, S.,
1961   "Explorations in the social psychology of language choice", *Human Relations* 14, 149-164.
Hess, R. D., and Virginia Shipman,
1965   "Early experience and the socialization of cognitive modes in children", *Child Development* 36, 869-886.
Homans, G. C.,
1950   *The Human Group* (New York: Harcourt, Brace, and World).
1958   "Social behavior as exchange", *American Journal of Sociology* 62, 597-606.
Horikawa, K., Y. Ohwaki, and T. Watanabe,
1956   "Variation of verbal activity through different psychological situations", *Tohoku Psychologica Folia* 15, 65-90.
Howell, R. W.,
1967   "Linguistic choice as an index to social change", Ph.D. dissertation, University of California, Berkeley.
Hymes, D.,
1962   "The ethnography of speaking" in T. Gladwin and W. C. Sturtevant (eds.), *Anthropology and Human Behavior* (Washington, D. C.: Anthropological Soc. Washington), pp. 13-53.
1964a   "Directions in (ethno-) linguistic theory", *American Anthropologist* 66, No. 3, Part 2, 6-56.
1964b   *Language in Culture and Society* (New York: Harper and Row).
1964c   "Toward ethnographies of communication", *American Anthropologist* 66, No. 6, Part 2, 1-34.
1967   "Models of the interaction of language and social setting", *Journal of Social Issues* 23, No. 2, 8-28.

Jakobson, R.,
1960 "Linguistics and poetics", in T. Sebeok (ed.), *Style in Language* (Cambridge, Mass.: MIT Press), pp. 350-377.
John, Vera, and Tomi D. Berney,
1967 "Analysis of story retelling as a measure of the effects of ethnic content in stories", OEO Project No. 577, Yeshiva University, New York.
Joos, M.,
1962 "The five clocks", *International Journal of American Linguistics* 28, Part 5.
Kantorovich, V.,
1966 *Ty i vy: Zametki pisatelya* (*Ty* and *vy*: a Writer's Notes) (Moscow: Izd-vo pol. lit.).
Katz, Evelyn,
1966 "A content-analytic method for studying themes of interpersonal behavior", *Psychological Bulletin* 66, 419-422.
Kjolseth, J. R.,
1967 "Structure and process in conversation", Paper at American Sociological Society meetings, San Francisco.
Klima, E. S.,
1964 "Relatedness between grammatical systems", *Language* 40, 1-20.
Knutson, A. L.,
1960 "Quiet and vocal groups", *Sociometry* 23, 36-49.
Kostomarov, V. G.,
1967 "Russkiy rechevoy stiket (Russian speech etiquette)", *Russkiy yazyk za rubezhom* 1, 56-62.
Krauss, R. M., and S. Weinheimer,
1964 "Changes in reference phrases as a function of frequency of usage in social interaction; a preliminary study", *Psychonomic Science* 1, 113-114.
Labov, W.,
1963 "The social motivation of a sound change", *Word* 19, 273-309.
1964 "Phonological correlates of social stratification", *American Anthropologist* 66, No. 6, 164-176.
1966 *The Social Stratification of English in New York City* (Washington, D. C.: Center for Applied Linguistics).
Labov, W., and P. Cohen,
1967 "Systematic relations of standard and nonstandard rules in the grammars of Negro speakers", *Project Literacy Reports*, No. 8, Cornell University, Ithaca, New York.
Labov, W., and J. Waletzky,
1967 "Narrative analysis: Oral versions of personal experience", in June Helm (ed.), *Essays on the Verbal and Visual Arts* (Seattle: University of Washington Press), pp. 12-44.
Lambert, W. E.,
1963 "Psychological approaches to the study of language. II. On second-language learning and bilingualism", *Modern Language Journal* 47, 114-121.
1967a "A social psychology of bilingualism", *Journal of Social Issues* 23, No. 2, 91-109.
1967b "The use of *Tu* and *Vous* as forms of address in French Canada: A pilot study", *Journal of Verbal Learning and Verbal Behavior* 6, 614-617.
Lambert, W. E., M. Anisfield, and Grace Yeni-Komshian,
1965 "Evaluational reactions of Jewish and Arab adolescents to dialect and language variations", *Journal of Personality and Social Psychology* 2,

84-90.
Lambert, W. E., and G. R. Tucker,
in press "A social-psychological study of interpersonal modes of address:
    I. A French-Canadian illustration".
Lawton, D.,
1964 "Social class language differences in group discussions", *Language and
    Speech* 7, 183-204.
Leary, T.,
1957 *Interpersonal Diagnosis of Personality* (New York: Ronald Press).
Lennard, H. L., and A. Bernstein,
in press *Patterns in Interaction* (San Francisco: Jossey-Bass Press).
Levine, L., and H. J. Crockett, Jr.,
1966 "Speech variation in a Piedmont community: Postvocalic r", *Socio-
    logical Inquiry* 36, No. 2, 204-226.
Lieberson, S. (ed.),
1966 "Explorations in sociolinguistics", *Sociological Inquiry* 36, No. 2.
McCormack, W.,
1960 "Social dialects in Dharwar Kannada", *International Journal of Ameri-
    can Linguistics* 26, No. 3, 79-91.
McDavid, R. I.,
1951 "Dialect differences and inter-group tensions", *Studies in Linguistics* 9,
    27-33.
Maclay, H., and S. Newman,
1960 "Two variables affecting the message in communication", in Dorothy
    K. Wilner (ed.), *Decisions, Values, and Groups* (New York: Pergamon
    Press), pp. 218-219.
McNeill, D.,
1963 "The psychology of *you* and *I*: A case history of a small language
    system", Paper presented at American Psychological Association
    meeting.
1966 "Developmental psycholinguistics", in F. Smith and G. A. Miller (eds.),
    The Genesis of Language (Cambridge, Mass.: MIT Press), pp. 15-84.
Markel, N. N.,
1965 "The reliability of coding paralanguage: pitch, loudness, and tempo".
    Journal of Verbal Learning and Verbal Behavior 4, 306-308.
Marsden, G.,
1965 "Content-analysis studies of therapeutic interviews: 1954-1964", *Psy-
    chological Bulletin* 63, 298-321.
Matarazzo, J. D., A. N. Wiens, and G. Saslow,
1965 "Studies in interview speech behavior", in L. Krasner and P. Ullman
    (eds.), *Research in Behavior Modification: New Developments and
    Their Clinical Implications* (New York: Holt, Rinehart, and Winston),
    pp. 179-210.
Mauer, D. W.,
1962 *The Big Con* (New York: New American Library).
Mehrabian, A., and M. Wiener,
1967 "Decoding of inconsistent communications", *Journal of Personality
    and Social Psychology* 6, 109-114.
Meredith, G. M.,
1964 "Personality correlates of pidgin English usage among Japanese-
    American college students in Hawaii", *Japanese Psychological Research*
    6, 176-183.

Moscovici, S.,
  1967 "Communication processes and the properties of language", in L. Berkowitz (ed.), *Advances in Experimental Social Psychology*, Vol. 3 (New York: Academic Press), pp. 226-271.
Nichols, M., and Elaine May,
  1959 "Conversation at breakfast", *Echo Magazine* 1, No. 1.
O'Neil, W. A.,
  in press "Transformational dialectology", *Proceedings of the Second International Congress of Dialectologists*, Marburg.
Peisach, Estelle C.,
  1965 "Children's comprehension of teacher and peer speech", *Child Development* 36, 467-480.
Pfuderer, Carol,
  1968 "A scale of politeness of request forms in English", Term paper for Speech 164A, University of California, Berkeley, 1968.
Piaget, J., and B. Inhelder,
  1956 *The Child's Conception of Space* (London: Routledge and Kegan Paul).
Pittenger, R. E., C. F. Hockett, and J. J. Danehy,
  1960 *The First Five Minutes* (Ithaca, N. Y.: Martineau).
Pool, I.,
  1959 *Trends in Content Analysis* (Urbana, Ill.: University of Illinois Press).
Post, Emily,
  1922 *Etiquette* (New York: Funk and Wagnalls).
Poussaint, A. F.,
  1967 "A Negro psychiatrist explains the Negro psyche", *New York Times Magazine*, August 20, 52 ff.
Ramanujan, A. K.,
  1967 "The structure of variation: A study in caste dialects", in B. Cohn and M. Singer (eds.), *Social Structure and Social Change in India* (New York: Aldine), pp. 461-474.
Romney, A. K., and F. G. D'Andrade (eds.),
  1964 "Transcultural Studies in Cognition", *American Anthropologist* 66, No. 3, Part 2.
Rosenfeld, H. M.,
  1966 "Approval seeking and approval-inducing functions of verbal and nonverbal responses in the dyad", *Journal of Abnormal and Social Psychology* 4, 597-605.
Rosenthal, R., and Lenore Jackson,
  1966 "Teacher's expectancies: Determinants of pupil's I.Q. gains", *Psychological Reports* 19, 115-118.
Ross, I.,
  1956 "U and non-U: An essay in sociological linguistics", in Nancy Mitford (ed.), *Noblesse Oblige* (New York: Harpers), pp. 55-92.
Rubin, Joan,
  1962 "Bilingualism in Paraguay", *Anthropological Linguistics* 4, 52-58.
  in press *National Bilingualism in Paraguay* (The Hague: Mouton).
Sachs, Jacqueline S.,
  1967 "Recognition memory for syntactic and semantic aspects of connected discourse", *Perception and Psychophysics* 2, 437-442.
Sacks, H.,
  in press "On some features of a method used in selecting identifications: An exercise in the formal study of natural social activities", ms.

Samarin, W. J.,
   1967   Field Linguistics: A Guide to Linguistic Field Work (New York: Holt,
          Rinehart and Winston).
Schachter, S.,
   1951   "Deviation, rejection, and communication", Journal of Abnormal and
          Social Psychology 46, 190-207.
Schatzman, L., and A. Strauss,
   1955   "Social class and modes of communication", American Journal of
          Sociology 6, 329-338.
Schegloff, E.,
   in press "Sequencing in conversational openings", in J. J. Gumperz and
          D. Hymes (eds.), Directions in Sociolinguistics (New York: Holt, Rine-
          hart, and Winston).
Skinner, B. F.,
   1957   Verbal Behavior (New York: Appleton-Century-Crofts).
Slama-Cazacu, Tatiana,
   1960   "Some features of the dialogue of small children", Problems of Psy-
          chology 4, 377-387.
Slobin, D. I.,
   1963   "Some aspects of the use of pronouns of address in Yiddish", Word 19,
          193-202.
Slobin, D. I. (ed.),
   1967   A Field Manual for Cross-Cultural Study of the Acquisition of Com-
          municative Competence (University of California, Berkeley ASUC
          Bookstore).
Slobin, D. I., S. H. Miller, and L. W. Porter,
   1968   "Forms of address and social relations in a business organization",
          Journal of Personality and Social Psychology 8, 289-293.
Slobin, D. I., and C. A. Welsh,
   1967   "Elicited imitation as a research tool in developmental psycholinguis-
          tics", Language Behavior Research Laboratory Working Paper No. 10,
          Berkeley, California.
Soskin, W. F., and Vera John,
   1963   "The study of spontaneous talk", in R. G. Barker (ed.), The Stream of
          Behavior (New York: Appleton-Century-Crofts).
Stephan, F. F., and E. G. Mishler,
   1952   "The distribution of participation in small groups: An exponential
          approximation", American Sociological Review 22, 713-719.
Stewart, W. A.,
   1964   "Urban Negro speech: sociolinguistic factors affecting English teach-
          ing", in R. Shuy (ed.), Social Dialects and Language Learning (Cham-
          paign, Ill.: Nat'l Council of Teachers of English), pp. 10-18.
   1967   "Sociolinguistic factors in the history of American Negro dialects",
          The Florida FL Reporter 5, No. 2, 1-4.
Strodtbeck, F. L., Rita James, and C. Hawkins,
   1957   "Social status and jury deliberations", American Sociological Review 22,
          713-719.
Stross, B.,
   1964   "Waiter-to-cook speech in restaurants", Term paper, Speech 160B,
          University of California, Berkeley.
Tanner, Nancy,
   1967   "Speech and society among the Indonesian elite: A case study of a

multilingual community", *Anthropological Linguistics* 9, Part 3, 15-40.

Triandis, H. C., W. D. Loh, and Leslie Levin,
1966 "Race, status, quality of spoken English, and opinions about civil rights as determinants of interpersonal attitudes", *Journal of Personality and Social Psychology* 3, 468-472.

Tucker, G. R., and W. Lambert,
1967 "White and Negro listeners' reactions to various American-English dialects", paper presented at Eastern Psychological Association meeting.

Tyler, S.,
1965 "Koya language morphology and patterns of kinship behavior", *American Anthropologist* 67, 1428-1440.
1966 "Context and variation in Koya kinship terminology", *American Anthropologist* 68, 693-707.

Véron, E., C. E. Sluzki, F. Korn, A. Kornblit, and R. Malfe,
1965 *Communication and Neurosis* (University of Buenos Aires Inst. Sociologia) (mimeo.).

Watson, Jeanne,
1958 "A formal analysis of sociable interaction", *Sociometry* 21, 269-281.

Watson, Jeanne, and R. J. Potter,
1962 "An analytic unit for the study of interaction", *Human Relations* 15, 245-263.

Weinreich, U.,
1953 *Languages in Contact* (Linguistic Circle of New York).

Williams, Marion,
1964 "Restaurant syntax", Term paper, Speech 160B, University of California, Berkeley.

Wurm, S. A., and D. C. Laycock,
1961 "The question of language and dialect in New Guinea", *Oceania* 32, 128-143.

Allen D. Grimshaw

SOCIOLINGUISTICS *

> For without common language, it is hard to avoid the
> misfortune of Babel tower.
> – 'rom a paper by a Korean graduate student, 1968

Although signed by a single author, the paper following is – in much
more than the usual sense – a product of genuinely cooperative activity
by a number of scholars. I am deeply indebted to my colleagues on the
Social Science Research Council Committee on Sociolinguistics, who
have provided detailed written commentary on earlier drafts of this
paper and who have spent hours in discussing the questions examined
below. My particular *gurus* among Committee members have been John
J. Gumperz, Dell Hymes, and William Labov – each of whom has given
time beyond the proper demands of colleagueship in instructing a
neophyte in radically new 'thoughtways'. Irwin Deutscher's encouragement and thoughtful skepticism has been most helpful. Among colleagues at Indiana University I am grateful to Carl Voegelin and Wolf-
gang Wolck for continuing encouragement and to Owen Thomas for
friendly encouragement, professional advice, and an enduring editorial
wisdom. A number of people have been most helpful in sharing their
knowledge and wisdom with me; heretical persistence in error is my
responsibility alone. (November, 1967)

* From Wilbur Schramm, Ithiel Pool, Nathan Maccoby, Edwin Parker, Frederick Frey and Leonard Fein (eds.), *Handbook of Communication* (Rand McNally
and Co.) (1972). Reprinted with permission.

This paper was solicited in early 1967 and written and submitted in the fall of that year. During the several years since the original research and writing was completed, the field of sociolinguistics has continued its rapid growth. The article here presented, while inaccurate only in minor particulars, fails to reflect most of the developments – both in reported empirical research and in theoretical advances – which have occurred in the intervening period. In particular, the colleagues whose contributions have been acknowledged above should not be considered as endorsing the article as being representative of the field of sociolinguistics at the time of publication of this book. (February, 1970)

I. INTRODUCTION

Five years ago a handbook on communication would not have included a section on sociolinguistics. Ten years ago it is doubtful that many readers would even have heard the term. Although Hertzler sounded a call for work on the sociology of language in a pioneering paper at the 1952 meetings of the Midwest Sociological Society (Hertzler 1953), sociolinguistics as an activity specifically directed to an examination of the interaction of language structure and social structure and of the interimplications of speech behavior and social behavior has developed only since the beginning of the sixties. This is true, even though sociologists have not ignored language as data. The contemporary phenomena of 'doing ethnomethodology', and the concerns central to the social psychologies of socialization and learning are all adumbrated in the work of early sociologists – Mead and Cooley, Bain and Bossard – and are continued into the present in the work of students of Park, Blumer and Hughes.[1]

Within the last few years there has been a marked acceleration of activity and publication. The SSRC Committee on Sociolinguistics, established in 1963, has moved from early interests primarily in autonomous linguistics and occasionally in anthropological linguistics to an increasingly broad concern with the entire range of sociolinguistic phenomena. During 1964 there were two major conferences on sociolinguistics. In May a conference on sociolinguistics was held at UCLA; most of the participants were linguists or anthropologists (the proceedings were published as Bright: 1966). During that same summer the

---

[1] Sociological readers of early drafts of this paper were quick to note the lapse of historical memory which suggests that a concern with language is new for sociologists. It is interesting to note, however, that the several sociological commentators referred to different sets of historical forebears and to different sets of current activities as representing sociological concern with language. Historical concern there may very well have been; interest until very recently has been meagre and unsystematic.

SSRC Committee on Sociolinguistics sponsored a summer seminar in conjunction with the Institute on Cultural Linguistics, held at Indiana University. Several of the participants were sociologists; and although there were occasional problems in communication between linguists and sociologists, almost all of the participants were now clearly moving toward a focus on language structure *and* social structure. (Several of the papers prepared for this seminar, along with others, were published as Lieberson: 1966). Since 1964 the SSRC Committee has sponsored two additional conferences, one in 1966 on language problems of developing nations (Fishman, Ferguson and Das Gupta: 1968) and a second, in 1968 on pidgin and creole languages (Hymes: 1970). Social scientists as well as linguists participated in both these conferences.

Sociolinguistic papers have been presented for many years at meetings of the American Anthropological Association and the American Ethnological Society; since 1966 there have been multiple sessions on sociolinguistics and on related topics in ethnomethodology at the Annual Meetings of the American Sociological Association. Sociolinguistics, and the interesting new collateral activity know as 'doing ethnomethodology', now seem to be as firmly established in sociology as anthropological linguistics is in anthropology. (For an interesting discussion of the 'naming' of such activities as sociolinguistics, ethnolinguistics, anthropological linguistics, and other 'linguistics' see Hymes: 1966b and Gumperz: 1966b.)

There are several standard collections of readings on sociolinguistics (see, especially, Hymes: 1964a and Fishman: 1969); a number of symposia and collections of specially written papers (Gumperz and Hymes: 1964; 1970, Bright: 1966b, Lieberson: 1966a), an excellent monograph focusing on micro-sociolinguistics (Ervin-Tripp: 1969), and a series of review articles in the *Biennial Review of Anthropology* (Lounsbury: 1959 and 1961 and especially, Bright: 1963, Gumperz: 1965, and Durbin: 1968). Several other edited collections are widely cited in the sociolinguistic literature. Three of the most recent are those by Hymes on pidgins and creole languages (1970); by Fishman and his colleagues on language problems of developing nations (1968) and by Macnamara on problems of bilingualism (1967a). Two volumes published early in the decade, Ferguson and Gumperz' collection on linguistic diversity in South Asia (1960) and Rice's on the role of second languages (1962) contain articles which have been of substantial influence in defining the field. Several of these sources contain bibliographies of considerable length and breadth; this bibliographic work has been supplemented by Pride's general overview (1967) in which he draws on citations from a number of writers in the field in order to delineate some principal problems and critical contrasts in perspectives.

Sociolinguistic papers have only recently begun to be published in sociological journals and the bulk of such papers continue to appear primarily in linguistic, language, educational and anthropological journals.[2] This is unfortunate, since it will leave many sociologists with the impression that J. O. Hertzler's, *A Sociology of Language* (1965), represents the extent of the potential contribution sociolinguistics can make to the two parent disciplines. It is not, a fact attested to by scholars representing a wide range of sociolinguistic perspectives (Fishman: 1967; Grimshaw: 1967a; 1969b; Gumperz: 1967b; Hymes: 1967b) as well as by materials included in the remainder of this review article.

II. THEORETICAL APPROACHES

Social interaction is a reciprocal process involving communication and most human communication requires the use of language. No two men use language in precisely the same way and some men use language in ways obviously very different from those of other men. Thus, to state that language structure and social structure are intimately related is to reiterate a fundamental fact known to all men who participate in social interaction. It is difficult to think of a single social characteristic which is not related to differentiation in language use though some, for example nativity, regional provenience, class, and education at first glance seem more important than others, for example, political party preference (at least between indifferent Republicans and indifferent Democrats, in some states), home ownership (but what of tax rates and crabgrass?) and marital status (though having children may make a difference in some societies).

There seem to be four principal perspectives on the causal relationship between social structure and language: (1) that which sees language as fundamental (or as source, cause, independent variable [or set of independent variables]), a position which is at the same time congenial with interpretations of Whorf (1956, see also Fishman: 1960) and of Chomsky (see citations in bibliography), (2) that which sees social structure as determinant or as independent variable [or set of independent variables], (3) that which sees neither as prior to the other, both being seen as co-occurring and co-determining, and (4) that which

[2] The index of the *American Sociological Review* lists eight articles under the subject heading "language". It does not list Bossard's two papers on "talk" in the family (1945a; 1945b). No article on "language" has been listed since 1951. *Social Forces* and *Sociological Inquiry*, however, have both recently published sociolinguistics papers (Wittermans: 1967 and Levine-Crockett: 1967, respectively). While there are other recent exceptions, sociolinguistics has clearly not been a flourishing speciality in sociology.

sees both as determined by a third factor, whether that third factor be
Weltanschauung, the human condition, the organization of the human
mind (a position which again is congenial with interpretations of
Chomsky) or the intrinsic demands of an ordered universe (this paradigm is adapted from that of Hymes: 1966a. Hymes uses the term culture rather than social structure. For present purposes the meaning of
the two terms is conceptually equivalent).[3] Depending upon whether

[3]   Much of the discussion in the pages following is directed to an examination of
several perspectives on relationships between language and social structures and
behavior; the conclusion will be drawn that the mutual embeddedness view has
the highest theoretical potential. It should be emphasized, however, that given the
acceptance of a sphere of speaking — of interest in sociolinguistics as contrasted
to language structure *per se* — a variety of different interests can be profitably
pursued. It is possible and legitimate to simply abstract from such study certain
correlations of interest. It is also true, however, that some correlations are not apparent without close study of speech behavior.

While the emphasis in this paper is on the interrelationships between linguistic
and other social phenomena, it should be clear that there are elements of language
structure which operate according to autonomously linguistic rules with no demonstrable influences on or from social structure and social interaction. Thus,
Labov writes (personal communication): "Most elements of linguistic structure are
rules which are quite abstract and quite categorical — they are independent of
social influences, show no subjective correlates, do not register caste, class, or
ethnic stratification and do not respond to stylistic shifts. They are invariant, absolute, and not subject to variation. Every linguist knows this — but in moments
of enthusiasm, they may become carried away.

"But this is a synchronic statement. In the course of many thousand years of
evolution, most of these linguistic rules probably underwent some type of variability, and during the course of their variation they may well have registered
social influence, shown stratification, even become markers or stereotypes. But
when the change was completed, the area of variability often shifted on to another
related section of the rules, and social effects evaporated. I would picture a linguistic structure as open to social influence at a few specific points which are
variable — some of these points are utilized by linguists as social variables and
may actually enter into social structure at the point of variation."

Labov is emphasizing the fact that there are certain aspects of language which
are totally independent of any social constraints, aspects in which variation is
governed solely by linguistic rules. This is true, for example, of the linguistic fact
that certain consonants cannot follow one another serially without the interven-
tion of vowel sounds. It is doubtful, however, that there is any variety of social
interaction which is not, in some way, conditioned by linguistic — or at least
semiotic — constraints.

In another personal communication (1967), Lieberson warns against any view
which sees language structure and social structure as being, in some instances,
so interrelated as to be identical. He suggests that if this were indeed the case there
would be no research problem, viz., "If they are identical . . . there is no possibility
of analyzing or decomposing them." There is, of course, the possibility that two
structures can be 'isomorphic' and that neither is understood. Equally likely, given
the current state of liaison between sociology and linguistics, is that one structure
has been 'decomposed' but that students of the other discipline neither know this
or, if they do, don't understand the implications for their own work.

one starts from the language end or the social structural end, there is evidence supporting either of the first two perspectives. The fourth perspective, of whichever subvariety, would seem to be untestable given the current and immediately prospective state of knowledge. It seems reasonable to conclude, therefore, that the first two perspectives represent incomplete examination of the evidence, or unsatisfactory rigor in research design, and that findings gained from these two perspectives can probably be properly subsumed under the third perspective – that of co-determination, which has earlier been labelled mutual embeddedness.

Correlations between speech (as contrasted to language) and the characteristics of its users are easy to determine. Correlations between language structure and social structure are more subtle but can also be identified. As in all correlational analyses, however, the difficult problems begin when attempts are made to isolate the direction of cause and effect. Moreover, while Bright (1966c) has suggested that sociolinguistics is essentially a study of the covariation of aspects of social structure which have traditionally concerned sociologists and anthropologists and aspects of language structure which have traditionally been of interest primarily to linguists, there is a question as to whether or not an interest in correlations alone exhausts the explanatory richness to be found in the study of relationships between social structure and language structure. Several scholars – most noticeably Gumperz and Hymes – have taken the position that there is a far more fundamental embedding of the two structures in one another. One purpose of this paper is to review these two perspectives, *viz.*, that which attempts to explain covariation in language structure and social structure from a corelational point of view and that which looks at the two structures as being in themselves so inextricably interrelated so as to require not separate but integrated study as a unitary phenomenon.

The interrelationship between speech and other social behavior is an extremely complex one, that between language structure and social structure may turn out to be even more complicated. There are some instances in which the usefulness of language or speech as data is primarily as an indicator of individual social characteristics or of the characteristics of social structures. This is the case, for example, where in the work of Bernstein class position is indicated by the use of elaborated or restricted codes (or formal or public languages) or where, more elegantly, Labov is able to identify both class position and aspiration for mobility through phonological analyses.[4] Analysis of

---

[4] The work of Bernstein and Labov goes far beyond simple correlational analysis; Bernstein has attacked fundamental problems of learning and of social control,

this sort has its most obvious usefulness in helping us to locate individuals in the social structure; it does not automatically provide an explanation of why particular usages are associated with particular positions. In such instances it can be said that language behavior *reflects* social structure. Aside from the work of social psychologists, particularly symbolic interactionists concerned with socialization and motivation, most sociologists who have used language as data, until very recently, have used it in this way.

There are other instances in which it may be said that social structure *determines* speech and/or language behavior (*infra.*, IV., B). This has been neatly documented in studies by John Gumperz in which he has shown the intricacies of code shifting between standards and dialects which occur as social contexts and conversational topics change. (See Blom and Gumperz: 1966, pp. 26ff.) Drawing on the work of Gumperz, Geertz and others, I have indicated some of the complexities which are introduced by varying characteristics of actual participants, their audience, the location of the interaction (social as well as physical), the topic under discussion, and so forth (Grimshaw: 1966). Moving to the level of speech communities and even nations it can be shown that historical and structural features of societies are crucial in the determination as to whether or not one or another language will become standardized, whether creoles or pidgins can move toward standardization, what are the likely outcomes of language conflict and of language planning, and so on (see III, infra.).

While Goffman, and more recently a growing number of ethnomethodologists, have attended to situations in which speech behavior along with gesture and other communicative symbols *defines* social structure and thereby constrains subsequent social interaction, this is, in spite of the early work of W. I. Thomas, a relatively new kind of activity in sociology. People frequently experience situations where they simply do not know what is going on and what expectations there may be for their behavior until conversation has been initiated. The topic of conversation chosen clearly is important in defining the situation. This is the case, for example, in one of Harvey Sacks's texts where the statement is made, "We were having an automobile discussion" (1966b; see also Bossard 1945a, b). Similarly, at a social gathering a new arrival can get many clues about patterns of interaction as he becomes aware of the topics which each small group is discussing. Sociologists have frequently neglected, however, the fact that how someone talks may be more important in defining a situation than what

---

Labov has investigated learning and social change. Some of their work in these areas will be noted below.

he talks about. Perhaps the most thoroughly documented and systematic instances of such definitions can be found in studies of pronominal usage and of honorifics (*infra.*, IV., A). However, the shifting of gears which is necessary when external clues as to social identity such as dress and demeanor are discovered to be incorrect identifiers (the high ranking officer in a combat team, indistinguishable in dress and appearance from his men; the dirty college professor working in his yard, addressed as if he were a servant; the butler addressed with respect) has been experienced by everybody. Differences in usage are indicators here as well as in those cases where lexical and phonological selection tells us something about the location of individuals in the social structure. In this instance, however, they are indicators which are useful to participants in the interaction in defining the situation as well as to students who are collecting data.

Those few sociologists who have given any thought to the relationships between language structure and social structure have generally examined it from one of the several correlational perspectives suggested above. Each of these several perspectives interests itself in a part of what, collectively, would be an adequate and general view of the interrelation between language structure (and speech) on the one hand, and social structure (and social interaction) on the other. Hymes (personal communication: 1967) has suggested that there is "a continuum of possible studies and interests, from the less language-involved to the more language-involved ... from the more correlational to the more embedded." The kind of data used determines in large part where on the continuum a study will fall; Gumperz, Hymes and Labov believe that respresentative samples of natural speech must be collected, and that with such samples of speech the researcher can move from gross identification of class correlates to apperception of situational-emotional interrelatedness (*viz.*, embeddedness) of increasingly high degrees of predictability. Such students, who are working towards the generation of an integrated theory of sociolinguistic description, find the identification of simple co-occurrence relationships to be interesting and suggestive but, at the same time, to fall short of a goal of full utilization of sociolinguistic data. According to these scholars there is a sense in which *the study of language is inseparable from the study of society* (Hymes, *loc. cit.*) or, as Gumperz has phrased it (personal communication: 1967), *linguistic interaction is social interaction*.

Such a view is in contrast to that of the Chomskyans who are at present interested in language structure as directly embedded in the fundamental character of the human mind in such a way as to exclude an interest in social life and social structure.[5] Chomsky says that the

[5] Gumperz comments here (personal communication: 1967): "In contrasting the

structure of the mind constrains the number of possible ways in which
humans may communicate and that there is, therefore, a bounded inventory of potential language behavior from which all actual languages
draw. Minimally, all human languages contain the nominative-predicative relationship. No natural language has been found which does not
contain this relationship. It is equally true, of course, that no symbolic
or logical system has been invented which does not contain this relationship. It would seem to be a moot question as to whether it is the mind
of man or a fundamental logic of communication which limits certain
fundamental sets of alternatives in language structure.

We do have data, however, which indicates that there are very close
similarities between social structure and language structure. At the same
time, while all societies seem to share certain institutions which are
directed to meeting the needs of their members, it would seem that
social structures vary too widely to be linked to any feature of the
human psyche common to all mankind. If all languages in certain fundamental characteristics were – because of some biological condition
of man – the same, we should expect all social structures to also be
the same (at least in equivalent 'deep' social structures which would
be equivalent to the deep structure of language). We know, however,
that man has met his social needs in a variety of ways and that differences among social structures are not random. It may be that there is
no fundamental contradiction here and that ultimately we will learn that
social structures and the ways in which they meet the needs of societal
members are substantially less dissimilar than now seems to be the
case.[6] Until this has been demonstrated, however, sociologists can not

---

sociolinguistic view with that of Chomsky you might note that the two don't necessarily conflict. They are complementary in the sense that they have different
types of goals, deal with different kinds of data and use different types of field
techniques. To be fair to Chomsky you might point to his distinctions between
languages and grammars. Grammars reflect competence and languages performance. All grammars are related in the sense that they share certain highly abstract
rules but this is not necessarily true of languages. So far no one has attempted to
draw a distinction similar to that between languages and grammars in the realm
of social processes. Ethnomethodologists are making a beginning but it's not yet
clear where they are going."

For a lucid and fairly non-technical introduction to transformational grammar,
the best source is probably Thomas (1965). Keith Schap of the Department of English, Indiana University, has suggested a series of readings at a middle-range of
difficulty and coverage, including: Gleitman: 1961, Katz: 1964, Klima 1964, Lees
1960; 1961; 1962, Postal: 1964; 1966, Rosenbaum: 1967, Smith: 1961; 1964.
Students with some background in linguistics and/or logic can begin directly with
Chomsky (1965) himself.

[6] I discuss this topic more thoroughly in chapter 6, "The Search for Universals",
Grimshaw: 1970c.

treat the differences among societies as being irrelevant nor can they treat differences in language use associated with differences in societies as being irrelevant. Moreover, it may very well be that the logic of communication does indeed limit the number of ways in which ideas can be communicated. An integrated theory of sociolinguistic description would attempt to indicate that the 'selection' of one or another such alternative is neither predetermined by man's mental structure nor independent of similar 'choices' which must be made in determining social structure in meeting social needs.

There is as yet no integrated theory of sociolinguistic description although the scholars mentioned are working in that direction. Meanwhile, language as a source of data can be far more effectively utilized by social scientists. Here again, adapting from Gumperz, we can see that there are two perspectives. The first of these sees language variously as an instrument in data collection or as an obstacle; the second emphasizes its use as data in a correlational examination of relationships between language structures and social structures. The methodological or instrumental concern with language is primarily with increasing the accuracy of language use in reporting aspects of social structure or individual motives or attitudes and secondarily in reducing the obfuscation and 'noise' attendant upon working across languages. These are meaningful problems and their solutions require sociolinguistic work. It should be noted, moreover, that the very difficulties attendant upon working across languages and in selecting adequate words for use in instruments indicate something about the cultures in which the student is working. If there is no way of saying "thank you" in Marathi, this says something about social structure in the area in which Marathi is spoken (Grimshaw: 1969a).

Psycholinguistic topics are treated elsewhere in this volume, and in the discussion which follows the emphasis will be on the interaction of social structure and language structure as they mutually influence one another rather than on questions which are more generally considered to be social-psychological, to wit, those having to do with socialization, motivation, and so on.[7] Thus, we are more interested in the consequences of bilingualism for social integration and in the development of social movements than we are with the immediate problems of interference in learning. Broadly speaking, perhaps too broadly, research on the covariation of language and social structure has focused on problems of social differentiation and social change. An interest in social and linguistic change leads one automatically to the study of languages

[7] For an analysis of these topics, a discussion of methods of data collection and attention to more 'micro' problems in sociolinguistics, see Ervin-Tripp: 1969, op. cit.

in contact, of bilingualism, of language conflict, and language planning (Grimshaw: 1969b). More recently, we have had the appearance of studies which examine changes in languages explicitly as a consequence of social changes. Contrasted to studies of change are studies more directly attending to relationships between language and social structure with particular reference to social differentiation.

III. LANGUAGES IN CONTACT

During the early decades of the Twentieth Century when millions of immigrants were coming to the United States, American sociologists had an opportunity to do a vast amount of research on problems of language contact and its social consequences.[8] Studies of language loyalty and language maintenance, of bi- and multilingualism, of adoption of prestige standards – could have been undertaken in one of the best 'natural' laboratories which has ever been available. Unfortunately, from the perspective of contemporary sociolinguists, sociologists studying the experience of these new Americans were interested almost exclusively in problems of 'the assimilation of ethnic minorities'. Similarly, linguists during the period were doing historical linguistics and were not interested in the variety of problems, particularly those related to interference, which have subsequently attracted the attention of Weinreich and other scholars.

When there was a concern with the language problems of immigrants, it was primarily one with language as a hindrance to assimilation and sociologists directed their attention to such studies as Thorsten Sellin's, *Culture Conflict and Crime* (1938). There were a few studies of the foreign language press, but with the exception of Robert E. Park (1955) such studies were generally from a perspective which viewed the press as hindering assimilation. Now, in the decade of the sixties when sociologists have become interested in language contact and when linguists have provided students of language contact with far more sophisticated linguistic techniques, there are no longer large immigrant groups in the United States; and with increasing frequency scholars are looking elsewhere for the particular problems of bilingualism which are of interest to them (see, however, fn. 8).

---

[8] Bilingualism has by no means disappeared in the United States, cf., Fishman 1966a and the extensive corpus on ghetto dialects (especially work of Labov cited in the Bibliography).

A. Bilingualism

Einar Haugen (1966b, see also the other citations to Haugen in the bibliography) has, in a discussion largely directed to dialects and standards and their meaningfulness in the context of a nation, made a distinction between the interests of linguists and of sociologists or sociolinguists in language. This distinction holds equally well for other areas of language contact. He writes:

Our discussion has shown that there are two clearly distinct dimensions involved in the various uses of 'language' and 'dialect'. One of these is *structural*, that is, descriptive of the language itself; the other is *functional*, that is, descriptive of its social uses in communication. Since the study of linguistic structure is regarded by linguists as their central task, it remains for sociologists, or more specifically, sociolinguists, to devote themselves to the study of the functional problem.

Haugen continues by stating that by structural use of "language" and "dialect" the overriding consideration is one of genetic relationship. This is in contrast to a concern with the *functional* use of "language" and "dialect", where the overriding consideration is the uses the speakers make of the codes they master.[9] Codification in a standard language he defines as minimal variation in form, elaboration as maximal variation in function. The particular issues of interest in studying movement from dialects to standards or the acceptance of one or another dialects as standard or the creation or crystallization of new languages are those of: (1) selection of norm, (2) codification of form, (3) elaboration of function, and (4) acceptance by the community. Haugen states that the first two refer primarily to the form, the last two to the function of language and claims that the interaction of the four form a matrix within which it is possible to discuss all the major problems of language and dialect in the life of a nation:

	Form	*Function*
Society	Selection	Acceptance
Language	Codification	Elaboration

This same organization is useful for discussion of most other problems of language contact, at least on the level which will be possible in this paper.

[9] Haugen's distinction between "structural" and "functional" is related to, but not synonymous with, other dichotomies: code structure-code, use, language-speech, competence-performance. What is new in all these emphases is attention not simply to a further facet of grammatical structures, but to the functional problem itself — one which brings into view aspects of language and other social behavior which would otherwise be neglected.

Since its original publication in 1953, Uriel Weinreich's, *Languages in Contact: Findings and Problems* (1966), has become the standard work in this area: his premature death was a major loss to the developing field of sociolinguistics. As a linguist, Weinreich was primarily concerned with what Haugen labels as the structural problem. However, Weinreich was among the pioneers in linguistics in his increasing awareness of what he called the psychological and socio-cultural setting of language contact, and in this volume specified a number of sociological questions which are of importance in language contact. In discussing non-structural factors Weinreich distinguished between those inherent in the bilingual person's relation to the languages he brings into contact – such as the generalized language facility of the individual, his relative proficiency in each language, and the manner of learning the languages – and his attitudes towards them. He continues, however, by noting that non-structural factors are not restricted to bilinguals as individuals, but that bilingualism is generally a group phenomenon. Thus, the size of the bilingual group and its socio-cultural characteristics, the prevalence of bilinguals with different characteristics of speech, the generalized attitudes towards the languages, attitudes towards bilingualism specifically, tolerance about varying patterns of language use, and the relations between bilingual groups and the language communities are singled out as being important to the socio-cultural study of bilingualism and language contact. In a caveat to his linguistic colleagues who insisted on doing 'pure' linguistics, Weinreich wrote, "The linguist who makes theories about language influence but neglects to account for the socio-cultural setting of the language contact, leaves his studies suspended, as it were, in mid air" (loc. cit.).

The principal concerns of the linguist in examining language contact and its consequences are with a variety of types of interference: phonic, grammatical, and lexical. While these need not be discussed here, many nonlinguists will find Weinreich's examination of these types of interferences an interesting and useful introduction into some of the nonsocial aspects of linguistic studies. Weinreich then examines the problem of the bilingual individual, reviewing psychological theories of bilingualism and such characteristics as the aptitude and switching facility of the individual as well as the relative status of the languages involved for the speaker himself in terms of such things as proficiency, motive use, characteristics of the situation in which the language was learned, its usefulness in communication, and matters of emotional involvement. As he moves closer to an examination of what he has labelled socio-cultural setting, he notes the importance of the speech situation itself insofar as interference for the individual speaker is concerned. Perceptions of one or another of the languages as being stigmatized may in certain situations cause the individual to shift, thus creating problems of interference. Again, situations of emotional stress may produce problems of interference particularly when the use of one language has been associated with the management of certain social situations.

Weinreich notes that it is reasonable to expect that those socio-cultural factors which determine personality traits, preferred language habits and the structuring of speech situations, will also be relevant to the control of interference. His concern is with interference. In the process of examining possible sources of interference he outlines the main topics of interest generally in the study of language structure and social structure. His discussion of the functions of language in bilingual groups anticipates some of the discussion below on the differentiation of language use. His discussion of parallels between group divisions and language divisions anticipates correlational studies between group and social characteristics and language and speech use. His discussion of the development and operation of language loyalty is relevant for a whole series of issues related to language conflict, language planning, and language maintenance. Finally, his brief discussion of the crystalization of new languages raises a series of interesting questions about the social structural features which are important in determining the acceptance or rejection of creoles, pidgins, and standards.

In addition to Weinreich's theoretical overview, there have been several other important publications in the areas of linguistic diversity and multilingualism in recent years.[10] Ferguson and Gumperz (1960) edited a special issue on regional, social and functional variation; Rice (1962) edited a volume emphasizing the role of second languages; Macnamara (1967a) recently edited a special issue on problems of bilingualism. Aside from Weinreich's volume and Hymes's recent paper (1967a) there are few explicitly theoretical treatments of multiple code usage and diversity although there have been important theoretical considerations in the writing of, e.g., Ervin-Tripp (1961); Friedrich (1962a); Lambert (1967); MacKey (1962) and in another, earlier, paper by Weinreich (1953). Ferguson (1962b, 1966), Kloss (1966b) and Stewart 1962a, b) have attacked typological problems. Several authors have attempted to measure either the extent of linguistic diversity in territorial units (Greenberg: 1956; Lieberson: 1964, 1965, 1966b; Hymes: 1968a)

---

[10] Researchers on bi- or multilingualism can be roughly dichotomized along two dimensions. The first of these dimensions distinguishes between a research focus on the individual as contrasted to one on groups or societies. The second distinguishes between situations in which standard languages are in contact and those in which there are either a variety of dialects or where there is a situation which has been labelled by Ferguson as *diglossia* (Ferguson: 1964, see also Fishman: 1967), one in which there is both a standard language present and one or more dialects.

or of code-switching facility and individual bilingualism (Diebold: 1963; Gumperz: 1964b, c, 1966b, 1967a, n.d.). Other studies, such as that of Rubin on Guarani in Paraguay, have combined several of these perspectives (1962, 1963). Banks and Textor (1963) used linguistic homogeneity as one of the raw characteristics in their *Cross-Polity Survey.* (see also Russett, et. al.; 1964).

The great bulk of the psychological and social psychological literature on bilingualism (and bidialectism), however, has been devoted to two problems. The first of these is second language learning (Center for Applied Linguistics: 1961, Ervin-Tripp: 1967, Ervin-Tripp and Osgood: 1954, Ferguson: 1962a, b, Gaarder: 1967, Gardner and Lambert: 1959, Lambert-Gardner-Barik-Tunstall: 1963,   Lambert-Havelka-Crosby: 1958, Macnamara: 1966, 1967b, c), a topic which has only very recently received attention from sociologists (see, especially, Cicourel: forthcoming). The second problem, which has more obvious implications for traditional sociological concerns, involves considerations of differences in statuses of languages in problems of self-concept and in judgements of personality and status attributes (Anisfeld-Bogo-Lambert: 1962, Anisfeld-Lambert: 1964, Bossard: 1945b, Lambert-Anisfeld-Yeni-Komshian: 1965, Lambert-Frankel-Tucker: 1966, Lambert-Hodgson-Gardner-Fillenbaum: 1960, Pieris: 1951, Rona: 1966, Sawyer: 1959, Tucker-Lambert: 1967). These studies have been concerned primarily with prestige factors associated with bilingualism. (There is a separate and rich literature on prestige differentiation related to bidialectism, see, especially, work of McDavid and Labov; and a smaller corpus of materials on the status aspects of creoles, e.g., Samarin: 1966.) To cite only one instance of the sociological relevance of this literature, Lambert's interesting studies of attitudes related to language problems of bilinguals have shown that primary users of the lower status standard language tend to denigrate the language and in some instances themselves and, moreover, that when such bilinguals listen to taped presentations (by identical speakers) in the two languages they are likely to ascribe higher status and more positively valued personality characteristics to the 'speakers' of the higher status standard.

More specifically sociological investigations into bilingualism or multilingualism whether on the level of contacts between standards or that of diglossia have focused on the problems of selection in the matrix presented by Haugen (*supra.*). Gumperz and others working with the concept of linguistic repertoire and switching have attempted to isolate the characteristics of social setting in which one or another type of language will be used. This literature will be discussed below during the examination of structural constraints on language use. Such research is generally on a microsociological or group level.

B. Language Conflict

Contrasted to this is a larger literature which involves both social and political questions and examines such topics as language conflict, language planning and language maintenance. These issues have to do with the displacement of languages by each other and with language dominance. Haugen (1966a) has shown the turmoil which accompanied the long struggle in Norway over the pattern of standardization to be followed in a common language accepted by all citizens of that small country. In a country like India, in which each of a dozen different languages is spoken by many millions of loyal speakers, the implications of dominance or subordination of one or another language has vast social and political implications. Harrison (1960) in his thoughtful study, *India: The Most Dangerous Decades*, showed how a host of political and power considerations have been superimposed on language nationalism, on concerns about the literary heritages of the many languages involved, and on simple needs for standard media of communication. After careful study of the centripetal potential and consequences of linguistic chauvinism in that troubled country, he concluded that India's experiment in democracy might founder from inability to deal with language problems. Other observers (Das Gupta: 1968, Kelley: 1966, McCormack: 1967, Weinreich: 1957, Windmiller: 1954) and subsequent events in India (viz., language rioting and governmental hesitance and inconsistency) have done little to encourage a more optimistic perspective. Das Gupta and Gumperz (1968), however, have suggested on the basis of Indian data that language conflict is elite conflict and does not necessarily involve the interests of unmobilized populations and, moreover, that language conflict – to the extent that it involves appeals for mass support – may in itself have the positive consequence of furthering the mobilization process. Das Gupta (1968) has also suggested that language associations frequently provide an institutional framework for the training of future political leaders (see also, E. Gumperz: 1967). In the initial chapter of his excellent and judicious study of the conflict in Norway first between *Riksmål* and *Landsmål* and later between *Bokmål* and *Nynorsk*, Einar Haugen (1966a) lists a litany of names of nations in Europe which underwent bitter and protracted struggles over language: Norway, Greece, Belgium, Rumania, Hungary, Bulgaria and Albania (all starting before the First World War); Finland, Estonia, Latvia, Lithuania, Iceland and the Irish Republic (all starting after World War I). As Haugen puts it, "Each of these added its own language to the concert of Europe, or rather to its bedlam". Some of these struggles have had to do with the search for a national identity, others have had even more profound consequences, as in the case of Turkey, where a shift of scripts generated a shift in national cultural orientation which had lasting consequences for the nation in its pattern of development. Turning his attention to the details of the Norwegian case, Haugen shows how national sentiment, rural-urban schisms, political infighting, a scholarly concern for clarity in expression and an occasional intellectual snobbery were intricately interrelated in the language struggle in Norway beginning after the achievement of independence in 1814 and continuing up to the present.

In Norway, and in most other European countries, the language problem was debated in literary circles, the national press and in parliaments. With the emergence of newly independent and multilingual nations in the years since the Second World War struggles over language have frequently taken on more sanguinary overtones. The Indian case, mentioned above, with its clash between supporters of Hindi and related Indo-European languages of the North and proponents of the languages of the South is more public but no more bitter than other cases in Africa and in other countries in Asia. Sociologists simply have not given sufficient attention to these problems of language conflict. While some aspects of language differentiation may be too subtle for the sociologist and observable only to the trained linguist, there are many other instances in which language serves as the most obvious clue to a whole host of other system boundaries.

Other scholars have examined the fissive and integrative impact of language loyalties in a variety of settings (Alisjahbana: 1949, Bidwell: 1962, Blom and Gumperz: 1966, Brosnahan: 1963, Buck: 1916, Chowdhury: 1960, De Francis: 1950, Deutsch: 1942; 1953, Fishman: 1968c, R. Hall: 1959, Haugen: 1952; Jakobson: 1945, Kloss: 1967, LePage: 1964, Maza: 1957, Nugroho: 1957, Rona: 1966, Rundle: 1946, Samarin: 1962, Sutherlin: 1962, Tanner: 1967, Taylor: 1961, van den Berghe: n.d.). Almost without exception these studies deal with whole societies or major sectors of societies or even with societies in contact. With only occasional exceptions, this literature has been neglected by social scientists interested in problems of societal integration.

C. Language Loyalty and Language Maintenance

Major immigration to the United States was completed shortly after the end of the first decade of the Twentieth Century. In 1966 (Fishman: 1966a, see also 1964a), with the publication of the report of the Language Resources Project (under the general direction of Joshua Fishman), the study of the role of minority languages in the United States was rescued from a half century of neglect. *Language Loyalty in the United States* includes three types of papers. First, there are papers by Fishman and his immediate associates on the actual status and distributions of immigrant languages in the United States and on the success or failure of a variety of institutions in fostering language loyalty and maintenance. There are chapters on the role of the ethnic press, of foreign language broadcasting, of ethnic group schools, of ethnic parishes, and of other organizational activities. A second major section consists of studies of the language maintenance experience of four different language communities in the United States: German-Americans (Heinz Kloss: 1966a); Franco-Americans (Herve-B. Le-Maire: 1966); Spanish-American (Christian and Christian: 1966); and Ukrainian-American (Nahirny and Fishman: 1966). In a third section and in a series of appendices, Fishman discusses problems of research on language maintenance and suggests both new research and direct action. He believes that language maintenance activities can be defended not only on the basis of values associated with cultural pluralism but also because there are immediate and practical reasons for maintaining linguistic diversity in a world in which Americans are continuously and increasingly in contact with peoples speaking other languages.

Theoretical materials of interest to students of language structure and social structure are to be found largely in the second section. Kloss discusses a series of factors which have contributed to language maintenance. One of them, religio-societal insulation, is sufficiently powerful that groups so endowed can resist assimilation. It is to be found, however, only among small groups. Other factors, which are only analytically distinguishable from each other, include the time of immigration, the existence of language islands, affiliations with denominations fostering parochial schools, pre-immigration experience with language maintenance efforts, and the former use of a language as the *only* official tongue during the pre Anglo-American period. Kloss's chapter is particularly interesting because of a section in which, paralleling Westie's study of pre-supposed empirical assumptions underlying studies of racial attitudes (1957), he takes up a series of factors which are ambivalent in their affects on language maintenance. Thus, for example, he states that there are both favorable and unfavorable effects of the high or low level of education of immigrants – a high level of education encourages a lively intellectual life, a flourishing vernacular press, the establishment of schools – but at the same time encourages occupational and frequently geographic mobility and rapid urbanization. The numerical size of a group speaking a language and the permissiveness or lack of it in the host society Kloss finds to have similarly ambivalent effects on language maintenance.

Christian and Christian in their discussion of Spanish language in the American Southwest emphasize cultural factors rather than the socio-demographic and organization features discussed by Kloss. In the view of these authors, the past history and the future prospects for the maintenance of Spanish in the Southwest can be understood only by understanding the culture of Spanish speakers and the difference of that culture from that of the Anglos. They state:

The nature of Hispanic culture seems to be *embedded in the language* of Spanish speakers in the Southwest. Furthermore, their culture and the language both seem to be *based upon and derived from* the reality in which they live; at the same time both language and culture seem to *create and mold* that reality.

In the view of the Christians language and culture together provide the basic orientation toward the real world of persons or groups of persons and the process of forming this orientation is circular. Their view is represented in the following diagram:

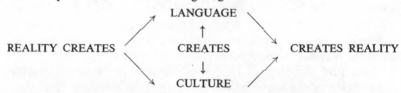

```
                        LANGUAGE
                            ↑
REALITY CREATES          CREATES            CREATES REALITY
                            ↓
                        CULTURE
```

They emphasize that the shift from one language to another means the shift from one culture to another and that this has implications for acceptance in the subordinated group. Unquestioned assumptions in cultures mean that the languages associated with those cultures are only partially translatable and the greater the differences in structure, the more difficulty there is in translating across the languages. They comment:

This observation has many implications for maintenance of Spanish in the Southwest. It would explain the almost total inaccessability of the mind of the 'chicano' to that of the 'gringo' or 'gabacho'. It would suggest that the acceptance of English by the Mexican-American implies the direct and immediate submission to a foreign culture and frame of reference, as well as to a foreign language. Those who do submit are called *pochos*, bleached or faded.

One of the implications of this observation is that of the desirability of research into the use of epithet as a mechanism in social control of those who have denied their cultural background and perhaps more generally.

In a summary chapter, Glazer (1966) reviews the factors suggested by Kloss and others as important in language maintenance and adds the further factor of ideology. He also discusses several counter-maintenance factors. Among these factors he emphasizes mass, free education and mass culture generally; the openness of American politics; and the organization of the economy with its possibilties for mobility. Most important, however, among these counter-maintenance factors is the fact that many natural supports for language use are cut off in America.

The process of assimilation in the United States with its accompanying consequences for the maintenance of immigrant languages occasionally provoked some bitterness; that bitterness did not begin to compare with the prolonged acrimony which has accompanied struggles over language selection in dozens of nations throughout the world which have gained their independence in the last one-and-one-half centuries.

D. Pidgins and Creole Languages

Among the sociologically more interesting instances of language contact are those where speakers of linguistically sharply variant languages representing sharply dissimilar cultures come into contact. In numerous historical instances, these differences have been accompanied by sharp discrepancies in power as well. Diebold, in writing about incipient bilingualism (1964) and Dozier, in writing about linguistic acculturation (1951) have examined a number of social structural variables which influence two sets of patterns consequent upon such contact.

More recently a number of sociolinguists and linguists have turned their attention to situations in which creoles and pidgins have developed (R. Hall: 1955, 1959, 1962; LePage: 1960, 1961; Stewart: 1962a, b). While these marginal patterns of communication through speech (in some instances early linguists were loath to dignify them by labelling them as languages) must have come into existence from the time of the first conquest of one group by another or of the first sustained trading contact which went beyond barter, systematic study was not started until long after linguistic traditions had been established for the European languages. The early reports of missionary and other visitors to Haiti mentioned by Goodman (1964) in his comparative study of creole French dialects are hardly more than collections of exotica. Only in the 1930's did serious attention begin to be given to these languages and dialects and it was only thirty years ago that Reinecke (1938) wrote his brief anticipatory article in *Social Forces* (based on an excellent and well documented dissertation, Reinecke: 1937) in which he noted, for the first time, some of the variety of these languages and some of the social factors which have produced them.

The publication of Robert A. Hall, Jr.'s, *Hands Off Pidgin English!* (1955), marked a turning point in the study of these 'exotic' languages. Hall, who had been working on Melanesian Pidgin for over a decade, had been increasingly impressed by the role of the pidgins of the area not only in facilitating communication between natives and Europeans,

but particularly in breaking down barriers which had been created by
the multiplicity of languages in eastern New Guinea – in which even adjacent clusters of villages had mutually unintelligible languages. The
immediate impetus for this technically excellent yet eminently readable
book was a demand by a United Nations Commission that Pidgin be
abolished – forthwith. The principal grounds for this were that pidgin
was a mechanism for the permanent social subordination of natives,
that it was not and could not be a language but was simply a corruption
of English, and that it would not be used as a vehicle for moving its
speakers into the modern period. Hall, in responding, demonstrated
that pidgin was indeed an intelligible language capable of carrying
refined thought (he gives examples), that it had its own unique grammar
which was not even remotely a corruption of English syntax, and, most
importantly, that it was playing a major role in the social and political
mobilization of the populations using it. He demonstrated that processes
were in motion such that pidgins were becoming creolized and that
standardization of a new language could be anticipated. He observed
the parallel with the standardization of Bazar Malay into Bahasa Indonesia – in part as a consequence of a refusal of the Dutch to respond
to natural language developments and needs. Any attempt to abolish
pidgins, he indicated, might only heighten their use as a vehicle for
a nationalist struggle for independence, perhaps precipitating that event
before the populations in question were ready.

Although Hall has been an exception, most students of creoles have
reported on technical investigations of patterns of interference, or
have published texts and other descriptive materials, or have written
historical chronologies. Only recently have scholars begun to attend
to processual patterns of development which lead to the dominance of
one or another speech variety in the movement toward standardization.
William Stewart has written a pioneering article on the creoles of the
Caribbean (1962b) in which he has examined the functional distribution
of standards and creoles and the contexts in which different speech
varieties are used. He diagrams the distribution in terms of two axes,
public-private and formal-informal:

	FORMAL	INFORMAL
PUBLIC	Standard	Creole (Standard)
PRIVATE	Standard (Creole)	Creole

Stewart is sensitive both to the mutual influence of language and social structures and to the value of changes in language usages in indexing social change. He writes:

For well over two centuries, Creoles and Standards have been used side by side in the Caribbean. Reflecting a traditionally rigid social structure, the relationship between Creoles and Standards has been one of a well defined mutually exclusive social and functional distribution. As long as Caribbean society remained essentially an extension of colonial plantation social structure, little motivation existed for equalizing the linguistic opportunities for participation in local cultural and administrative affairs. More recently, however, social and technological changes have begun to penetrate the region, and this has prompted among other things the adoption of policies aimed at reducing those linguistic differences which it is felt promote social and political equality, i.e., the contrast between literate and illiterate, and between use of the Creole and of the Standard.

It is possible that phonological and syntactic changes in creoles and pidgins can be inter-correlated with patterns of social change and that each of these types of change can be used to predict the other. (Grimshaw: 1970b; Mintz: 1970). It has been suggested, for example, that the appearance of new patterns in creolization and pidginization should be studied in the context of contemporary patterns of foreign relations of the society under study. It is increasingly coming to be recognized that there is a complex interplay between the economic, political, social and educational context of the development of special languages and that both linguists and sociologists could profit from an examination of this interaction. Thus it should be possible to isolate probable patterns of special language development in latifundiary *versus* mercantile systems; in instances of colonial domination *versus* simple culture contact; in instances where there are intersections of multiple colonial spheres of domination; and in instances where there are varying patterns of urban-rural differentiation and different kinds of demands for involvement in industrializing labor forces.

Linguists have generally examined patterns of creolization and pidginization in a frame of reference which emphasizes phono-grammatical and lexical interference. The social bases for support of or resistance to such interference are to be found in the social organization of the several societies themselves (including the ways in which conflict groups are bounded) and in the intra-societal power structure (Barth: 1964, Gumperz: 1964b). Social structure and power distribution are, in turn, influenced by macro-societal variables. It should be at least equally profitable to attempt to predict the appearance of varieties of such languages on the basis of historical-sociological as contrasted to solely linguistic analysis. One might, for example, examine the character of

the independence movement and of post-independence relations between
the ex-colonial power and the new domestic government. It might be
fruitful also to see the consequences of attaining independence at different historical periods, with or without the use of force, and to
examine the role of transportation and communication in the Nineteenth
as contrasted to the Twentieth Century.

IV. LANGUAGE STRUCTURE AND SOCIAL STRUCTURE: SOCIAL BEHAVIOR AND LANGUAGE BEHAVIOR

Linguists make a clear distinction between language structure (rules,
competence) and language behavior (speech, performance). Sociologists
distinguish between social structure and social behavior or interaction;
the distinction is less clear. One reason for the lesser clarity in the case
of social structure is that social structure not only includes norms (in
the sense of a syntax for social behavior), but also incorporates the
realities of differential distribution of power. The rules for language,
in the sense of competence, change only very slowly. (Some linguists
would substitute 'grammar' for 'competence' on the grounds that there
are other varieties of *linguistic* competence and that the term grammar
specifically bounds the phenomena to be considered.) The consequences
of conflict in a society may be to generate new structural arrangements
(or at least shifts in power distribution) in very short periods of time.
Thus, while relationships between social structure and language structure and between language behavior and social behavior will be found
in every micro- or macro-social situation, it will frequently be difficult
to identify and measure the mutual influence and co-determination of
the two structures and two types of behavior.

Among possible relationships between language structure and language behavior and social structure and social behavior suggested above
were the following: language behavior can *reflect* social structure; language behavior can *define or condition* social behavior (and social
structure); social structure can *determine* language behavior; *language
structure and behavior can be inseparable from social structure and
behavior.* These perspectives are all correct and only analytically se-
parable; they do, however, represent some extremely subtle differences
in ways of looking at the same phenomena. An outside observer, for
example, may see the ways in which different speech patterns (whose
users may or may not be conscious of the differences) *reflect* users'
positions in the social structure. On the other hand, the use of honorifics
may *define* proper behavior and *identify* social relationships for a person
just entering a conversation, as well as for an outside observer. A

complex set of social structural variables may *determine* code selection and repertoire shifts – and the speaker may or may not be consciously aware of them. On a deeper level of analysis, there may be inter-relationships between language structure and social structure in which directionality is no more discernible to the observer than to naive speakers.

The possible relationships suggested are by no means exhaustive of the intricate patterns which link language and social structure and behavior. Another perspective can also be suggested, that which sees language usages as reflecting social structure and at the same time determining other patterns of social behavior. Others could be added, depending upon the sociological or linguistic interests of the researcher. The theoretically most important questions, however, have to do with the cases of language definitions of social structure, of social structural definitions of language usages and with the far more difficult issue of causality or isomorphism of language and other social phenomena. Most sociolinguistic work up until quite recently, however, has been directed towards essentially correlational studies, and variation in language (particularly speech) behavior has been used to indicate social differences.

A. Language as Reflecting Social Structure

The 'pure' linguist is concerned with language 'competence', not with language 'performance'. This position is best summarized in a quotation from Chomsky's *Aspects of the Theory of Syntax* (1965):

Linguistic theory is concerned primarily with an ideal speaker-listener in a completely homogeneous speech-community, who knows its language perfectly, and is unaffected by such *grammatically irrelevant conditions* as memory limitations, distractions, shifts of attention and interest, and errors (random or characteristic) in applying his knowledge of language in actual performance. [emphasis added].

Chomsky's position represents the fundamental posture of 'structural' linguistics; sociologists are clearly more interested in 'functional' linguistics (Hymes: 1966b, 1967a, b, nd). (Hymes: 1966b. *Note to linguist readers:* 'Structural' is used here not in the Bloomfieldian sense of structural linguistics but rather in the sociological sense of dichotomy between structure and function – as in the citation from Haugen, p. 103, *supra*.). Sociologists are committed, axiomatically, to the belief that *no* social behavior is random and that *no* social behavior is irrelevant. Speech behavior (language codes and speech behavior should be distinguished) is social behavior. Following Hymes, the distinction between the structural and the functional positions (and the labels are unimportant) is that the former takes the concepts of speech community, speech act, fluent native speaker, and the functions of speech and of languages for granted or as arbitrarily postulated while the latter position takes them as problematic and to be investigated. Gumperz has defined socio-linguistic study as:

attending to those reflections of social structure which are revealed in language, particularly in speech usages, and . . . are concerned neither with motivation nor with conscious behavior. (Personal conversation.)

Simply defined, a speech community is a population whose members share the same set of evaluative norms with respect to language behavior. According to Labov, who has perhaps contributed most to refinements of research on the correlations between phonological and social differentiation, this community shares norms about language structure, style and production – norms which are usually followed unconsciously but which can be made explicit. If then, there are variations in speech usage, these variations reflect either normative variation among speech sub-communities or, possibly, the presence of underlying, covert and competitive sets of normative values.[11] In a

---

[11] Continuing use in the growing research and theoretical literature of sociolinguistics has required refinements of the concept of speech community, and the usage suggested here is being replaced by others with far more complex dimensions (see, e.g., Hymes: 1967a). Hymes (personal communication) has suggested that the principal definitional problem is a choice between definitions which emphasize *shared homogenous codes* as contrasted to those which emphasize *shared norms of interpretation of use* (whatever position is taken as to numbers and repertoires of codes). He observes that "evaluative norms" may suggest either too little or too much, that it might exclude shared code (in the narrow sense of language structure) and include only norms for the handling of conversation. In some instances language behavior could even be taken as implicitly opposed to language code.

Neither the definitional problem nor the realities of diversity can be ignored. Hymes (personal communication) specifies this in the following manner: "Perhaps the accurate thing to say is that the sociolinguist *faces* the problem of defining the speech community — cannot theoretically take the easy way out of bracketing diversity, and postulating a homogeneous simplified unreal object (as Chomsky: 1965). And must take into account both diversity of codes, variety within repertoires, and the problem of shared norms for use as well a shared norms for structure of code(s) proper. . . . The problem of *types* of speech community is a very real one for comparative sociology/sociolinguistics: as to repertoires, norms of use (Haugen's functional problem), valuation of speaking as an activity. What must be rejected is the simplistic equation of a language=communication=community. The three vary independently in relation to each other." (first emphasis added)

Labov (personal communication) emphasizes the fact that the sociolinguist is not solely concerned with the identification of norms and writes: "In a word, I agree with Homans that the object of study is not behavior, nor norms alone, but rather to account for the extent to which people deviate from these norms." Gumperz (personal communication) underlines the ways in which actual speech behavior

series of careful and ingenious studies (1963a, b; 1964; 1966a, b, c; 1968a) Labov has demonstrated: (1) the existence of speech sub-communities which are associated with social class strata; (2) shifts (whether conscious or not) to patterns of speech usage associated with higher strata by persons actually mobile or aspiring to mobility; and (3) marked shifts in speech patterns as contexts of speech production become more formal. In studying the prestige marker /r/, for example, he found the following percentage distribution for three individuals (1964b):

3 Individuals	(r) Casual Speech	Careful Speech	Reading Style	Word Lists
Upper middle class	69	85	96	100
Middle class	00	19	24	53
Working class	00	05	14	29

In his stratification studies Labov has examined instances in which the variations between speech sub-community norms are minor and non-competitive. In more recent studies of lexical and syntactic shifts, as well as phonological variants, in urban dialects of the very poor in New York City, he has identified a situation in which there are strong social structural supports in the sub-cultures using those dialects which have the immediate effect of enhancing the development of a competitive and sharply differentiated speech community with an entirely different set of language norms (1967a, b; Labov and Robins: 1968). Teachers of children who use these dialects understand neither the normative structure of the language of the speech community nor the sub-culture which supports it. The consequences are well-known.[12]

---

can reflect not shared evaluation of codes but shared norms about social relationships: "Although members of a speech community may have the same unconscious norms about speech usage, these vary or are variously interpreted depending on speakers, audiences and special situations. Speech variation, along with gestures, posture and other communicative signs serve as signals which tell speakers which social relationships are to be enacted and how norms are to be interpreted in a particular instance. ... From the sociolinguistic point of view speech variation is an essential signaling device which provides important information about interlocutors and guides us in evaluating their messages.

[12] Teachers are not the only ones who do not understand. Labov writes (personal communication): "The sociolinguistic structure for a community appears to show a relatively uniform set of evaluative norms as the subjective correlate of a highly stratified behavior pattern. This is true in the Negro community as well as the white. Those outside the community may understand the referential content of the dialect, but have no accurate view of the social significance of the language choices made within the dialect. Thus an excellent speaker of British West Indian standard will hear no pattern at all in response to our subjective reaction tests based on Negro or white sociolinguistic variables.

Labov has used quantitative methods in attempting to isolate patterns of social stratification and mobility in large populations. While his current studies on urban dialects are illuminating the quality of social relationships in ghetto populations, his stratificational studies have examined language and social behavior in the aggregate and have been less concerned with the social consequences of language differentiation than with the identification of patterns of differentiation themselves. Roger Brown and a number of other students of the use of honorifics in address have attempted to move from the identification of status differences in micro social interaction to the understanding of the quality of social relationships in whole societies.

Study of situations in which there is differentiation in use of terms of address is both doubly useful and perilous for the sociolinguist. It is useful both because the observer can quickly grasp something about the structure of the role relationship between speakers and because the perceptions by those observed of the situation in which they are interacting can influence usage choices. There is an apparent dilemma as to whether the observed speech behavior *reflects* social structure or whether perceptions of social structure are influencing speech behavior.[13]

In a series of publications (Brown: 1965; Brown and Ford: 1961; Brown and Gilman: 1960; see also, Geertz: 1960; Howell: 1967) Brown and his associates have examined the subtleties of symmetry and asymmetry in forms of inter-personal address. They have demonstrated that the choice of familiar or formal forms and their functional equivalents of first names and last names with titles, indicate those dimensions of intimacy and solidarity, on the one hand, and of social distance and status, on the other, which characterize an interpersonal relation-

---

[13] Hymes (personal communication: 1967) suggests that the dilemma *is* only apparent. He distinguished between *normal* usages across roles, statuses and situations — which, to a great extent, *reflect* social structure — and *marked* usages across different domains, again of roles, statuses, and situations. What may be normal usage in talking to a baby may be an insulting marked usage in talking with an adult; nonetheless, this would not be a rule violation but rather the use of a rule about *the appropriate way to insult*. Marked usages, in other words, are used to *define* social relationships.

Thus, Hymes continues, both things are continually going on. "The system in use reflects social structure and is being used to define situations at the same time, thus feeding back into the social structure." He suggests that social interaction can be presumed to lead social usage of speech in this ongoing system of definitions and redefinitions. He concludes: "Given the perception of the relationships, there will be a range of appropriate ways to be normal, condescending, insulting, ingratiating, etc. Not everyone in every situation will have the same choices, so that the behavior, in its possibility of alternates, will both manifest perceptions and the actual structures of the relationship."

ship. While there are exceptions, the general norm is for superiors to address inferiors and intimate equals familiarly and non-intimate equals formally, and for inferiors to address superiors and non-intimate equals formally and intimate equals familiarly. This *norm* holds in all languages which have been examined.[14]

Elaborations of this perspective have taken two directions. Friedrich has shown, using Russian novels as sociological source materials (the translation of novels into English, with its singular 'you' form removes a substantial amount of useful data from such materials), that the uses of *ty* and *vy* (roughly equivalent to *tu* and *vous*) can serve not only as indicators of status differentials and of shifting patterns of interpersonal relationships, but of extremely subtle subjective personal response as well. (Friedrich: 1966b). Other scholars have shown the ways in which forms of address in other languages reflect even more subtle differentiations of hierarchy and intimacy. Martin (1964; see also Howell: 1965, 1967), for example, has shown that Japanese must make choices of speech level on two axes, those of reference and those of address. The axis of address – permitting choices of plain, polite, or deferential forms – reflects status differences. The axis of reference – permitting choices of humble, neutral or exalted forms – reflects characterizations of the subject of expression. In Korean the complexity is compounded by a distinction between address to ingroup or outgroup members; in the latter case the axis of address includes polite, authoritative and deferential forms. Selection of forms, Martin reports, is differentially determined by factors of age, sex, social position and outgroupness. Martin feels that the importance of politeness is so great in these societies that shifts in patterns of social distance and even of intimacy and solidarity will not be automatically accompanied by a diminution in the fineness of distinctions on speech levels.

Howell (1967) has pointed out some additional subtleties of the meaning of usages within dyads. He has noted that the full exchange of forms of address must be available, that there are cases in which proffered exchange of the familiar is refused, and that this refusal will be taken as an affront even in those instances in which the intent of the refusal is to signify the higher status of the person proffering the usage. He has also pointed out that in situations of ambiguous status there may simply be an avoidance of the use of any terms of address. His example is of changing patterns of race relations in the American South. An example of equivalent ambiguity might be that of relations between senior graduate students and some of their senior professors.

Attention by linguists to characteristics of sender and receiver has

[14] Ervin-Tripp (1969) has a comprehensive discussion of this literature and develops implications not discussed in this paper.

focused largely on those attributes associated with hierarchical ordering and, to a lesser extent, with degrees of intimacy. Other variables may tend to override the hierarchical, for example, participation in a common work situation (Negro and white miners below ground, Minard: 1952) or shared danger and concern in crisis situations, for example, the well-known shifts in degree of familiarity and formality in military address in and out of combat. Aside from this, however, sociologists are well aware of possibilities of status inconsistencies (which may characterize social identities of either sender or receiver or both) and of simple errors in perceiving another's, say receiver's, statuses. Folk literatures are rich with cases of mistaken status identity, and frequently detail the language shifts as well as the other behavior changes which occur when perceptions are corrected. The bulk of studies which have attended to conditioning factors have been done in societies where the statuses of each and every individual are known or where clues are clear and unambiguous. This is clearly not the case in urban areas of complex, industrialized, urban societies where there are additional complexities in the meaning of 'social identity'. (Adapted from Grimshaw: 1966.)

Linguistic data on several levels can be used to identify the boundaries of significant social aggregates. Lieberson (1966b) has listed a number of the uses to which language censuses can be put in studying such problems as creolization, multilingualism and language standardization. He has further noted that linguistic developments in smaller communities will be increasingly influenced by language characteristics of the larger social units of which they are parts. He has also specified a large number of possible errors which can be introduced by the uncritical use of census materials on language.

On a more intensive level of research, dialectologists working on isoglosses have long been able to identify boundaries which frequently have social as well as linguistic significance. McDavid (1964, see also Levine and Crockett: 1966, 1967), in work on the post vocalic -r in the Piedmont has combined highly sophisticated phonological analysis with an equally insightful perspective into the social factors environing linguistic differentiation. Gumperz, in his work (on the relationship between languages as socially defined entities and grammars as theories of language and proto-languages as generic constructs) on the Mysore-Maharashtra border has incidentally demonstrated the potential of linguistic analysis in identifying cultural and regional boundaries in areas of extremely complex patterns of language use, where both multilingualism and diglossia are found within individual villages. (1967a, see also 1961).

Limitations of space preclude the inclusion of numerous other studies which have demonstrated ways in which language usages reflect social structure and social relationships. No treatment, however, would be complete without reference to Friedrich's innovative and convincing study of changes in kinship terminologies in Russia as consequent upon major social changes in Russian society (1966). In one of the very few genuinely diachronic researches in the sociolinguistic literature, Friedrich demonstrates how a series of cataclysmic changes in Russian society (the Emancipation of the Serfs, the Revolution and the two World Wars) have radically transformed the social structure of Russian kinship, and thereby have caused a drastic diminution in both the size of the repertoire of kinship terminology and in the semantic specialization of individual terms. In the mid Nineteenth Century every Russian used easily a minimum of about sixty-five core kin terms – in 1950 the number of terms used had been reduced to about thirty. Friedrich concludes:

It is obviously true that the relation of the social system of behavior and principles to the several levels of languages is not by any means unidirectional in the sense that the second is an entirely dependent variable. On the contrary, as Sapir and others have argued, the semantic categories and conceptual interrelationships implicit in everyday speech to some extent precondition and in that sense determine our real decisions and our experience of life. Nevertheless, the available evidence indicates beyond cavil, I think, that the covert design and the audible stimuli of language function primarily as a conservative, stabilizing force, as a peripheral feedback system; in other words, it is change in social systems that *primarily* precedes and predetermines change in the corresponding semantic systems.

B.   *Social Structural Determinants of Repertoire Selection*

Social restraints on language choice ... are also a part of social structure. They are thus susceptible to analysis in terms of generalized relational variables which apply to interaction in all human groups. The study of particular sets of grammatical systems and cultural norms in terms of these variables enables us to treat linguistic behavior as a form of social behavior, and linguistic change as a special case of social change. (Gumperz: 1964b)

The researches discussed immediately above have generally been directed toward ways in which analysis of language usages can be used to determine the identities of speakers and persons spoken to and the relative positions of interlocutors. Characteristic *patterns of speech of individuals* have been used to locate their users in the social structure; characteristic uses of *speech in situations* have been used to identify patterned social relationships (as in the use of honorifics). The study of linguistic repertoires and of code-switching has shown that many individuals can handle more than one acceptable pattern of speech and that the pattern chosen is determined by the definition of the situation.

Gumperz introduced the concept of linguistic repertoire – defined as the totality of styles, dialects, and languages used within a socially defined community – as a unit of analysis for the cross-cultural comparison of language behavior. (Gumperz: 1964b. There are a variety of ways in which sociolinguistic analysis could strengthen and enrich comparative sociological research. Unfortunately, there is not space in this review for a systematic review of either work already done or of needed developments.) After studying communities in India and in Norway, Gumperz concluded that social structure influenced repertoire selection on two levels. In summary, he showed:

> While the choice between dialect use or the use of the standard language in each case is conditioned by such factors as the social occasion, the setting, the formal or informal roles of participants, their audiences, and the topic of conversation, in the Indian case the existence of sharply defined social barriers of caste and status has the effect of separating the repertoire into highly discrete, nonoverlapping varieties. In Norway, on the other hand, where social barriers are more fluid, the standard and the dialect are more like poles defining the end points of a continuum of linguistic variants. (Grimshaw, 1967a)

The greater importance of shifting in India reflects the greater and more rigid hierarchization of Indian society, a fundamental embedding of lingual and social structures. In both societies, however, within the specified ranges of permissibility of repertoire selection, setting and topic determine choice.

Linguists who have discussed the influence of setting on choice of speech patterns and/or dialects have done so most frequently in cases of diglossia or in other situations where there are sharp distinctions between literary and/or ritual uses and those of everyday life. (See, e.g., Opler and Hoijer's oft-cited 1940 study of Apache war language and Gumperz' treatment of the Indian case cited above.) Moreover, as suggested above, the bulk of studies which have investigated conditioning factors have been done in societies where the statuses of conversational participants are clear and unambiguous, a situation which does not hold in most complex, industrialized, urban societies.

I have suggested elsewhere (Grimshaw, 1966, includes a fuller review of the topic here under consideration) that the presence of and variable characteristics of audiences may have as substantial an influence on style selection as the topic of discussion and the actual physical setting. Using the cross-status interaction of professor and janitor as an example, I suggested that the choice of style by the actor of higher status could be considered as a consequence of the interplay of variables suggested in Table 1 *viz.*, audience characteristics and the role-taking ability of the speaker. In the absence of role-taking ability, status consciousness becomes a determining factor. Three possible responses were posited: (1) style adoption (however incorrect), (2) simplification, and (3) depersonalization.

TABLE 1

Speech Pattern or Style by High Status Sender to Low Status Receiver, by Type of Audience and Ability to Take Receiver's Role

Audience Characteristics	Willingness and/or Ability to Take Role of Receiver		
	Yes	No	
		Highly Status Conscious	Low Status Consciousness
None	Style Adoption	Nonpersonal Communication	Simplification
Higher than Sender	Lexical and Grammatical Simplification	Nonpersonal Communication	Simplification
Same as Sender	Style Adoption[a]	Nonpersonal Communication	Simplification
Lower than Sender	Lexical and Grammatical Simplification	Nonpersonal Communication	Simplification
Same as Receiver	Style Adoption	Nonpersonal Communication	Simplification

[a] Posits perceived role-taking on the part of audience.

In a further discussion of the Table, I wrote:

Willingness and ability to take the role of the receiver are not, of course, randomly distributed. Shared military service experience may heighten this ability, increasing age along with increasing increments of status may be associated with a diminution of such skills. It is also possible that highly motivated and status conscious individuals may possess the requisite skills but repress their use and permit them to atrophy. In the presence of such skills and willingness to use them, however, audience characteristics can become crucial. In the instance under discussion suppose the janitor comes into the office while the academician is (1) alone, (2) with a senior member of the administration, (3) with a colleague of peer status, (4) with an under-graduate student, or (5) with another maintenance man. The ensuing patterns of interaction, including speech, could vary widely. Additional changes might be anticipated with the entrance of still other actors into the situation – the professor's wife, for example. Indeed in all the above situations it might be well to assume that all the participants were male, and then to speculate on different speech styles which might emerge with the introduction of females into the situation. Before other audiences, say, the parents of students, other variations could be anticipated. Similarly, a shift from the academician's own office to another physical setting – elevator, classroom, coffee-shop, etc. – would produce other changes.

I believe my concluding comment still holds:

What has been suggested here is more than an additional taxonomic paradigm. If it is true that this kind of conceptual framework helps to organize and explicate linguistic behavior, and that audience is an important element in the social structure *between* language and speech, it should be equally true that sociologists could take linguistic data of the sort suggested here and use it to illuminate varieties of social structures more thoroughly. Few sociologists have ever attended to language shifts. Important and easily obtainable data are being wasted. (Grimshaw: 1966)

Gumperz' paper on dialect differentiation and social stratification in North India (1958) and working papers by Bright (1968, see also Bright: 1960), McCormack (1968), and Ramanujam (1968), focus their attention on social (status) characteristics of senders in multidialectical diversity. A second focus in these papers is on the relation of intensity of communication to diffusion of linguistic phenomena. (See, especially, Gumperz: 1967b, an excellent review article which became available too late for fuller incorporation into this paper.) Geertz' extremely interesting and illuminating discussion of linguistic etiquette in Modjokuto (1960) underlines the importance of receiver as well as sender and notes in passing some of the elements of setting which parallel the axis of reference in Japanese discussed by Martin (*supra.*). Sociologists, particularly Goffman (1959; 1961; 1963; 1964), but more recently some of those doing ethnomethodology as well, have concentrated on the influence of setting on a variety of social behaviors, including language use. The most succinct review and summary of the influence of social structural factors involved in communicative events – including the interactive effects of channels, codes, settings, message-forms, topics and events – is to be found in two articles by Hymes (1964e and 1967a). In these two articles, Hymes is moving toward a general theory of descriptive sociolinguistics and increasingly emphasizes the isomorphic nature of the relationships between language structure and social structure.

C. *The Case for Isomorphism*

It was suggested above, at the beginning of Section II., that there are four principal perspectives on the causal relationship between language and social structure: those which variously see language as 'causing' social behavior – or social structure as somehow determining language; that which sees both language and social structure as determined by some third factor; and that which sees neither as prior to the other, both being seen as co-occurring and co-determining. The studies reviewed in Parts A. and B. of this section would seem, at the very least, to demonstrate beyond reasonable argument the fact that there are causal relationships between the two sets of behavior under consideration. At least some of the data adduced – for example, the Friedrich study of social change and kinship terminology – seems to support the causal priority of the social structural features of the phenomena being examined. More generally, however, assessment of causal priority seems to reflect the original point of departure; and the more closely a set of speech behavior and social behavior is scrutinized, the more likely that the researcher will conclude that there is influence in both directions. If this is the case, then it seems probable that both these two perspectives may, in the final analysis, be subsumable under the perspective of co-determination, earlier labelled mutual embeddedness.

It is difficult to select a point of departure from which to move in an attempt to answer this question. This difficulty has currently been exacerbated by a fundamental change in orientation of American linguistics, brought about both by the Chomskyan revolution itself and by the new perspectives of the sociolinguists, particularly Hymes, who writes of this change:

In the recent past, American linguistics and anthropology seem to have emphasized invariance of structure in analysis of a single language; variation of structure as between languages; variation in the handling of use with regard to a single language (the intrusion of data dependent on special functions being handled as deviation from a norm); and invariance of use as between languages. At the present time, there seems to be coming to the fore a pattern of emphasis which is the converse of that just described. There is an emphasis on recognition of variation in the analysis of a single language; on invariance as between languages (universals of language); on invariance in the handling of speech functions in relation to a single system (language a 'system of systems', or subcodes, with data dependent on special uses handled positively in terms of additional norms); and on variation as across languages. Part of this second pattern of emphasis is projected. Sociolinguistics seems to be rapidly establishing an emphasis on variation of structure in the analysis of individual languages; emphasis on variation of function across languages is the special concern of the present paper. (1966a)

Adapting from Hymes' presentations (1966a, n.d.), this shift càn be shown as follows:

PRE-SOCIOLINGUISTIC ORIENTATION

	Descriptive (Intracultural)	Comparative (Crosscultural)
Structure	Invariance	Variation
Function	Variation	Invariance

POST-SOCIOLINGUISTIC ORIENTATION

	Descriptive (Intracultural)	Comparative (Crosscultural)
Structure	Variation	Invariance
Function	Invariance	Variation

Hymes has been quoted above as summarizing the difference between 'structural' and 'functional' perspectives as one in which "concepts of speech community, speech act, fluent native speaker, functions of speech and of language" are in the first case "taken for granted or arbitrarily postulated", and in the second "taken as problematic and to be investigated". The sociolinguistic perspective assumes a considerable diversity in ways in which language and speech can be used to meet needs which are to be found within individual social structures. Needs may vary across social structures; the structure of language and speech to meet the same communicative need will not vary. This perspective does not deny the likelihood of linguistic universals and insist upon an uncritical linguistic relativity. If the nominative-predicative relationship is a necessity for all human communication, it will appear in the same structural form in all languages. The sociolinguist, however, insists that there are other types of relationships which are not common to either all language structures or to all social structures and that in these instances language and social structures reflect each other rather than intrinsic human psychological needs.

We have reviewed research above in which speech usage is seen as reflecting social structure, social structure is seen as determining speech usage and correlations of linguistic and social structures are reported without attempting to assess causal priority. There have been no researches explicitly designed to test the hypothesis of codetermination or mutual embeddedness and only a few which can be used as evidence for the validity of that hypothesis. In the remainder of this section I will review two sets of studies, each of which offers indirect evidence for this point of view. The first is synchronic and deals with cross-societal differentiation of linguistic and social structures in 'near' cultures – Truk and Ponape (on "near" cultures, see Smelser: 1966). The evidence here is phonological and syntactic and comes closest to meeting the demands of more traditional linguists. The second case is also synchronic and intracultural although comparative for subcultures.

In two recent reports on his cross-societal study of Truk and Ponape, Fischer (1965; 1966, see also Garvin and Riesenbert: 1952; Goodenough: 1964) has attempted to demonstrate the manner in which variations in social structure in the two societies are linked to varying patterns of phonological and syntactic differentiation. If his analysis is correct, he has shown the phonological and syntactic differences between the two related but mutually intelligible languages to be isomorphic to differences in the social structures of the two societies and has, moreover, in the phonological study suggested the possibility of a universal expressive value of different varieties of consonant clusters.

In the syntax study Fischer examines patterned differentiation of noun modifiers by position within the sentence. This analysis reveals that while the two languages are closely related (lexico-statistical analysis indicates that the languages have been geographically isolated for approximately eight centuries), Ponapean noun phrases are "constructed more tightly" than those of Trukese. Fischer reports that as a consequence of this difference there is a greater chance in the second language "for the listener to decide that the speaker has come to a point at which he may be interrupted, when actually the speaker intends to say more". This difference in syntax, with its accompanying consequences for speech behavior and closure in intellectual discourse, he attributes to differences in the social structure of the two societies which have developed in the long years since the two societies have become isolated. In our view, of course, the differences in social structure have been reinforced by the differences in language structure. Fischer characterized Ponapean social structure as being more differentiated than Trukese. There is a greater variety of clearly demarcated social roles on Ponape (particularly kinship and political roles). These roles are not only more differentiated, but individuals may change their position from one role to another through the exercise of individual initiative. Ponapean social structure is not only more hierarchical and

more differentiated, but more flexible and characterized by greater
social mobility. Fischer concludes that differences in syntax between
Trukese and Ponapean are moderate, but at the same time consistently
and significantly in the same direction – a direction which is best explained in terms of *social* differences which favor a different balance
between two types of thought habits, variously labelled as 'concrete'
versus 'abstract', or with other polar distinctions. He observes that
there may be other variables of general thought patterns which are
relevant to syntax but functionally unrelated to differential location of
noun modifiers. Clues to the nature of such patterns, Fischer asserts,
"may be found by careful consideration of small groups of related languages in relation to the social structure of the speech communities".
In conclusion he states what may well be a 'sociolinguistic universal':

As societies become more complex and social roles become more differentiated, the realized meaning of words in particular contexts becomes less
important than the common or basic meaning. Speakers are forced to assume
a greater cognitive gap between themselves and their listeners. At the same
time, the basic meaning of the items of the lexicon tends to become more
abstract and attenuated, since speakers have less need for words which can
express much meaning in compact form to listeners who are conceived of
as being much like the self; they have more need, instead, for words which
can be used in many different contexts with many different listeners who
are conceived of as being very different from the self and from each other.
Of course, it is still necessary to speak precisely about detailed matters much
of the time, but this kind of concreteness can be achieved through the
combination of several words which in themselves are relatively abstract.

Sociologists who have attended at all to linguistic and speech variation
have, with the exception of those doing ethnomethodology and some
social psychologists who have done work in semantics, generally limited
their investigations to the examination of lexical inventories and to
class differences in style. Analysis of syntax is beyond the competence
of most sociologists; the phonological data used by Fischer in the
second paper to be reviewed must seem even more esoteric.

   In all languages phonetic adjustments are made at the boundaries of
adjacent words during fluent speech – an example in English might
be the variant handling of the terminal consonants in the two word
phrases tota*l* lapse or tota*l* time, moto*r* repair or moto*r* failure. In some
instances there is simple alternation of phonetic forms that are usually
assigned to the same underlying consonant, quite automatic and predictable from the relations of the articulators, or one consonant is
dropped entirely if it is followed by the same consonant. In other
instances, however, the change is more radical, leading to a form which
would be considered a different consonant if it occurred initially. (The

latter changes are referred to as *sandhi*, following the usage of Sanskrit grammarians.) Fischer has examined the different rules for consonantal sandhi in Trukese and Ponapean and associated these rules with the same differences in social structural complexity which he explicated in his syntactic study. He has gone beyond the cross-societal comparison in this study, however, to suggest that changing patterns of sandhi within languages may reflect internal differentiation, and that the types of changes found within these two languages may reflect some universal expressive value of this form of phonological shift.

Fischer's findings on sandhi in Truk and Ponape are summarized in Tables Two through Four. Table Two shows the pattern which sandhi takes in each of the two societies. In Truk underlying forms which are characterized by double stops retain them, while nasal-stop patterns are shifted to double-stops. In Ponape a converse pattern holds, with all underlying forms ending up as nasal-stop patterns. He shows that the Ponapean pattern is associated with an emphasis on precision in speech which is consonant with and supported by the greater complexity of Ponapean society already indicated in the syntax study. In contrast, the greater emphasis on fluency and quantity in speech which is consonant with the double-stop pattern in Truk is also paralleled by a lesser complexity in that society.

TABLE 2

Cross-Societal Variation in Sandhi

	TRUK		PONAPE	
Underlying forms	Nasal-stop	Stop-stop	Nasal-stop	Stop-stop
Result of Sandhi	Stop-stop	Stop-stop	Nasal-stop	Nasal-stop
	Less complex social structure; emphasis on fluency in speech.		More complex social structure; emphasis on precision in speech.	

Adapted from Fischer: 1965.

Table Three, which is based on what Fischer characterizes as more fragmentary evidence, shows the association of a sandhi differentiation within each of the two societies in association with different speech contexts.

TABLE 3
Intracultural Variation in Sandhi

	TRUK	PONAPE
Free expression including aggression	Double-stop (Normal sandhi)	Double-stop (Sandhi eliminated)
Restraint, gentleness, politeness	Nasal-stop	Nasal-stop

In both societies free expression, including the expression of aggression, seems to be associated with the use of the double-stop pattern and more restrained, gentle and polite speech contexts demand the use of the nasal-stop pattern. In other words in Trukese, which generally emphasizes freedom and fluency of expression, normal sandhi is maintained in contexts of non-constraint and the nasal-stop pattern is used in more restrained contexts. The same result is achieved in Ponapean, on the other hand, by the elimination of sandhi to produce the double-stop pattern in more relaxed speech contexts and in cases of the free expression of aggression. Thus, the phonological pattern which favors double-stops is associated in cross-societal comparison with the society which is less complex and in which fluency in speech is preferred and within both these societies the same pattern is associated with freer, more expressive interaction. Conversely, the nasal-stop pattern is associated in cross-societal comparison with the society which is more complex and in which precision in speech is preferred and within both these societies the same pattern is associated with restrained, precise and more formal interaction. The cross-societal and intra-societal comparisons are summarized in Table Four.

TABLE 4
Nasal-stop and Double-stop: Cross-societal and Intrasocietal 'Function'

	Function	
Structure	Cross-societal	Intra-societal
Nasal-stop	More complex society	Restrained, precise interaction
Double-stop	Less complex	Free, expressive interaction

Fischer is careful to point out that there are, of course, great variations in speech situations within both cultures. The overall evidence is impressive, however, and the pattern of cross-societal and intra-societal variation is surely consonant with Fischer's speculation that similarities in the expressive value of the two types of consonant clusters "may lead us to consider . . . whether there may not be something appropriate in these cultural meanings from the point of view of a potentially universal phonetic symbolism".

These examples show, first how detailed linguistic analysis can be combined with ethnographic information (sociological data) actually to demonstrate the "reciprocal relationship between language and human society". Secondly, they show how sociolinguistic research can lead to statements of relationships which are generalizable beyond the confines of single social structures and which at the same time have important methodological implications (phonology and syntax as indicators of social structural complexity *and* internal differentiation of contexts).[15]

There has been one major sociological contributor to the growing corpus of the literature on sociolinguistics, the British sociologist Basil Bernstein (for full citations, see bibliography. It should be noted that Bernstein's work has created considerable controversy and that both linguists and sociologists have been critical of his methods and his interpretations. This was particularly true of some of his earlier work, see, *inter alia*, John: 1966 and 1967. More recent work has been both linguistically and sociologically more sophisticated and has had a substantial impact on the work of scholars in both fields). Bernstein's fun-

---

[15] There have been two principal types of criticisms of Fischer's papers. The first is that his interpretation of his data is *ex post facto*; the second, that he may be guilty of a naive neo-Whorfianism in seeking reflections of social structure within the grammatical structure of a single code or speech variety.

The papers *were* written after data had been collected; quite clearly, further studies will be needed to further document his interpretations. The kind of relationships posited are, however, singularly amenable to testing: do Trukese take the opportunity to break in, does the difference in noun structure function as Fischer suggests? Hymes notes, however: "The basic model, of differential selection in linguistic features together with differential trends in social structure — the linguistic features being clearly such as could be motivated in interaction — seems . . . important and valid" (personal communication). In the absence of contrary data both the underlying delineation of the problem and the suggested solutions are of great heuristic value.

It seems to me that the answer to the charge of neo-Whorfianism is to be found in the quotation from Fischer's paper itself (pp. 56-57). The situation which he describes as being typical of increasingly complex societies with greater role differentiation is clearly one in which semantic constraints of lexical choice are correspondingly reduced as the cognitive gap between interlocutors increases. Indeed, the achievement of precision through word combination has been observed for developing languages in less complex societies as well (note Hall on pidgin).

damental view is that social structure constitutes a set of intervening variables between languages (which represent the world of the possible in lexical and structural options, 1964b), and speech, which encapsulates the choices among the available options. This speech system, labelled by Bernstein as a linguistic code, in turn reinforces the selective perceptions of its users of what is relevant in their environment. In this way definitions of the social structure are again reinforced and again influence code selection. In actuality, Bernstein himself demonstrates that position in the social structure automatically limits the range of possible selection from the total world of lexical and structural (and phonological) options; codes or speech systems then are isomorphic to societal sub-systems. In relatively homogeneous social systems and speech communities such as Truk and Ponape there is little intrasocietal differentiation in speech behavior because there is little or no subcultural or sub-systemic variation in the social system.[16] In more heterogeneous social systems, which will also be characterized by greater diversity in speech systems, particular 'levels' of the social system will be associated with particular sectors of choice among all possible options in language.

Bernstein has used the polar concepts of what he has variously labelled as *elaborated* and *restricted* codes or *formal* and *public* languages in the elucidation of a wide range of situations and uses of language but has attended particularly to problems of learning and process of social control (in my treatment of Bernstein I have drawn heavily on my earlier discussion, Grimshaw: 1966). In his earlier papers, Bernstein was interested primarily in problems of learning (see especially, 1958; 1961a, b, c; 1970). He suggested that users of what he called elaborated codes are more able to think abstractly, particularly in terms of relationships, and are therefore more able to handle complex materials than the rote learning of the early years of school. The restricted code is restricted in that, while it facilitates the exchange of solidarity and permits transmission of concrete information, its user cannot think conceptually, hypothetically, or speculatively about worlds and events which might

---

[16]   This is, of course, a relative statement. There is greater stratification and differentiation generally in Ponape than in Truk; both societies are characterized by lesser differentiation than is found in contemporary urban and industrialized nations.

Fishman (1965) and Gumperz (1962) both deal with the relationship between language and complexity of social systems. More generally, Gumperz writes (personal communication): "I would say that small isolated groups tend to show a minimum of stylistic or dialect diversity. Highly stratified groups show diversity, i.e., either multi-dialectism or multilingualism (of the diglossia variety) and compartmentalization of language usage. More egalitarian or democratic westernized or urbanized societies may show linguistic diversity or speech variation but it tends to be of the fluid type."

exist... if. It is a world of addition without algebra, of historical chronology without historical causation, of melodies as tunes without motif or orchestration.[17] Consequently, restricted code users are able to handle schoolwork during those years in which there is emphasis on rote learning (two times two is four; Look, Jane, look!), but they cannot keep up with their middle-class age peers when materials are introduced which require understanding and articulation of relational abstract concepts.

If possession of facility in elaborated codes enhances learning skills and provides its user with a richer conceptual world (in an almost Whorfian sense), it also brings some disadvantages. Bernstein (n.d.) has made the propositions that there are four principal modes of social control in the family: normative-oriented, parent-oriented, child-oriented, and status-oriented. The primary distinction is between person-oriented and status-oriented, a distinction which carries with it the occurrence of either *guilt* or *shame* as sanctions. Social control in the restricted mode, Bernstein suggests, relies on status and authority but may provide the child with security. The elaborated mode, with its emphasis on personal characteristics and specific situations, may confuse the child while contributing to the long-range development of greater flexibility and individuality. Bernstein has suggested (1964a), that it is this difference in social control along with the restricted code user's relative inability to articulate meaning or individual experience verbally, which makes it so difficult for the elaborated code-using therapist to deal successfully with restricted code-using patients (For another perspective on communication problems see Grimshaw: 1970a).

The social world of the restricted code user is one constituted by membership in a small, closely-knit group sharing a high sense of identification; shared experience and mutuality of expectation; and, implicitly, lesser need for highly developed ability to manipulate concepts associated with problem-solving. In his earlier papers Bernstein had suggested an explicit continuum in which higher class position would be positively correlated with greater possession of and use of elaborated codes. As his research has broadened, however, he has come to conclude that social subsystems with these characteristics are located *throughout the society* and not just at the bottom. He has presented no evidence but has suggested that the examination of performance of upper class boys in public schools (in England) might be similar to that of lower- and working-class users of restricted codes. Insofar as a principal characteristic of restricted codes is the exchange of solidarity

---

[17] Somewhat more technically, it is a pattern which emphasizes now-coding as contrasted to then-coding, with different types of hesitation pauses, with different (and more limited) lexical choices, with a simpler syntax.

cliches rather than relational statements, this may be true. It is likely, however, that in upper class groups there would be a richer range of lexical choices and greater awareness of grammatical properties. Restricted codes probably exist to some extent in all relatively small, 'exclusive' social systems – and this may very well include certain groups of college students as well as occupational groups and the working classes. The use of such codes may be determined more by the predominance of positional (status-oriented) rather than person-oriented modes of social control than by the user's command over richer or poorer lexical inventories and syntactical inventories (for an explication of further developments in Bernstein's thought in this area see Bernstein: 1970).

It is also true that while the bulk of the interaction carried on by restricted code users exhibits what might be called the 'Marty' syndrome ("Wha d'ya wanna do tonight? I dunno, wh d'ya wanna do?"), there is probably more concrete content and exchange of individuated experience in their communication than Bernstein had originally reported (see later papers, e.g. 1964b). Bernstein recently has given greater importance to the role of non-verbal signals in transmitting content within this group (there is, unfortunately, no space in this paper to treat the growing literature on paralinguistics and proxemics; see, however, Deutscher: 1967; Grimshaw: 1970a; E. Hall: 1959, 1963, 1964, 1966; and Sebeok: 1964). Facial expressions, minor phonological shifts, changes in rhythm, tone and loudness may all, under certain circumstances, serve as highly significant data for other restricted code users. Although Bernstein's early work nowhere refers to Goffman, the inter-implications of his discussion with Goffman's "giving impressions" and "giving off impressions" are obvious (Goffman: 1959).

Bernstein's early work was generally limited to analysis of vocabulary and grammatical usages of youth in small populations with limited characteristics (see, however, Grimshaw, 1969). His work has been done with the spoken language (one of his students has done analysis of a small number of cases of written work, see Lawton: 1963). Nonetheless, his work in an urban society presents some preliminary evidence for a reflexitivity of language structure and social structure in complex societies which had previously been available primarily for simpler groups.

The current state of sociolinguistic knowledge does not permit any final conclusion on the causal relationships between social structure and language structure.[18] The research evidence is scanty, and what little

[18] There is simply no space in this paper to discuss all the literature bearing on this question. The interested reader should, however, examine Labov: 1965 for a rich and useful explication of three problems which must be considered: the transition, embedding and evaluation problems.

there is has seldom been collected for the specific purpose of isolating relationships between linguistic and social structures. While there seems to be some strength to the assertion that social factors may have precedence over autonomously linguistic factors, it also seems to be possible to demonstrate that there are processes of linguistic change which generate their own momentum through phonological or syntactical laws. What is important is that the research reviewed above clearly demonstrates that the social sciences need the linguist and that his work and research can be markedly improved and simplified by attending to social structural variables.

V. TOWARD AN INTEGRATED THEORY OF DESCRIPTIVE SOCIOLINGUISTICS

Sociolinguistics is a hybrid discipline with a short and largely atheoretical history. Generated largely as a consequence of the 'startle effect' resulting from the rediscovery by sociologists (and some linguists) that certain linguistic events and certain social behavior seemed to be correlated, its propositional inventory developed initially through statements of empirical relationships and then to somewhat more ambitious theories of the 'lower-middle range'. The researches reviewed in the pages above have been the source of the data which has provided a direction to these preliminary, and frequently halting, steps toward a more general theory of sociolinguistics. That an integrated theory of descriptive sociolinguistics is an attainable and reasonable goal has been demonstrated by Hymes, who in two articles (1964e; 1967a) has presented an outline of the form such an integrated theory must take. Any student who undertakes to grasp the full richness of the possibilities of the sociolinguistic enterprise must read these two articles. Hymes (1967a) summarizes the need as one of "a study of speaking that seeks to determine the native system and theory of speaking; whose aim is to describe the communicative competence that enables a member of the community to know when to speak and when to remain silent, which code to use, when, where and to whom, etc.". The concepts with which such a theory must deal, he continues (*ibid.*) are those of "speech community, speech situation, speech act, speech event, fluent speaker, native speaker, factors (or components) of speech events, functions of speech, rules of speaking, types of speech event and act".

Three types of elements must be included in either a taxonomic or more developed relational sociolinguistic theory (1967a). There must be, first, a set of concepts for dealing with the characteristics of the social structure itself, what Hymes has labelled as *the social unit of*

analysis. Secondly, there must be a conceptual apparatus which identi-
fies the *components of speech* itself. In Hymes' proto-taxonomy several
of these components are closely linked to social characteristics. This is
particularly the case when status characteristics of participants in a
speech act are distinguished. Finally, for every instance of communication, or possible communication, there are formal *"rules of speaking"*.
Rules of speaking are generalizations about relationships among components, e.g., code choice may be determined by status characteristics
of participants in the speech act alone, by the setting in which the act
occurs, or by a combination of these and other components. The
problem of generating formal rules can only be resolved by full specification of the components themselves (e.g., consider code choices of
priest and high status and wealthy parishioner in (1) the confessional,
(2) free interaction in a golf game, and (3) a conversation concerning
bequests to the church). Much of the research reviewed above has had
to do with precisely this type of specification of speech components.

The principal notions involved in defining the social unit of analysis
are *speech community* (see Gumperz' definition, *supra,* p. 122), *speech
field* (essentially the range of interactions possible given knowledge of
a set or sets of code(s) and rule(s)), *speech network* (linkages actually
operative within the speech field), *speech situation* (there are also
situations in which communication is non-verbal; these are no less important for a full understanding of communicative interaction, see, e.g.,
the references to paralinguistic phenomena, *supra,* p. 134), *speech event*
(a complete speech activity governed by rules for speech usage), and
speech act (any sub-unit of a speech event).

Hymes has adopted a mnemonic device for listing the components of
speech: SPEAKING. The letters represent, serially: (1) setting or scer ,
(2) participants or personnel, (3) ends (as both goals and outcomes.
[Hymes gives an intriguing example of the interaction of purpose and
outcomes in an example adapted from a forthcoming paper by Frake
(1970) on speech events among the Yakan of the Philippines. The four
varieties are as follows:

(a) [Purpose]   [talk about a topic]
    Outcome   [no special outcome]   / *miting*

That is, the type of speech event called *miting* has as its theme simply
talk about some topic; no special outcome is expected.

(b) [Purpose]   [talk about an issue]   / *gisun*
    Outcome   [decision]   (conference)

That is, the type of speech event called *gisun* has as its theme simply talk about something regarded as an *issue*, as when to plant rice, when to take a trip, and a *decision* is expected as the outcome.

(c) [Purpose]   [talk about a disagreement]   / *mawpakkat*
Outcome   [Settlement]   (negotiation)

That is, the type of speech event called *mawpakkat* has as its theme talk about a *disagreement* involving conflicting interests, and as its expected outcome, a legally binding resolution, or *settlement*.

(d) [Purpose]   [talk about a dispute]   / *hukum*
Outcome   [ruling]   (litigation)

That is, the type of speech event called *hukum* has as its theme a dis-agreement arising from a charge that an offense has been committed, and as its expected outcome, a legal ruling, based on precedent and carrying special sanctions.]), (4) art characteristics (form and content of message), (5) key (the manner or spirit in which the speech act is done [Hymes observes that the importance of key can be shown by the fact that when content and key or manner are in conflict, it is the manner which carries the true significance of the message, e.g., in cases of sarcasm, etc. He also observes that non-verbal behavior such as facial expressions and the like may carry the key]), (6) instrumentalities (channel [oral, written or other medium of transmission] and code [see, *supra*, pp. 121–4, section on linguistic diversity and repertoire selec-tion]), (7) norms of interaction and interpretation, and (8) genres (con-versation, curse, professional paper, etc.).

As has been noted, several of the components of speech are them-selves clearly social structural factors. This serves to underline the in-extricably interrelated character of the relationships between speech and the social unit within which it occurs. Relationships between the compo-nents of speech can be generalized into formal rules of speaking. As Hymes notes, the process of the specification of these rules will de-monstrate:

the inseparability of sociolinguistic analysis from the fullscale analysis of social life itself, for it is in the analysis of social life that the requisite rules of selection for sociolinguistic features are to be found and stated.

VI. A POSTSCRIPT

In the researches reviewed above, the linguistic variables which have been examined have been phonological, grammatical, or lexical. These sociolinguistic data have been variously used in the examination of substantive empirical questions (e.g., those related to social differentiation and social change) and directed to the development of propositional statements to be incorporated into general theory about social structure and social behavior. They have also been used in an examination of possible relationships between social structure and language structure – whether these relationships be simply correlational; whether they be causal in one or another direction; or whether they represent some more fundamental set of linkages between the two structures. They have *not* been used in an attack upon essentially methodological questions.

Hymes (1966d) has observed that some sociologists have a primarily methodological interest in the study of language while others are interested in language itself, either as data for substantive research on social structure or as itself a social phenomenon. This paper has been directed almost solely to the second set of perspectives, languages as data and as social phenomenon. The methodological questions related to language are primarily semantic rather than phonological, grammatical, or lexical (at least in the sense of simple lexical selection within codes, the way in which the term has been used most often above).

This essay, as originally written three years ago, contained a brief treatment of some of these semantic problems. In the time elapsed since there has been a considerable growth of interest in these problems and several treatments are available elsewhere (see., e.g., Deutscher: 1967; Cicourel: 1969; Grimshaw: 1969a, 1970a). For this reason, and because of limitations of space, no attempt has been made to review that literature in this article.

BIBLIOGRAPHY

Alisjahbana, T.,
    1949   "The Indonesian language – by-product of nationalism", *Pacific Affairs* 22, 388-392.
Anisfeld, M.,
    n.d.   A review of John B. Carroll, *Language and Thought, International Journal of American Linguistics* 32, Part 1, 285-288.
Anisfeld, M., N. Bogo, and W. E. Lambert,
    1962   "Evaluation reactions to accented English speech", *Journal of Abnormal and Social Psychology* 65, 223-231.
Anisfeld, E., and W. E. Lambert,
    1964   "Evaluational reactions of bilingual and monolingual children to spoken languages", *Journal of Abnormal and Social Psychology* 69, 89-97.
Banks, A. S., and R. B. Textor,
    1963   *A Cross-Polity Survey* (Cambridge, Mass.: MIT Press).
Barth, F.,
    1964   "Ethnic processes in the Pathan-Baluchi boundary in Indo-Iranica", in *Melanges presente a George Morgenstierne a l'occasion de son soixante dixième anniversaire* (Wiesbaden: Otto Harassowitz), 13-20.

Bernstein, B.,
1958 "Some sociological determinants of perception", *British Journal of Sociology* 9, 159-174.
1960 "Language and social class", *British Journal of Sociology* 11, 271-276.
1961a "Social class and linguistic development: A theory of social learning", in A. H. Halsey, J. Floud, and C. A. Anderson (eds.), *Education, Economy and Society* (Glencoe: Free Press), 288-314.
1961b "Aspects of language and learning in the genesis of the social process", *Journal of Child Psychology and Psychiatry* 1, 313-324.
1961c "Social structure, language and learning", *Educational Research* 3, 163-176.
1962a "Linguistic codes, hesitation phenomena and intelligence", *Language and Speech* 5, 31-46.
1962b "Social class, linguistic codes and grammatical elements", *Language and Speech* 5, 221-233.
1964a "Social class, speech systems and psycho-therapy", *British Journal of Sociology* 15, 54-64.
1964b "Elaborated and restricted codes: Their social origins and some consequences", in J. J. Gumperz and D. Hymes (eds.), *The Ethnography of Communication*, special publication of *American Anthropologist* 66, Part 2, 55-69.
1966 "Elaborated and restricted codes: An outline", in S. Lieberman (ed.), *Explorations in Sociolinguistics*, special issue of *Sociological Inquiry* 36, 254-261.
1970 "A socio-linguistic approach to socialization: With some reference to educability", in J. J. Gumperz and D. Hymes (eds.), *Directions in Sociolinguistics*, in press. Also in *Human Context*, Vol. 1, Part 2, in press.
n.d. "Family role systems socialization and communication", Paper read at the Conference of Cross-Cultural Research into Childhood and Adolescence, University of Chicago.
Bidwell, C. E.,
1962 "Language, dialect, and nationality in Yugoslavia", *Human Relations* 15, 217-225.
Blom, J. P., and J. J. Gumperz,
1970 "Some social determinants of verbal behavior", in J. J. Gumperz and D. Hymes (eds.), *Directions in Sociolinguistics* (New York: Holt, Rinehart and Winston), in press.
Bossard, J. H. S.,
1945a "Family modes of expression", *American Sociological Review* 10, 226-237.
1945b "The bilingual as a person – linguistic identification with status", *American Sociological Review* 10, 699-709.
Bright, W.,
1960 "Linguistic change in some Indian caste dialects", *International Journal of American Linguistics* 26, 19-26.
1963 "Language" in B. J. Siegel (ed.), *Biennial Review of Anthropology, 1963* (Stanford: Stanford University Press), 1-29.
1966a "Language, social stratification, and cognitive orientation", in S. Lieberson (ed.), *Explorations in Sociolinguistics*, special issue of *Sociological Inquiry* 36, 313-318.
1966b Introduction: "The dimensions of sociolinguistics", in W. Bright (ed.),

Sociolinguistics: Proceedings of the UCLA Sociolinguistics Conference, 1964 (The Hague: Mouton), 11-15.

1968 "Social dialect and semantic structure in South Asia", in M. Singer and B. Cohn (eds.), *Structure and Change in Indian Society* (Chicago: Aldine), 455-460.

Bright, W. (ed.),
1966 *Sociolinguistics: Proceedings of the UCLA Sociolinguistics Conference, 1964* (The Hague: Mouton), 11-15.

Brosnahan, L. F.,
1963 "Some historical cases of language imposition", in J. F. Spencer (ed.), *Language in Africa* (Cambridge, England: Cambridge University Press), 7-24.

Brown, R.,
1965 *Social Psychology* (New York: The Free Press).

Brown, R., and M. Ford,
1961 "Address in American English", *Journal of Abnormal and Social Psychology* 62, 375-385.

Brown, R., and A. Gilman,
1960 "The pronouns of power and solidarity", in T. A. Sebeok (ed.), *Style in Language* (New York: John Wiley), 253-276.

Buck, C. D.,
1916 "Language and the sentiment of nationality", *American Political Science Review* 10, 44-69.

Center for Applied Linguistics,
1961 *Second Language Learning as a Factor in National Development in Asia, Africa, and Latin America* (Washington, D. C.: Center for Applied Linguistics).

Chomsky, N.,
1961 "Some methodological remarks on generative grammar", *Word* 17, 219-239.
1964 *Current Issues in Linguistic Theory* (The Hague: Mouton).
1965 *Aspects of the Theory of Syntax* (Cambridge, Mass.: MIT Press).
1968 *Syntactic Structures* (The Hague: Mouton).

Chomsky, N., and M. Halle,
1965 "Some controversial questions in phonological theory", *Journal of Linguistics* 1, 97-138.

Chowdhury, M.,
1960 "The language problem in East Pakistan", *International Journal of American Linguistics* 26, 64-78.

Christian, J. M., and C. C. Christian, Jr.,
1966 "Spanish language and culture in the Southwest", in J. Fishman (ed.), *Language Loyalty in the United States* (The Hague: Mouton), 280-317.

Cicourel, A. V.,
1964 *Method and Measurement in Sociology* (New York: The Free Press).
1969 "Generative semantics and the structure of social interaction", a paper read at the International Days of Sociolinguistics, Rome, Italy.
in press "The acquisition of social structure: Towards a developmental sociology of language and meaning", in H. Garfinkel and H. Sacks (eds.), *Contributions in Ethnomethodology* (Bloomington: Indiana University Press).

Das Gupta, J.,
1967 "Language associations and political development", unpublished paper

presented at the annual meeting of the American Sociological Association.

in press "Official language: Problems and policies in South Asia", in T. Sebeok (ed.), *Current Linguistics* (The Hague: Mouton).

Das Gupta, J., and J. J. Gumperz,
1968 "Language communication and control in North India", in J. A. Fishman, C. A. Ferguson and J. Das Gupta (eds.), *Language Problems of Developing Nations* (New York: Wiley and Co.), 157-166.

De Francis, J.,
1950 *Nationalism and Language Reform in China* (Princeton: Princeton University Press).

Deutsch, K. W.,
1942 "The trend of European nationalism – the language aspect", *American Political Science Review* 36, 533-541.
1953 *Nationalism and Social Communication: An Inquiry into the Foundations of Nationality* (published jointly by Cambridge, Mass.: MIT Press, and New York: Wiley and Sons).

Deutscher, I.,
1967 "Notes on language and human conduct: Some problems of comparability in cross-cultural and interpersonal contexts", unpublished paper (Syracuse, N. Y.: The Maxwell Graduate School of Social Sciences and the Youth Development Center, Syracuse University). Partially published as, "Asking questions cross-culturally: Some problems of linguistic comparability", in H. Becker, et al., *Institutions and the Person* (Chicago: Aldine).

Diebold, A. R., Jr.,
1963 "Code switching in Greek-English bilingual speech", in E. E. Woodworth and R. J. de Prieto (eds.), *Report of the Thirteenth Annual Roundtable Meeting on Linguistics and Language Studies* (Washington, D. C.: Georgetown University Press).
1964 "Incipient bilingualism", in D. Hymes (ed.), *Language in Culture and Society* (New York: Harper and Row), 495-510.

Dozier, E. P.,
1951 "Resistance to acculturation and assimilation in an Indian Pueblo", *American Anthropologist* 53, 55-56.

Durbin, M.,
1968 "Language", in B. J. Siegel (ed.), *Biennial Review of Anthropology, 1967* (Stanford: Stanford University Press).

Ervin-Tripp, S. M.,
1961 "Semantic shift in bilingualism", *American Journal of Psychology* 74, 78-90.
1967 "An Issei learns English", *Journal of Social Issues* 23, 78-90.
1968 "Sociolinguistics", in L. Berkowitz (ed.), *Advances in Experimental Social Psychology* (New York: Academic Press).

Ervin-Tripp, S. M., and C. E. Osgood,
1954 "Second language learning and bilingualism", *Journal of Abnormal and Social Psychology* 49, supplement, 139-146.

Ferguson, C. A.,
1962a "Background to second language problems", in F. A. Rice (ed.), *Study of the Role of Second Languages in Asia, Africa, and Latin America* (Washington, D. C.: Center for Applied Linguistics), 1-7.
1962b "The language factor in national development", in F. A. Rice (ed.),

Study of the Role of Second Languages in Asia, Africa, and Latin America (Washington, D. C.: Center for Applied Linguistics), 8-14.

1964 "Diglossia", in D. Hymes (ed.), *Language in Culture and Society* (New York: Harper and Row), 429-439.

1966 "National sociolinguistic profile formulas", in W. Bright (ed.), *Sociolinguistics: Proceedings of the UCLA Sociolinguistics Conference, 1964* (The Hague: Mouton), 309-324.

Ferguson, C. A., and J. J. Gumperz (eds.),

1960 "Linguistic diversity in South Asia: Studies in regional, social and functional variation", special issue of *International Journal of American Linguistics* 26.

Fischer, J. L.,

1965 "The stylistic significance of consonantal sandhi in Trukese and Ponapean", *American Anthropology* 67, Part 1, 1495-1502.

1966 "Syntax and social structure: Truk and Ponape", in W. Bright (ed.), *Sociolinguistics: Proceedings of the UCLA Sociolinguistics Conference, 1964* (The Hague: Mouton), 168-187.

Fishman, J. A.,

1960 "A systematization of the Whorfian hypothesis", *Behavioral Science* 4, 323-339.

1964a *Language Loyalty in the United States*, mimeographed report in three volumes prepared for the Language Research Section, U. S. Office of Education (New York: Yeshiva University).

1964b "Language maintenance and language shift as a field of inquiry", *Linguistics* 9, 32-70.

1965 "Varieties of Ethnicity and Varieties of Language Consciousness", *Georgetown University Monograph Series, Languages and Linguistics* No. 18, 69-79.

1966 "Language maintenance and language shift: The American immigrant case", *Sociologus* NS 16, 19-39.

1967a "Bilingualism with and without diglossia: Diglossia with and without bilingualism", *Journal of Social Issues* 23, 29-38.

1967b "Basic issues in the sociology of language: A review of J. O. Herzler's *Sociology of Language*", *Language* 43, 586-604.

1968 "Nationality-nationalism and nation-nationism", in J. A. Fishman, C. A. Ferguson, and J. Das Gupta (eds.), *Language Problems of Developing Nations* (New York: Wiley), 39-52.

Fishman, J. A. (ed.),

1966 *Language Loyalty in the United States* (The Hague: Mouton).

1969 *Readings in the Sociology of Language* (The Hague: Mouton).

Fishman, J. A., C. A. Ferguson, and J. Das Gupta (eds.),

1968 *Language Problems of Developing Nations* (New York: Wiley).

Frake, C. O.,

1970 "Struck by speech: The Yakan concept of litigation", in J. J. Gumperz and D. Hymes (eds.), *Directions in Sociolinguistics* (New York: Holt, Rinehart and Winston), in press.

Friedrich, P.,

1962a "Multilingualism and socio-cultural organization", *Anthropological Linguistics* 4.

1962b "Language and politics in India", *Daedalus*, 543-559.

1966a "The linguistic reflex of social change: From Tsarist to Soviet Russian kinship", in S. Liberson (ed.), *Explorations in Sociolinguistics*, special issue of *Sociological Inquiry* 36, 31-57.

1966b "Structural implications of Russian pronominal usage", condensed from a contribution to W. Bright (ed.), *Sociolinguistics: Proceedings of the UCLA Sociolinguistics Conference, 1964* (The Hague: Mouton), 214-259.

Gaarder, A. B.,
1967 "Organization of the bilingual school", *Journal of Social Issues* 23, 110-120.

Gardner, R. C., and W. E. Lambert,
1959 "Motivational Variables in second-language acquisition", *Canadian Journal of Psychology* 13, 266-272.

Garfinkel, H.,
1964 "Studies of the routine grounds of everyday activities", *Social Problems* 11, 220-250.
1967 *Studies in Ethnomethodology* (Englewood Cliffs: Prentice Hall).

Garvin, P. L., and S. H. Riesenbert,
1952 "Respect behavior on Ponape: An ethnolinguistic study", *American Anthropologist* 54, 201-220.

Geertz, C.,
1960 *The Religion of Java* (New York: The Free Press).

Glazer, N.,
1966 "The process and problems of language-maintenance: An integrative review", in J. A. Fishman (ed.), *Language Loyalty in the United States* (The Hague: Mouton), 358-368.

Glietman, L. R.,
1961 "Pronominals and stress in English conjunctions", *Language Learning* 11, 157-169.

Goffman, E.,
1959 *The Presentation of Self in Everyday Life* (New York: Doubleday Anchor).
1961 *Encounters: Two Studies in the Sociology of Interaction* (Indianapolis: Bobbs-Merrill).
1963 *Behavior in Public Places* (Glencoe: Free Press).
1964 "The neglected situation", in J. J. Gumperz and D. Hymes (eds.), *The Ethnography of Communication*, special publication of *American Anthropologist* 66, Part 2, 133-136.

Goodenough, W. H.,
1964 "Property and language on Truk: Some methodological considerations", in D. Hymes (ed.), *Language in Culture and Society* (New York: Harper and Row), 185-188.

Goodman, M. F.,
1964 *A Comparative Study of Creole French Dialects* (The Hague: Mouton).

Greenberg, J. H.,
1956 "The measurement of linguistic diversity", *Language* 32, 109-115.

Grimshaw, A. D.,
1966 "Directions for research in sociolinguistics: Suggestions of a nonlinguist sociologist", in S. Lieberson (ed.), *Explorations in Sociolinguistics*, special issue of *Sociological Inquiry* 36, 319-332.
1967 "A review of Joyce O. Hertzler, *A Sociology of Language*", *Harvard Educational Review* 37, 302-308.
1969a "Language as obstacle and as data in sociological research", *Items* 23, 17-21.

1969b "Sociolinguistics and the sociologist", *The American Sociologist* 4, 312-321.

1970a "Some problematic aspects of communication in cross racial research in the United States", *Sociological Focus*.

1970b "Some social sources and some social functions of Pidgin and Creole languages", in D. Hymes (ed.), *Proceedings of the Social Science Research Council Conference on Creolization and Pidginization* (Cambridge: Cambridge University Press), in press.

1970c *An Introduction to Sociolinguistics* (Chicago: Aldine), in press.

Gumperz, E. M.,
1967   "Growth of regional consciousness in Maharashtra", a paper presented to the Interdisciplinary Graduate Seminar on South Asian Studies, University of California at Berkeley, October, 1967.

Gumperz, J. J.,
1958   "Dialect differences and social stratification in a North Indian village", *American Anthropologist* 60, 668-681.

1961   "Speech variation and the study of Indian civilization", *American Anthropologist* 63, 976-988.

1962   "Types of linguistic communities", *Anthropological Linguistics* 4, 28-40.

1964a "Religion and social communication in village North India", *Journal of Asian Studies* 23, 89-97.

1964b "Linguistic and social interaction in two communities", in J. J. Gumperz and D. Hymes (eds.), *The Ethnography of Communications*, special publication of *American Anthropologist* 66, Part 2, 137-153.

1964c "Hindi-Pinjabi code switching in Delhi", *Proceedings of the Ninth International Congress of Linguists* (The Hague: Mouton).

1965   "Language", in B. J. Siegel (ed.), *Biennial Review of Anthropology, 1965* (Stanford: Stanford University Press).

1966a "On the ethnology of linguistic change", in W. Bright (ed.), *Sociolinguistics: Proceedings of the UCLA Sociolinguistics Conference, 1964* (The Hague: Mouton).

1966b "Linguistic repertoires, grammars and second language instruction", in *Report of the Sixteenth Round Table Meeting on Linguistics and Language Teaching* (Washington: Georgetown University) Monograph no. 18, 81-88.

1967a "On the linguistic markers of bilingual communication", *Journal of Social Issues* 23, 48-57.

1967b "Language and communication", *The Annals of the American Academy of Political and Social Science* 373.

in press "The measurement of bilingualism in social groups", in *Proceedings of the International Seminar on the Description and Measurement of Bilingualism*. Canadian National Commission for UNESCO.

Gumperz, J. J., and D. Hymes (eds.),
1964   *The Ethnography of Communication*, special publication of *American Anthropologist* 66, Part 2.

1970   *Directions in Sociolinguistics* (New York: Holt, Rinehart and Winston), in press.

Hall, E. T.,
1959   *The Silent Language* (Garden City: Doubleday).

1963   "A system for the notation of proxemic behavior", *American Anthropologist* 65, 1003-1026.

1964   "Adumbration as a feature of intercultural communication", in J. J.

Gumperz and D. Hymes (eds.), *The Ethnography of Communication*, special publication of *American Anthropologist* 66, Part 2, 154-163.
1966   *The Hidden Dimension* (Garden City: Doubleday).
Hall, R. A., Jr.,
1955   *Hands Off Pidgin English!* (Sydney: Pacific Publications, Pty.).
1959   "Colonial policy and Melanesian", *American Linguistics* 1, 22-27.
1962   "The life cycle of pidgin languages", *Lingua* 11, 151-156.
Harrison, S. S.,
1960   *India: The Most Dangerous Decades* (Princeton: Princeton University Press).
Haugen, E.,
1946   *Bilingualism in the Americas: A Bibliography and Research Guide* (University of Alabama: American Dialect Society).
1952   "The struggle over Norwegian", in *Norwegian-Amercian Studies*, XVII (Northfield, Minn.: Norwegian-American Historical Association).
1953   *The Norwegian Language in America*, two volumes (Philadelphia: University of Pennsylvania Press).
1954   "Some pleasures and problems of bilingual research", *International Journal of American Linguistics* 20, 116-122.
1963   "Schizoglossia and the linguistic norm", in E. D. Woodworth (ed.), *Report of the Thirteenth Annual Round Table Meeting on Linguistics and Language Studies* (Washington, D. C.: Georgetown University).
1965   "Construction and reconstruction in language planning: Ivar Aasen's grammar", *Word* 21, 188-207.
1966a   *Language Conflict and Language Planning: The Case of Modern Norwegian* (Cambridge: Harvard University Press).
1966b   "Semicommunication: The language gap in Scandinavia", in S. Lieberson (ed.), *Explorations in Sociolinguistics*, special issue of *Sociological Inquiry* 36, 280-297.
1966c   "Dialect, language, nation", *American Anthropologist* 68, 922-935.
1966d   "Linguistics and language planning", in W. Bright (ed.), *Sociolinguistics: Proceedings of the UCLA Sociolinguistics Conference, 1964* (The Hague: Mouton), 50-71.
Hertzler, J. O.,
1953   "Toward a sociology of language", *Social Forces* 32, 109-119.
1965   *A Sociology of Language* (New York: Random House).
Howell, R. W.,
1965   "Linguistic status markers in Korean", *The Kroeber Anthropological Society Papers* 55, 91-97.
1967   "Linguistic choice as an index to social change", unpublished doctoral dissertation, Berkeley, University of California.
Hymes, D.,
1964a   *Language in Culture and Society: A Reader in Linguistics and Anthropology* (New York: Harper and Row).
1964b   "Directions in ethno-linguistic theory", in A. K. Romney and R. G. D'Andrade (eds.), *Transcultural Studies of Cognition* (Washington, D. C.: American Anthropological Association), 1-34.
1964c   "A perspective for linguistic anthropology", in S. Tax (ed.), *Horizons of Anthropology* (Chicago: Aldine).
1964d   "A discussion of Burling's paper", *American Anthropologist* 66, 116-119.
1964e   "Introduction: Toward ethnographies of communication", in J. J. Gum-

perz and D. Hymes (eds.), *The Ethnography of Communication*, special publication of *American Anthropologist* 66, Part 2, 1-34.

1966a "Two types of linguistic relativity (with examples from American ethnography)", in W. Bright (ed.), *Sociolinguistics: Proceedings of the UCLA Sociolinguistics Conference, 1964* (The Hague: Mouton).

1966b "On 'anthropological linguistics' and congeners", *American Anthropologist* 68, 143-153.

1966c "Teaching and training in sociolinguistics", unpublished paper prepared for SSRC Committee on Sociolinguistics.

1967a "Models of the interaction of languages and social setting", *Journal of Social Issues* 23, 8-28.

1967b "The anthropology of communication", in F. Dance (ed.), *Human Communication Theory* (New York: Holt, Rinehart and Winston).

1968a "Linguistic problems in defining the concept of 'tribe' ", in J. Helm (ed.), *Essays on the Problem of Tribe* (Seattle: University of Washington Press), 23-48.

1968b "Linguistics", *International Encyclopedia of the Social Sciences* (New York: MacMillan).

1968c "Why linguistics needs the sociologist", *Social Research* 34, 632-647.

n.d.   "On communicative competence", unpublished manuscript. An enlarged and revised version is to appear in the *Proceedings of a Conference on Mechanisms of Language Development*, held in May, 1968, sponsored by the Center for Advanced Study in the Developmental Sciences and the Ciba Foundation, London. In press.

Hymes, D. (ed.),
1970   *Proceedings of the Social Science Research Council Conference on Creolization and Pidginization* (Cambridge: Cambridge University Press), in press.

Jakobson, R.,
1945   The beginning of national self-determination in Europe", *Review of Politics* 7, 29-42.

John, V. P.,
1966   "The Basil Bernstein Fad: A critical look at theories of language and educability", a paper presented at the AAA symyposium on Culture of Poverty: A Critique, November, 1966, Pittsburgh.

1967   "Communicative competence of low-income children: Assumptions and programs", a report to the Language Development Study Group of the Ford Foundation, March 30, 1967.

Katz, J. J.,
1964   "Mentalism in linguistics", *Language* 40, 124-137.

Katz, J. J., and P. M. Postal,
1964   *An Integrated Theory of Linguistic Descriptions* (Cambridge: MIT Press).

Kelley, G.,
1966   "The status of Hindi as a lingua franca", in W. Bright (ed.), *Sociolinguistics: Proceedings of the UCLA Sociolinguistics Conference, 1964* (The Hague: Mouton).

Klima, E. S.,
1964   "Relatedness between grammatical systems", *Language* 40, 1-20.

Kloss, H.,
1966a "German-American language maintenance efforts", in J. A. Fishman (ed.), *Language Loyalty in the United States* (The Hague: Mouton),

206-252.
1966b "Types of multilingual communities: A discussion of ten variables", in
S. Lieberson (ed.), *Explorations in Sociolinguistics*, special issue of
Sociological Inquiry 36, 135-145.
1967 "Bilingualism and nationalism", *Journal of Social Issues* 23, 39-47.
Labov, W.,
1963a "The social motivation of a sound change", *Word* 19, 273-309.
1963b "Phonological indices of stratification", a paper presented at the annual
meeting of the American Anthropological Association, San Francisco,
November 22, 1963.
1964 "Phonological correlates of social stratification", in J. J. Gumperz and
D. Hymes (eds.), *The Ethnography of Communication*, special publication of *American Anthropologist* 66, Part 2, 164-176.
1965 *On the Mechanism of Linguistic Change* (= *Georgetown University
Language and Linguistics Series*, Monograph 18), 91-114.
1966a *The Social Stratification of English in New York City* (Washington,
D. C.: Center for Applied Linguistics).
1966b "The effect of social mobility on linguistic behavior", in S. Lieberson
(ed.), *Explorations in Sociolinguistics*, special issue of *Sociological Inquiry* 36, 186-203.
1966c "Hypercorrection by the lower middle class as a factor in linguistic
change", in W. Bright (ed.), *Sociolinguistics: Proceedings of the UCLA
Sociolinguistics Conference, 1964* (The Hague: Mouton), 84-113.
1967a "Some sources of reading problems for Negro speakers of non-standard
English", *New Directions in Elementary English*, 140-167.
1968a "Reflections of social processes in linguistic structures", in J. A. Fishman (ed.), *Readings in the Sociology of Language* (The Hague:
Mouton), 240-251.
1968b "The non-standard vernacular of the Negro community: Some practical
suggestions", in *Positions Paper from Language Education for the Disadvantaged*. Report No. 3 of the NDEA National Institute for Advanced Study in Teaching Disadvantaged Youth, June, 1968, 4-7.
Labov, W., and C. Robins,
1968 "A note on the relation of reading failure to peer-group status in urban
ghettos", *Teachers College Record*, Fall.
Lambert, W. E.,
1967 "A social psychology of bilingualism", *Journal of Social Issues* 23,
91-109.
Lambert, W. E., M. Anisfeld, and G. Yeni-Komshian,
1965 "Evaluational reactions of Jewish and Arab adolescents to dialect and
language variations", *Journal of Personality and Social Psychology* 2,
84-90.
Lambert, W. E., R. C. Gardner, H. C. Barik, and K. Tunstall,
1963 "Attitudinal and cognitive aspects of intensive study of a second language", *Journal of Abnormal and Social Psychology* 66, 358-368.
Lambert, W. E., J. Havelka, and C. Crosby,
1958 "The influence of language acquisition contexts on bilingualism",
Lambert, W. E., R. C. Hodgeon, R. C. Gardner, and S. Fillenbaum,
1960 "Evaluation reactions to spoken languages", *Journal of Abnormal and
Social Psychology* 60, 44-51.
Lawton, D.,
1963 "Social class language differences in language development: A study of

some samples of written work", *Language and Speech* 6, 120-143.

LeMaire, H. B.,
1966 "Franco-American efforts on behalf of the French language in New England", in J. Fishman (ed.), *Language Loyalty in the United States* (The Hague: Mouton), 251-279.

Lees, R. B.,
1960 "A multiple ambiguous adjectival construction in English", *Language* 36, 207-221.
1961 "Grammatical analysis of the English comparative construction", *Word* 17, 171-185.
1962 *The Grammatical Basis of Some Semantic Notions (= Monograph Series on Languages and Linguistics)*, No. 13, 5-20.

LePage, R. B.,
1964 *The National Language Question: Linguistic Problems of Newly Independent States* (London: Oxford University Press).

LePage, R. B. (ed.),
1960 *Creole Language Studies*, Vols. I and II (New York: St. Martin's Press).

Levine, L., and H. J. Crockett, Jr.,
1966 "Speech variation in a Piedmont community: Post-vocalic 'r' ", in S. Lieberson (ed.), *Explorations in Sociolinguistics*, special issue of *Sociological Inquiry* 36, 204-226.
1967 "Friends' influence on speech", *Sociological Inquiry* 37, 109-128.

Lieberson, S.,
1964 "An extension of Breenberg's linguistic diversity measures", *Language* 40, 526-531.
1965 "Bilingualism in Montreal: A demographic analysis", *The American Journal of Sociology* 71, 10-25.
1966 "Language questions in censuses", in S. Lieberson (ed.), *Explorations in Sociolinguistics*, special issue of *Sociological Inquiry* 36, 262-279.

Lieberson, S. (ed.),
1966 *Explorations in Sociolinguistics*, special issue of *Sociological Inquiry* 36. Republished as Publication 44, Indiana University Research Center in Anthropology, Folklore, and Linguistics (1967) and also as Part II, 33, 2, *International Journal of American Linguistics* (1967).

Lounsbury, F. G.,
1959 "Language", in B. J. Siegel (ed.), *Biennial Review of Anthropology 1959* (Stanford: Stanford University Press), 185-209.
1961 "Language", in B. J. Siegel (ed.), *Biennial Review of Anthropology 1961* (Stanford: Stanford University Press), 279-322.

Mackay, W. F.,
1962 "The description of bilingualism", *Canadian Journal of Linguistics* 7, 51-85.

Macnamara, J.,
1966 *Bilingualism in Primary Education* (Edinburgh: Edinburgh University Press).
1967a "The bilingual's linguistic performance – A psychological over-view", in J. Macnamara (ed.), *Problems of Bilingualism*, special issue of *Journal of Social Issues* 23, 58-77.
1967b "The effects of instruction in a weaker language" in J. Macnamara (ed.), *Problems of Bilingualism*, special issue of *Journal of Social Issues* 23, 121-135.

Macnamara, J. (ed.),
1967   *Problems of Bilingualism*, special issue of *Journal of Social Issues* 23.
Martin, S.,
1964   "Speech levels in Japan and Korea", in D. Hymes (ed.), *Language in Culture and Society: A Reader in Linguistics and Anthropology* (New York: Harper and Row), 407-415.
Maza, H.,
1957   "Language differences and political integration", *Modern Language Journal* 41, 365-372.
McCormack, W. C.,
1967   "Language identity: An introduction to India's language problems", in J. W. Elder (ed.), *Chapters in Indian Civilization: Volume II, British and Modern Period* (Madison: Department of Indian Studies, University of Wisconsin), 435-465.
1968   "Occupation and residence in relation to Dharwar dialects", in M. Singer and B. S. Cohn (eds.), *Structure and Change in Indian Society* (Chicago: Aldine Publishing Co.), 475-486.
McDavid, R. I., Jr.,
1964   "Postvocalic -r in South Carolina: A social analysis", in D. Hymes (ed.), *Language in Culture and Society: A Reader in Linguistics and Anthropology* (New York: Harper and Row), 473-482.
Minard, R. D.,
1952   "Race relationships in the Pocahontas coal field", *Journal of Social Issues* 8, 29-44.
Mintz, S.,
1970   "Comments on the socio-historical background to pidginization and creolization", in D. Hymes (ed.), *Proceedings of the Social Science Research Council Conference on Creolization and Pidginization* (Cambridge: Cambridge University Press), in press.
Nahirny, V. C., and J. A. Fishman,
1966   "Ukranian language maintenance efforts in the United States", in J. A. Fishman (ed.), *Language Loyalty in the United States* (The Hague: Mouton), 318-357.
Nugroho, R.,
1957   "The origins and development of Bahasa Indonesia", *Publications of the Modern Language Association* 72, 23-28.
Opler, M. E., and H. Hoijer,
1940   "The raid and warpath language of the Chiricahua Apache", *American Anthropologist* 42, 617-634.
Park, R. E.,
1955   "The collected papers of ... (*Society*)", in E. C. Hughes et al. (eds.) (Glencoe: The Free Press).
Phillips, H. P.,
1959   "Problems of translation and meaning in field work", *Human Organization* 18 (1959-60 Winter), 184-192.
Pieris, R.,
1951   "Bilinguality and cultural marginality", *British Journal of Sociology* 2, 328-339.
Postal, P. M.,
1964   "Underlying and superficial linguistic structure", *Harvard Educational Review* 34, 246-266.

Pride, J. B.,
  1967 "A guide to the study of language in culture and society", unpublished paper.
Ramanujam, A. K.,
  1968 "The structure of variation: A study of caste dialects", in M. Singer and B. S. Cohn (eds.), *Structure and Change in Indian Society* (Chicago: Aldine Publishing Co.), 461-474.
Reinecke, J. E.,
  1938 "Trade jargons and creole dialects as marginal languages", *Social Forces* 17, 107-118.
Rice, F. A. (ed.),
  1962 *Study of the Role of Second Languages in Asia, Africa, and Latin America* (Washington, D. C.: Center for Applied Linguistics).
Rona, J. P.,
  1966 "The social and cultural status of Guarani in Paraguay", in W. Bright (ed.), *Sociolinguistics: Proceedings of the UCLA Sociolinguistics Conference, 1964* (The Hague: Mouton), 277-298.
Rosenbaum, P. S.,
  1967 "Phrase structure principles of English complex sentence formation", *Journal of Linguistics* 3, 103-118.
Rubin, J.,
  1962 "Bilingualism in Paraguay", *Anthropological Linguistics* 4, 52-58.
  1963 "Stability and change in a bilingual Paraguayan community", paper presented at the Meeting of the American Anthropological Association, November 21, 1963, San Francisco, California.
Rundle, S.,
  1946 *Language as a Social and Political Factor in Europe* (London: Faber and Faber).
Russett, B. M. et al.,
  1964 *World Handbook of Political and Social Indicators* (New Haven: Yale University Press).
Sacks, H.,
  1968 "On some features of a method used in selecting identification: An exercise in the formal study of natural social activities", in J. J. Gumperz and D. Hymes (eds.), *Directions in Sociolinguistics* (New York: Holt, Rinehart and Winston).
Samarin, W. J.,
  1962 "Lingua Francas, with special reference to Africa", in F. A. Rice (ed.), *Study of the Role of Second Languages in Asia, Africa, and Latin America* (Washington, D. C.: Center for Applied Linguistics), 54-64.
  1966 "Self-annulling prestige factors among speakers of a Creole language", in W. Bright (ed.), *Sociolinguistics: Proceedings of the UCLA Sociolinguistics Conference, 1964* (The Hague: Mouton), 188-213.
Sawyer, J. B.,
  1959 "Aloofness from Spanish influence in Texas English", *Word* 15, 270-281.
Sebeok, T. A., A. S. Hayes, and M. C. Bateson (eds.),
  1964 *Approaches to Semiotics: Transactions of the Indiana University Conference on Paralinguistics and Kinesics* (The Hague: Mouton).
Sellin, T.,
  1938 *Culture, Conflict, and Crime* (New York: Social Science Research Council), 20-40.

Smelser, N. J.,
  1966 "The methodology of comparative analysis", unpublished paper.
Smith, C. S.,
  1961 "A class of complex modifiers in English", *Language* 37, 342-365.
  1964 "Determiners and relative clauses in a generative grammar", *Language* 40, 37-52.
Stewart, W. A.,
  1962a "An outline of linguistic typology for describing multilingualism", in F. A. Rice (ed.), *Study of the Role of Second Languages in Asia, Africa, and Latin America* (Washington, D. C.: Center for Applied Linguistics), 15-25.
  1962b "Creole languages in the Caribbean", in F. A. Rice (ed.), *Study of the Role of Second Languages in Asia, Africa, and Latin America* (Washington, D. C.: Center for Applied Linguistics), 34-53.
Sutherlin, R. E.,
  1962 "Language situation in East Africa", in F. A. Rice (ed.), *Study of the Role of Second Languages in Asia, Africa, and Latin America* (Washington, D. C.: Center for Applied Linguistics), 65-78.
Tanner, N.,
  1967 "Speech and society among the Indonesian elite, a case study of a multilingual community", *Anthropological Linguistics* 9, 15-40.
Taylor, D.,
  1961 "New languages for old in the West Indies", *Comparative Studies in Sociology and History* 3, 277-288.
Thomas, O.,
  1965 *Transformational Grammar and the Teacher of English* (New York: Holt, Rinehart and Winston).
Tucker, G. R., and W. E. Lambert,
  1967 "White and Negro listeners' reactions to various American-English dialects", a taped speech given at McGill University.
van den Berghe, P. L.,
  n.d. "Language and 'nationalism' in South Africa", unpublished paper.
Weinreich, U.,
  1953 "Functional aspects of Indian bilingualism", *Word* 13, 203-233.
  1957 "The troubles of Hindi", paper given at the American Anthropological Association, Chicago, December, 1957.
  1966 *Languages in Contact: Findings and Problems* (The Hague: Mouton).
Westie, F. R.,
  1957 "Toward closer relations between theory and research: A procedure and an example", *American Sociological Review* 22, 149-154.
Whorf, B. L.,
  1956 *Language, Thought, and Reality. Selected Writings of Benjamin Lee Whorf*, J. B. Carroll (ed.), (Cambridge, Mass.: The Technology Press, and New York: John Wiley and Sons).
Windmiller, M.,
  1954 "Linguistic regionalism in India", *Pacific Affairs* 27, 291-318.
Wittermans, E. P.,
  1967 "Indonesian terms of address in a situation of rapid social change", *Social Forces* 46, 48-51.

William Labov

THE STUDY OF LANGUAGE IN ITS SOCIAL CONTEXT*

0. FOREWORD

In recent years, there has developed an approach to linguistic research which focuses upon language in use within the speech community, aiming at a linguistic theory adequate to account for this data. This type of research has sometimes been labelled as 'sociolinguistics', although it is a somewhat misleading use of an oddly redundant term. Language is a form of social behavior: statements to this effect can be found in any introductory text. Children raised in isolation do not use language; it is used by human beings in a social context, communicating their needs, ideas and emotions to one another. The egocentric monologues of children appear to be secondary developments derived from the social use of language (Vygotsky 1962:19) and very few people spend much time talking to themselves. It is questionable whether sentences that communicate nothing to anyone are a part of language. In what way, then, can 'sociolinguistics' be considered as something apart from 'linguistics'?

One area of research which has been included in 'sociolinguistics' is perhaps more accurately labelled 'the sociology of language'. It deals with large-scale social factors, and their mutual interaction with languages and dialects. There are many open questions, and many practical problems associated with the decay and assimilation of minority languages, the development of stable bilingualism, the standardization of languages and the planning of language development in newly emerging nations. The linguistic input for such studies is primarily that a

* From *Studium Generale*, 1970, 23, 30-87. Reprinted with permission.

given person or group uses language X in a social context or domain Y. A number of recent reviews have discussed work in this area (Fishman 1969) and I will not attempt to deal with these questions and this research in this paper.

There is another area of study sometimes included in 'sociolinguistics' which is more concerned with the details of language in actual use – the field which Hymes has named "the ethnography of speaking" (1962). There is a great deal to be done in describing and analyzing the patterns of use of languages and dialects within a specific culture: the forms of 'speech events'; the rules for appropriate selection of speakers; the interrelations of speaker, addressee, audience, topic, channel and setting; and the ways in which the speakers draw upon the resources of their language to perform certain functions. This functional study is conceived as complementary with the study of linguistic structure. Current research and the aims of the field have been well reviewed by Hymes (1966); in our discussion of methodology, some of the material of this descriptive study will be involved, but this review will not attempt to cover the ethnography of speaking as a whole. A number of readers and reviews of this larger field of 'sociolinguistics' have appeared recently; and the reader will find a number of excellent and penetrating studies in Bright 1966; Gumperz and Hymes 1966; Lieberson 1966; Fishman 1968; Ervin-Tripp 1968; and Grimshaw 1968.

This paper will deal with the study of language structure and evolution within the social context of the speech community. The linguistic topics to be considered here cover the area usually named 'general linguistics', dealing with phonology, morphology, syntax and semantics.[1] The theoretical questions to be raised will also fall into the category of general linguistics. We will be concerned with the forms of linguistic rules, their combination into systems, the co-existence of several systems, and the evolution of these rules and systems with time. If there were no need to contrast this work with the study of language out of its social context, I would prefer to say that this was simply *linguistics*. It is therefore relevant to ask why there should be any need for a new approach to linguistics with a broader social base. It seems natural enough that the basic data for any form of general linguistics would be language as it is used by native speakers communicating with each other in every-day life. Before proceeding, it will be helpful to see just why this has not been the case.

---

[1] We have also extended these studies into the area of discourse analysis, which has not been considered a part of general linguistics or seriously investigated in the past. Section 4 of this paper gives a brief indication of the nature of this work.

THE SAUSSURIAN APPROACH TO "LANGUE"

The basic orientation to the structural analysis of language as most linguists pursue it today departs from the point of view first expressed by Ferdinand de Saussure at the beginning of this century. Linguists often begin theoretical discussions with reference to Saussure's concept of *langue,* to be distinguished from *parole* or 'speech' on the one hand, and *langage* or 'language as a whole' on the other. According to Saussure, *langue* "est la partie sociale du langage . . . elle n'existe qu'en vertu d'une sorte de contrat passé entre les membres de la communauté" (1962: 321). For this reason, Saussure's Geneva school is often referred to as the 'social' school of linguistics. Saussure conceived of linguistics as one part of "une science qui étudie la vie des signes au sein de la vie sociale". Yet curiously enough, the linguists who work within the Saussurian tradition (and this includes the great majority) do not deal with social life at all: they work with one or two informants in their offices, or examine their own knowledge of *langue.* Furthermore, they insist that explanations of linguistic facts be drawn from other linguistic facts, not from any 'external' data on social behavior.[2]

This development depends on a curious paradox. If everyone possesses a knowledge of language structure, one should be able to obtain the data from the testimony of any one person – even oneself.[3] On the other hand, data on *parole*, or speech, can only be obtained by examining the behavior of individuals as they use the language. Thus we have the SAUSSURIAN PARADOX: the social aspect of language is studied by observing any one individual, but the individual aspect only by observing language in its social context. The science of *parole* never developed, but this approach to the science of *langue* has been extremely successful over the past half-century.

The study of this abstract 'language' – the knowledge available to every native speaker – has received new impetus from Chomsky, who has re-emphasized the Saussurian dichotomy, opposing *competence,* or

---

[2] Saussure's contemporary Meillet thought that the twentieth century would see the development of historical explanation based on the examination of language change embedded in social change (1905). But students of Saussure such as Martinet (1964) actively repudiated this notion, and urged that linguistic explanation be confined to the interrelations of internal, structural factors.

[3] Thus Bloomfield presents a structural analysis of "standard English, as spoken in Chicago" without further identification (1933:90-92); we assume that he is speaking of his own system, though he does not reach a level of detail where this would become an issue. Benjamin L. Whorf wrote a paper on the "Phonemic analysis of the English of Eastern Massachusetts" (1943) which was again a report based on his way of speaking.

the abstract knowledge of the rules of language, to *performance*, or the selection and execution of these rules (1965)[4]. For Chomsky, linguistics is properly the study of competence, and he makes explicit the practice which followed from the Saussurian paradox: that the proper object of linguistic study is an abstract, homogeneous speech community in which everyone speaks alike and learns the language instantly (1965:3). Furthermore, Chomsky insists that the data of linguistics is not the utterance spoken by the individual to be studied, but his intuitions about language – primarily his judgments as to which sentences are grammatical and which are not – but also judgments on the relatedness of sentences – which sentences mean 'the same'. Theories of language are to be constructed to explain these intuitions.

This theoretical development is based upon two more or less explicit assumptions:

(1) that linguistic structure is closely associated with homogeneity. (Weinreich, Labov and Herzog 1968). Saussure says that "tandis que le langage est hétérogène, la langue ainsi délimitée est de nature homogène". (1962:32).[5] The general view then, is that linguistic theories can be fully developed on the basis of that portion of language behavior which is uniform and homogeneous; though language variation may be important from a practical or applied viewpoint, such data is not required for linguistic theory – and in fact will be best understood when the theory of competence is fully developed.

(2) Speakers of the language have access to their intuitions about *langue* or competence, and can report them.

Linguistics has thus been defined in such a way as to exclude the study of social behavior or the study of speech. The definition has

---

[4] Although Chomsky criticized Saussure's conception of *langue* as somewhat limited (1964:59-60), he sees no difference between Saussure's *langue/parole* dichotomy and his own *competence/performance* terminology. "The generative grammar internalized by someone who has acquired a language defines what in Saussurian terms we may call *langue* ... Clearly the description of intrinsic competence provided by the grammar is not to be confused with an account of actual performance, as de Saussure emphasized with such lucidity" (1964:52).
[5] In a recent introductory textbook by John Lyons, representing a viewpoint quite independent of generative grammar, we find: "When we say that two people speak the same language we are of necessity abstracting from all sorts of difference in their speech. ... For simplicity of exposition, we shall assume that the language we are describing is uniform (by 'uniform' is meant 'dialectally and stylistically' undifferentiated: this is, of course, an 'idealization' of the facts ...) and that all native speakers will agree whether an utterance is acceptable or not." (1968:140-1). It should be noted that Lyons' textbook is an introduction to "Theoretical Linguistics" and this idealization does not represent a response to any practical problems.

been convenient for the formulators, who by disposition preferred to work from their own knowledge, with individual informants, or with secondary materials. But it has also been a successful strategy in our attack on linguistic structure. There is no *a priori* reason why one *must* enter the speech community to search for data. The large expenditure of time and effort needed would have to be justified, and the success of abstract linguistic analysis in the past five decades has plainly precluded such a development. Indeed, the limiting of our field of inquiry has certainly been helpful in the development of generative grammar – the working out of abstract models based upon our intuitive judgments of sentences. We cannot afford any backward steps: anyone who would go further in the study of language must certainly be able to work at this level of abstraction. At the same time, it is difficult to avoid the common-sense conclusion that the object of linguistics must ultimately be the instrument of communication used by the speech community; and if we are not talking about *that* language, there is something trivial in our proceeding. For a number of reasons, this kind of language has been the most difficult object for linguistics to focus on. Some of the reasons for this difficulty will be outlined below.

PROBLEMS IN DEALING WITH SPEECH

Despite the general orientation of the field towards the study of language in isolation, there have been many situations where linguists have hoped to obtain confirmation from the study of speech. There are four distinct difficulties that have been cited, and which have had profound effects upon linguistic practice.

(1) *The ungrammaticality of speech*

At one time, linguists of the Bloomfieldian school asserted that native speakers never made mistakes. But the opposite point of view prevails today: that speech is full of ungrammatical forms, since the difficulties of performance stand in the way of the full display of the speaker's competence.[6] It is generally believed that a corpus drawn from spoken language does not form good evidence, since it will contain many examples of badly formed sentences which the speakers themselves condemn and change when their attention is drawn to them.

[6] Chomsky has asserted that the "degenerate" character of the every-day speech which the child hears is a strong argument in support of the nativist position. The child must have an inborn theory of language, since he could not induce rules from the ungrammatical speech with which he is surrounded (1965:58).

(2) *Variation in speech and in the speech community*

It is common for a language to have many alternate ways of saying 'the same' thing. Some words like *car* and *automobile* seem to have the same referents; others have two pronunciations, like *working* and *workin'*. There are syntactic options such as *Who is he talking to?* vs. *To whom is he talking?* or *It's easy for him to talk* vs. *For him to talk is easy*.[7] In each of these cases, we have the problem of deciding the place of this variation in linguistic structure. Current formal analysis provides us with only two clear options: (1) the variants are said to belong to different systems, and the alternation is an example of 'dialect mixture' or 'code switching'. (2) the variants are said to be in 'free variation' within the same system, and the selection lies below the level of linguistic structure. Both approaches place the variation outside of the system being studied. There are of course many cases which fall appropriately under one or the other of these labels. But to demonstrate that we have a true case of code-switching, it is necessary to show that the speaker moves from one consistent set of co-occurring rules to another; to demonstrate 'free variation' one has to show that he has not moved at all. It is rare for either of these claims to be established empirically. Most cases are not easily described under either heading; consider for example an actual example of language in use.[8]

An' den like IF YOU MISS ONESIES, de OTHuh person shoot to skelly; ef he miss, den you go again. An' IF YOU GET IN, YOU SHOOT TO TWOSIES. An' IF YOU GET IN TWOSIES, YOU GO TO tthreesies. An' IF YOU MISS tthreesies, THEN THE PERSON THa' miss skelly shoot THE SKELLIES an' shoot in THE ONESIES: an' IF HE MISS, YOU GO f'om tthreesies to foursies.

In this extract, a 12-year-old Negro boy is explaining the game of Skelly. We can treat his variations as examples of code-switching; each time he uses a different variant, he moves into the system containing that variant. Lower case would then indicate 'Non-standard Negro English' and upper case 'Standard English'. But it is an unconvincing effort: there is no obvious motivation for him to switch eighteen

---

[7] It is customary to say that these expressions have the same *meaning*, which we define narrowly by some criterion such as 'having the same truth value'. The end result of our studies of syntactic variation will be to assign a certain meaning or *significance* to a transformation, a type of functional load which we may want to distinguish sharply from representational meaning.

[8] This quotation is from an interview with "Boot", the verbal leader of a pre-adolescent group of Negro boys in South Central Harlem, New York City (Labov et al. 1968).

times in the course of this short passage. But on the other hand, can we treat the difference between *de* and *THE* as 'free variation'? Such a decision would make no sense to either the speaker or the analyst, who both know that *de* is a stigmatized form. Without any clear way of categorizing this behavior, we are forced to speak of 'stylistic variants', and we are then left with no fixed relation at all to our notion of linguistic structure. What is a style if not a separate sub-code, and when do we have two of them? We normally think of language as a means of translating meaning into linear form. Where and how do stylistic meanings enter into this process? We speak of the need for communicating meaning as a controlling factor in linguistic evolution. What kind of control if any is exerted by the need to communicate 'stylistic' messages?

An even more puzzling problem arises when we consider a variable phenomenon such as consonant cluster simplification in non-standard Negro English – a process which lies on the intersection of grammar and phonology. A word such as *bold* is often simplified to *bol'*, but not always. This is also the case with *rolled*. We immediately want to know if past tense clusters CVC + D can be treated in the same way as simple CVC forms, without losing the past tense inflection. Careful investigation shows us that the distinction is never lost – the past tense forms are simplified *less* often by everyone. But our theory has no way of registering this fact formally: both *bold* and *rolled* fall under the same 'optional' rule, and our observations have no theoretical status in the rules of *langue*.

(3) *Difficulties of hearing and recording*

Record of speech observed in actual use is often very poor in quality. Acoustic phoneticians gather their data in sound-proof rooms, under the best possible conditions. In the field, we find that room noise, street noise, and other interference reduces the phonetic value of our data. If the informant is brought to record under ideal conditions, then his speech has the properties of formal, elicited speech we tried to avoid.[9] The fundamental problem is that most linguistic signals are supported by a great many redundant signals, and it is rare that any one of them carries a heavy burden of meaning; it is not essential to

---

[9]   This situation is not so damaging for phonological analysis as for grammatical research. In phonology, we can wait for the clear, stressed forms to emerge from the background noise. But many grammatical particles are reduced to minimal consonants or even features of tenseness or voicing which are difficult to hear in less than the best conditions, and many are rare enough that we cannot afford to let one escape us.

the over-all message that listeners receive any one signal. Yet to record this item in full form, the linguist would like to hear it at its clearest, as if it were the only means of signaling that message. It would therefore follow that the elicited forms given in the laboratory give the clearest indication of the underlying system.

(4) *The rarity of syntactic forms*

The data based on what speakers actually say may be adequate for the most common phonological and syntactic forms. For any deep analysis of the sound pattern of a language, it will be necessary to elicit such rare words as *adz* (the only English morpheme ending in a cluster of voiced obstruents). In the study of syntax, the inadequacy of the average corpus is even plainer. Any attempt to specify syntactic rules inevitably involves forms which one could not expect to hear in any limited investigation. For example, an analysis of the *got* passive may depend upon whether it is possible to say such sentences as "He got kicked out of the army by playing the trumpet", where we are looking for such rare forms as X *got Verb* $+$ *ed* ... *by* $\emptyset$ *Verb.* $+$ *ing.* $- Z$.

These difficulties make clear the basic motivation behind the *langue-parole* or competence-performance arguments. Given the fact that considerable progress has been made in the abstract study of *langue*, and given these difficulties of work in a natural setting, it should not be surprising that linguistics has turned firmly away from the speech community. But there are also disadvantages to the abstract study of language. Some of its limitations have recently become painfully prominent; the difficulties of developing linguistic theory with this limited data base are perhaps even greater than those outlined above for the study of the speech community.

PROBLEMS IN THE STUDY OF INTUITIONS

When Chomsky first made the explicit proposal that the subject matter of linguistics be confined to the intuitive judgments of native speakers, he hoped that the great majority of these would be clear judgments (1957:14). It was expected that the marginal cases, which were doubtful in the mind of the theorist and/or the native speaker, would be few in number and their grammatical status would be decided by rules formed from the clear cases. The situation has not worked out in this way, for it is difficult to find doubtful cases which have not remained problematical for the theory. It is not the number of doubtful cases which is at issue here: it is their locations at crucial points needed to argue a question of grammatical theory. One can see examples of this problem at any linguistic meeting, where paper after paper will cite crucial data as acceptable or unacceptable without obtaining agreement from the audience. This is not due to carelessness or lack of linguistic ability on the part of the authors: in their earnest intent to explore linguistic theory on the basis of their intuitions, they inevitably reach the point that their data take this form. The two assumptions of the homogeneity and accessibility of *langue* which led to this situation are seriously brought into question by this development.

When challenges to data arise on the floor of a linguistic meeting, the author usually defends himself by stating that there are many 'dialects' and that the systematic argument he was presenting held good for his own 'dialect'. This is an odd use of the term, and it raises the question as to what the object of linguistic description can or should be.

THE OBJECT OF LINGUISTIC DESCRIPTION: 'DIALECT' AND 'IDIOLECT'

The use of the term 'dialect' in the discussions of the variability of judgments is difficult to justify. No evidence is given of a systematic set of rules used by a group of speakers; what we observe are differences of opinion on an individual point. As we will see, individuals are not at all consistent from one judgment to the next. The question arises, what is being described? Or more generally, what should be the object of linguistic description? In the search for a homogeneous object to conform to the needs and assumptions of the Saussurian model, linguists have gradually contracted their focus to smaller and smaller segments of language. Thus Bloch introduced the term 'idiolect' to represent the speech of one person talking on one subject to the same person for a short period of time (1948). Although this term has been widely adapted, it is doubtful if anyone has found within such an 'idiolect' the homogeneous data which Bloch hoped for. But it must be noted that the very existence of the concept 'idiolect' as a proper object of linguistic description represents a defeat of the Saussurian notion of *langue* as an object of uniform social understanding.

It was hoped that by concentrating upon the judgments of the native speaker rather than his actual speech, that much of this variation could be bypassed. In some ways, this hope is justified: members of a speech community do share a common set of normative patterns even when we find highly stratified variation in actual speech (Labov

1966:4-35 ff.). But such uniformity in intuitive judgments is characteristic only of well-developed sociolinguistic variables which have received overt social correction. Most linguistic rules are well below the level of social correction, and have no overt social norms associated with them. This is certainly the case with many of the detailed rules of pronominalization and co-reference. In a recent informal study of the reflexive, we obtained judgments from 167 native speakers of English on whether the following sentences were grammatical (where the subscripted pronouns refer to the same person).

(1) He stuck the knife into himself.   (reflexive, same clause)

(2) He was shot by himself.   (passive, reflexive)

(3) He$_i$ stuck the knife into him$_i$.   (no reflexive, same clause)

(4) Himself was shot by him.   (reflexive, passive)

To the linguist, (1) is completely grammatical, and (4) is "crashingly" ungrammatical, in Postal's term.[10] But on a three-point scale where 3 is perfectly grammatical, 1 is ungrammatical, and 2 is intermediate, the best our subjects could average for (1) was 2.62 and the worst for (4) was 1.40. The others were intermediate at 2.00 for (2) and 1.75 for (3). Misunderstandings, mistakes, and different conceptions of grammaticality may have contributed to the failure to achieve categorical judgments; but there is other evidence that judgments of grammaticality are gradient behavior (Quirk 1966), and in some cases they may show very little regularity at all.

In a recent paper on co-reference "Cross-over Constraints" Postal (1968) reported that there were at least four distinct "dialects" of English with relation to the following four types of sentences, in which a pronoun crosses over a co-referent pronoun embedded in various positions, which may or may not be deleted by a later rule. (Again the subscripts identify the same referent).

	Dialect			
	A	*B*	*C*	*D*
(5) Who$_i$ did he$_i$ claim I saw?	No	No	No	No
(6) Who$_i$ did his$_i$ realization I was sick disturb?	No	No	Yes	Yes

[10]   In his discussion of the reflexive, Postal points out that example (4) where the passive and reflexive transformations are wrongly ordered, is a much more violent violation to our intuitions than example (2), which breaks the weak cross-over rule (1968b).

(7) Who did the realization I was
     sick disturb?   No   Yes   No   Yes
(8) Who did finding that out
     disturb?   No   Yes   No   Yes

These four dialects were said to represent consistent judgments which speakers could reliably reproduce. But in two sets of questions submitted at different times to 38 subjects, we obtained consistent answers from only four. There were no examples of the C or D patterns, and two each of A and B. The rest varied widely with many internal contradictions in their replies.

Again, one must pay tribute to the difficulty and subtlety of the questions posed. Obviously techniques for investigation must be developed further. Yet there is no evidence that consistent and homogeneous judgments can be obtained from native speakers on such crucial matters. Variation in syntactic judgments can be studied with profit and the implicational series within them analyzed to decide the form of the rules (Elliott, Legum and Thomson 1969). But it is now evident that *the search for homogeneity in intuitive judgments is a failure.* Once this result is accepted, the strongest motivation for confining linguistic analysis to such judgments disappears. In many ways, intuition is less regular and more difficult to interpret, than what speakers actually say. If we are to make good use of speakers' statements about language, we must interpret them in the light of unconscious, unreflecting productions. Without such control, one is left with very dubious data indeed – with no clear relation to the communicative process we recognize as language itself.

PROBLEMS IN THE RELATION OF THEORY TO DATA

The procedures of generative grammar, working with intuitions about language, have enabled us to elaborate elegant and insightful models of linguistic structure. We have unearthed a great fund of problems which had never been touched on or discussed before. It is now commonplace to assert that *generative grammar is the best discovery procedure we have.* The study of intuitive judgments focuses our attention on important relations between sentences and the deeper structures which underlie them. But as a theory of language this approach is seriously defective, since it offers us no means of discovering whether our model is right or wrong. Originally, the generative grammar was constructed to produce all the acceptable sentences of the language and none of the unacceptable ones. But if we now compare the model with what speakers say, we cannot draw any decisive conclusions from the way it matches or fails to match the data.

(1) If someone uses a sentence structure that is not generated by the grammar, there is nothing to prevent us from setting it aside as a mistake or a dialect difference.

(2) If no one ever uses a sentence structure which is predicted by the grammar, this fact can be discounted because most complex syntactic forms are known to be very rare – the occasion simply has not arisen.

This second situation can be extremely embarrassing when the syntactic forms concerned are at the very center of the theoretical argument. Chomsky's original argument against finite state grammars (1957) depended on the existence of self-embedded structures in natural language. Everyone seems to accept such sentences as

(9) The man (that) the girl (that) I used to go with married just got drafted.

as grammatical (in competence) though a bit difficult to follow (in performance). But now that Peter Reich has challenged the grammatical status of this pattern and reasserted the finiteness of natural language (1969) one looks in vain for empirical evidence of the use of such doubly embedded forms.[11] In all of the thousands of hours of interviews and conversations we have recorded, no such example from unreflecting, natural speech has yet emerged, (though we have just begun to search seriously for one). I am not sure of how to interpret the grammaticality of (9) in the absence of any solid evidence of its use.

The problems we as linguists face in dealing directly with the data of language are not peculiar to our discipline. This is a general problem for all the social sciences. Garfinckel (1968) has demonstrated that there exists in every field of research an inevitable gap between the raw data as it occurs and the protocols in which the data are recorded as input to the theoretical pursuit. In the sociolinguistic literature cited, we find many kinds of data used to provide information about language in actual use: census data; questionnaires; extracts from plays and novels; psychological tests; ethnographic reports of community norms. No matter how insightful or productive these studies may be, they do not bring us much closer to the fundamental data of language in use than we were before. There are many open questions we simply cannot answer. What is the relation between the novelist's stereotype and the language behavior of the people in question? what is the con-

---

[11] A finite state grammar may produce single embeddings such as "The girl I used to go with just got married". The problem only arises when the grammar must be in a state to "remember" that it has two subjects stored for which it must produce predicates.

nection between word association tests and the semantics of natural language? how do we discover when a speaker uses *tu* from his statement of when he uses it, or discover when he speaks French from his report of when he does so? what is the relation between the norms which the anthropologists report and the practice of members in conforming to those norms? There are many acts of perceiving, remembering, selecting, interpreting and translating which lie between the data and the linguist's report, and these are almost all implicit in these papers. As Garfinckel has pointed out every coding and reporting procedure that transforms the data will show an ineradicable residue of common-sense operation which cannot be reduced to rule. To come to grips with *language,* we must look as closely and directly at the data of every-day speech as possible, and characterize its relationship to our grammatical theories as accurately as we can, amending and adjusting the theory so that it fits the object in view. We can then turn again and re-examine the methods we have used, an inquiry which will greatly increase our understanding of the object we are studying.

THE DIRECT STUDY OF THE LINGUISTIC DATA

The critique of the conventional linguistic methods just given must not be taken as a suggestion that they be abandoned. The formal elicitation of paradigms, the exploration of intuitive judgments, the study of literary texts, experimentation in the laboratory, and questionnaires on linguistic usage are all important and valuable modes of investigation. The first two procedures must be mastered by anyone who hopes to do significant linguistic analysis. The techniques to be discussed below for the direct observation of language in use presuppose that the outlines of the grammar have been sketched in – that the main possibilities are known. Thus the phonetic transcription of an unknown language (or even unknown words) is quite beyond our capacity. The ear is a very poor instrument for judging the absolute quality of isolated sounds. But given an understanding of the syntax and the morphemes intended, the ear is a superb instrument for judging which of several possibilities are realized.[12] In syntax, our first analyses of a given form are relatively superficial; but when many relationships with other sentence forms are noted, a rich field of possible

[12] Our own recent work in tracing sound changes in progress through spectrographic measurements confirms the remarkable accuracy of impressionistic phonetics used to compare two sounds. See Labov 1963 for preliminary indications of this finding.

underlying structures begins to emerge. There is a second CUMU-
LATIVE PARADOX involved here: *the more that is known about a language, the more we can find out about it.*

The limitations placed upon the input data by Chomsky have led
him to the conviction that the *theory is undetermined by the data*
(1966) – that there will always be many possible analyses for each
body of data, and we will need internal evaluation measures to choose
among them. We take the opposite view. Through the direct study of
language in its social context, the amount of available data expands
enormously, and offers us ways and means for deciding which of the
many possible analyses is right. In our preliminary operations upon
the initial data, considerations of simplicity will always find a place;
in suggesting the correct line of attack,[13] it is always possible to prove
whether the simple hypothesis constructed is the correct one. The
studies of co-variation and change in progress discussed below will
provide considerable support for this claim.

RESOLUTION OF PROBLEMS IN THE STUDY OF EVERY-DAY
LANGUAGE

Among the motivations discussed for the restriction of linguistic data
to intuitions were difficulties in working with every-day speech. Fortunately for our studies, many of these problems turned out to be il-
lusory, or greatly exaggerated.

(1) *The ungrammaticality of every-day speech* appears to be a
myth with no basis in actual fact. In the various empirical studies that
we have conducted, the great majority of utterances – about 75 per
cent – are well-formed sentences by any criterion. When rules of ellipsis are applied, and certain universal editing rules to take care of
stammering and false starts, the proportion of truly ungrammatical and
ill-formed sentences falls to less than two percent. (Labov 1966) When
non-academic speakers are talking about subjects they know well –
narratives of personal experience – the proportion of sentences which
need any editing at all to be well-formed drops to about ten per

---

[13] Watson's discovery of the structure of DNA is one of the most striking cases
of the role of simplicity in scientific research. Watson was convinced that the
solution must be a simple one, and this conviction motivated his persistent attempts at model-building (1969). But simplicity merely suggested the best approach: the validity of his model was established by the convergence of many
quantitative measures. Hafner and Presswood (1965) cite another case in the
theory of weak interactions where considerations of simplicity led to a new theoretical attack; but again, as in all other cases I know, the acceptance of the theory
as correct depended upon new quantitative data.

cent. I have received confirmation of this general view from a great many other linguists who have worked with ordinary conversation. The myth of the ungrammaticality of spoken language seems to have two sources: data taken from transcripts of learned conferences, where highly educated speakers are trying to express complex ideas for the first time; and the usual tendency to accept ideas that fit into our frame of reference without noticing the data with which we are surrounded.

(2) The existence of *variation and heterogeneous structures* in the speech communities investigated is certainly well-established in fact. It is the existence of any other type of speech community which may be placed in doubt. There is a kind of folk-myth deeply embedded among linguists that before they themselves arrived on the scene there existed a homogeneous, single-style group who really 'spoke the language'. Each investigator feels that his own community has been corrupted from this normal model in some way – by contact with other languages, by the effects of education and pressure of the standard language, or by taboos and the admixture of specialized dialects or jargons. But we have come to the realization in recent years that this is the *normal* situation, that heterogeneity is not only common, it is the natural result of basic linguistic factors. We argue that it is the absence of style-shifting and multi-layered communication systems which would be dysfunctional (Weinreich, Labov and Herzog 1968: 101).

Once we dissolve the assumed association between structure and homogeneity, we are free to develop the formal tools needed to deal with inherent variation within the speech community. Again, we find ourselves fortunate in that the patterning within this variation is by no means obscure: it does not require the statistical analysis of hundreds of speakers' records as linguists traditionally feared (Hockett 1958:444). On the contrary, we find that the basic patterns of class stratification, for example, emerge from samples as small as 25 speakers.[14] Extremely regular arrays of stylistic and social stratification emerge even when our individual cells contain as few as five speakers and we have no more than five or ten instances of the given variable for each speaker. With this regular and reproducible data, we are in a position to specify what we mean by the 'stylistic' or 'social'

---

[14] This conclusion is supported throughout Labov 1966a and Labov et al. 1968, but most strikingly in Shuy, Wolfram and Riley 1967. From a very large sample of seven hundred interviews, twenty-five were selected for analysis, and extremely regular patterns of social stratification emerged for a number of linguistic variables. See also Kucera 1961:97-98, where 19 subjects are stratified into at least four classes.

meaning which seems so elusive when language is studied out of context.

(3) *The problem of recording speech in natural settings* is a technical one: and the development of professional battery-operated tape recorders has made it possible to obtain excellent results in the field. Given a good microphone, the primary problem is to reduce mouth to microphone distance for each speaker.[15] In general, it may be said that the problem lies primarily in the failure of linguists to respond to the invention of the magnetic tape recorder in Germany in the 1930's. There is no tradition in linguistics of solving technical or experimental problems, of assessing technological developments and responding to them; otherwise the nature of linguistic operations would have been transformed thirty years ago.

(4) The fourth problem to be resolved is the *rarity of crucial grammatical forms* needed for evidence. There is no immediate solution on hand but the direction of the answer is beginning to appear. A deeper understanding of the communicative function of grammatical forms will enable us to enrich the data of ordinary conversation. The ideal mode of operation is for the linguist to engage in a normal conversation with an informant, and be able to elicit the informant's natural use of a given form without using it himself. Obviously there is feedback here between abstract analysis and field methods: the ability to control the production of a given form confirms our analysis and provides contextual data on its use. We have had some success in eliciting and controlling items such as the English passive and present perfect forms in this way. Eventually, we will be in a position to assert that a speaker does not have a given form in his system because of his consistent failure to use it in a context where other members of the community do so regularly.

SOURCES FOR THE STUDY OF LANGUAGE IN ITS SOCIAL CONTEXT

There are now in print a number of empirical studies which demonstrate convincingly that the direct study of language is a practical and fruitful procedure. The research to be discussed in the following pages is relatively recent: it is limited to the work of seven investigators or groups of investigators who use as their primary data accurate records of language in its normal social context. The first two are brief studies incidental to other research; the others are large scale undertakings, specifically designed for the study of the speech community.

[15] See section 1 below for some difficult consequences of this fact.

(1) John L. Fischer's brief study of the *-ing* suffix used by children in a New England community (1958).

(2) Henry Kucera's observations of the use of Common Czech and Literary Czech variables in the speech of 19 exiles on French radio stations (1961).

(3) John Gumperz' investigations of dialect stratification and code switching in Khalapur, India and Hemnes, Norway (1966, 1967), and his study of Marathi-Kannada bilingualism in Kupwad, India (1969).

(4) Lewis Levine and Harry Crockett's report on the use of post-vocalic *r* in their sociolinguistic survey of Hillsboro, N.C. (1966; Frank Anshen's study of four phonological variables in the Negro population of that city (1969).

(5) Investigations of Spanish-English bilingualism in the Puerto Rican community of New York City and Jersey City by Joshua Fishman, Robert Cooper and Roxana Ma (Fishman et al. 1968) and particularly Ma and Herasimchuk's study of Spanish and English variables.

(6) Roger Shuy, Walt Wolfram and Ralph Fasold's study of the social stratification of phonological and grammatical variables in Detroit English (Shuy 1967, Wolfram and Riley, Fasold 1968) and Wolfram's analysis of Negro speech within that study (1969).

(7) My own study of a sound change on Martha's Vineyard (1963); of the social stratification of English in New York City, focusing on five phonological variables (1966); with Paul Cohen, Clarence Robins, and John Lewis, an investigation of phonological and grammatical structure of non-standard Negro English in urban ghetto areas (Labov et al. 1968, Vol. I) and a parallel study of the use of language in those communities (1968, Vol. II).

In addition, I will be drawing on studies of social attitudes towards languages and dialects by Lamberts and his colleagues (1968). Though these are based entirely on test reactions, they fit in and help to explain the other data cited above. There are also smaller studies carried out by students, and a number of major studies now in progress which add to our understanding of the principles involved.

We can best understand the value of this empirical research if we apply it to the kind of specific theoretical problems of linguistic structure which concern all linguists. The study of language in its social context takes up the same range of linguistic problems as other approaches to linguistic theory. We can isolate five general questions:

1. What is the form of the linguistic rule? and what constraints may be placed upon it?

2. What are the underlying forms upon which rules operate, and how can they be determined accurately in any given case?

3. How are rules combined into systems? and how are they ordered within these systems?

4. How are systems related to each other in bilingual and poly-systemic situations?

5. How do rules and rule systems change? what is the mechanism of the fundamental processes of language acquisition, or how do rules change in the larger course of linguistic evolution?

Section 1 will present methods for gathering reliable data within the speech community; section 2 will deal with the methods used for analyzing this data and show the kind of solutions to internal linguistic problems that are possible; section 3 will deal with the broader sociolinguistic structures and the interaction of social and linguistic factors. The theoretical analysis and the formal approach is primarily my own, based to a large extent on the studies listed under (7), but the convergence of findings and principles in the field is very striking indeed. In all of these discussions we will make use of the facts of inherent variation to resolve abstract questions which would otherwise remain as undecided, moot possibilities. The aim here is not necessarily to provide linguistics with a new theory of language, but rather to provide a new method of work.

1. METHODOLOGY

In any academic course that deals with research in the speech community, there is always a great deal of interest in the first steps to be taken: "What do you say to people?" This is not a trivial question. The elementary steps of locating and contacting informants, and getting them to talk freely in a recorded interview, are formidable problems for students. It is an error for anyone to pass over these questions, for in the practices and techniques that have been worked out are embodied many important principles of linguistic and social behavior. Close examination of these methodological assumptions and findings will tell us a great deal about the nature of discourse and the functions of language.

The fundamental sociolinguistic question that must be posed here is: "Why does anyone say anything?" and more specifically, "Under what conditions will they say it to us?" There are subsidiary questions of sampling and recording which must be handled, but they merely set the stage for the basic problem. Our initial approach to the speech community is governed by the need to obtain large volumes of well-recorded, natural speech.

We can isolate five methodological axioms that are supported by the combined findings of the research projects cited above. These five axioms lead to a methodological paradox, and the solution to this paradox is the central problem for field work in the speech community.

1. Style shifting.   As far as we can see, there are no single-style speakers. Some informants show a much wider range of style shifting than others, but every speaker we have encountered shows a shift of some linguistic variables as the social context and topic change. Some of these shifts can be detected immediately in the minor self-corrections of the speaker, which almost always show a uniform direction.

2. Attention.   There are a great many styles and stylistic dimensions that can be isolated by analytical means. But we find that *all such styles can be ranged along a single dimension, measured by the amount of attention paid to speech.* The most important way in which this attention is exerted is in audio-monitoring one's own speech, though other forms of monitoring also take place.[16] This axiom (really an hypothesis) receives strong support from the fact that speakers show the same level for many important linguistic variables in casual speech, when they are least involved, and excited speech, when they are deeply involved emotionally. The common factor for both styles is that the minimum attention is available for monitoring one's own speech.

3. The vernacular.   Not every style or point on the stylistic continuum is of equal interest to linguists. Some styles show irregular phonological and grammatical patterns, with a great deal of 'hyper-correction'. In other styles, we find more systematic speech, where the fundamental relations which determine the course of linguistic evolution can be seen most clearly. This is the 'vernacular' – the style in which the minimum attention is given to the monitoring of speech. Observation of the vernacular gives us the most systematic data for our analysis of linguistic structure.

4. Formality.   *Any systematic observation of a speaker defines a formal context in which more than the minimum attention is paid to speech.* In the main body of an interview, where information is requested and supplied, we would not expect to find the vernacular used. No matter how casual or friendly the speaker may appear to us,

---

[16] Experiments with white noise which eliminate audio-monitoring show much the same kind of style shift as we observe when attention to speech is distracted by other means.

we can always assume that he has a more casual speech, another style
in which he jokes with his friends and argues with his wife.

5. *Good data.*   No matter what other methods may be used to
obtain samples of speech (group sessions, anonymous observation), the
only way to obtain sufficient good data on the speech of any one
person is through an individual, tape-recorded interview: that is through
the most obvious kind of systematic observation.[17]

6. We are then left with the OBSERVER'S PARADOX: the aim of
linguistic research in the community must be to find out how people
talk when they are not being systematically observed; yet we can only
obtain this data by systematic observation. The problem is of course
not insoluble: we must either find ways of supplementing the formal
interviews with other data, or change the structure of the interview
situation by one means or another. Of the various research projects
mentioned above, not all have been successful in overcoming this
paradox. Many investigators have completed their work with only a
limited range of stylistic data, concentrated in the more formal ends
of the spectrum. Systematic study of the vernacular has been accomplished primarily in Gumperz' work, in our own work in New York
City and in urban ghetto areas, and in the Fishman-Cooper-Ma
project in Jersey City.

One way of overcoming the paradox is to break through the constraints of the interview situation by various devices which divert attention away from speech, and allow the vernacular to emerge. This can
be done in various intervals and breaks which are so defined that
the subject unconsciously assumes that he is not at that moment
being interviewed (Labov 1966). We can also involve the subject in
questions and topics which recreate strong emotions he has felt in the
past, or involve him in other contexts. One of the most successful
questions of this type is one dealing with the "Danger of Death":
"Have you ever been in a situation where you were in serious danger
of being killed?" Narratives given in answer to this question almost
always show a shift of style away from careful speech towards the
vernacular.[18]

---

[17]   There are some situations where candid recording is possible and permissable,
but the quality of the sound is so poor that such recordings are of confirmatory
value at best.
[18]   One of the most interesting aspects of this question is that it involves a yes-no
answer, which we normally avoid. The mechanism seems to be that the informant
is willing to commit himself to the fact of having been in such a situation, though
he may be unwilling to volunteer an account. But having so committed himself, he
finds it very difficult to avoid giving a full account when the interviewer asks,
after some delay, "What happened?" Otherwise, he would appear to have made a
false claim.

One cannot expect that such devices will always be successful in obtaining a radical shift of style. A more systematic approach uses the normal interaction of the peer-group to control speech instead of the one-to-one confrontation of subject and interviewer. In Gumperz' work in Hemnes (1966), the fundamental data was obtained through recorded sessions with natural groups. In our work in South Central Harlem, (Labov et al. 1968) we studied adolescent peer groups through long-term participant observation. Individual interviews were carried out with all members of the group, yielding the individual data we needed on each individual. A series of group sessions were held in which the speech of each member (picked up from a lavaliere microphone) was recorded on a separate track. There was no obvious constraint in these group sessions; the adolescents behaved much as usual, and most of the interaction – physical and verbal – took place between the members. As a result, the effect of systematic observation was reduced to a minimum.

Rapid and anonymous interviews. In the methods just described, the identity and demographic position of each subject is well known. One can also carry out systematic observation anonymously, in conversations which are no' defined as interviews. In certain strategic locations, a great many subjects can be studied in a short period of time, and if their social identity is well defined by the objective situation, the findings can be very rich. In the study of the New York City community, I confirmed the results of a sociolinguistic survey by rapid and anonymous interviews with employees of three large, well-stratified department stores. (Labov 1966a: 63-87). The data was easily transcribed in writing, since only one variable was studied: postvocalic (r) in the expression 'Fourth floor'. The sources of error in this study were exactly complementary to those of survey interviews: the data on the demographic characteristics of the population was very rough, but the bias of the interview situation was absent. Subjects did not consider that they had been interviewed or observed, or that any conversation out of the ordinary had occurred. Other such studies have been carried out since in this model, asking for various kinds of information from a stratified population.

Unsystematic observations. The crucial question to be asked in any of these studies in whether one has indeed obtained data on the fundamental, systematic vernacular form of the language. Unsystematic and candid observation of speech at various strategic points can tell us a great deal about our success in this regard. One can record a number of constant and variable features from large numbers of people in public places such as trains, buses, lunch counters, ticket lines, zoos – wherever enough members of the speech community are gathered together so that their speech is naturally and easily heard by others. There are many biases built into such observations – loud and less educated talkers, for example, are strongly selected. But as a corrective to the bias of the interview situation, such data can be very valuable.

Mass media. It is also possible to obtain some systematic data from radio and television broadcasts, although here the selection and the stylistic constraints are very strong. In recent years, we have had a great many direct interviews at the scene of disasters, where the speakers are too strongly under the immediate influence of the event to monitor their own speech. Conversation programs and speeches at public events can give us a good cross-section of a population, but here the style is even more formal than that we would obtain in a face-to-face interview.

The formal end of the stylistic range. It is relatively easy to extend the range of styles used by the speaker towards the formal end of the spectrum, where more attention is given to speech. There are many questions which naturally evoke more careful speech (such as questions about speech itself). In most of the urban studies carried out so far, reading texts were used to study phonological variations. In general, linguistic variables show a marked shift from the most formal speech to the least formal reading. One can obtain a wide stylistic range within types of reading texts. A well-written text that reads well, focusing on vernacular or adolescent themes, will yield much less formal speech than a list of isolated words. Minimal pairs can be embedded in such a text, so that the speaker is not made aware of the contrast; his pronunciation can be compared to his reading of an isolated minimal pair where his attention is directed specifically to the variable being studied, and its use in differentiating words. One can observe the minimal pair *god* ∼ *guard* in a passage such as "... I told him to ask a subway guard. My god! I thought, that's one sure way to get lost in New York City." Secondly, *god* and *guard* may be included in a long list of other words. Finally, the speaker may be asked to pronounce the two words and say whether they sound the same or different to him. We thus have five stylistic levels for the study of post-vocalic (r):

    a. Casual speech
    b. Careful speech
    c. Reading
    d. Word lists
    e. Minimal pairs

Levine and Crockett (1966) and Anshen (1969) used another method to extend the stylistic range of readings. Sentences were constructed in which the variables were embedded, and at other points blanks were inserted for the subject to fill in lexical items as he read, diverting his attention from the variables. The pronunciation of the phonological variables in this context showed less [r] than in the reading of isolated words.

A number of formal tests do not require any reading on the part of the subjects. *Perception tests* of the ABX form provide useful information: in the case of total merger of a phonological distinction, speakers cannot hear whether X is closer to A or B; but where variable rules are operating, and the merger is not complete, they will show partial success. A surprising amount of grammatical information can be obtained by repetition tests with older subjects. Psycholinguists have long used such repetition tests with children 2 to 5 years old, but we found to our surprise that with speakers of non-standard dialects the underlying grammatical rules of much older speakers, 10 to 17 years old, controlled the form of their repetitions. Speakers of non-standard Negro English had no difficulty in repeating back accurately long sentences within their own grammatical system, but many sentences in standard English were repeated back instantly in vernacular form (Labov et al. 1968, 3.9).[19]

A number of formal tests have been developed to isolate social attitudes towards language, and the social information carried by dialect forms. One can play taped sections of 'typical' speakers, and ask subjects to identify their ethnic background, race, social class (Labov et al. 1968 4.4; Shuy 1969; Brown 1969). This tells us whether or not the listeners can obtain this social information from speech, but not where the information is located – in the speaker's grammar, phonology, intonation, or voice qualifier. *Subjective reaction tests* allow us to separate the linguistic variables from personal factors. The "matched guise" technique used by Lambert and his students (Lambert 1968, Lambert et al. 1968) presents for the subject a series of tape recorded sections in which voices of the same speakers are heard using different languages or dialects. The subjects are asked to make judgments of the speakers' personalities. As long as they cannot know how they have rated the same speakers before, they unconsciously translate their social attitudes towards language into differential judgments of the speaker's honesty, reliability, intelligence, etc. In our own subjective reaction tests (Labov 1966a:405-450, Labov et al 1968:4.6) the same speakers are heard reading sentences which differ

[19]   These observations have since been confirmed by larger scale tests carried out with school populations, where the subjects' relation to the vernacular was not well known.

principally by their treatment of the linguistic variable being studied. The subjects' evaluation of the social significance of this variable is registered by their differential responses to the matched sentences, on such scales as "What is the highest job the speaker could hold, talking as he does?" or "If the speaker was in a street fight, how likely would he be to come out on top?"

Speakers' attitudes towards well-established linguistic variables will also be shown in *self-evaluation tests*. When asked which of several forms are characteristic of their own speech, their answers reflect which form they believe has prestige or is 'correct', rather than the form they actually use. Here again, this kind of test data cannot be interpreted without data on the subjects' actual speech patterns.

We can investigate speakers' awareness of stigmatized well-marked social variants by *Classroom Correction Tests*, asking them to correct sentences which depart from school or classroom models (Labov et al. 1968:4.4). But it is almost impossible to obtain interpretable results on the reverse type of *Vernacular Correction Tests*, in which the subject is asked to correct standard prestige forms to the non-standard vernacular. The influence of the formal test situation is such that the subject cannot perceive accurately the non-standard rules. There is some evidence that the audio-monitoring norm which governed production of the non-standard form in childhood is replaced by the prestige norm, so that it is not possible in general for most speakers to direct their attention accurately to non-standard rules. This result reflects an important axiom of *Vernacular shifting: whenever a subordinate dialect is in contact with a superordinate dialect, answers given in any formal test situation will shift from the subordinate towards the superordinate in an irregular and unsystematic manner*. The terms 'superordinate' and 'subordinate' here refer to any hierarchical social dimension, equivalent to 'prestige' and 'stigmatized'. Some linguists hope that by 'educating' the informant in the goals of the analysis, it will be possible to diminish this effect, and gradually obtain answers characteristic of the pure vernacular. But this is an illusion. Instead, the subject may use his knowledge of the prestige dialect to avoid giving any 'vernacular' form which is identical or similar to the standard, and so produce stereotyped forms which are simply a collection of the 'most different' or 'worst' sentence types. Speakers who have had extensive contact with the superordinate form, no longer have clear intuitions about their vernacular available for inspection.[20]

---

[20] This is obviously true in the case of children. One cannot ask young children whether a non-standard sentence of theirs is well-formed, nor ask adults to reconstruct their childhood grammars. It is true in general that learning one series

There is further reason to regard as suspect data on a non-standard vernacular gathered from an 'educated' informant. Usually the investigator speaks the standard superordinate dialect which is dominant in this face-to-face interviewing situation. The informant's capacity to learn languages is operating at all times, and there is evidence that his grammatical rules will be heavily influenced by the standard during this period of elicitation.[21]

Once in a great while we encounter an informant who seems almost immune to 'correction' of this sort – who seems to have direct access to his intuitions, despite his knowledge of the standard dialect. An important task for psycholinguists is to identify other traits which accompany or determine this behavior, so that we will be able to search a given population for "ideal" informants. But it will always be necessary to calibrate the informant's responses against other data of the vernacular to see if he does indeed have access to his original rules. To evaluate this data, we must already know the rules of the vernacular from the direct observation of casual speech. But the procedure is not entirely circular; for if we have confidence in the introspections of 'immune' informants, we may obtain crucial data on forms which are too rare to find in any body of casual speech. Whether or not we are safe in extrapolating from observed stability on common forms to unobserved stability on rare forms is an open question.

These considerations do not necessarily apply to linguists studying languages through an intermediate language which is not marked socially with regard to their object language.[22] It is normal for a linguist who approaches a language for the first time to work with bilingual informants, who may not even be good speakers of the object language. Such preliminary steps in formal elicitation are of course necessary prerequisites to the accurate study of language in its social context. Good linguists can go further than this, and draw their best data from recordings of native speakers talking to each other – parallel to the group sessions mentioned above. The study of language in its social context can only be done when the language is 'known' in the sense that the investigator can understand rapid conversation. When an anthropological linguist enters into this more

---

of rules closely related to the older series makes it impossible to reconstruct the earlier situation.

[21] Our own field worker in South Central Harlem, John Lewis, showed a strong shift of the non-standard variables we were investigating from the time that he was first interviewed (1965) to the time that he finished interviewing others (1967).

[22] In his first approach to Lahu, a Lolo-Burmese language of Thailand and Burma, J. Matisoff used an English-Lahu bilingual speaker. It is his opinion that if he had used a more closely related language such as Thai, the distortion of the data would have been much greater.

advanced study, then the axiom of vernacular shifting will apply, for there will inevitably be stylistic levels which he will want to distingush.

Although one can achieve a certain amount of insight working with bi-lingual informants, it is doubtful if as much can be said for 'bi-dialectal' informants, if indeed such speakers exist. We have not encountered any non-standard speakers who gained good control of a standard language, and still retained control of the non-standard vernacular. Dialect differences depend upon low-level rules which appear as minor adjustments and extensions of contextual conditions, etc. It appears that such conditions inevitably interact, and although the speaker may indeed appear to be speaking the vernacular, close examination of his speech shows that his grammar has been heavily influenced by the standard. He may succeed in convincing his listeners that he is speaking the vernacular, but this impression seems to depend upon a number of unsystematic and heavily marked signals.[23]

There are speakers in every community who are more aware than others of the prestige standard of speech, and whose behavior is more influenced by exterior standards of excellence. They will show greater style shifting than those who do not recognize such a standard. This trait can be measured by *linguistic insecurity tests*. For a selected list of socially marked variants, the subject is asked which of two forms, is correct; and then which he actually uses himself. The index of linguistic insecurity is simply the number of items for which these two answers are different: that is, the extent to which the speaker recognizes an exterior standard of correctness different from his own speech (Labov 1966a: 474-480).

2. RESOLVING PROBLEMS OF LINGUISTIC STRUCTURE

This section will present three distinct problems of linguistic structure which have arisen in the study of non-standard Negro English: problems concerning the internal rules and the underlying elements upon which the rules operate. Within the abstract study of linguistic possibilities, these problems are only partly decidable. Data from the study of speech in its social context, obtained by the methods outlined above, will be used to provide what seems to us decisive solutions for each of these problems.

Each of these solutions is re-inforced by the convergence of data drawn from many sources. Within our own studies, we have parallel data for six different adolescent NNE peer groups, several adult

---

[23]   The ways in which such speakers convince their listeners that they are speaking the vernacular is an important problem for sociolinguistic study. Educated leaders of the black community in the United States provide many examples of this phenomenon.

populations, and many exploratory samples in other cities. On each of these problems, independent confirmation is provided by the work of Wolfram in Detroit (1969) with a completely different population and different analysts. The regular convergence of data drawn from completely different studies provides the kind of strong evidence that leads us to assert that these are indeed correct solutions.

2.1. Consonant cluster simplification and the past tense suffix. As noted above, non-standard Negro English [NNE] shows a marked pattern of consonant cluster simplification at the ends of words. Words which show in standard English [SE] consonant clusters ending in −*t,d,*[24] frequently appear in NNE with only the first consonant. Thus *bold, find* and *fist* are frequently pronounced *bol' fin'* and *fis'*. The question arises, is this indeed a case of cluster simplification, or are these final consonants simply absent in NNE? The existence of plurals such as *lisses* for *lists* suggests that some such words have the underlying forms without *t*. We can put this question sharply only after a series of preliminary investigations which enable us to define the variable as we have done here. The argument presented here outlines the solution given in detail in Labov et al. 1968:3.2. Given a proper definition of the variable, any small body of speech from any NNE group or individual will provide the following evidence:

(a) There are no speakers who never have these clusters: nor are there any who always preserve them: it is a case of inherent variation in NNE.

(b) For every speaker and every group, the second consonant is absent more often when the following word begins with a consonant than when it begins with a vowel. This regular effect of a following vowel is a characteristic feature of other phonological rules: it also constrains the vocalization of final *r*, *l* or nasals in many dialects.

(c) There is little or no hypercorrection: that is, final −*t*, or −*d* are not supplied for the wrong word class, giving us *mold* for *mole* or *lipt* for *lip*.

These facts show that the full cluster is present in the underlying form of *act, bold* or *find*, and that a variable rule deletes the second consonant. In our formal representation of this process, fact (c) can easily be shown by supplying the correct underlying forms in the dictionary. Fact (a) can be shown by making the deletion rule optional. But in conventional generative terms, there is no way to show formally fact (b). If we wrote:

---

[24] As Wolfram points out, clusters which are simplified are those which have homogeneous voicing. Words such as *jump, belt* and *else* are not included in this pattern.

(10) t, d → (∅) / C — # # (∼V)

we would be stating that *t* or *d* is deleted optionally after a consonant and before a word boundary if the next word does not begin with a vowel. This rule holds quite well for the colloquial speech of many middle-class speakers, who often say *firs' thing* and *las' month* but not *firs' of all* or *las' October*. But (10) is not at all adequate for non-standard dialects where clusters *are* simplified some 30 to 50 percent of the time, when the next word begins with a vowel. Since the existence of phonological conditioning is crucial data in determining the nature of this rule, it seems essential that our formal representation of rules show this fact. We do so by assigning to every rule a quantity φ representing the proportion of cases in which the rule applies out of all those cases in which it might do so. In a categorical, in-variant rule, $\varphi = 1$; in a variable rule, $\varphi = 1 - k_0$ where k_0 represents some constraint upon the rule. If a vowel does not follow, the rule is favored, so k_0 is reduced by a factor k_1 smaller than k_0 and $\emptyset = 1 - (k_0 - \alpha k_1)$ where α is plus or minus depending on whether the following environment is not a vowel or is a vowel. This interpretation is automatically provided by showing the rule for —*t,d* deletion as

(11) t,d → (∅) / C ___ # # α(∼V)

This form of the rule is quite satisfactory for many non-standard white dialects, whose speakers do occasionally say *firs' of all*. But it applies only to clusters of the form _CC without a morpheme bound-ary between the two consonants; it does not apply to clusters in *passed* [pæst] or *rolled* [rold] of the abstract form —C#C where the second consonant represents the past tense. In NNE, these past tense clusters are also deleted. We can show this by inserting the boundary optionally in our rule:

(12) t,d → (∅) / C (#) ___# # α(∼V)

This is an odd situation, for if the consonant is deleted, then the entire signal of the past tense disappears for regular verbs.[25] The question arises whether the boundary # is indeed present in NNE: do speakers 'know' in any linguistic sense that the [-*st*] cluster in *passed* represents the past tense? Grammatical searching of our group sessions and individual interviews, shows that for every individual and for every group the following facts hold:

(a) There are no speakers who always delete the *-ed* in these clus-ters, and no speakers who never do.

(b) There is phonological conditioning for these clusters as well: a following vowel has a strong effect in preserving them.

(c) In each phonological environment, past tense clusters are deleted less often than monomorphemic clusters.

(d) There is no hypercorrection: the *–ed* ending is not supplied wrongly where the present tense would be expected.

For any samples of speech of even moderate length, we then find the following relations holding:

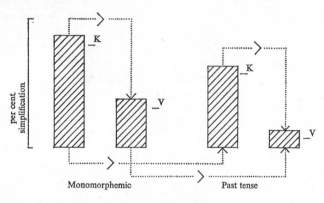

Figure 1

If we divide *–t,d* clusters into these four classes, we find in every case that past tense clusters are simplified less often, and clusters before vowels less often than other clusters. These relations are remarkably uniform: they hold for every individual and every group. The constraints upon the rule then appear as (13):

$$(13)\ \text{t,d} \quad (\emptyset) / C - \beta(\#) \underline{\qquad} \# \# \alpha(\sim V)$$

where we read automatically that $\varphi = 1 - (k_0 - \alpha k_1 - \beta k_2)$. In this case, the α effect of the following vowel is greater than the β grammatical constraint. But as the speaker gets older, or as he talks more formally, the grammatical environment has a stronger effect, until the positions of α and β are reversed. This alternation in the ordering of constraints upon rules represents one of the elementary forms of linguistic change, genetically or diachronically. It is one of the most important reasons for incorporating variable constraints into our representation of rules, for otherwise we have no formal way of registering this fundamental aspect of language development.

[25] Whenever the consonant deleted represents a whole morpheme, then the effect of a following vowel will not allow native speakers to reconstruct the underlying form. For even if the [t] is preserved in *I passed Edith,* this does not tell us anything about whether the *-ed* signal is present in *I passed Mike.* For monomorphemic clusters in *first,* etc., such an alternation does tell us what the underlying form of the word is.

The existence of variation does not itself tell us that the variable element is present in our underlying grammar. For example, third singular –*s* also appears variably in NNE clusters, as in *He works* vs. *He work*. But in contrast with the –*t,d* situation, our grammatical searching establishes the following facts:

(a) There are some speakers who show no third singular –*s* at all even in casual speech, and other individuals vary widely in the amount of –*s* they use.

(b) There is no general phonological process operating on clusters ending in –*s* or –*z*, for the plural is almost completely intact in NNE.

(c) A following vowel does not act to preserve third singular –*s*. If anything, this –*s* is present *less* often when a vowel follows.

(d) There is a great deal of hypercorrection: the –*s* appears unpredictably in other persons and numbers (*We works there*) or even in non-finite positions (*He can gets hurt*).

Evidence from formal tests confirms in many ways the analysis given here. Repetition tests, perception tests, and comprehension tests all show that the –*ed* suffix is easily supplied by NNE speakers of all ages, like the plural –*s* suffix, but that third-singular –*s* is very difficult for them to perceive, produce reliably, or comprehend.[26]

The independent investigation of Wolfram in Detroit provides precisely the same set of facts as shown here. Table 1 shows the percentages of –*t,d* clusters simplified in the four environments for three adult social classes and four peer groups in New York City, and four social classes in the Detroit study.[27] Here we see that for every group, the relations given in Figure 1 hold. Column 1 is greater than column 2, and column 3 is greater than column 4, showing the effects of a following vowel. Column 1 is greater than column 3, and column 2 is greater than column 4, showing the effect of the past tense boundary. As with all the other sociolinguistic data to be presented here, it is immediately obvious to the sophisticated statistician that tests of significance are irrelevant. The original data is given in a form that statistical analysis can be carried out if desired, but it is plain that even if a particular case were below the level of significance, the convergence of so many independent events carries us to a level of confidence which is unknown in most social or psychological research.

The confirmation of the New York study by the Detroit study of

---

[26] Recent work of Jane Torrey with younger children in South Central Harlem shows that the third singular -s can be used as a signal of the present tense, but not to distinguish singular from plural, as in *The cat splashes* vs. *The cats splash*.

[27] This data is given for the individual interviews in New York City and in Detroit. The relations of Figure 1 are preserved in the group sessions in New York, with the grammatical constraint operating at a lower level.

TABLE 1

Convergence of New York City and Detroit
Studies of Constraints on Consonant Cluster
Simplification in the Negro Speech Community

	Percent		simplified	
	Clusters in single morphemes		Past tense clusters	
	— K	— V	— K	— V
NEW YORK CITY				
Adults				
Middle class	60	28	19	04
Upper working class	90	40	19	09
Lower working class	89	40	47	32
Adolescents				
Thunderbirds (10-12)	91	59	74	24
Aces	98	64	85	43
Cobras	97	76	73	15
Jets	90	49	44	09
DETROIT				
Upper middle class	79	23	49	07
Lower middle class	87	43	62	13
Upper working class	94	65	73	24
Lower working class	97	72	76	34

(from Labov, *et al.* 1968: Table 3-9, and Wolfram 1968: Figs 7 and 9)

–t,d deletion leaves no doubt as to the existence of the underlying *–ed*
form in NNE, and the nature of the rule which is operating. The contrast between *–ed* and third singular *–s* is also delineated clearly in the
Detroit data (Wolfram 1969:161ff.). Since Wolfram's data does not
include group sessions or casual speech, we do not find the lowest
levels of third singular *–s*, as noted under (a) above. But we do find
(b) the absence of any general phonological process affecting *–s,z*: not
only are other inflections preserved, but the third singular *–s* is absent
just as often after verbs ending in vowels as verbs ending in consonants. Again, (c) there is no clear effect of a following vowel in preserving the *–s:* on the contrary, it is present in 38 per cent of the cases
before a consonant, and only 33 per cent before a vowel. Finally,
(d) Wolfram notes frequent but irregular hypercorrection, with the *–s*
appearing in other persons and in non-finite positions. These examples
give only some indication of the precision and detail of the con-

vergence between the New York and Detroit studies, which allows us to write both variable and categorical rules with confidence.

Is variation inherent in the system? Before proceeding, one must take into account the possibility that we have not really succeeded in isolating the basic vernacular. Even the wild and uncontrolled group sessions with adolescents may show the effect of observation, which may be responsible for some unsimplified clusters. Or perhaps children at the age of ten have already begun to show dialect mixture with standard English in their most casual speech, and to find the pure vernacular we must look to even younger children. Two findings make this possibility immediately unlikely. First, our work with younger children does not show us any greater homogeneity in their speech.[28] Secondly, we have already noted that the systematic character of –*t,d* deletion makes it most probable that these final consonants are present in the underlying representation. But there is a more important theoretical reason why we posit the variable rule (13) as the most accurate characterization of the basic vernacular. If the underlying rule in some 'pure' system was a categorical rule which went to completion, eliminating all final –*t,d* clusters, then it would eliminate itself. There would be no basis for positing the form *bold* in the dictionary of this dialect; instead children would infer that the word was *bole* and the rule would have nothing to operate on; the same would be said for *rolled*. A categorical rule would eliminate the regular past tense inflection.[29]

It is important to note that in the course of language evolution, change does go to completion, and variable rules have become invariant. When this happens, there is inevitably some other structural change to compensate for the loss of information involved. I would like to cite three examples of such dramatic structural change to support this claim.

(a) In a number of English-based Creoles, phonological and grammatical simplification has effectively reduced clusters so that final inflections are typically eliminated altogether. Whereas NNE preserves the past tense accurately with irregular verbs such as *give – gave, keep – kep', tell – tol'*, and the –*ed* ending in *rolled* remains embedded in a variable rule, Trinidad English and Jamaican Creole use the invariant simple forms *roll, give, keep, tell*, for the simple past. How

[28]   Work done with children four to seven years old by Jane Torrey in South Central Harlem shows the same patterns of variation in the -*ed* suffix and -*t, d* clusters as with older children, and similar patterns with the copula and negative concord to be discussed below.

[29]   This would be the case even if the categorical rule was context-restricted so that it did not operate before vowels. As noted in footnote 25 above, there is no way to reconstruct the underlying form if the morpheme disappears entirely in most positions.

is the past then distinguished from the present? In Trinidad, the auxiliary *do* is used, so that now the present tense becomes the marked form, *I do give* as opposed to the past *I give* (Solomon 1965).

(b) In the English dialects of Scotland, the simplification of *–t,d* clusters after voiceless stops has become categorical, giving a uniform *ac'* for *act,* and *ap'* for *apt.* The same rule would have eliminated the past tense in *liked* and *stopped.* But a different rule of epenthesis preserves these past tense morphemes so that they do not form clusters, and we have [laɪkɪt] and [stapɪt] for *liked* and *stopped* (Grant and Dixon 1921).

(c) In the evolution of the French language, a sound change moving down from the North eliminated final *–p, –t, –k* and *–s.* When final *–s* was lost for most dialects the normal way of distinguishing singular from plural in articles, adjectives and nouns was lost as well. Thus the singular article *la* could no longer be opposed to the plural article *las,* except when a vowel followed. In most cases, radical changes in the plural forms preserved the singular-plural distinction. The *Atlas Linguistique de France* shows that in one area of South Central France, near the southern limit for the loss of final *–s,* another sound change was taking place: unstressed *a* was changing to *o.* Normally, this change took place in both singular and plural forms. But in a sizeable sub-region to the northward, where *–s* was lost, this sound change was differentiated so that *a* changed to *o* only in the singular, opposing *lo* (singular) to *la* (plural). This recent finding of Dorothy Eckert (1969) is of the greatest importance in showing how grammatical functions can directly modify a sound change for communicative needs. it is also relevant for our discussion here that this compensating differentiation of the *a → o* change only took place where the loss ·f *–s* had become a uniform and categorical rule. In the area of '*–s* disturbance', there is no compensating effect on the *a → o* rule. This implies that if a variable rule is regular enough, it provides language learners with enough information to preserve the basic distinctions and the underlying forms.

If a sociolinguistic study of *–s* were carried out in that area, we would no doubt have found a variable rule similar to (13). The deletion of final *–s* in France was not recorded in any detail by the dialect geographers. But a similar variable rule in Puerto Rican Spanish has been studied by Roxana Ma and Eleanor Herasimchuk (Fishman et al.:689-703). They found regular patterns of variable constraints similar to those just given for *–t,d* deletion. The phonological constraint of a following vowel was strong, as well as grammatical constraints which favored the retention of the plural inflection on articles and adjectives over the plural attached to nouns, especially before a

The Study of Language in its Social Context 185

vowel. The form of the Puerto Rican s → h → ∅ rule is probably quite similar to the French s → ∅

We conclude that variation such as is shown in the deletion of *–t,d* clusters is not the product of irregular dialect mixture, but an inherent and regular property of the system. The status of variable rules in a grammar may be questioned on another ground: they involve a fundamental asymmetry between production and perception. We can argue that the speaker displays his knowledge of the past tense suffix by simplifying fewer *–ed* clusters than others (and presumably preserving *–ed* more often when it carries a heavy semantic load). But all that the listener has to know is whether or not the *–ed* is optional, since he interprets each past signal as it comes. (There is strong evidence that listeners can and do react to frequency, but it would be difficult to connect this capacity with the grammatical function of the past; such reactions have to do with over-all characterization of the speaker.) There is no question but that variable rules are rules of *production*. The issue is whether or not the symmetry of production and perception is a well-founded assumption about linguistic structure, or even an attainable goal of theory construction. As attractive as this might seem, there is now solid evidence that it is an invalid assumption. In repetition tests with NNE speakers 14 to 17 years old, we find that sentences such as *I asked him if he did it* are repeated instantly as *I axed him did he do it.* The meaning of the sentence is grasped perfectly, but it is produced automatically by NNE rules – there is evidently a deep asymmetry between perception (SE and/or NNE) and production (NNE only).

Finally, one may set aside variable rules on the ground that they are rules of performance. The less said about this 'wastebasket' use of the performance concept the better. It may only be noted that the great majority of our transformational and phonological rules may also be characterized as 'performance' rules. Extraposition, *wh*-attraction, adverbial postposing, etc., are all means of facilitating the linearization of the phrase structure input, eliminating discontinuities and left-hand embedding, coordinating and assimilating elements to one another so as to make the 'performance' of the sentence that much easier.

The ability of human beings to accept, preserve, and interpret rules with variable constraints is clearly an important aspect of their linguistic competence or *langue*. But no one is aware of this competence, and there are no intuitive judgments accessible to reveal it to us. Instead, naive perception of our own and others' behavior is usually categorical [30], and only careful study of language in use will demonstrate the existence of this capacity to operate with variable rules.

[30] Given a continuous range of frequency in the application of a rule, such as

2.2.   The deletion of the copula in NNE. We now turn to a much more complex problem, concerning the variable appearance of the present copula and auxiliary *is* in NNE. We frequently hear in this dialect such sentences as *He wild,* and *She out the game,* and *He gon' try to get up* corresponding to SE *He is wild, She is out of the game,* and *He is going to try to get up.* These copula-less sentences are similar to those of many languages like Russian, Hebrew or Hungarian, which have no present copula; to Jamaican English or Creole which has the copula only before noun phrases (and locatives) or to the speech of young children who say *That a lamb,* and *Mommy busy.* The question arises whether or not a copula is present in the deep structure or higher level structure of NNE; and if so, whether it is then deleted as a whole on the morphological level or by lower level phonological rules. It is an important question for both theoretical and applied linguistics, for it bears on the question of how dialects of a language differ, and how they are to be taught. The brief outline of the argument as presented here is abstracted from a detailed presentation in Labov 1969 and Labov et al. 1968:3.4.

(a) We first find that there are no speakers of NNE who always delete the copula, and none who never do so. Everyone shows some full forms, some contracted forms, and some zero forms. The regularity of this behavior, and the pattern of the variable constraints discussed below, show that we are dealing with a variable rule within the NNE system.

(b) There are syntactic positions where deletion never takes place: in elliptical forms (*He is too*), after wh-attraction (*That's what he is*). In general, we find that wherever standard English can contract, NNE can delete the copula, and wherever SE cannot contract, NNE cannot delete.

(c) This connection between contraction and deletion makes it necessary to explore the general conditions for English contraction,

---

"dropping the g" in *-ing,* we observe listeners reacting in a discrete way. Up to a certain point they do not perceive the speaker "dropping his g's" at all; beyond a certain point, they perceive him as always doing so. This is equally true with the (th) and (dh) rules discussed below, and any other well-developed linguistic variable. The same categorical judgments appear in the perception of others' eating habits ("She eats like a bird; he never knows when to stop") or housekeeping ("She cleans night and day; the dust could be that thick . . ."). Whenever there are strong social values associated with standards of role performance, we tend to get such categorical perception. But note that even this sudden reversal of judgments requires the observer to be (unconsciously) sensitive to frequency. We can speculate that each occurrence of the marked form sets up an unconscious expectation, which becomes overt if reinforced within a given period of time, but is otherwise extinguished without effect.

analyzing the evidence of our own intuitions within the generative model. We find that contraction of *am, is, are, will, has, have, had* is the removal of a lone initial schwa before a single consonant in a word which contains the tense marker. This process, which yields *He's here, I'm coming, You're there, I'll go, He's got it*, etc., is dependent upon rules which delete initial glides, and upon the vowel reduction rule which reduces unstressed lax vowels to schwa. The vowel reduction rule is in turn dependent upon the stress assignment rules which are determined by the syntax of the surface structure as developed by Chomsky and Halle (1968). The rules for contraction fit in with and confirm by independent evidence Chomsky and Halle's construction of the transformational cycle in English phonology.

(d) That deletion of the copula is related to contraction is also indicated by our finding that NNE does not delete forms with tense vowels which cannot be reduced to schwa: *be, ain't, can't* are not contracted. That deletion is a phonological process is also shown by the fact that the *m* of *I'm* is rarely deleted: in general, final nasals are not deleted in NNE.

(e) The variable rules which control contraction and deletion in NNE show a series of variable constraints according to grammatical environment. The rule is favored if the preceding noun phrase is a pronoun. The following grammatical environment constrains the rules in the order (from least favorable to most) predicate noun phrase; adjectives and locatives; verbs; and the auxiliary *gonna* before a verb. If we take the view that contraction operates first, and deletion removes the lone consonant which remains after contraction, then we see that these constraints operate in the same way on both rules, and contraction in NNE will show a pattern similar to contraction in other English dialects. The fact that there are two separate rules is indicated by the fact that the quantitative effects of these grammatical environments is intensified with deletion: the constraints have applied twice.

(f) Although the same grammatical constraints operate upon contraction and deletion in NNE, the phonological effect of a preceding vowel or consonant is reversed. For contraction, the rule is favored if the subject ends in a vowel; for deletion, if it ends in a consonant. This reversal matches the phonological difference between contraction and deletion, for the former is the removal of a vowel and the latter of a consonant, and in each case the favored context leads to a CVC structure.

We thus conclude that the basic form of the contraction and deletion rules for *is* are:

(14) CONTRACTION

$$\text{ə} \rightarrow (\emptyset) \ / \ \begin{bmatrix} \alpha \ \text{pro} \\ \gamma \ \text{V} \end{bmatrix} \ \#\# \ \begin{bmatrix} \overline{} \\ +\text{T} \end{bmatrix} \ \text{Z} \ \#\# \begin{bmatrix} \beta \ \text{Verb} \\ -\gamma \ \text{Noun} \end{bmatrix}$$

(15) DELETION

$$\text{Z} \rightarrow (\emptyset) \ / \ \begin{bmatrix} \alpha \ \text{pro} \\ \gamma \ \text{V} \end{bmatrix} \ \#\# \ \underline{} \ \#\# \begin{bmatrix} \beta \ \text{Verb} \\ -\gamma \ \text{Noun} \end{bmatrix}$$

Here, as in many other cases, our conclusions agree with the general point of view expressed by Chomsky that dialects of a language are apt to differ from each other in low-level rules, and that superficial differences are greater than those differences found (if any) in their deep structures.

This finding makes an important difference in the teaching of standard English to NNE speakers. If the copula were simply missing, then one would begin teaching basic sentence structure S → NP + VP. But since the absence of the copula is due to a low level deletion rule which is dependent on contraction, the problem is to teach the reading and writing of the contracted forms, and give the student practice in contraction without deletion.[31]

These conclusions are confirmed by a number of formal tests. Subjects have no difficulty in repeating back the copula in imitation tests (Labov et al. 1968: 3.9), and they show very few problems in comprehension tests for the copula.[32] This contrasts sharply with third singular –s, which does not correspond to any element in the grammatical structure of NNE.

The results of Wolfram in Detroit provide striking confirmation of the abstract relations outlined above. The variable constraints on copula deletion appear in the Detroit study in strikingly similar form. Wolfram's figures show for each sub-group the same effect of the preceding pronoun, and for the following grammatical environment he shows the effects upon deletion in the same order. Table 2 compares the New York City and Detroit figures for the effect of the following grammatical environment on the deletion of *is*.

---

[31] Teachers will correct *He wild* by saying "He *is* wild". But if a Negro child wanted to say "He *is* wild" he would have done so, since the stressed *is* is never reduced, contracted or deleted. His expression *He wild* is equivalent to SE *He's wild*.

[32] Again, we find from Jane Torrey's results that the full form of the copula is more common with children 4 to 7 years old than with adolescents.

TABLE 2

Convergence of New York City and Detroit Studies
of Effect of Following Grammatical Environment on
Deletion of is in NNE with Pronoun Subjects

	Percentage		deletion	
NEW YORK CITY	Noun phrase	Adj, Loc	Vb	gonna
Thunderbirds	35	51	74	91
Cobras	53	77	80	100
Jets	63	72	78	95
DETROIT Working class	37	46	50	79

(from Labov *et al.* 1968: 3.4, and Wolfram 1969: 211)

It must be emphasized here that the absolute value of these figures is not the data being compared. The relations among them are the fundamental structural facts we are examining. The absolute level at which these rules operate (that is, the initial value of k_0) is determined by factors of social context and status (style, socioeconomic class, age and ethnic group) which we will consider in section 3. The relations expressed by the variable constraints are constant for almost every individual, group and community, within the NNE sub-culture. As the study of language in its social context develops, we would expect that the focus will be on higher level relations among the variables and more precise quantitative formulations will be required.

2.3. Negative concord. For the third example of the analysis of linguistic structure in its social context, I will consider the problem which revolves around the sentence:

(16) It ain't no cat can't get in no coop

This was said by Speedy, the leader of the 'Cobras' in one of our group sessions, in a discussion about pigeon coops. Speakers of any other dialect of English besides NNE interpret (16) as meaning 'There is no cat that can't get into any coop'. They are more than a little surprised to discover from the context that Speedy was denying that cats were a problem, and that *his* meaning was 'There isn't any cat that can get into any coop'. At first glance, it seems that the NNE dialect is behaving in an illogical, contradictory way. If dialects do not differ radically in their deep structure, as suggested above, how can it be that a negative in one is a positive in another?

First, one might ask if Speedy had simply made a mistake. This is not the case, for we have encountered a half dozen other examples of the same construction in our work in the Negro community. Most convincing is the example from a long epic poem of Negro folklore: speaking of a whore, the narrator says, *There wasn't no trick couldn't shun her,* meaning that she was so good that 'there wasn't any trick (customer) that could shun her'.

We noticed that all of the examples we found had three features in common: (a) there were two clauses, and contradictory negative appeared in the second; (b) there was another negative in the first clause, and (c) the first clause also contained an indefinite adverb such as *one, ever* or *any* (negative plus *any* = *no*). These three facts lead us to connect the phenomenon with 'negative concord', the process by which negatives are attracted to indefinites. In this investigation, we again found it necessary to develop the argument further in terms of our grammatical intuitions (as native speakers of standard English and of several non-standard white dialects). We can begin with the generative formulation provided by Klima (1965) of the observation of Jesperson and others, that in English the negative is obligatorily attracted to the first indefinite if it precedes the verb, and optionally to the first indefinite thereafter. Thus in place of **Anybody doesn't sit there,* we have by obligatory rule, *Nobody sits there.* On the other hand, it is merely an optional (and somewhat formal) rule which shifts *He doesn't sit anywhere* to *He sits nowhere.* If we continued to consider only standard English, we might write a rule which takes the initial negative as a feature of the sentence and distributes it directly to the various positions with the conditions indicated. But study of a variety of English dialects leads us to the conclusion that the negative attraction rule which incorporates the negative with the first indefinite is of a very different character from the others. It seems there are three distinct rules, all operating *after* the negative is placed in its normal pre-verbal position. The first rule is the categorical one of negative attraction:

(17)   NEGATIVE ATTRACTION (obligatory for all dialects)

$$\text{Indef} - \text{X} - \text{Neg}$$
$$1 \qquad 2 \qquad 3 \;\rightarrow\; 1{+}3 \quad 2$$

Not only is this rule obligatory for all dialects, but sentences where it has not applied, such as **Anybody doesn't sit there* are un-English in a very striking way; in repetition tests (Labov et al.: 3.9) sentences like this provoke only confusion and no one can repeat them back. I believe that this rule reflects a cognitive requirement for the re-organization of the features [+ definite, distributive, + partitive, + hypothetical] when combined with a negative (Labov 1968).

The next two rules are of a different character:

(18a) NEGATIVE TRANSPORT (optional; Standard Literary English only)

$$\text{Neg} - \text{X} - \text{Indef}$$
$$1 \quad 2 \quad 3 \ \rightarrow 2 \ \ 1+3$$

(18b) NEGATIVE CONCORD (optional, for non-standard dialects only)

$$\text{Neg} - \text{X} - \text{Indef}$$
$$1 \quad 2 \quad 3 \ \rightarrow 1 \ \ 2 \ \ 1+3$$

These two rules are complementary and perform the same emphatic function. Instead of *He doesn't sit anywhere*, the first rule gives us *He sits nowhere*, and the second pleonastic rule yields *He don't sit nowhere*. Rule (18b) applies without regard to clause boundaries: thus we can have *He don't like nobody that went to no prep school* = SE *He doesn't like anybody that went to any prep school*. There are also some non-standard white dialects [WNS] which can transfer the nega-tive back to pre-verbal position, so that we have **Anybody doesn't sit there* → *Nobody sits there* → *Nobody don't sit there*. NNE shares this property.

Careful grammatical searching of our interviews and group sessions now shows us that NNE differs surprisingly in one other way from other dialects. Rule (18b) is not variable, but obligatory for NNE within the same clause. For core members of the NNE peer groups, we find that negative concord operates not at a 95 or 98 per cent level, but at 100 per cent in 42 out of 42 cases, 63 out of 63, etc., whereas our corresponding white groups show inherent variation. This means that the emphatic function of negative concord is entirely lost for NNE: if the rule is obligatory, it has no stylistic or contrastive significance. This emphatic function is supplied by NNE through several extensions of the negative rules not used by Northern dialects, such as *negative inversion*: *Nobody can do it* → *Ain't nobody can do it. Nobody saw him* → *Didn't nobody see him*. NNE also extends rule (18b) to permit transferring the negative to the pre-verbal position *in a following clause*. It is this emphatic usage which yields (16) *It ain't no cat can't get in no coop*.

We see finally that the apparent 'contradiction' of (16) is not a difference in logical operations among dialects, but only a slight re-adjustment of the conditions on a transformation. We may re-write (18b) now as

(18b′) NEGATIVE CONCORD

$$\text{Neg} - X - \begin{array}{c} \text{Verb} \\ \text{Indef} \\ 3 \end{array} \quad \rightarrow \quad 1 \quad 2 \quad 1+3$$
$$\begin{array}{cc} 1 & 2 \end{array}$$

and set up a table of conditions as follows. This table is in the form of values of φ, where 0 means the rule never applies, $\sim$ means it is a variable rule with $0 < \varphi < 1$, and 1 means the rule is obligatory.

3 =	Indef		Verb	
1 and 3 clause mates?	Yes	No	Yes	No
DIALECT SE	0	0	0	0
WNS$_1$	$\sim$	$\sim$	0	0
WNS$_2$	$\sim$	$\sim$	$\sim$	0
NNE	1	$\sim$	$\sim$	$\sim$

Here we distinguish two white non-standard dialects, one of which permits *Nobody don't sit there*. We here make use of the distinction between a variable rule and an obligatory one in a new way: the variable rule has a communicative function – 'stylistic', 'expressive' or 'emphatic' value in this case, while the invariant rule has none. Once again, a structural compensation appears as a variable rule becomes invariant and information is lost: NNE extends negative concord to new environments to supply this loss. NNE thus has the properties of a separate sub-system, in that changes in one part of the system seem to be inevitably accompanied with compensating changes in another to maintain the same functional operation.

3. SOCIOLINGUISTIC STRUCTURE

We may define a *sociolinguistic variable* as one which is correlated with some non-linguistic variable of the social context: of the speaker, the addressee, the audience, the setting, etc. Some linguistic features (which we will call *indicators*) show a regular distribution over socio-economic, ethnic, or age groups, but are used by each individual in more or less the same way in any context. If the social contexts concerned can be ordered in some kind of hierarchy (like socio-economic or age groups), these indicators can be said to be *stratified*. More highly developed sociolinguistic variables (which we will call *markers*) not only show social distribution, but also stylistic differentiation. As noted in section 1, stylistic contexts can be ordered along a single dimension according to the amount of attention paid to speech, so that we have *stylistic* as well as *social stratification*. Early studies such as those of Fischer (1958) or Kucera (1961) observed linguistic variables only one dimension at a time, but more recent studies (Labov 1966, Wolfram 1969, Anshen 1969) look at the interrelation of both dimensions.

1. A stable sociolinguistic marker: (th). One of the most general and simple sociolinguistic markers in English is (th): the phonetic form of the voiceless interdental fricative /Θ/ in *thing, thick,* etc. The prestige form is universally the fricative, while affricates and stops are stigmatized. The influence of other languages without this interdental fricative may reinforce the development of the stop form in various large cities of the United States, in Anglo-Irish and in NNE; but we also find this sociolinguistic variable in a great many other rural and urban areas in England and the United States. It has apparently had roughly the same status for at least two centuries, and probably more.

There are a number of technical questions in the definition of this variable: the simplest approach is to consider only initial position [33]. In the numerical index to be used here, a stop [t] is counted as 2 points, the affricate [tΘ] as 1, and the prestige variant [Θ] as 0. Invariant use of the stop form would yield an index score of (th) –200; of the prestige form, (th) –00. Figure 2 shows both stylistic and social stratification of (th) in New York City displayed on one diagram (Labov 1966a: 260).

The vertical axis is the (th) index, and the horizontal axis shows contextual style; ranging from the most informal on the left to the most formal on the right as described in section 1. On the figure, the average (th) values for five different socio-economic groups are plotted, and scores for each group connected with straight lines. Figure 2 thus

[33] This is one of the most striking findings of sociolinguistic research, since essays about social usage, written from 'common-sense' knowledge, have tried to distinguish "functional varieties" and "cultural levels" as completely independent dimensions. But their interdependence is shown in this and every other careful empirical study to date. Though it may seem inconvenient to have one variable operate on both dimensions, it seems to be an inevitable result of the sociolinguistic processes involving attention to speech and perception of norms, as outlined below.

shows regular stratification of the (th) variable for each contextual style. This is merely one of many such sociolinguistic structures which might be displayed here; there are a number of common properties which Figure 2 exemplifies:

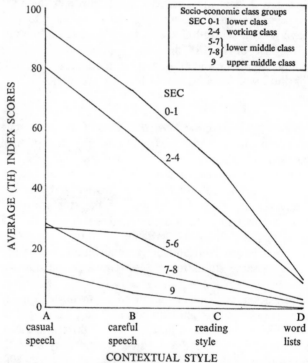

Figure 2. Stylistic and social stratification of (th) in *thing, three,* etc. in New York City

(a) In every context, members of the speech community are differentiated by their use of (th).

(b) Every group is behaving in the same way, as indicated by the parallel slope of style shifting for (th).

(c) Since Figure 2 is not visible as a whole to members, facts (a) and (b) are not part of general knowledge. The portion of Figure 2 visible to any given individual is usually one vertical and one horizontal section: the range of style shifting used by his own group, and the stratified behavior of other groups in the one context where he interacts with them. He is not aware that others shift in the same way he does.

(d) The same sociolinguistic variable is used to signal social and stylistic stratification. It may therefore be difficult to interpret any signal by itself – to distinguish, for example, a casual salesman from a careful pipefitter.

(e) Althought it is impossible to predict for any one utterance which variant a speaker will use, the striking regularity of Figure 2 emerges from samples with as few as five individuals in one sub-group, and no more than five or ten utterances for each individual.

The pattern of Figure 2 shows us the exterior, sociolinguistic controls on the variable rule represented as (19):

$$(19) \quad \begin{bmatrix} +\text{cons} \\ -\text{voc} \end{bmatrix} \rightarrow ([-\text{cont}]) \; / \begin{bmatrix} - \\ -\text{strid} \\ -\text{back} \\ +\text{cor} \end{bmatrix}^{34}$$

The variable input to this rule may be shown as a function of socio-economic class and style:

$$(20) \quad k_o = f(\text{SEC}, \text{Style}) = a(\text{SEC}) + b\,(\text{Style}) + c$$

These general traits hold for a number of sociolinguistic markers which have now been studied in the research groups cited. The complete view of social stylistic stratification is not available in most of these studies: some provide data on relatively small sections of Figure 2 and its equivalents, while others cover a wider range. But all of this data can be interpreted in terms of the configuration shown in Figure 2, and fitted into this framework consistently.

The variable (th) is one of a pair which are remarkably similar and parallel. The other member is the voiced interdental fricative (dh) in *this, then,* etc, which has been charted in the general study of New York City (Labov 1966a) and in the Negro community (Labov et al. 1968 and Anshen 1969).[35] A very similar stable sociolinguistic pattern appears for unstressed (ing) in *working, nothing,* etc. Almost univer-

[34] The notation used here differs from that of Chomsky and Halle (1968) only in the use of parentheses around the right hand member to indicate a variable rule. This parenthesis convention provides the automatic interpretation that $\varrho = 1 - k_o$, developed further in (20). The rule may be read as "Consonants variably lose their continuant or fricative character if they are non-strident and articulated with the forward part of the tongue". In this form, the rule applies to the voiced counterpart (dh) which shows the same structure, and to all environments. Variable constraints may appear to indicate the difference between (th) and (dh) (as -*a* tense in the environment shown here) or as variables attached to the preceding or following segments. Our discussion here concerns the variable input k_o, and such details are left unspecified.

[35] The (dh) variable (in initial position) is more regular in the Negro community than (th). Final (th) is realized as [f] more often than as [t], though initially it is not realized as [f] in the Cockney pattern. It should be noted that (th) and (dh) are examples of inherent variation by the same criteria as used in section 2: in particular, we note the absence of hypercorrection, even though the phonetic forms overlap with /t/ and /d/ in some cases. See Wolfram 1969:100ff. for a detailed analysis of the (th) variants.

sally, the [ɪn] variant is considered non-standard, and the sociolinguistic structure duplicates Figure 2. (Labov 1966a:398). Confirming data appears in Fischer 1958, and Anshen 1969. Such stigmatized variables as negative concord and pronominal apposition have been studied by Shuy, Wolfram and Riley 1968 for Detroit. Ma and Herasimchuk examined style shifting of a number of Puerto Rican variables: final (S) as noted above; (R), the neutralization of *r* and *l*; (RR), the alternation of [r:] and [ð]; and (D), the deletion of intervocalic [d].

Figure 2 also has some features that are not shared by all sociolinguistic variables. One can observe a sharp break between the working-class groups and the middle-class groups – a pattern which I have termed 'sharp' stratification. (see also Wolfram 1969:147). There is very little overlap between the working-class treatment of (th) and the middleclass values, while that is not the case for other variables. (see Figure 3 below). In a stable sociolinguistic marker, this may reflect discontinuities in the over-all pattern of socio-economic stratification in the society.

Men vs. women. There is another aspect to the social stratification

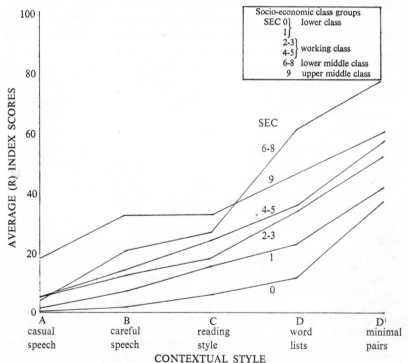

Figure 3. Class stratification of (r) in *guard, car, beer, beard*, etc. for native New York City adults

of (th) which is not shown on Figure 2. In careful speech, women use fewer stigmatized forms than men, (Labov 1966:288), and are more sensitive than men to the prestige pattern. They show this in a sharper slope of style shifting, especially at the more formal end of the spectrum. This observation is confirmed innumerable times in Fischer (1958), throughout Shuy and Fasold's work in Detroit, in Levine and Crockett, and in Anshen's study of Hillsboro. The pattern is particularly marked in lower middle-class women, who show the most extreme form of this behavior. There is some question as to whether lower class women are also more sensitive to social norms of speech: the evidence is not clear here.

The hypercorrect pattern of the lower middle class. One of the most solidly established phenomena of sociolinguistic behavior is that the second-highest status group shows the most extreme style shifting, going beyond that of the highest status group in this respect. To see this most clearly, it is necessary to examine the sociolinguistic structure of a change in progress. Figure 3 shows the pattern for final and pre-consonantal (r) in New York City (Labov 1966a:240). This community has a basically *r*-less vernacular, but shortly after the end of World War II, *r*-pronunciation became the prestige norm (as to a lesser extent, in other *r*-less areas of the United States). The vertical axis is the (r) index – the percentage of constricted [r] in words like *ear, where, car, board,* etc.[36] Higher scores reflect greater use of prestige form [r]. Note the sharp cross-over of the lower middle class group in the two most formal styles. This pattern recurs in several other variables from New York City. One of the most striking instances of quantitative convergence is supplied by Levine and Crockett's study, as shown in Table 3.

TABLE 3

R Scores by Sentence and Word-List and by Education and Sex

	Sentence-List	Word-List	Net Increase
Education			
Any College	52.7	58.9	6.2
High School Graduate	54.6	65.6	11.0
Some High School	50.0	57.0	7.0
Grade School or None	52.6	57.3	4.7
Sex			
Male	52.3	57.4	5.1
Female	52.9	61.1	8.2

[36] This variable does not include *r* following the mid-central vowel of *her, heard,* etc., which follows a different pattern with either a palatal up-glide or more constriction.

Here data from a completely independent study with a more limited stylistic range shows the same cross-over phenomenon. The second highest status group – in this case, high school graduates – show a much greater shift towards the prestige norm in their more formal style. The significance of this pattern for mechanism of linguistic change has been dealt with specifically in Labov 1966c. Here it will be helpful to see what formal simplification can be achieved for this complex pattern, abstractly:

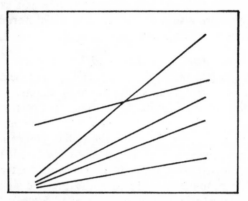

The slope of style shifting is very complex. The highest and lowest group have the shallowest slope. The interior groups follow behind the lead of the second highest group which is the steepest. How can this be formalized? The rule for the vocalization of (r) in the white community has the general form:

(21) $[+\text{cen}] \rightarrow ([-\text{cons}]) / [-\text{cons}] \underline{\quad} \sim V$ [37]

The problem here is to write a formula for the basic constraint on the input variable k_0 comparable to the simple and straightforward (20). The solution lies in an understanding of the significance of style shifting: it is governed by the recognition of an exterior standard of correctness. The strength of such behavior can be measured by an index of Linguistic Insecurity (see section 1) which gives us precisely the curvilinear pattern we need to describe the slope of style shifting in Figure 3, with the lower middle class at a maximum (Labov 1966a: 477). We can then write for (21)

(22) $k_0 = f(\text{Class, Style}) = a(\text{SEC}) + b(\text{ILI}) (\text{Style}) + c$

---

[37]   This rule is the formal equivalent of "A central consonant (r) variably loses its consonantal character after a vowel or glide if a vowel does not follow directly." If a word boundary follows directly, and then a vowel, this rule is constrained so that [r] appears more often in *four o'clock*.

Problems of sociolinguistic structure. Perhaps the most immediate problem to be solved in the attack on sociolinguistic structure is the quantification of the dimension of style. If quantitative studies of attention can be related to style shifting, we will then be able to give more precise form to rules such as (20) or (22) and specify the constants a, b, and c. Such quantification may possibly be obtained by studies of pupil dilation, or of systematic divisions of attention through mechanical and measurable tests, or by quantitatively reducing audiomonitoring through noise level.

It is also evident that the studies cited do not have enough data from the direct study of the vernacular. The methodological task is to combine surveys of individuals which give us a representative sample with longer-term studies of groups. The ideal study of a community would randomly locate individuals, and then study several groups of which that individual was a member. That is quite impossible in a normal social survey, given the numbers required, but since we have established that sociolinguistic studies require a smaller population to begin with, such a model is not beyond the realm of possibility.

A third problem lies in dealing with rules which show irregular lexical distribution. There is now good evidence that the course of linguistic change involves the temporary dissolution of word classes.[38] The most difficult problem here is that there are distributions across word classes which we would want to describe which are not a part of the knowledge of the native speaker. In most cases, he only needs to know in what class a given word falls. The proportion of the original word class which has been affected by the incoming rule is of no immediate interest to him if he has no choice in the pronunciation of any given item. It may be that we will enter rules into our grammar which are *not* a part of the 'knowledge' of native speakers. This particular metaphor may have lost its value at this point in our investigations.

A fourth major challenge is to enter more deeply into the study of higher level syntactic variables, such as extraposition, nominalization, placement of complementizers, negative raising, wh-attachment or relativization. The two chief stumbling blocks to investigating these

---

[38] Although Figures 2 and 3 show word classes moving as a whole, we have encountered some rules which show a great deal of irregular lexical variation. The tensing of short /a/ in *bad, ask,* etc., now being investigated in New York City by Paul Cohen, shows such irregularity, while the raising rule which follows does not (Labov 1966a:51-2). It is the existence of a variable rule which allows the word class to be re-constituted when the change is completed, since it is defined as the class of lexical items which can vary between X and Y, as opposed to the classes which are always X or always Y. For some possible structural causes of such lexical variation, see Wang 1969.

features in their social context is the low frequency of occurrence of the critical sub-cases, and the lack of certainty in our abstract analyses. But some beginning has been made in our recent work in urban ghetto areas, and the challenges to work with more abstract matters cannot be ignored. The study of language in its social context cannot remain at the level of such phonological variables as (th), if it is to make a significant contribution to the problems outlined in the first part of this article.

The fifth problem is to enlarge the scope of these studies beyond individual speech communities, and relate them to larger grammars of the English speech community as a whole. The discussion of negative concord in section 2 indicates one way in which this might be done. The work of C. J. Bailey is most challenging here: particularly his penetrating studies of phonological rules in Southern dialects (1969), and his broader attempts to incorporate all English phonology into a single, pandialectal set of rules (1969b). Though these studies of Bailey are not based upon the study of language in context, one must eventually hope to provide reliable data to support work of this generality and level of abstraction.

The relation of norms to behavior. So far, in our consideration of sociolinguistic structure, we have taken into account only what people say, and only incidentally what they think they *should* say. These are "secondary responses" to language that Bloomfield suggested that we might well observe (1944) as one part of popular lore. There is a very small vocabulary available to most people for talking about language: the same few terms recur over and over for we hear that the other people's pronunciation has a 'nasal twang', is 'sing-song', is 'harsh' or 'gutteral', 'lazy' or 'sloppy'. Grammar is said to be 'mixed-up', 'illogic.'.

A small number of sociolinguistic markers rise to overt social consciousness, and become *stereotypes*. There may or may not be a fixed relation between such stereotypes and actual usage. The variables (ing) and (dh) are such stereotypes in the United States: someone may be said to 'drop his g's' or to be one of those 'dese, dem and dose guys'. Most communities have local stereotypes, such as 'Brooklynese' in New York City which focuses on 'thoitythoid' for *thirty-third;* in Boston, the fronted broad *a* in 'cah' and 'pahk' receives a great deal of attention. Speakers of the isolated Cape Hatteras, North Carolina, dialect are known as 'hoi toiders' because of the backing and rounding of the nucleus in *high, tide,* etc.

Such social stereotypes yield a sketchy and unsystematic view of linguistic structure to say the least. In general, we can assert that overt *social correction* of speech is extremely irregular, focusing on the most frequent lexical items, while the actual course of linguistic evolution,

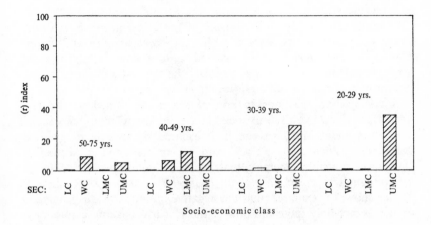

Figure 4a. Social stratification of (r) in *ear, board, car,* etc. for four age levels in casual speech: New York City [Labov 1966a:344]

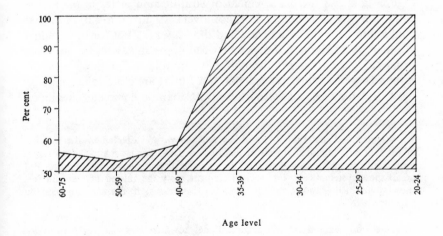

Figure 4b. Percent showing (r)-positive response on subjective reaction test by age level (two-choice test): New York City [Labov 1966a:435]

which has produced the marked form of these variables, is highly systematic. This is the basic reason why the vernacular, in which minimum attention is paid to speech, gives us the most systematic view of linguistic structure. For example, the evolution of the New York City vernacular has led to the raising of the vowel in *off, lost, shore, more*, etc. until it has merged with the vowel of *sure* and *moor*. This high vowel has been stigmatized, and is now being corrected irregularly by middle-class speakers. But the same vowel, raised simultaneously in the nucleus of *boy, toy*, etc., is never corrected.[39]

But subjective reactions to speech are not confined to the few stereotypes that have risen to social consciousness. Unconscious social judgments about language can be measured by techniques such as Lambert's "matched guise" test, and others described in section 1. One basic principle emerges: that *social attitudes towards language are extremely uniform throughout a speech community.*[40] Lambert's studies show, for example, that the negative attitude towards Canadian French is not only quite uniform in the English-speaking community, but almost as unanimously held among French speakers in Quebec (1968). In our study of unconscious subjective reactions to markers such as (r), we find the most extraordinary unanimity in speakers' reactions. There is a general axiom of sociolinguistic structure which can be stated as: *the correlate of regular stratification of a sociolinguistic variable in behavior is uniform agreement in subjective reactions towards that variable.* This may be illustrated by Figure 4, which compares behavior and subjective reactions for (r) in New York City. Figure 4a shows the development of stratification of (r) in the vernacular for young adults. For those over 40, there is no particular connection between social class and the use of (r), but for those under 40, there is a striking difference between upper middle class and other groups. Figure 4b shows the normative correlate. For those over 40, responses to the subjective reaction test for (r) are close to the random level. But for those between 18 and 39, there is complete unanimity:

[39] We also find that the vowels of *my* and *mouth* are affected by the rotation of the long and ingliding vowels of *bad, bar, lost*. As *bar* moves to the back, *my* moves with it, and *mouth* moves in the opposite direction towards the front. But of all these systematically interrelated changes, only the raising of *bad* and *lost* shows style shifting and correction. Even for these cases, the correction is lexically irregular.

[40] In fact, it seems plausible to define a speech community as a group of speakers who share a set of social attitudes towards language. In New York City, those raised out of town in their formative years show none of the regular pattern of subjective reactions characteristic of natives when a New York City variable such as the vowel of *lost* is concerned (Labov 1966a:651).

42 out of 42 subjects showed responses that unconsciously registered the prestige status of *r*-pronunciation.

As we re-examine the structures shown in Figures 2 and 3, it is apparent that the uniform slope of style shifting also reflects the uniform attitudes held in the community. But for a stable sociolinguistic marker like (th), we can raise the question, what maintains this structure for such a long period of time? Why don't all people speak in the way that they obviously believe they should? The usual response is to cite laziness, lack of concern, or isolation from the prestige norm. But there is no foundation for the notion that stigmatized vernacular forms are easier to pronounce [41]; there is strong evidence of concern with speech, and in large cities, everyone is exposed to the prestige norm. Careful consideration of this difficult problem has led us to posit the existence of an opposing set of covert norms, which attribute positive values to the vernacular. In most formal situations in urban areas, such as an interview or a psycholinguistic test, these

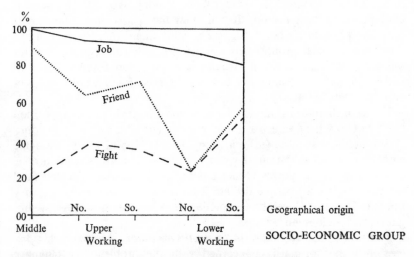

Figure 5. Per cent rating middle-class speaker (S2) higher than working-class speaker (S1) on three scales for five social groups.
[Labov *et al.* 1968:242]

[41] Some of the extreme developments of vernacular vowel shifts in New York City, Detroit or Chicago are tense vowels which seem to involve a great deal of muscular effort compared to the standard. Spectographic analysis indicates that such vowels as short /a/ rising to the height of *here* are extremely fronted. An interesting correlate of such extreme movements is the pattern of subjective reaction tests which shows that those who use the highest percentage of stigmatized forms are quickest to stigmatize them in the speech of others.

norms are extremely difficult to elicit. Middle-class values are so dominant in these contexts that most subjects cannot perceive any opposing values, no matter how strongly they may influence behavior in other situations. In our recent work in the Negro community, we have recently been able to uncover evidence of the existence of such opposing norms. Figure 5 shows responses to the first two items on our subjective reaction test, opposing a working-class speaker to a middle-class speaker on 'zero' sentences (which contain none of the variables to be tested). The upper line shows the percent of those who rated the middle-class speaker higher on the scale of 'job-suitability'. It begins very high with middle-class subjects, and falls off slightly as we move to lower socio-economic groups. The lower line is the converse: this registers judgments to the 'fight' or 'toughness' scale: "If the speaker was in a street fight, how likely would he be to come out on top?" There is a simple inverse relationship here; a stereotype that is probably reinforced by school teachers but also shows some recognition of social reality. But the third set of reactions to the 'friendship scale' shows that there is more involved. This scale is in response to the question "If you knew the speaker for a long time, how likely would he be to become a good friend of yours?" For the three upper social groups, this follows the job scale closely; but for the lower working class, it switches abruptly, and follows the fight scale. The same phenomenon can be observed for a whole range of variables tested (Labov et al. 1968: 3.6).

We have therefore some empirical support in positing the opposition between two sets of values as the normative correlate of stable sociolinguistic markers such as (th) and (ing). In this type of study, we agree with Homans (1955) that the proper object of study should not be behavior alone, or norms alone, but rather the extent to which (and the rules by which) people deviate from the explicit norms which they hold. It is at this level of abstraction that we can best develop linguistic and sociolinguistic theory.

The role of social factors in linguistic evolution. Although this discussion is not primarily concerned with the problems of language change, I have already introduced some data which bears on this question. In speaking of the role of social factors influencing linguistic evolution, it is important not to overestimate the amount of contact or overlap between social values and the structure of language. Linguistic and social structure are by no means co-extensive. The great majority of linguistic rules are quite remote from any social value; they are part of the elaborate machinery which the speaker needs to translate his complex set of meanings or intentions into linear form. For example, the rules governing the cross-over of co-referent pronouns discussed above (section 0) are well below the level of social affect, and their irregular, idiosyncratic distribution in the population reflects this fact.

Variables closer to surface structure frequently are the focus of social affect. In fact, social values are attributed to linguistic rules only when there is variation. Speakers do not readily accept the fact that two different expressions actually 'mean the same' and there is a strong tendency to attribute different meanings to them.[42] If a certain group of speakers uses a particular variant, then the social values attributed to that group will be transferred to that linguistic variant. Sturtevant (1948) has proposed a general model of linguistic change showing the opposition of two forms, each favored by a particular social group. When the issue is resolved, and one form becomes universal, the social value attached to it disappears.

We may think of social meaning as parasitic upon language. Given a uniform set of linguistic rules used to express certain meanings, language may be considered as a neutral instrument. But in the course of change, there are inevitably variable rules, and these areas of variability tend to travel through the system in a wave-like motion. The leading edge of a particular linguistic change is usually within a single group, and with successive generations the newer form moves out in wider circles to other groups. Linguistic *indicators* which show social distribution but no style shifting represent early stages of this process. *Markers* which show both stylistic and social stratification represent the development of social reaction to the change and the attribution of social value to the variants concerned. *Stereotypes*, which have risen to full social consciousness, may represent older cases of variation which may in fact have gone to completion; or they may actually represent stable oppositions of linguistic forms supported by two opposing sets of underlying social values.

Many of the individual sociolinguistic variables are members of a complex network of linguistic relations, and as change spreads slowly throughout this system (Labov 1965), there is a gradual shift of social values. Generally speaking, it seems to take about thirty years for a change in one part of a system (as in a front vowel) to be generalized fully to a parallel member (as a back vowel). But social structures are seldom stable over such a period of time. For example, in Martha's Vineyard we see the development of the raising of the nucleus of the

---

[42] When New York City *cruller* (Dutch *kroeller*) was replaced by the standard term *doughnut*, the term *cruller* was variously assigned to other forms of pastry. Similarly the local *pot cheese* (Dutch *pot kaas*) was replaced by *cottage cheese* and was differentiated to indicate a drier form. The oscillation of socially marked pronunciations of *vase* led one informant to say, "These small ones are my [vezɪz] but these big ones are my [vazɪz]".

diphthong in *nice, right, side,* etc., among Yankee speakers (Labov: 1963). This sound change was generalized to the corresponding diphthong in *out, proud,* etc. But in the interval, a large number of second and third generation Portuguese-Americans entered into the speech community, and for various reasons we find that they favor the raising of the second vowel much more than the first, moving the whole process to higher levels. Thus succeeding generations re-interpret the on-going course of a linguistic change in terms of a changing social structure. It is the oscillation between the internal process of structural generalization, and interaction with the external social system, which provides the impetus for continuous linguistic evolution (Labov 1965).

As far as the synchronic aspect of language structure is concerned, it would be an error to over-emphasize the importance of social factors. Generative grammar has made great progress in working out the invariant relations within this structure, even though it wholly neglects the social context of language. But it now seems clear that one cannot make any major advance towards understanding the mechanism of linguistic change without serious study of the social factors which motivate linguistic evolution.[43]

4. SOME INVARIANT RULES OF DISCOURSE ANALYSIS

This presentation has so far concentrated almost entirely upon the variable rules of language: their use in providing decisive evidence on questions of linguistic structure, their place in sociolinguistic structure, and more briefly, their role in the evolution of language. But a very great number of linguistic rules are not variable in the least: they are categorical rules which, given the proper input, always apply. More than any other field, linguistics has succeeded in isolating the invariant structures underlying behavior, and it is upon this foundation that we have been building in the work outlined in sections 2 and 3. The formal representation of variable rules presented there depend upon, and interlock with, a number of invariant rules of grammar derived from studies of language quite apart from any social context.

There are some areas of linguistic analysis in which even the first steps towards the basic, invariant rules cannot be taken unless the

---

[43] It is Lévi-Strauss who testifies most eloquently to the advantage of linguistics over other social sciences in its grasp of invariant relations (1963:31ff). The invariant rules we speak of here play the same role as the "structural relations" which Lévi-Strauss admires in the work of Troubetzkoy and Jakobson. One hopes that anthropology will be able to absorb the advantage of that linguistic approach without its limitations.

social context of the speech event is considered. The most striking examples are in the analysis of discourse. The fundamental problem of discourse analysis is to show how one utterance follows another in a rational, rule-governed manner – in other words, how we understand coherent discourse. We rely upon our intuitions to distinguish coherent from incoherent discourse; for example, the following is plainly not governed by any rules that we can immediately recognize.

(23) A: What is your name?
      B: Well, let's say you might have thought you had something from before, but you haven't got it any more.
      A: I'm going to call you Dean.

                                        [from Laffal 1965:85]

This is an excerpt from a conversation between a doctor and a schizophrenic patient. Our first data in dealing with such a passage will be our intuitive reactions to it, and the first challenge in discourse analysis is to account for our intuitions (as confirmed by the response of participants as in (23)). The question is: how much and what kind of data do we need in order to form sound judgments and interpret sequences of utterances as the participants in the conversation do? The simplest case is that of elliptical responses, as in (24).

(24) A: Are you going to work tomorrow?
      B: Yes.

Here our normal knowledge of English syntax is sufficient to allow us to derive B's utterance from *Yes, I am going to work tomorrow*. There is a simple rule of discourse of the following form:

(25) If A utters a question of the form Q-S_1, and B responds with an existential E (including *yes, no, probably, maybe*, etc.), then B is heard as answering A with the statement E-S_1.

But now let us consider sequences of the following form:

(26) A: She never helps at home.
      B: Yes.

(27) A: She told you what we are interested in.
      B: Yes.

(28) A: You live on 115th St.
      B: No. I live on 116th.

We encounter many such examples in our analyses of therapeutic interviews and in every-day speech. Rule (25) obviously does not apply: there is no Q-S₁ in the A form. Is it true that any statement can be followed with a *yes* or *no*? The following sequences seem to indicate the opposite.

(29) A: I don't like the way you said that.
      B: *Yes.

(30) A: I feel hot today.
      B: *No.

It is not only that (29-30) do not require or tolerate a *yes* or *no* answer, but even more strikingly that statements like (25-28) seem to demand such a response. We find many cases where speakers will not let the conversation continue unless a *yes* or *no* answer is given to such statements. The rule which operates here is one of the simplest invariant rules of discourse. Given two parties in a conversation, A and B, we can distinguish as 'A-events' the things that A knows about but B does not; as 'B-events' the things which B knows but A does not; and as 'AB-events' knowledge which is shared equally by A and B. The rule then states:

(31) If A makes a statement about a B-event, it is heard as a request for confirmation.

Note that in (29-30), A is making a statement about an A-event, but in (26-28) about a B-event. Anyone can immediately test this rule in an ordinary conversation and observe the force of its operation. This rule contains the social construct of 'shared knowledge' which is not normally part of a linguistic rule. This is merely one of many rules of interpretation which relate 'what is said' – questions, statements, imperatives – to 'what is done' – requests, refusals, assertions, denials, insults, challenges, retreats, and so on. There are no simple one-to-one relations between actions and utterances; rules of interpretation (and their nearly symmetrical rules of production) are extremely complex and relate several hierarchical levels of 'actions' to each other and to utterances. Sequencing rules do not operate between utterances, but between the actions performed with those utterances. In fact, there are usually no connections between successive utterances at all. The over-all pattern of discourse analysis may be sketched as:

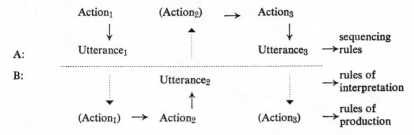

It may be helpful to consider a more difficult case, drawn from a therapeutic interview we have been investigating in some detail.[44]

(32) A: Well, when do you plan to come home?
     B: Oh why-y?

There is no syntactic connection between these two questions and no amount of abstract analysis will relate them correctly. One cannot interpret B as $Q-S_1$: "Why do I plan to come home?" One might interpret B as addressed to an implicit underlying form, A: [I ask you] when do you ... B: Why [do you ask me. . . .]? But this would be a wrong interpretation; without detailed knowledge of the speakers and the situation, one could not hope to arrive at the appropriate intuitive judgments to begin analyzing. We must be aware that A is a college student, and that B is her mother; that B has been away for four days helping a married daughter; that A and B both know that A wants B to come home; and that B has said many times in the past that A cannot take care of herself, which A denies. It is then clear that (32-A) is a request for action, not for information: A is requesting that her mother come home.

There is a general rule for interpreting any utterance as a request for action (or command) which reads as follows:

(33)   If A requests B to perform an action X under conditions Z, A's utterance will be heard as a valid command only if the following pre-conditons hold: B believes thet A believes (= it is an AB-event that)

    1. X should be done for a purpose Y
    2. B has the ability to do X
    3. B has the obligation to do X
    4. A has the right to tell B to do X.

[44] From studies of therapeutic interviews being conducted by the author and David Fanshel of the Columbia School of Social Work.

Where the four pre-conditions do not hold in some obvious way, we have jokes or joking insults such as: "Drop dead!" "Go jump in the lake!" or "Get this dissertation finished by the time I get back from lunch!"[45] These pre-conditions appear in almost every rule of interpretation and production which concern making or responding to commands. Note that the primitive terms of (33) include *rights* and *obligations* which are plainly social constructs. Given rule (33), there is a rule of interpretation operating for B in responding to A's question in (32):

(34)   If A makes a request for information of B about whether an action X has been performed, or under what conditions Z X will be performed, and the four pre-conditions of (33) hold, then A will be heard as making a mitigated request for action with the underlying form *B: do X!*

B's response "oh, why?" is then aimed not at the surface request for information, but rather at the pre-condition 1 of the more abstract request for action: "Why are you asking me to come home?" By asking a question about pre-condition 1, B puts off A's request: since if any of the preconditions are not shared knowledge, the request is obviously not valid by rule (33). A's next move in this discourse is to respond to B's request for information: she explains that the housework and her studies are altogether too much for her to do. Thus the content of A's response shows that she interprets B's question as we do here.

We now find intuitively that the original request of (32) is still in force, under the operation of a further invariant rule which states generally that

(35)   If A has made a request, and B responds with a request for information, A re-instates the original request by supplying that information.

Since the original request is put again, B must now respond a second time. This time B puts off the request by asking another question involving pre-condition 2–B's ability to do X.

---

[45]   Harvey Sacks has pointed out the first decision to be made in the interpretation of any utterance is whether it is serious or not (or we might say, the degree of seriousness involved). Appropriate reactions to jokes are limited, and almost independent of context, but if the utterance is serious more complex rules must be invoked. Rule (33) shows us one formal basis for this decision.

(36) A: Well, things are getting just a little too much . . . [laugh]
      This is – it's just getting too hard . . .
    B: Well, why don't you tell Helen that?

It is obvious that the complexities of the situation do not end here. These illustrations of discourse rules should serve to show the form of such rules and the kind of primitive elements which they require. Although this exposition is based upon several years of analysis of therapeutic interviews and other speech events, it is not put forward with the same confidence as the solutions to the problems of sections 2 and 3. On the contrary, discourse analysis is at a much more primitive stage, analogous to the earliest developments in syntax and morphology. It is a matter of some interest that the most significant advances in this field have not been made by linguists, but by sociologists. The work of Sacks (1969) and Schegloff (1968) has located many fundamental questions concerning the selection of speakers, the identification of persons, and isolated a number of sequencing rules. Linguists have been handicapped in their approach to this field by their inability to utilize such essential social constructs involving the roles of speaker and listener, obligations, power relationships, membership categories, and the like.

It should be evident that the approach to the study of language in its social context outlined in sections 2-3 of this paper can easily accommodate the full range of elements which we need for discourse rules. The linguistic approach can contribute a number of concepts which are not well developed in anthropology or sociology. First there is the distinction between utterances and actions, and the hierarchical relations of actions whereby a question may be seen as a request for information, which is in turn interpreted as a request for action, which may appear on a higher level as a challenge. Further advancement of this field may proceed from the linguistic concept of an invariant rule, and the linguistic approach to the formalization of such rules.

Eventually, the exploration of discourse rules will reach a quantitative phase in which variable rules may be constructed and in which large bodies of data can be introduced to confirm or reject the tentative rules we have written. One area which plainly involves variable rules is in the degree of mitigation or aggravation which governs the selection of rules for making requests. We observe that in (32) the daughter *must* mitigate her request; to say to her mother "Come home right now!" would be violating a strong social constraint, although a mother can easily say this to her daughter. The exact degree of mitigation, and the way in which the request is executed involve a number of variables: age, socio-economic class, relative status of speaker and listener, and the form of the preceding utterance. Such variable constraints will eventually appear in rules comparable to those written in sections 2 and 3. But our present knowledge is too fragmentary to make such attempts fruitful.[46] Quantitative research implies that one knows what to count, and this knowledge is reached only through a long period of trial and approximation, and upon the basis of a solid body of theoretical constructs. By the time the analyst knows what to count, the problem is practically solved.

In recent years, there have been many attempts by social psychologists to characterize differences in the use of language by middle class and working class speakers (Bernstein 1966, Lawton 1968). There is little connection between the general statements made and the quantitative data offered on the use of language. It is said that middle class speakers show more verbal planning, more abstract arguments, more objective viewpoint, show more logical connections, and so on. But one does not uncover the logical complexity of a body of speech by counting the number of subordinate clauses. The cognitive style of a speaker has no fixed relation to the number of unusual adjectives or conjunctions that he uses. As the example given above shows, no useful purpose would be served by counting the number of questions that someone asks in an interview. The relation of argument and discourse to language is much more abstract than this, and such superficial indices can be quite deceptive. When we can say what is being done with a sentence, then we will be able to observe how often speakers do it.

5. THE STATE OF LINGUISTICS

In the introduction to this review, I suggested that linguistics was suffering from difficulty in coming to grips with the fundamental data of language. In this respect, our field is no different from any other social science. Linguists did take the somewhat unusual step of redefining their field so that the every-day use of language in the community would be placed outside of linguistics proper – to be called *speech,* not language. Rather than worry about the difficulties of dealing with this material, we concluded that it was quite unnecessary, on theoretical grounds, for us to account for it; indeed, it was argued that a linguist *should* not be concerned with the facts of speech.

---

[46] The most thorough examination of a speech event which we have carried out so far is the analysis of ritual insults in the Negro community (Labov et al. 1968:4.3, Labov 1969b). Although the discourse rules given there seem to be sound, we do not have the means of corroboration which are available in our studies of linguistic structure.

Just how long such a program can continue to be productive is an open question. Clearly linguistics has benefited from a restriction of its field of view. If at this point linguistics is more advanced than any other study of social behavior, it is no doubt due to the highly structured nature of our object rather than the peculiar excellence of our strategy. In this paper, I have taken up a number of problems where progress has been blocked, where a broader field of view seems to be required to come to a decisive solution. The analysis of language out of context will undoubtedly continue as a separate pursuit; as before, we will find some linguists who spend all of their time analyzing their intuitions about language, as others will work with texts or carry out laboratory experimentation. My own view is that such activity will be increasingly valued as a necessary preliminary to the development of linguistic research. But linguistic theory can no more ignore the social behavior of speakers of a language than chemical theory can ignore the observed properties of the elements.

The penalties for ignoring data from the speech community are a growing sense of frustration, a proliferation of moot questions, and a conviction that linguistics is a game in which each theorist chooses the solution that fits his taste or intuition. I do not believe that we need at this point a new 'theory of language'; rather, we need a new way of doing linguistics that will yield decisive solutions. By enlarging our view of language, we encounter the possibility of being right: of finding answers that are supported by an unlimited number of reproducible measurements, in which the inevitable bias of the observer is cancelled out by the convergence of many approaches. There are many linguists who do not believe that there is a 'right' or 'wrong'; the nature of their work does not allow such convergence or confirmation.

I do not mean, of course, that a particular solution offered is right in any absolute sense. No one can doubt that his best effort will be criticized, modified, replaced, or perhaps re-emerge in an almost unrecognizable form. But within the framework provided, the solutions offered to the problems of consonant cluster simplification, copula deletion, and negative concord represent abstract relations of linguistic elements that are deeply embedded in the data. It is reasonable to believe that they are more than constructions of the analyst – that they are properties of language itself. The state of linguistics is indeed promising if we can assert this about any single result of our research.

BIBLIOGRAPHY

Anshen, Frank
    1969   "Speech Variation Among Negroes in a Small Southern Community",
           Unpublished N. Y. U. dissertation.

Bailey, Charles-James N.
1969a "The Integration of Linguistic Theory: Internal Reconstruction and the Comparative Method in Descriptive Linguistics", with an Appendix of 107 pan-dialectal ordered rules. Paper given before Conference on Historical Linguistics in the Light of Generative Theory, Los Angeles.
1969b "Introduction to Southern States Phonetics", University of Hawaii Working Papers in Linguistics 4-5.

Bernstein, Basil
1964 "Elaborated and Restricted Codes", In Gumperz and Hymes 1964, pp. 55-69.

Bloch, Bernard
1948 "A Set of Postulates for Phonemic Analysis", *Language* 24:3-46.

Bloomfield, Leonard
1933 *Language* (New York: Henry Holt). Chapters "Secondary and Tertiary
1944 Responses to Language", *Language* 20:45-55.

Bright, W. (ed.)
1966 *Sociolinguistics* (The Hague: Mouton).

Chomsky, Noam
1955 *Syntactic Structures* (The Hague: Mouton)
1965 *Aspects of the Theory of Syntax* (Cambridge, Mass.: MIT Press).
1966 "Topics in the Theory of Generative Grammar", in (T. Sebeok, ed.) *Current Trends in Linguistics 3: Linguistic Theory* (Bloomington, Ind.: Indiana University Press).

de Saussure, Ferdinand
1962 *Cours de Linguistique générale* (Paris: Payot).

Elliott, Dale, Stanley Legum and Sandra Thompson
1969 "Syntactic Variation as Linguistic Data", mimeographed.

Ervin-Tripp, Susan
1967 'Sociolinguistics", Working Paper No. 3, Language Behavior Research Laboratory, Berkeley.

Fischer, John L.
1958 "Social Influences on the Choice of a Linguistic Variant", *Word* 14:47-56.

Fishman, Joshua A.
1969 "Sociolinguistics" in (Kurt W. Back, ed.) *Social Psychology* (New York: Wiley).

Fishman. Joshua A. (ed.)
1968 *Readings in the Sociology of Language* (The Hague: Mouton).

Fishman, Joshua A., Robert L. Cooper, Roxana Ma, et al.
1968 *Bilingualism in the Barrio*. Final Report on OEC-1-7-062817. Washington, D.C.: Office of Education. Published version: 1971 (Indiana University) Language Science Monographs, 7. .

Garfinckel, Harold
1967 *Studies in Ethnomethodology* (Englewood Cliffs, N.J.: Prentice-Hall)

Grant, W. and J. Dixon
1921 *Manual of Modern Scots* (Cambridge).

Grimshaw, Allen D.
1968 "Sociolinguistics", in (Wilbur Schramm et al., eds.) *Handbook of Communication* (New York: Rand McNally and Co).

Gumperz, John J.
1967 "On the Linguistic Markers of Bilingual Communication", in (John Mcnamara, ed.), *Problems of Bilingualism (The Journal of Social Is-*

sues Vol. 23, No. 2) pp. 48-57.

Gumperz, John and Dell Hymes (eds.)
1964   *The Ethnography of Communication, American Anthropologist,* Vol. 66, No. 6, Part 2.

Hafner, E. M. and Susan Presswood
1965   "Strong Inference and Weak Interactions", *Science* 149:503-509.

Hockett, Charles F.
1958   *A Course in Modern Linguistics* (New York: Macmillan).

Homans, George C.
1958   *The Human Group* (New York: Harcourt, Brace and Co.).

Hymes, Dell
1966   "Introduction: Toward Ethnographies of Communication", in Gumperz and Hymes 1964, pp. 1-34.

Hymes, Dell
1962   "The Ethnography of Speaking", in (T. Gladwin and W. C. Sturtevant, eds.) *Anthropology and Human Behavior* (Washington, D.C.: The Anthropological Society of Washington) pp. 13-53. Reprinted in Fishman 1968.

Klima, Edward S.
1964   "Negation in English", in (J. A. Fodor and J. J. Katz eds.), *The Structure of Language* (Englewood Cliffs, N. J.: Prentice-Hall).

Kučera, Henry
1961   *The Phonology of Czech* (The Hague: Mouton).

Labov, William
1963   "The Social Motivation of a Sound Change", *Word* 19:273-309.
1965   "On the Mechanism of Linguistic Change", *Georgetown University Monograph No. 18, Language and Linguistics* (Washington, D.C.: Georgetown University).
1966a *The Social Stratification of English in New York City* (Washington, D.C.: Center for Applied Linguistics).
1966b "On the Grammaticality of Every-Day Speech", Paper given before the Linguistic Society of America, New York City.
1969a "Contraction, Deletion, and Inherent Variability of the English Copula", *Language* 45.
1969b "Rules for Ritual Insults", in (D. Sudnow, ed.), *Studies in Social Interaction* (New York: MacMillan).

Labov, William, Paul Cohen, Clarence Robins, and John Lewis
1968   "A Study of the Non-Standard English of Negro and Puerto Rican Speakers in New York City". Final Report, Cooperative Research Project 3288. Vols. I and II. Washington, D.C.: Office of Education.

Lambert, Wallace E.
1967   "A Social Psychology of Bilingualism", in (J. Macnamara, ed.) *Problems of Bilingualism (The Journal of Social Issues* 23:2) pp. 91-109.

Levine, Lewis and Harry J. Crockett, Jr.
1966   "Speech Variation in a Piedmont Community: Postvocalic r", in Lieberson 1966, pp. 91-109.

Lieberson, Stanley (ed.)
1966   *Exploration in Sociolinguistics, Sociological Inquiry* 36:2. Reprinted as Publication 44, *International Journal of American Linguistics.*

Lawton, Denis
1968   *Social Class, Language and Education* (London: Routledge and Kegan Paul).

Lévi-Strauss, Claude
  1963 *Structural Anthropology*, tr. C. Jacobson and B. Schoepf (New York: Basic Books).
Lyons, John
  1968 *Introduction to Theoretical Linguistics* (Cambridge: Cambridge University Press).
Martinet, Andre
  1965 *Economie des changements phonétiques* (Berne: Francke).
Meillet, Antoine
  1921 *Linguistique historique et linguistique générale* (Paris: La Société Linguistique de Paris).
Postal, Paul
  1968a "Cross-over Constraints", Paper given at the Linguistic Society of America, New York City.
  1968b "The Cross-Over Principle", mimeographed (Yorktown Heights, N.Y.: I.B.M.)
Quirk, Randolph
  1966 "Acceptability in Language", *Proceedings of the University of Newcastle upon Tyne Philosophical Society* 1:79-92.
Reich, Peter
  1968 "On the Finiteness of Natural Language", mimeographed.
Sacks, Harvey
  1969 "The Search for Help", in (D. Sudnow, ed.) *Studies in Social Interaction* (New York: MacMillan).
Schegloff, Emmanuel
  1968 "Sequencing in Conversational Openings", *American Anthropologist* 70:1075-1095.
Shuy, Roger, Walt Wolfram and William K. Riley
  1967 *A Study of Social Dialects in Detroit.* Final Report, Project 6-1347. Washington, D.C.: Office of Education.
Solomon, Denis
  1966 "The System of Predication in the Speech of Trinidad", unpublished Columbia University Master's Essay.
Vygotsky, L. S.
  1962 *Thought and Language*, tr. by E. Hanfmann and G. Vakar (Cambridge, Mass.: M. I. T. Press).
Wang, William S.-Y.
  1969 "Competing changes as a cause of residue", *Language* 45:9-25.
Watson, James D.
  1969 *The Double Helix* (New York: New American Library).
Weinreich, Uriel, William Labov and Marvin Herzog
  1968 "Empirical Foundations for a Theory of Language Change", in (W. P. Lehmann and Y. Malkiel, eds.), *Directions for Historical Linguistics* (Austin, Tex: University of Texas Press).
Whorf, Benjamin L.
  1943 "Phonemic Analysis of the English of Eastern Massachusetts", *Studies in Linguistics* 2:21-40.
Wolfram, Walter
  1969 "Linguistic Correlates of Social Stratification in the Speech of Detroit Negroes", Hartford Seminary Foundation Thesis.

Joshua A. Fishman

THE SOCIOLOGY OF LANGUAGE: AN INTERDISCIPLINARY SOCIAL SCIENCE APPROACH TO LANGUAGE IN SOCIETY*

1.0 INTRODUCTION

Man is constantly using language – spoken language, written language, printed language – and man is constantly linked to others via shared norms of behavior. The sociology of language examines the interaction between these two aspects of human behavior: use of language and the social organization of behavior. Briefly put, the sociology of language focuses upon the entire gamut of topics related to the social organization of language behavior, including not only language usage per se but also language attitudes, overt behaviors toward language and toward language users.

1.1 Sociolinguistic Headlines

The latter concern of the sociology of language – overt behavior toward language and toward language users – is a concern shared by political and educational leaders in many parts of the world and is an aspect of sociolinguistics that frequently makes headlines in the newspapers. Many French-Canadian university students oppose the continuation of public education in English in the Province of Quebec. Many Flemings in Belgium protest vociferously against anything less than full equality – at the very least – for Dutch in the Brussels area. Some Welsh nationalists daub out English signs along the highways in Wales and many Irish revivalists seek stronger governmental support for the restoration of Irish than that made avail-

* From Current Trends in Linguistics, 12, in press. Reprinted with permission.

able during half a century of Irish independence. Jews throughout
the world protest the Soviet government's extermination of Yiddish
writers and the forced closing of Yiddish schools, theaters and publications.

Swahili, Philipino, Indonesian, Malay and the various provincial
languages of India are all being consciously expanded in vocabulary
and standardized in spelling and grammar so that they can increasingly
function as the exclusive language of government and of higher culture and technology. The successful revival and modernization of
Hebrew has encouraged other smaller communities – the Catalans, the
Provencals, the Frisians, the Bretons – to strive to save *their* ethnic
mother tongues (or their traditional cultural tongues) from oblivion.
New and revised writing systems are being accepted – and at times,
rejected – in many parts of the world by communities that hitherto had
little interest in literacy in general or in literacy in their mother tongues
in particular.

Such examples of consciously organized behavior toward language
and toward users of particular languages can be listed almost endlessly.
The list becomes truly endless if we include examples from earlier
periods of history, such as the displacement of Latin as the language
of religion, culture and government in Western Christendom and the
successive cultivation of once lowly vernaculars – first in Western
Europe, and then, subsequently, in Central, Southern and Eastern
Europe, and, finally, in Africa and Asia as well. Instead of being
viewed (as was formerly the case) as merely fit for folksy talk and
for common folk the vernaculars have come to be viewed, used and
developed as *independent* languages, as languages suitable for *all*
higher purposes, and as languages of state-*building* and state-*deserving*
nationalities. All of these examples feed into modern sociology of
language, providing it with historical breadth and depth in addition to
its ongoing interest in current language issues throughout the world.

1.2 Subdivisions of the Sociology of Language

However, the subject matter of the sociology of language reaches far
beyond interest in case studies and very far beyond cataloging and
classifying the instances of language conflict and language planning
reported in chronicles, old and new. The ultimate quest of the sociology of language is pursued diligently in many universities
throughout the United States and other parts of the world, and is
very far from dealing directly with headlines or news reports. One
part of this quest is concerned with describing the generally accepted social organization of language usage within a speech community

(or, to be more exact, within speech and writing communities). This part of the sociology of language – *descriptive sociology of language* – seeks to answer the question "who speaks (or writes) what language (or what language variety) to whom and when and to what end?" Descriptive sociology of language tries to disclose the norms of language usage – that is to say, the generally accepted social patterns of language use and of behavior and attitude toward language – for particular social networks and communities, both large and small. Another part of the sociology of language – *dynamic sociology of language* – seeks to answer the question "what accounts for different rates of change in the social organization of language use and behavior toward language?" Dynamic sociology of language tries to explain why and how the social organization of language use and behavior toward language can be selectively different in the *same* social networks or communities on two different occasions. Dynamic sociology of language also seeks to explain why and how once similar social networks or communities can arrive at quite different social organizations of language use and behavior toward language.

These two subdivisions taken together i.e. descriptive sociology of language *plus* dynamic sociology of language constitute the sociology of language, a *whole* which is *greater than the mere sum of its parts*.

1.3 Language IS Content; the Medium IS (at Least Partly) the Message

Newspaper headlines with all of their stridency may serve to remind us of a truism that is too frequently overlooked by too many Americans, namely, that language is not merely a *means* of interpersonal communication and influence. It is not merely a *carrier* of content, whether latent, or manifest. Language itself *is* content, a referent for loyalties and animosities, an indicator of social statuses and personal relationships, a marker of situations and topics as well as of the societal goals and the large-scale value-laden arenas of interaction that typify every speech community.

Any speech community of even moderate complexity reveals several varieties of language, all of which are functionally differentiated from each other. In some cases the varieties may represent different occupational or interest specializations ('shop talk', 'hippie talk', etc.) and, therefore, contain vocabulary, pronunciation and phraseology which are not generally used or even known throughout the broader speech community. As a result, the speakers of specialized varieties may not always employ them. Not only must they switch to other varieties of language when they interact in less specialized (or differently specialized) networks within the broader speech community of which they are a part, but most of them do not even use their specialized varieties all of the time with one another. On some occasions, interlocutors who *can* speak a particular specialized variety to one another nevertheless do not do so, but, instead switch to a different variety of language which is either in wider use or which is indicative of quite a different set of interests and relationships than is associated with their specialized variety. This type of switching represents the raw data of descriptive sociology of language, the discipline that seeks to determine (among other things) who speaks what variety of what language to whom, when and concerning what.

The varieties of language that exist within a speech community need not all represent occupational or interest specializations. Some varieties may represent social class (economic, educational, ethnic) distinctions within coterritorial populations. 'Brooklynese' and 'Cockney' English within New York and London, respectively, do not connote foreignness or even a particular section of the city as much as lower class status in terms of income, education or ethnicity. Nevertheless, many individuals who have left lower class status behind can and do switch back and forth between Brooklynese and more regionally standard New York English when speaking to each other, depending on their feelings toward each other, the topic under discussion, where they happen to be when they are conversing and several other factors, all of which can exhibit variation and, as a result, can be signalled by switching from one variety of English to another.

A speech community that has available to it several varieties of language may be said to possess a *verbal repertoire*. Such repertoires may not only consist of different specialized varieties and different social class varieties but may also reveal different regional varieties (Boston English, Southern English, Midwestern English and other widely, and roughly, designated dialects of American English are regional varieties), if the speech community is sufficiently large such that enclaves come to arise within it on a geographic basis alone. Furthermore, multilingual speech communities may employ, for the purpose of *intragroup* communication, all of the above types or varieties of language within each of the codes that the community recognizes as 'distinct' languages (e.g. within Yiddish *and* Hebrew, among most pre-World War II Eastern European Jews; within English *and* Hindi, among many upper-class individuals in India today, etc.).

Regardless of the nature of the language varieties involved in the verbal repertoire of a speech community (occupational, social class, regional, etc.) and regardless of the interaction between them (for initially regional dialects may come to represent social varieties as well, and vice versa) descriptive sociology of language seeks to disclose their linguistic and functional characteristics and to determine how much of the entire speech community's verbal repertoire is available to various smaller interaction networks within that community since the entire verbal repertoire of a speech community may be more extensive than the verbal repertoire controlled by sub-groups within that community. Dynamic sociology of language on the other hand seeks to determine how changes in the fortunes and interactions of networks of speakers alter the ranges (complexity) of their verbal repertoires.

All in all, the sociology of language seeks to discover not only the societal rules or norms that explain and constrain language behavior and *the behavior toward language* in speech communities but it also seeks to determine the symbolic value of language varieties for their speakers. That language varieties come to have symbolic or symptomatic value, in and of themselves, is an inevitable consequence of their functional differentiation. If certain varieties are indicative of certain interests, of certain backgrounds, or of certain origins, then they come to represent the ties and aspirations, the limitations and the opportunities with which these interests, backgrounds and origins, in turn, are associated. Language varieties rise and fall in symbolic value as the status of their most characteristic or marked functions rises and falls. Varieties come to represent intimacy and equality if they are most typically learned and employed in interactions that stress such bonds between interlocutors. Other varieties come to represent educated status or national identification as a result of the attainments associated with their use and their users and as a result of their realization in situations and relationships that pertain to formal learning or to particular ideologies. However, these functions are capable of change (and of being consciously changed), just as the linguistic features of the varieties themselves may change (and may be consciously changed), and just as the demographic distribution of users of a variety within a particular speech community may change.

The step-by-step elevation of most modern European vernaculars to their current positions as languages of culture and technology is only one example of how dramatically the operative and symbolic functions of languages can change. Similar changes are ongoing today:

Since the preservation of adequate control over the labour force loomed so large in the minds of the early planters, various devices have evolved, of which the maintenance of castelike distance was perhaps the one most significantly affecting race relations. One thinks immediately of the frequently cited admonition in the *Rabaul Times* of August 8, 1926, by a veteran

Territorian, "Never talk to the boys in any circumstances. Apart from your house-boy and boss-boy, never allow any native to approach you in the field or on the bungalow veranda." This free advice to the uninitiated planters was, no doubt, intended to preserve "White prestige", but it was also conceived as a protective device to "keep labour in its place". So also the Melanesian Pidgin, which had come into being as a medium of interchange in trade, subsequently acquired, on the plantations, the character of a language of command by which the ruling caste "talked down" to its subordinates and "put them in their place". A wide range of plantation etiquette symbolizing proper deference by workers toward their masters and expressed in expected form of address and servile conduct gave further protection to the system and any signs of insubordination or "cheekiness" on the part of the workers might be vigorously punished and rationalised by the planter as a threat to the system." (Lind 1969, p. 36)

Yet today, barely half a century since Melanesian Pidgin began to expand, it has been renamed Neo-Melanesian and is being groomed by many New Guineans to become their country's national language, and, as such to be used in government, education, mass media, religion and high culture more generally (Wurm 1961/62).

The sociology of language is the study of the characteristics of language varieties, the characteristics of their functions, and the characteristics of their speakers as these three constantly interact, change, and change one another, both within and between speech communities.

2.0 SOME REASONS WHY THE SOCIOLOGY OF LANGUAGE HAS ONLY RECENTLY BEGUN TO DEVELOP

Given the obvious importance of the sociology of language, given its apparent interest for all who are interested in either or both of its parent disciplines (as well as for all who wish better to understand events and processes all over the world), and, finally, given the substantial applied promise of the sociology of language for educational and governmental use, it is quite natural to ask: why is the sociology of languages only now coming into its own? Actually, the sociology of language, as a field of interest within linguistics and the social sciences, is not as new as its recent prominence may suggest. The 19th and early 20th century witnessed many studies and publications that belonged to this field (many are cited in Hertzler 1965). Nevertheless, it is quite true that the disciplinary priorities and biases of both fields were such that those earlier attempts were prematurely set aside and only recently has momentum been attained in this field to enable it to attract and train specialists devoted to it per se (Ferguson 1965, Fishman 1967b).

2.1 Invariant Behavior

Linguistics has classically been interested in completely regular or fully predictable behavior. The *p* in "pun" is always aspirated by native speakers of English. The *p* in "spin" is always unaspirated by these speakers. This is the kind of entirely determined relationship that linguistics has classically sought and found – to such an extent that a highly respected linguist wrote a few decades ago: "if it exists *to some degree,* it's not linguistics" (Joos 1950). The implication of this view is quite clear: linguistics is not interested in 'sometime things'. The phenomena it describes are either completely determinable occurrences or non-occurrences. Wherever some other lesser state of determinacy was noted, e.g. in usage, this was defined as 'exolinguistic', as 'free variations' that was outside of the realm or the heartland of linguistics proper.

The social sciences on the other hand, were (and remain) singularly uninterested in apparently invariant behavior. Any such behavior could only prompt the observation "so what?" from the social sciences since their preserve was and is societally patterned *variation* in behavior and the locations of those factors that parsimoniously explain and predict such variation. If one were to observe to a social scientist that the *same* individuals who *always* wore clothing when they were strolling on Fifth Avenue *never* wore any when they were bathing or showering, his reaction to his brand of societal invariance would be "so what?"

Given the above basic difference in orientations between its two parent disciplines, it is not even necessary to add that linguistics was classically too code-oriented to be concerned with societal patterns in language usage, or that sociology, e.g., was classically too stratificationally oriented to be concerned with contextual speaking (or writing) differences *within* strata. Fortunately, both fields have recently moved beyond their classical interests (see Figure 1) and, as a result, fostered the kinds of joint interests on which the sociology of language now depends.

2.2 Moderately Variable Behavior

Linguistics has, in recent years, plunged further and further into 'sometimes things' in the realm of language behavior. Some of the same speakers who say "aint" on certain occasions do *not* use it on others, and some of the same cotton-pickers who have such a colorful and unique vocabulary, phonology and grammar on occasions also

Type of Behavior	Linguistics	Social Sciences
Invariant	*Classical Interest*	*No Interest*
Moderately Variable	*Recent Growing Interest*	*Classical Interest*
Highly Variable	*Possible Future Interest*	*Recent Growing Interest*

Figure 1. The Changing Interests and Emphases of Linguistics and the Social
Sciences with Respect to Variation in Behavior
(after Labov)

share other varięties with their many non-cotton-picking friends and
associates. This is the kind of societally patterned variation in behavior
that social scientists not only recognize and understand, but it is the
kind they are particularly well prepared to help linguists study and
explain. When such behavior is reported the social scientist is oriented
toward locating the smallest number of societal factors that can account
for or predict the usage variation that has been reported.

2.3 Highly Variable Behavior

Finally, and even more recently, even more complex societally patterned variation in behavior has come to be of interest to the social
scientist. This behavior is so complexly patterned or determined that
a goodly number of explanatory variables must be utilized and combined, with various quantitative weights and controls, in order that
their total impact as well as their separate contributions can be gauged.
This kind of highly variable and complexly patterned societal behavior obviously exists (and plentifully so) with respect to language
too. However, linguists generally lack the skills of study design, data
collection and data analysis that are required in order to undertake
to clarify such multiply determined language behavior. At this level,
more than at any other, the corpus of language per se is insufficient
to explain a major proportion of the variation in language behavior
that obtains. Nor are a few demographic (age, sex, education), nor a
few contextual (formality-informality in role relationships), nor a few
situational factors sufficient for this purpose. Rather, predictors of all of these kinds are needed and, to the extent that this is so,
their joint or combined use will result in far greater explanatory or
predictive power than would any two or three of them alone. The
social sciences themselves have only rather recently become accustomed

to working with large numbers of complexly interrelated and differentially weighted variables. This is obviously a level of analysis which will become available to the sociology of language only if there is genuine cooperation between linguists and social scientists.

The sociology of language is thus a by-product of a very necessary and very recent awareness on the part of linguistics and the social sciences that they do indeed need each other in order to explore their joint interests in a productive and provocative manner. This cooperative attitude has yielded important results in the few years that it has been actively pursued (Grimshaw 1969, Hymes 1967a) and we may expect even more from it in the future when a greater number of individuals who are themselves specialists in *both fields simultaneously* (or in the joint field per se) will have been trained.

2.4 Variability and Predictability

While it is, of course, true that the more variable behavior is, the more the factors that need to be located in order to account for it in any substantial way, the less predictable the behavior is until the proper factors have been located and combined or weighted in the most appropriate ways. Ultimately, however, if the quest of rigorous data collection and data analysis is successful, as high a level of predictability or explainability may be attained with respect to complexly determined and highly variable behaviors as with the far less and the somewhat less complexly determined and variable ones. Thus, the methodological differences that have existed between linguistics and sociology have been primarily differences in the extent to which a very few well chosen parameters could account substantially for the behaviors that the respective disciplines choose to highlight. Ultimately, all disciplines of human behavior – including linguistics and sociology – strive to locate and to interrelate the most parsimonious set of explanatory-predictive variables in order to maximally account for the variability to which their attention is directed.

With respect to societally patterned language behavior, there is doubtlessly variability that can be well-nigh perfectly accounted for by a very few well selected intra-code positional factors. Social scientists should recognize such behavior for it not only leads them to a recognition of linguistics per se but to the clearer realization that the entire world of socially patterned variability in language behavior still remains to be explored – and to be explored by linguists and social scientists together – after 'the variability explainable on the basis of intra-code factors alone has been accounted for. However, at that level of inquiry it is *not* possible to simply put linguistics aside and, turning to more exciting and difficult tasks, simply to 'do social science'. Studies of more complexly determined and more highly variable socially patterned language behaviors still require rigorous descriptions and analyses of language usage per se and for such analyses the social sciences will always be dependent on linguistics.

3.0 SOME BASIC SOCIOLINGUISTIC CONCEPTS

The sociology of language deals with quite a range of topics: small group interaction and large group membership, language use and language attitudes, language-and-behavior norms as well as changes in these norms. We expect to deal with all of these topics, at least briefly, in this presentation, and, necessarily, to introduce the technical terms and concepts which specialized fields of discourse inevitably require. However, before moving into any of these more specialized substantive topics there are a number of basic sociolinguistic concepts that are of such general intertopic utility that we had best pause to consider them here, rather than to permit them to remain as primitives any longer.

3.1 Language-Dialect-Variety

The term *variety* is frequently utilized in sociology of language as a nonjudgemental designation. The very fact that an objective, unemotional, technical term is *needed* in order to refer to 'a kind of language' is, in itself, an indication that the expression 'a language' is often a judgmental one, a term that is *indicative* of emotion and opinion, as well as a term that *elicits* emotion and opinion. This is an important fact about languages and one to which we will return repeatedly. As a result, we will use the term 'variety' in order not to become trapped in the very phenomena that we seek to investigate, namely, when and by whom is a certain variety considered to be a language and when and by whom is it considered something else.

Those varieties that initially and basically represent divergent geographic origins are known as *dialects* (Ferguson and Gumperz 1960; Halliday 1964b). It is in this purely objective sense of the word that it is used in such terms as *dialectology* and *dialect geography* within linguistics, and it is in this sense that the sociology of language employs it as well. However, dialects may easily come to represent (to stand for, to connote, to symbolize) other factors than geographic ones. If immigrants from region A come to be a large portion of the poor, the disliked and the illiterate in region B, then their speech variety (Dialect A) will come to stand for much more than geographic origin alone in the minds of the inhabitants of region B. Dialect A will come to stand for lower social status (educationally, occupationally) than will dialect B. In this way what was once a *regional variety* (in the sense that a particular time its speakers were viewed as merely concentrated in a particular area) may come to be viewed (and to function) much more importantly as a *social variety* or *sociolect* (Blanc 1964). Furthermore, if the speakers of variety A are given hardly any access into the interaction networks of region B, if they marry primarily only each other, engage primarily in their original regional customs and continue to value only each other's company, they may, in time, come to consider themselves a different society, with goals, beliefs and traditions of their own. As a result, variety A may no longer be viewed as a social variety but, rather, as an *ethnic* or *religious* variety and, indeed, it may come to be cultivated as such to the point of being viewed as a separate *language* (Kloss 1967; Fishman 1968c). However, within the community of A speakers there may come to be some who have learned B as well. They may utilize A with each other for purposes of intimacy and in-group solidarity but they may also use B with each other for occupational and deferential purposes. Thus, for them, A and B will be contrasted and complementary *functional varieties*, with B also being (or including) a *specialized* (occupational or other experiential) *variety* and, therefore, in some ways different than variety B as used by others (Weinreich M. 1953).

The above theoretical sketch has more than general didactic value. It represents the route that many varieties – regional and social – have travelled in the past and the route on which still others are embarked at this very time (Haugen 1966c; Deutsch 1966). Nevertheless, it is the *general* point that is of particular value to us at this juncture. Varieties may be viewed as regional at one time and social at another. Varieties may be reacted to as regional within the speech community of their users and as social (or ethnic) by outsiders. Varieties may have additional functional uses for some of their users that they do not have for others who possess fewer contrasted varieties in their verbal repertoires. Thus, the term variety – unlike the term dialect – indicates no particular linguistic status (other than difference) vis-a-vis other varieties. A dialect must be a regional *sub*-unit in relation to a language, particularly in its vernacular or spoken realization. 'Language' is a superordinate designation; 'dialect' is a subordinate designation. Both terms require that the entire taxonomy to which they pertain be known before they themselves can be accepted.

The sociology of language is interested in them only in so far as members of speech communities contend over which is which, and why. As the result of such contention varieties hitherto considered to be dialects may throw off their subordination and be 'promoted' by their speakers to official and independent status, whereas formerly independent languages may be subordinated. The term variety, on the other hand, merely designates a member of a verbal repertoire. Its use implies only that there are other varieties as well. These can be specified by outsiders on the basis of the phonological, lexical and grammatical differences that they (the varieties) manifest. Their functional allocations, however – as languages or as dialects – are derivable only from societal observation of their uses and users rather than from any characteristics of the codes themselves.

Varieties change over time but varieties are also *changed*, either by drift or by design. Varieties that have been used in palaces and universities may later come to be used only by the rural and unlettered. In this process their lexicons may well become impoverished (hundreds or thousands of the terms once needed dropping into disuse). At the same time lexicons, grammars as well as phonologies may become much influenced by other temporarily more prestigeful and possibly genetically unrelated varieties. Conversely, varieties that had never been used outside of the most humble speech networks may be elevated in function, increased in lexicon and purified or enriched in whatever direction their circumstantially improved speakers may desire (Kloss 1952, 1967; Fishman 1968c). All varieties of all languages are equally expandable and changeable; all are equally contractable and interpenetrable under the influence of foreign models. Their virtues are in the eyes (or ears) of their beholders. Their functions depend on the norms of the speech communities that employ them. These norms, in turn, change as speech communities change in self-concept, in their relations with surrounding communities and in their objective circumstances. Finally, such changes usually lead to changes in the varieties themselves. Speech communities and their varieties are not only interrelated systems; they are completely interdependent systems as well. It is this interdependence that the sociology of language examines.

3.2 Major Types of Attitudes and Behaviors toward Language

One of the best known societal behaviors toward language is *Standardization,* i.e., "the codification and acceptance, within a community of users, of a formal set of norms defining 'correct' usage " (Stewart 1968). Codification is, typically, the concern of such language 'gatekeepers' as scribes, storytellers, grammarians, teachers and writers, i.e., of certain groups that arise in most diversified societies and whose use of language is professional and conscious. Given codification as a goal, this desired 'good' is formulated and presented to all or part of the speech community via such means as grammars, dictionaries, spellers, style manuals, and exemplary texts, whether written or oral. Finally, the acceptance of the formally codified (i.e. the standardized) variety of a language is advanced via such agencies and authorities as the government, the educational system, the mass media, the religious institutions and the cultural 'establishment'. The standard variety then becomes associated with such institutions, the types of interactions that most commonly occur within them, and the values or goals they represent (Haugen 1966a).

Note that not all languages have standard varieties. Note also, that where a standard variety does exist it does not necessarily displace the non-standard varieties from the linguistic repertoire of the speech community for functions that are distinct from but complementary to those of the standard variety. Note, additionally, that there may be several competing standard varieties in the same speech community. Note, finally, that hitherto non-standard varieties may themselves undergo standardization whereas hitherto standardized varieties may undergo de-standardization as their speakers no longer view them as worthy of codification and cultivation. Standardization is not a property of any language per se, but a characteristic societal treatment of language given sufficient societal diversity and need for symbolic elaboration.

Another common societal view of language is that which is concerned with its *autonomy*, i.e., with the uniqueness and independence of the linguistic system or, at least, of some variety within that system. *Autonomy* is often of little concern to speech communities whose languages differ markedly from each other. These may be said to be autonomous by dint of sheer *abstand* or linguistic distance between them (Kloss 1952; Kloss 1967). On the other hand, where languages seem to be quite similar to each other – phonologically, lexically and grammatically – it may be of great concern to establish their autonomy from each other, or at least that of the weaker from the stronger. Were such autonomy not to be established it might occur to some that one was 'no more than' a dialect (a regional variety) of the other, a subservience which may become part of a rationale for political subservience as well.

A major vehicle of fostering autonomy views concerning a language is its standardization. The availability of dictionaries and grammars is taken as a sure sign that a particular variety is 'really a language'. However, the availability of dictionaries and grammars not only *represents* autonomy, but also cultivates and increases it by introducing new vocabulary and stressing those phonological and grammatical alternatives that are most different from those of any given autonomy-threatening contrast language. "Heroes are made, not born." The same is true of the autonomy of genetically (historically) related languages. Their autonomy has to be worked on. It is not autonomy by *abstand*, but, rather, by *ausbau* (by effort, and, often, by fiat or decree), and pertains particularly to their standard (and most particularly to their written standard) varieties.

It is a characteristic of the newly rich to supply their own ancestors. In a similar vein those speech communities, the autonomy of whose standard variety is based most completely on *ausbau*-activity, are also most likely to be concerned with its *historicity*, that is with its 'respectable' ancestry in times long past. As a result, many speech communities create and cultivate myths and genealogies concerning the origin and development of their standard varieties in order to de-emphasize the numerous components of more recent vintage that they contain (Ferguson 1959b). As a result of the widespread preference for historicity, currently utilized (and recently liberated or standardized) varieties are found to be derived from ancient prototypes that had largely been forgotten, or are found to be the language of the gods, or to have been created by the same miraculous and mysterious forces and processes that created the speech community itself, etc. Thus, a variety achieves historicity by coming to be associated with some great ideological or national movement or tradition (Fishman 1965c). Usually, historicity provides the ex post facto rationale for functional changes that have transpired with respect to the verbal repertoire of a speech community.

Finally, a speech community's behavior toward any one or another of the varieties in its linguistic repertoire is likely to be determined, at least in part, by the degree to which these varieties have visible *vitality*, i.e., interaction networks that actually employ them natively for one or more vital functions. The more numerous and the more important the native speakers of a particular variety are the greater its vitality and the greater its potential for standardization, autonomy and historicity. Conversely, the fewer the number and the lower the status of the native speakers of a variety, the more it may be reacted to as if it were somehow a defective or contaminated instrument, unworthy of serious efforts or functions, and lacking in proper parentage or uniqueness. As usual such biased views are likely to be self-fulfilling in that when the numbers and the resources of the users of a given variety dwindle they are less likely to be able to protect its standardization, autonomy or historicity from the inroads of other speech communities and their verbal repertoires and language-enforcing resources.

ATTRIBUTES*

1	2	3	4	VARIETY-TYPE	SYMBOL
+	+	+	+	Standard	S
—	+	+	+	Vernacular	V
—	—	+	+	Dialect	D
—	—	—	+	Creole	K
—	—	—	—	Pidgin	P
+	+	+	—	Classical	C
+	+	—	—	Artificial	A

*1 = standardization, 2 = autonomy, 3 = historicity, 4 = vitality

Figure 2. Evaluations of different types of language varieties (Stewart 1968)

Given these four widespread patterns of societal belief and behavior toward language, it is possible to define seven different kinds of varieties, depending upon their absence or presence at any given time (Figure 2). Note, however, that any speech community may include in its repertoire a number of such varieties which are differentiable on the basis of the four widespread belief-and-behavior systems just discussed. Furthermore, occupational, social class and other experiential subvarieties are likely to exist within most of the varieties listed in Figure 2. Indeed, the members of any given community may not agree as to whether standardization, autonomy, historicity and/or vitality are absent or present in connection with one or more of the varieties in their repertoire. After all, these dimensions are highly evaluational, rather than objective characteristics of language varieties per se, and as such, variation in evaluations may be expected both synchronically (at any particular time) as well as diachronically (across time).

In some speech communities deference due an interlocutor with whom one stands in a particular role-relationship may be indicated by switching from one social class variety or from one dialect to another. In other speech communities this very same function may be realized by switching from a dialect to the standard variety (which latter variety, alone, may possess formal verb-forms and pronouns of respect). In yet another speech community a switch from one language to another (or from a dialect of one language to the standard variety of another) may be the accepted and recognized realization pattern for deferential interaction. While the precise nature of the switch will depend on the repertoire available to the speech community, switching as such and the differentia and concepts by means of which it may be noted and explained are of constant interest to sociolinguistic method and theory.

3.3 Speech Community

Speech community (a term probably translated from the German *Sprachgemeinschaft),* like variety, is a neutral term. Unlike other societal designations it does not imply any particular size nor any particular basis of communality. A speech community is one, all of whose members share at least a single speech variety and the norms for its appropriate use. A speech community may be as small as a single closed interaction network, all of whose members regard each other in but a single capacity. Neither of these limitations, however, is typical for speech communities throughout the world and neither is typical for those that have been studied by sociologists of language.

Isolated bands and nomadic clans not only represent small speech communities but speech communities that also exhaust their members' entire network-range while providing little specialization of roles or statuses. Such speech communities usually possess very limited verbal repertoires in terms of different varieties, primarily becau.ᶾ one individual's life experiences and responsibilities are pretty much like another's. Nevertheless, such similarity is likely to be more apparent than real. Even small and total societies are likely to differentiate between men and women, between minors and adults, between children and parents, between leaders and followers. Indeed, such societies are likely to have more contact with the 'outside world' than is commonly imagined, whether for purposes of trade or exogamy (Owens 1965). Thus, even small, total societies reveal functionally differentiated linguistic repertoires (and, not infrequently, intra-group bilingualism as well) based upon behaviorally differentiated interaction networks.

Such small and total (or nearly total) societies differ, of course, from equally small or even smaller family networks, friendship networks, interest networks, or occupational networks within such larger speech communities as tribes, cities or countries. In the latter cases the interaction networks are not as redundant as in the former (i.e., one more frequently interacts with *different* people in one's various roles as son, friend, work colleague, party member, etc.). However, varieties are needed not only by diverse small networks but also by large networks of individuals who rarely, if ever, interact but who have certain interests, views and allegiances in common. Thus, not only are network redundancy and network size attributes that characterize and differentiate speech communities but so is the extent to which their existence is experiential rather than merely referential.

One of the characteristics of large and diversified speech communities is that some of the varieties within their verbal repertoires are primarily experientially acquired and reinforced by dint of actual verbal interaction within particular networks, while others are primarily referentially acquired and reinforced by dint of symbolic integration within reference-networks which may rarely or never exist in any physical sense. The 'nation' or the 'region' are likely to constitute a speech community of this latter type and the standard ('national') language or the regional language is likely to represent its corresponding linguistic variety.

Many American cities present ample evidence of both of these bases – verbal interaction and symbolic integration – for the functioning of speech communities. Every day hundreds of thousands of residents of Connecticut, Up-State New York and various parts of Pennsylvania come to New York City to work and shop. In terms of waking hours of actual face-to-face verbal interaction these speakers of dialects that differ from New York City English may talk more, and more frequently, to New Yorkers than they do to inhabitants of their places of residence and to speakers of their local dialects. How then can we explain the fact that not only do most of them differentially utilize the markers of their local dialects (and not only during the evenings, week-ends and holidays when they are at home rather than at work) but the simultaneous fact that many of them can and do also employ a more regionally neutral variety, which is their approximation to 'Standard American', as distinct from New York City English on the one hand and Lower Connecticut Village English on the other? Obviously, the 'Standard American' of these commuters to New York City cannot be based on much verbal interaction with a separate network known as 'the American people'. Nor can it be based upon any other interaction network, however referred to, whose speakers use 'Standard American' and it alone. There is no other alternative but to conclude that the speech community of 'Standard American' represents a reference group for the denizens of Connecticut villages while 'Standard American' itself is a variety that has the functions of 'symbolic integration with the nation' in their linguistic repertoire.

Thus, some speech communities and their linguistic repertoires are preserved primarily by communication gaps that separate them from other communities and their repertoires. Other speech communities and their repertoires are preserved primarily by the force of symbolic (attitudinal) integration even in the absence of face-to-face interaction. Many speech communities contain networks of both types. Many networks contain both kinds of members. Societal norms that define communicative appropriateness can apply with equal force and regularity regardless of whether direct interaction or symbolic integration underlies their implementation.

As mentioned earlier, the standard variety of a language is likely to be that variety that stands for the nation as a whole and for its most exalted institutions of government, education and High Culture in general. It is this variety which comes to be associated with the mission, glory, history and uniqueness of an entire 'people' and, indeed, it is this variety which helps unite individuals who do not otherwise constitute an interaction network into a symbolic speech community or 'people'. Thus it is that standard varieties and larger-than-face-to-face speech communities are historically and functionally interdependent. While interaction networks of speakers of standard varieties doubtlessly do exist (literati, scholars, social and educational elites, etc.), these are likely to arrive at somewhat specialized usages, on the one hand, as well as to require a non-standard variety, on the other hand, if they are to engage in more intimate and informal kinds of interactions as well. Thus, the standard language per se, without further differentiation or accompaniment, is most fitted for communication across large but referential (or non-interacting) networks such as those involving the mass media, governmental pronouncements, legal codes and textbooks. The standard variety is the 'safest' for those communications in which a speaker cannot know his diversified and numerous listeners (Joos 1959). However, the more the communication is expected to live on, independently of both speaker and listener (or sender and receiver), over an appreciable period of time, the more it will be viewed as archaic (or classical) rather than merely 'standard'.

A basic definitional property of speech communities is that they are *not* defined as communities of those who "speak the same language' (notwithstanding Bloomfield 1933), but, rather, as communities set off by density of communication or/and by symbolic integration with respect to communicative competence *regardless of the number of languages or varieties employed* (Gumperz 1964a). The complexity of speech communities thus defined varies with the extent of variation in the experiential and attitudinal networks which they subsume. Speech communities can be so selected as to include greater or lesser diversity on each of these grounds. In general the verbal repertoire of a speech community is a reflection of its role repertoire (in terms of both implemented and ideologized roles). This reflection pertains not only to repertoire *range* but also to repertoire *access* and *fluidity*.

Speech communities with a larger role repertoire reveal a larger verbal repertoire as well (Gumperz 1962). Communities most of whose members are restricted in daily experiences and in life aspirations, will also tend to show little linguistic range in terms of differentiable varieties. This tends to be the case not only in the small, total communities that were mentioned earlier but also, some suspect, in large, democratic, industrialized communities of the most modern sort. Actually, both kinds of speech communities show more repertoire range (in terms of verbal repertoire and in terms of role repertoire) than is obvious on superficial inspection. Nevertheless, they both tend to have narrower (and less diversified) ranges than are encountered in the stratified speech communities that exist in intermediate societies of the traditional, non-Western World. Whereas the modern, relatively open speech community tends to reveal several varieties of the same language the more traditional speech community will typically reveal varieties of several languages (see Figure 3).

Societal *Domain*	Speech Community 1	Speech Community 2	Speech Community 3	Speech Community 4
Home	a_1	c_1	c_1	d_1
School and Culture	a_2	b_3/c_2	b_2/c_2	a_2
Work	a_3	c_3	d_2	d_2
Government	a_2	b_1	a_2	a_2
Church	e_1	b_2	b_2	e_1
	(Moscow, 1960) [Russians]	(Mea Shearim, 1966) [Jews]	(Ostropol, 1905) [Jews]	(Ostropol, 1905) [Ukrainians]

Some communities have more obviously diversified repertoires than others (e.g., SC*1* utilizes 3 varieties of one language and one of another, whereas SC*3* utilizes varieties of four different languages). Varieties that are related to one societal domain in one SC (e.g., b_2 in SC2) may be associated with more or different societal domains in another SC (e.g., b_2 in SC*3*). All speakers of varieties of a particular language do not necessarily constitute a single speech community.

Figure 3. Speech Communities and Verbal Repertoires
(based upon concepts of Gumperz, 1964a and elsewhere)

These two types of speech communities are also quite likely to differ in the extent to which their members have *access* to the roles and to the varieties available in the respective repertoires of their communities. In the more traditional speech communities access to certain roles is severely restricted and is attained, in those cases in which access to new roles *is* available, on the basis of *ascription*. Those whose ancestry is inappropriate cannot attain certain new roles, regardless of their personal achievement. Similarly, access to an expanded verbal repertoire is also severely restricted, most varieties not learned in childhood being available only to those who can afford to devote many years of patient and painstaking formal study to their acquisition. Both of these conditions are not nearly so likely to exist in modern, personal-achievement-oriented societies, although their lack of completely equal and open access is evident to all students of the disadvantaged (including Negro non-standard speech) in the midst of America's plenty.

In more traditional societies in which status is based on ascription there is also likely to be more role *compartmentalization*. Thus, not only are certain individuals barred from enacting certain roles but, in general, the rights and duties that constitute particular roles are more distinct and the transition from one role to the next, for members of those classes who may enter into them, are ritually governed, as are the roles themselves. Such societies also tend to reveal marked verbal compartmentalization as well (McCormack 1960). When an individual speaks language or variety A he takes great care not to switch into B and not to slip into traces of B, whether phonologically, lexically or grammatically. Each variety is kept separate and uncontaminated from the other just as is each role. How different such compartmentalization is from the fluidity of modern democratic speech communities in which there is such frequent change from one role to the other and from one variety to another that individuals are frequently father and pal, or teacher and colleague, simultaneously or in rapid succession! The result of such frequent and easy role shifts is often that the roles themselves become more similar and less distinctive or clearcut. The same occurs in the verbal repertoire as speakers change from one variety (or language) to another with greater frequency and fluidity. The varieties too tend to become more similar as the roles in which they are appropriate become more and more alike. This is particularly likely to occur, as we will see below, among lower class speakers whose mastery of the more formal roles and varieties available to their speech communities is likely to be marginal at best.

Thus, just as varieties are characterizable by a small number of attributes and their combinations, so is this true of the attributes that characterize speech communities at the most general level. The inter-actional basis of speech communities, their symbolic-integrative basis, their size, repertoire range, repertoire access and repertoire compart-mentalization are all concepts that we will need to refer to again and again in the pages that follow.

4.0 INTERACTIONAL SOCIOLOGY OF LANGUAGE:
    MICRO AND MACRO

Boss	Carmen, do you have a minute?
Secretary	Yes, Mr. Gonzalez.
Boss	I have a letter to dictate to you.
Secretary	Fine. Let me get my pen and pad. I'll be right back.
Boss	Okay.
Secretary	Okay.
Boss	Okay, this is addressed to Mr. William Bolger.
Secretary	That's B-o-r-g-e-r?
Boss	B-o-l
Secretary	Oh, oh, I see.
Boss	Okay. His address is in the files.
Secretary	Okay.
Boss	Okay. Dear Bill, Many thanks for telling me about your work with the Science Research Project. The information you gave me ought to prove most helpful.
Secretary	That was "The information you gave me ought to prove most helpful"?
Boss	Correct.
Secretary	Okay.
Boss	Okay, ah. I very much appreciate the time you gave me. Never mind, strike that out. Ah, enclosed are two of the forms that you let me borrow. I'll be sending back the data sheets very soon. Thanks again. I hope that your hospital stay will be as pleasant as possible and that your back will be soon in top shape. Will soon be in top shape. It was nice seeing you again. Sincerely, Louis Gonzalez.
Secretary	Do you have the enclosures for the letter Mr. Gonzalez?
Boss	Oh yes, here they are.
Secretary	Okay.
Boss	Ah, this man William Bolger got his organization to contribute a lot of money to the Puerto Rican parade. He's very much for it.

¿Tú fuiste a la parada?
(Did you go to the parade?)

Secretary   Sí, yo fuí.
(Yes, I went.)

Boss   ¿Sí?
(Yes?)

Secretary   Uh huh.
¿Y cómo te estuvo?
(and how did you like it?)

Secretary   Ay, lo mas bonita.
(Oh, very pretty.)

Boss   Sí, porque yo fuí y yo nunca había participado en la parada
(Yes, because I went and I had never participated in the parade

y este año me dió curiosidad por ir a ver como era y estuvo eso

and this year I became curious to go and see how it was and that was

fenómeno. Fuí con mi señora y con mis nenes y a ellos también

a phenomenon. I went with my wife and my children and they also

le gustó mucho. Eh, y tuve un día bien agradable. Ahora lo que

liked it very much. And I had a very pleasant day. Now me molesta a mí es que las personas cuando viene una cosa así,

what bothers me is that people when something like this comes along,

la parada Puertorriqueña o la fiesta de San Juan, corren de la

the Puerto Rican parade, or the festival of San Juan they run from

casa a participar porque es una actividad festiva, alegre, y sin

the house to participate because it is a festive activity, happy, and

embargo, cuando tienen que ir a la iglesia, o la misa para pedirle . . .

then, when they have to go to church or to mass, to ask . . .)

Secretary   (Laughter)

Boss   A Diós entonce no van
(God then they don't go.)

Secretary	Sí, entonces no van.
	(Yes, then they don't go.)
Boss	Pero, así es la vida, caramba.
	(But that's life, you know.)
	Do you think that you could get this letter out today?
Secretary	Oh yes, I'll have it this afternoon for you.
Boss	Okay, good, fine then.
Secretary	Okay.
Boss	Okay.

If we carefully consider the above conversation it becomes evident that it reveals considerable internal variation. Speaker A does not always speak in the same way nor does his interlocutor, Speaker B. Were it possible for us to listen to the original tapes of this conversation, several kinds of variation within each of them would become evident to us: variations in speed of speaking, variations in the extent to which Spanish phonology creeps into English discourse, and, vice versa, variations in the extent to which English phonology creeps into the Spanish discourse, etc. However, even from the conventionally (orthographically) rendered transcription available to us on the previous pages one kind of variation remains exceedingly clear: that from Spanish to English or from English to Spanish for each speaker. It is precisely because bilingual code switching is often more noticeable than other kinds of sociolinguistic variation that bilingualism is so commonly examined in sociolinguistic theory and research. However, the concepts and findings that derive from such examinations must be provocative and illuminating for the sociology of language more generally, and, indeed, that *is* the case, for the societal patterning of bilingual interaction is merely an instance (hopefully a more obvious and, therefore, pedagogically useful instance) of the vastly more general phenomenon of societal patterning of variation in verbal interaction.

How shall we describe or measure the phenomenon of interest to us: societal patterning of variation in verbal interaction? Usefully accurate description or measurement is certainly the basic problem of every scientific field of endeavor. Most of mankind has constantly been immersed in a veritable ocean of cross-currents of talk. Nevertheless, as with most other aspects of everyday social behavior, it is only in very recent days that man has begun to recognize the latent order and regularity in the manifest chaos of verbal interaction that surrounds him.

4.1   How should Talk be Described Contextually?

How should 'talk' be described contextually in order to best reveal
or discover its social systematization (assuming that its 'basic' linguistic description is already available)? Let us begin with some
passages of actual 'talk', making sure to preserve its verbatim form
(preferably by utilizing sensitive audio and visual recording equipment) rather than merely summarizing the content of such talk. The
smallest sociolinguistic unit that will be of interest to us is a *speech
act*: a joke, an interjection, an opening remark (Schegloff, 1968), a
question, in general – a segment of talk that is also societally recognizable and reoccurring. Speech acts are normally parts of somewhat
larger *speech events,* such as conversations, introductions, lectures,
prayers, arguments, etc. (Hymes 1967b), which, of course, must also
be societally recognizable and reoccurring.

    If we note that a switch has occurred from variery *a* to variety *b*
– perhaps from a kind of Spanish to a kind of English, or from more
formal English to less formal English, or from regionally neutral,
informal Spanish to Jíbarro (rural) informal Spanish – the first question
that presents itself is whether one variety tends to be used (or used
more often) in certain kinds of speech acts or events, whereas the other
tends to be used (or used more often) in others. Thus, were we aware
of the speech acts recognized by bilingual Puerto Rican youngsters in
New York, we might venture to explain a switch such as the following:

First Girl   Yes, and don't tell me that the United States is the only
             one that has been able to in Puerto Rico. . . . .
Boy   Okay so you have a couple of people like Moscoso **and**
             Luís Ferrer.
First Girl   ¡Un momento!
Boy   ¡Bueno!
First Girl   ¡Un Momento!
Boy   Have you got people capable of starting something like . . .
             like General Motors?

as being related to the act of interruption or disagreement in the
midst of a somewhat specialized argument. There may be a problem, however, when testing this interpretation, in determining the
speech acts and speech events that are to be recognized within a
speech community.

    Certainly, it is not appropriate to simply apply the system of
acts and events that has been determined for one speech community

in the study of another, without determining first its appropriateness in the second community. Similarly, it is not sufficient for the investigator, no matter how much experience he has had with the verbal behavior of a particular speech community, merely to devise as detailed a listing of speech acts and events as he can. Such a list runs the decided risk of being *etic* rather than *emic*, i.e., of making far too many, as well as behaviorally inconsequential, differentiations, just as was often the case with phon*etic* vs. phon*emic* analysis in linguistics proper. An *emic* set of speech acts and events must be one that is validated as meaningful via final recourse to the native members of a speech community, rather than via appeal to the investigator's ingenuity or intuition alone.

An *emic* set of speech acts and speech events is best approximated, perhaps along a never-ending asymptote, by playing back recorded samples of 'talk' to native speakers and by encouraging them to react to and comment upon the reasons for the use of variety *a* 'here' as contrasted with the use of variety *b* 'there'. The more the sensitive investigator observes the speech community that he seeks to sociolinguistically describe the more hunches he will have concerning functionally different speech acts and speech events. However, even the best hunches require verification *from within the speech community*. Such verification may take various shapes. The views of both naive and skilled informants may be cited and tabulated as they comment upon recorded instances of variation in 'talk' and as they reply to the investigator's patient probes and queries as to "Why didn't he say 'Just a minute!' instead of '¡Momento!'? Would it have meant something different if he *had* said that instead? When is it appropriate to say '¡Momento!' and when is it appropriate to say 'Just a Minute!' (assuming the persons involved known both languages equally well)?", etc. Once the investigator has *demonstrated* (not merely assumed or argued) the validity of his sets of functionally different speech acts and events he may then proceed to utilize them in the collection and analysis of samples of talk which are *independent* of those already utilized for validational purposes. Such, at least, is the rationale of research procedure at this micro-level of sociolinguistic analysis, although the field itself is still too young and too linguistically oriented to have produced many instances of such cross-validation of its *social* units selected for purposes of *socio*linguistic analysis.

4.2 *Micro-level Analysis in the Sociology of Language*

Sociolinguistic description may merely begin – rather than end – with the specification and the utilization of speech acts and events, depen-

ding on the purpose of a particular research enterprise. The more
linguistically oriented a particular study may be, the more likely it
is to remain content with micro-level analysis, since the micro-level in
the sociology of language is already a much higher (i.e., a more contextual and complicated) level of analysis than that traditionally employed within linguistics proper. However, the more societally oriented a particular sociolinguistic study may be, the more concerned
with investigating social processes and societal organization, per se,
the more likely it is to seek successively more macro-level analyses.
Micro-level sociology of language (sometimes referred to as ethno-
methodological) constitutes one of the levels within sociolinguistic
inquiry (Garfinkel 1967; Garfinkel and Sacks, in press). The various
levels do not differ in the degree to which they are correct or accurate.
They differ in purpose and, therefore, in method. We can trace only
a few of the successive levels in this SECTION, primarily in order to
demonstrate their similarities and their differences.

One of the awarenesses to which an investigator may come
after pondering a mountain of sociolinguistic data at the level of
speech acts and events is that variation in 'talk' is more common and
differently proportioned or distributed between certain interlocutors
than it is between others (Schegloff 1968). Thus, whereas either the
boy or the girl in Conversation 2 may initiate the switch from one
language to another, it may seem from Conversation 1 that the boss
is the initiator of switching far more frequently than is the secretary.
Therefore, while a great deal of switching is functionally *metaphorical*,
i.e., it indicates a contrast in emphasis (from humor to seriousness,
from agreement to disagreement, from the unessential or secondary to
the essential or primary, in any interchange already underway in a
particular language variety), interlocutors may vary in the extent to
which they may appropriately initiate or engage in such switching,
depending on their *role-relationship* to each other. Note, however, that
it is necessary for a certain appropriateness to exist between a variety
and certain characteristics of the social setting before it is possible to
utilize another variety for metaphorical or contrastive purposes.

4.3 Role-relationships

Any two interlocutors within a given speech community (or, more
narrowly, within a given speech network within a speech community)
must recognize the role-relationship that exists between them at any
particular time. Such recognition is part of the communality of norms
and behaviors upon which the existence of speech communities depend.
Father-son, husband-wife, teacher-pupil, clergyman-layman, employer-

employee, friend-friend: these are but some examples of the role-relationships that may exist in various (but not in all) speech communities (Goodenough 1965). Role-relationships are implicitly recognized and accepted sets of mutual rights and obligations between members of the same socio-cultural system. One of the ways in which members reveal such common membership to each other, as well as their recognition of the rights and obligations that they owe toward each other, is via appropriate variation (which, of course, may include appropriate non-variation) of the way(s) they talk to each other. Perhaps children should generally be seen and not heard, but when they *are* heard, most societies insist that they talk differently to their parents than they do to their friends (Fischer 1958). One of the frequent comments about American travelers abroad is that they know (*at most*) only one variety of the language of the country they are visiting. As a result, they speak in the same way to a child, a professor, a bootblack and a shopkeeper, thus revealing not only their foreignness, but also their ignorance (of the appropriate ways of signalling local role-relationships).

It is probably not necessary, at this point, to dwell upon the kinds of variation in talk that may be required (or prohibited) by certain role-relationships. In addition, and this too should require no extensive discussion at this point, whether the variation required is from one language to another or from one geographic, social or occupational variety to another, the functionally differential role-relationships must be *emically* validated rather than merely *etically* enumerated. There are certainly sociolinguistic allo-roles in most speech communities. However, two other characterizations of role-relationships do merit mention at this point, particularly because they have proved to be useful in sociolinguistic description and analysis.

Role-relationships vary in the extent to which their mutual rights and obligations must or must not be *continually stressed*. The king-subject role-relationship may retain more invariant stress than the shopkeeper-customer relationship. If shopkeepers and their customers may also interact with each other as friends, as relatives, as members of the same political party, etc., whereas kings and their subjects (in the same speech community) may not experience a similar degree of role change, access and/or fluidity *vis-a-vis each other*, then we would expect to encounter more variation in the 'talk' of two individuals who encounter each other as shopkeeper and customer than we would expect between two individuals who encounter each other as king and subject. In addition, a shopkeeper and his customer may be able to set aside their roles entirely and interact entirely on the basis of their individual and momentary needs and inclinations. This may not be permissible for the king and his subjects. Thus, we would say that a shopkeeper and his customer may engage in both *personal* and *transactional* interactions (Gumperz 1964a), whereas the king and his subjects engage only in transactional interactions. Transactional interactions are those which stress the mutual rights and obligations of their participants. Personal interactions are more informal, more fluid, more varied.

In part, speech acts and events are differentially distributed throughout various role-relationships because personal and transactional interactions are differentially permitted in various role-relationships. The sociology of language is necessarily of interest to those investigators who are concerned with determining the functionally different role-relationships that exist within a given community. Micro-level sociology of language, at least, is concerned with the validation of such relationships, via demonstration of differential role access, role range and role fluidity, as well as via the demonstration of differential proportions of personal and transactional interaction, through the data of 'talk'. Role-relationships may be used as data-organizing units both with respect to variation in talk as well as with respect to other variations in interpersonal behavior. That is the reason why role-relations are so frequently examined in the sociology of language.

4.4   The Situation: Congruent and Incongruent

It has probably occured to the reader that if the shopkeeper and his customer are not to interact only as such but, rather, also as friends, lovers, relatives, or party-members, that more than their roles are likely to change. After all, neither the *time* nor the *place* of the storekeeper-customer role-relationship is really ideal for any of the other relationships mentioned. Lovers require a time and a place of their own, and the same is true – or, at least, is typical – for other role-relationships as well. These three ingredients (the *implementation* of the rights and duties of a particular role-relationship, in the *place* (locale) most appropriate or most typical for that relationship, and at the *time* societally defined as appropriate for that relationship), taken together, constitute a construct that has proven itself to be of great value in the sociology of language: the *social situation* (Bock 1964; see Figure 4).

The simplest type of social situation for micro-level sociology of language to describe and analyze is the congruent situation in which all three ingredients 'go-together' in the culturally accepted way. This is not to say that the investigator may assume that there is only one place and one time appropriate for the realization of a particular role-relationship. Quite the contrary. As with the wakes studied by Bock

SITUATION: "CLASS"	*Time*: Class Meeting
Space: Classroom	*Roles*: + Teacher + Pupil ± Student-Teacher

+ indicates obligatory occurrence
± indicates optional occurrence

Figure 4. The Social Situation (Bock 1964)

on a Micmac Indian Reserve, there may be various times and various places for the appropriate realization of particular role-relationships (see Figure 5). Nevertheless, the total number of permissible combinations is likely to be small and, small or not, there is likely to be little ambiguity among members of the society or culture under study as to what the situation in question is and what its requirements are with respect to their participation in it. As a result, if there are language usage norms with respect to situations these are likely to be most clearly and uniformly realized in avowedly congruent situations.

However, lovers quarrel. Although they meet in the proper time and place they do not invariably behave toward each other as lovers should. Similarly, if a secretary and her boss are required to meet in the office at 3:00 a.m. in order to complete an emergency report, it may well be difficult for them to maintain the usual secretary-boss relationship. Finally, if priest and parishioner meet at the Yonkers Raceway during the time normally set aside for confessions this must have some impact on the normal priest-parishioner role-relationship. However, in all such instances of initial incongruency (wrong behavior, wrong time, or wrong place) the resulting interaction – whether sociolinguistic or otherwise – is normally far from random or chaotic. One party to the interaction or another, if not both, reinterpret(s) the seeming incongruency so as to yield a congruent situation, at least phenomenologically, for that particular encounter, where one does not exist socioculturally.

Because of incongruent behavior toward each other lovers may reinterpret each other as employer and employee and the date situation is reinterpreted as a dispassionate work situation. Because of the incongruent time, secretary and boss may view the work situation as more akin to a date than is their usual custom. Because of the incongruent place priest and parishioner may pretend not to recognize each other, or to treat each other as 'old pals'. In

M-14			T-1	T-2	T-3	T-4	T-5
S-1:	Bier	s-1.1: nucleus	R-1	R-1	R-1	R-1	R-1
	Area	s-1.2: margin	±R-2			±R-2	
S-2:	Front Area			R-3	R-4		r-2.1
S-3:	Audience Area			R-2	R-2	±R-2 ±R-4	r-2.2 R-4
S-4:	Marginal	s-4.1: kitchen				r-2.1	
	Area	s-4.2: outside	r-2.2			±r-2.2 ±R-4	

Figure 5. Situation-Matrix #14: Indian Wake (Bock, 1964)

14.SC-A: Place of Wake—External distribution into 9.S-A.1: House site (usually that occupied by deceased)

   S-1:   Bier Area
   s-1.1:   nucleus—contains coffin
   s-1.2:   margin—area immediately surrounding coffin
   S-2:   Front Area—focal region of performance during T-2, -3, and -5.
   S-3:   Audience Area—seating area for R-2: Mourner
   S-4:   Marginal Area—residual space, including
   s-4.1:   kitchen area
   s-4.2:   outside of house

14.TC-A: Time of Wake—External distribution (see discussion above).
   TC-A = //T-1/T-2//:T-3/T-4://±T-5//:T-3/T-4://

   T-1:   Gathering Time—participants arrive at SC-A: Place of Wake
   T-2:   Prayer Time—saying of the Rosary by R-3: Prayer Leader
   T-3:   Singing Time—several hymns sung with brief pauses in between
   T-4:   Intermission—longer pause in singing
   T-5:   Meal Time—optional serving of meal (about midnight)

14.RC-A: Participant Roles—External distribution noted for each:
   R-1:   Corpse—from 3:RC-A: Band Member
   R-2:   Mourner
   r-2.1:   Host—member of 9.RC-A: Household Group (of deceased)
   r-2.2:   Other—residual category
   R-3:   Prayer Leader
   r-3.1:   Priest—from 3.R-B.1.1: Priest
   r-3.2:   Other—from 14.R-4
   R-4:   Singer—usually from 11.R-A.4:   Choir Member

short, after a bit of 'fumbling around' in which various and varying tentative redefinitions may be tried out, a new congruent situation is interpreted as existing and *its* behavioral and sociolinguistic requirements are implemented (Blom and Gumperz, in press; Fishman 1968b). Thus, whereas bilingual Puerto Rican parents and their children in New York are most likely to talk to each other in Spanish at home when conversing about family matters, they will probably speak in English to each other in the Public School building (Fishman, Cooper and Ma 1968). As far as they are concerned, these are two different situations, perhaps calling for two different role-relationships and requiring the utilization of two different languages or varieties.

Situational contrasts need not be as discontinuous as most of our examples have thus far implied. Furthermore, within a basically Spanish speaking situation one or another member of a bilingual speech community may still switch to English (or, in Paraguay, to Guarani) in the midst of a speech event for purely metaphorical (i.e., for emphatic or contrastive) purposes. Such *metaphorical switching* would not be possible, however, if there were no general norm assigning the particular situation, as one of a class of such situations, to one language rather than to the other. However, in contrast to the frequently unilateral and fluid back-and-forth nature of metaphorical switching (perhaps to indicate a personal interlude in a basically transactional interaction) there stands the frequently more reciprocal and undirectional nature of *situational switching*.

More generally put, *situational switching is governed by common allocation*, i.e., by widespread normative views and regulations that commonly allocate a particular variety to a particular cluster of topics, places, persons and purposes. *Metaphorical switching, on the other hand, is governed by uncommon or contrastive allocation*. It is operative as a departure from the common allocations that are normally operative. Without well established normative views and regulations relative to the functional allocation of varieties within the repertoire of a speech community neither situational nor metaphorical switching could effectively obtain. A switch to Cockney where Received Pronounciation (and grammar) is called for may elicit a brief raising of eyebrows or a pause in the conversation – until it is clear from the speaker's demeanor and from the fact that he has reverted to RP that no change in situation was intended. However, such metaphorical switching can be risky. Someone might feel that Cockney for the situation at hand is in poor taste. Metaphorical switching is a luxury that can be afforded only by those that comfortably share not only the same *set* of situational norms but also *the same view as to their inviolability*. Since most of us are members of several speech networks, each with somewhat different sociolinguistic norms, the chances that situational shifting and metaphorical switching will be misunderstood and conflicted – particularly where the norms pertaining to variety selection have few or insufficiently powerful guardians – are obviously great.

4.5   The Transition to Macrolevel Sociology of Language

The situational analysis of language and behavior represents the boundary area between microlevel and macrolevel sociology of language. The very fact that a baseball conversation 'belongs' to one speech variety and an electrical engineering lecture 'belongs' to another speech variety is a major key to an even more generalized description of sociolinguistic variation. The very fact that humor during a formal lecture is realized through a metaphorical switch to another variety must be indicative of an underlying sociolinguistic regularity, perhaps of the view that lecture-like or formal situations are generally associated with one language or variety whereas levity or intimacy is tied to another (Joos 1959). The large-scale aggregative regularities that obtain between varieties and societally recognized functions are examined via the construct termed *domain* (Fishman 1965d; Fishman in press).

Sociolinguistic domains are societal constructs derived from painstaking analysis and summarization of patently congruent situations (See Fishman, Cooper, and Ma 1968, for many examples of the extraction of *emic* domains via factor analysis as well as for examples of the validation of initially *etic* domains). The macro-sociologist or social psychologist may well inquire: What is the significance of the fact that school situations and 'schoolish' situations (the latter being initially incongruent situations reinterpreted in the direction of their most salient component) are related to variety *a*? Frequently, it is helpful to recognize a number of behaviorally separate domains (behaviorally separate in that they are derived from discontinuous social situations) all of which are commonly associated with a particular variety or language. Thus, in many bilingual speech communities such domains as school, church, professional worksphere and government have been verified and found to be congruent with a language or variety that we will refer to as *H* (although for purely labelling purposes we may refer to it as *a* or *X* or *1*). Similarly, such domains as family, neighborhood and lower worksphere have been validated and found to be congruent with a language or variety that we will refer to as *L* (or *b*, or *Y* or *2*). All in all, the fact that a complex speech community contains various superposed varieties – in some cases, various languages, and, in others, various varieties of the same language – is now well documented. The existence of complementary varieties for intra-group purposes is known as *diglossia* (Ferguson 1959a) and the communities in which diglossia is encountered are referred to as *diglossic*. Domains are particularly useful constructs for the macro-level (i.e., community-wide) functional description of societally patterned variation in "talk" within large and complex diglossic speech communities, about which more will be said in Section 7, below.

Some members of diglossic speech communities can verbalize the relationship between certain broad categories of behavior and certain broad categories of "talk". More educated and verbally more fluent members of speech communities can tell an investigator about such relationships at great length and in great detail. Less educated and verbally limited members can only grope to express a regularity which they vaguely realize to exist. However, the fact that the formulation of a regular association between language (variety) and large scale situational behaviors may be difficult to come by is no more indicative of a dubious relationship than is the fact that grammatical regularities can rarely be explicitly formulated by native speakers is to be considered as calling the abstracted rules themselves into question.

As with all constructs (including situations, role-relationships and speech events), domains originate in the integrative intuition of the investigator. If the investigator notes that student-teacher interactions in classrooms, school corridors, school auditoriums and in school laboratories of elementary schools, high schools, colleges and universities are all realized via H as long as these interactions are focused upon educational technicality and specialization, he may begin to suspect that these hypothetically congruent situations all belong to a single (educational) *domain*. If he further finds that hypothetically incongruent situations involving an educational and a non-educational ingredient are, by and large, predictably resolved in terms of H rather than L if the third ingredient is an educational time, place or role-relationship, he may feel further justified in positing an educational domain. Finally, if informants tell him that the predicted language or variety would be appropriate in all of the examples he can think of that derive from his notion of the educational domain, whereas they proclaim that it would not be appropriate for examples that he draws from a contrasted domain, then the construct is as usefully validated as is that of situation or event – with one major difference.

Whereas particular speech acts (and speech excerpts of an even briefer nature) can be apportioned to the speech and social situations in which they transpire, the same cannot be done with respect to such acts or excerpts in relationship to societal domains. Domains are extrapolated from the *data* of 'talk', rather than being an actual component of the *process* of talk. However, domains are as real as the very social institutions of a speech community, and indeed they show a marked paralleling with such major social institutions (Barker 1947). There is an undeniable difference between the social institution, 'the family', and any particular family, but there is no doubt that the societal norms concerning the former must be derived from data on many instances of the latter. Once such societal norms are formulated they can be utilized to test predictions concerning the distributions of societally patterned variations in talk across all instances of one domain vs. all instances of another.

Thus, domains and social situations reveal the links that exist between microlevel and macrolevel sociology of language. The members of diglossic speech communities can come to have certain views concerning their varieties or languages because these varieties are associated (in behavior and in attitude) with particular domains. The H variety (or language) is considered to reflect certain values and relationships within the speech community, whereas the L variety is considered to reflect others. Certain individuals and groups may come to advocate the expansion of the functions of L into additional domains. Others may advocate the displacement of L entirely and the use of H solely. Neither of these revisionist views could be held or advocated without recognition of the reality of domains of language-and-behavior in the existing norms of communicative appropriateness. The high culture values with which certain varieties are associated and the intimacy and folksiness values with which others are congruent are both derivable from domain-appropriate norms governing characteristic verbal interaction.

4.6   On the Reality of Sociolinguistic Compositing

So little (if, indeed, any) microsociolinguistic data has been subjected to rigorous quantitative analysis or obtained via experimentally controlled variation that it is fitting that we pause to examine a study that has attempted to do so, even if it deals only with sociolinguistic normative views and claims. The study in question (Fishman and Greenfield, 1970) is concerned with the relative importance of persons, places and topics in the perception of congruent and incongruent situations and with the impact of perceived congruency or incongruency on claimed language use in different domains. Since domains are a higher order generalization from *congruent situations* (i.e. from situations in which individuals interact in appropriate role-relationships with each other, in the appropriate locales for these role-relationships, and discuss topics appropriate to their role-relationships) it was first necessary to test intuitive and rather clinical estimates of the widespread congruences that were felt to obtain. After more than a year of participant observation and other data-gathering experiences it seemed to Greenfield (1968) that five domains could be generalized from the innumerable situations that he had encountered. He tentatively labeled these "family", "friendship", "religion", "education" and "employment" and proceeded to determine whether a typical *situation* could be presented for each domain as a means of collecting self-report data on language choice. As indicated below each domain was represented by a congruent person (interlocutor), place and topic in the self-report instrument that Greenfield constructed for high school students.

Domain	*Interlocutor*	*Place*	*Topic*
Family	Parent	Home	How to be a good son or daughter
Friendship	Friend	Beach	How to play a certain game
Religion	Priest	Church	How to be a good Christian
Education	Teacher	School	How to solve an algebra problem
Employment	Employer	Workplace	How to do your job more efficiently

Greenfield's hypothesis was that within the Puerto Rican speech community, among individuals who knew Spanish and English equally well, Spanish was primarily associated with family and with friendship (the two, family and friendship constituting the intimacy value cluster), while English was primarily associated with religion, work and education (the three constituting the status-stressing value cluster). In order to test this hypothesis he first presented two seemingly congruent situational components and requested his subjects (a) to select a third component in order to complete the situation, as well as (b) to indicate their likelihood of using Spanish or English if they were involved in such a situation and if they and their Puerto Rican interlocutors knew Spanish and English equally well. Section I of Table 1 shows that Greenfield's predictions were uniformly confirmed among those subjects who selected congruent third components. Spanish was decreasingly reported for family, friendship, religion, employment and education, regardless of whether the third component selected was a person, place or topic.

However, as Blom and Gumperz (in press), Fishman (1968b) and others have indicated, seemingly incongruent situations frequently occur and are rendered understandable and acceptable (just as are the seemingly ungrammatical sentences that we hear in most spon-

TABLE 1

Spanish and English Usage Self-Ratings in Various Situations
for Components Selected

I. *Congruent Situations:* Two 'congruent' components presented; S selects third
congruent component and language appropriate to situation.   1=all Spanish,
5=all English.

Congruent Persons Selected

	Parent	Friend	Total	Priest	Teacher	Employer	Total
Mean	2.77	3.60	3.27	4.69	4.92	4.79	4.81
S.D.	1.48	1.20	1.12	.61	.27	.41	.34
N	13	15	15	13	13	14	15

Congruent Places Selected

	Home	Beach	Total	Church	School	Work Place	Total
Mean	2.33	3.50	2.60	3.80	4.79	4.27	4.27
S.D.	1.07	1.26	1.10	1.51	.58	1.34	.94
N	15	6	15	15	14	15	15

Congruent Topics Selected

	Family	Friend-ship	Total	Religion	Education	Employ-ment	Total
Mean	1.69	3.30	2.64	3.80	4.78	4.44	4.38
S.D.	.92	1.20	.95	1.47	1.53	1.12	.73
N	16	18	18	15	18	18	18

II. *Incongruent Situations:*   Two 'incongruent' components presented; S selects
third component and language appropriate to situation. 1=all Spanish, 5=all
English.

Persons Selected

	Parent	Friend	Total	Priest	Teacher	Employer	Total
Mean	2.90	3.92	3.60	4.68	4.77	4.44	4.70
S.D.	1.20	.64	.70	.59	.48	.68	.52
N	16	16	16	14	15	9	15

Places Selected

	Home	Beach	Total	Church	School	Work Place	Total
Mean	2.63	3.86	2.77	3.71	4.39	4.42	4.10
S.D.	.77	.94	.70	1.32	1.90	.96	.82
N	15	5	15	15	15	15	15

Topics Selected

	Family	Friend-ship	Total	Religion	Education	Employ-ment	Total
Mean	2.83	3.81	3.26	3.07	3.66	3.81	3.49
S.D.	1.04	1.13	1.02	1.00	1.20	.85	.76
N	18	16	18	18	17	18	18

taneous speech). Interlocutors reinterpret incongruencies in order to salvage some semblance of the congruency in terms of which they understand and function within their social order. Were this not the case then no seemingly congruent domains could arise and be maintained out of the incongruencies of daily life. In order to test this assumption Greenfield proceeded to present his subjects with two incongruent components (e.g., with a person from one hypothetical domain and with a place from another hypothetical domain) and asked them to select a third component in order to complete the situation as well as to indicate their likelihood of using Spanish or English in a situation so constituted. Greenfield found that the third component was overwhelmingly selected from either one or the other of any two domains from which he had selected the first two components. Furthermore, in their attempts to render a seemingly incongruous situation somewhat more congruent his subject's language preferences left the relationship between domains and language choice substantially unaltered (directionally), regardless of whether persons, places or topics were involved. Nevertheless, all domains became somewhat less different from each other than they had been in the fully congruent situations. Apparently, both individual indecisiveness as well as sociolinguistic norms governing domain regularity must be combined and compromised when incongruencies appear. Language choice is much more clear-cut and polarized in 'usual' situations governed neatly by sociolinguistic norms of communicative appropriateness than they are in 'unusual' situations which must be resolved by individual interpretation.

Yet, another (and, for this presentation, final) indication of the construct validity of domains as analytic parameters for the study of large scale sociolinguistic patterns is yielded by Edelman's data (1968). Here we note that when the word naming responses of bilingual Puerto-Rican children in Jersey City were analyzed in accord with the domains derived from Greenfield's and Fishman's data reported above significant and instructive findings were obtained. The most Spanish domain for all children was 'family' (Table 2A). The most English domain for all children was 'education'. The analysis of variance (Table 2B) indicates that not only did the children's res-

TABLE 2A

Mean number of words named by young schoolchildren (Edelman, 1968)

(N= 34)

Age	Language	Family	Education	Domain Religion	Friendship	Total
6-8	English	6.2	8.2	6.6	8.3	7.3
	Spanish	7.6	6.2	5.8	6.4	6.5
	Total	6.9	7.2	6.2	7.4	6.9
9-11	English	11.7	12.8	8.7	10.9	11.0
	Spanish	10.5	9.4	7.2	9.7	9.2
	Total	11.1	11.1	7.9	10.3	10.1
Total	English	9.0	10.5	7.7	9.6	9.2
	Spanish	9.0	7.8	6.5	8.0	7.8
	Total	9.0	9.1	7.1	9.0	8.5

TABLE 2B

Analysis of variance of young schoolchildren's word-naming scores

Source	Sum of Squares	df	Mean Square	F	F_{95}	F_{99}
Between Subjects	1844.12	33				
C (age)	689.30	1	689.30	19.67[a]	4.17	7.56
D (sex)	15.54	1	15.54	.44	4.17	7.56
CD	87.87	1	87.87	2.51	4.17	7.56
error (b)	1051.41	30	35.05			
Within Subjects	1795.88	238				
A (language)	123.13	1	123.13	9.73[a]	4.17	7.56
B (domain)	192.54	3	64.18	8.51[a]	2.71	4.00
AB	65.12	3	21.71	11.67[a]	2.71	4.00
AC	16.50	1	16.50	1.30	4.17	7.56
AD	42.08	1	42.08	3.32	4.17	7.56
BC	61.54	3	20.51	2.72	2.71	4.00
BD	2.89	3	.96	.13	2.71	4.00
ABC	23.99	3	8.00	4.30[a]	2.71	4.00
ABD	6.70	3	2.23	1.20	2.71	4.00
ACD	14.62	1	14.62	1.15	4.17	7.56
BCD	13.53	3	4.51	.60	2.71	4.00
ABCD	7.98	3	2.66	1.43	2.71	4.00
error (w)	1225.26	210				
$error_1$ (w)	379.88	30	12.66			
$error_2$ (w)	678.31	90	7.54			
$error_3$ (w)	167.07	90	1.86			
Total	3640.00	271				

[a] Significant at or above the .01 level.

ponses differ significantly by age (older children giving more responses in both languages than did younger children), by language (English yielding more responses than does Spanish), and by domain (church yielding fewer responses than does any other domain), but that these three variables *interact significantly* as well. This means that one language is much more associated with certain domains than is the other and that this is differentially so by age. This is exactly the kind of finding for which domain analysis is particularly suited. Its utility for inter-society comparisons and for gauging language shift would seem to be quite promising, but its major value should be in describing and demonstrating the dependence of communicative appropriateness on the composing appropriateness of members of speech communities, whether monolingual or bilingual.

One thing appears to be clear from the theoretical and empirical work cited: there are classes of events recognized by each speech network or community such that several seemingly different situations are classed as being of the same kind. No speech network has a linguistic repertoire that is as differentiated as the complete list of apparently different role relations, topics and locales in which its members are involved. Just *where the boundaries come* that do differentiate between the *class of situations* generally requiring one variety and another class of situations generally requiring another variety must be empirically determined by the investigator, and constitutes one of the major tasks of descriptive sociology of language. Such classes of situations are referred to as *domains*. The various domains and the appropriate usage in each domain must be discovered from the data of numerous discrete situations and the shifting or non-shifting which they reveal. This is a central task of descriptive sociology of language, and it can only be accomplished by painstaking research – utilizing *all* of the available social science methods: participant observation, interviews, surveys and experiments too. The compositing concerns of some researchers in the sociology of language are thus far from being research strategies alone. Ultimately they also seek to reveal the behavioral parsimony of members of speech communities all of whom inevitably come to rely on a relatively functional sociolinguistic typology to guide them through the infinite encounters of daily interaction.

4.7 Sociology of Language: Multilevel and Multimethod

The list of constructs utilized in the sociolinguistic description and analysis of samples of 'talk' is far from exhausted. We have not mentioned several of the social units long advocated by Hymes (1962), such as participant vs. audience roles, the purposes and the outcomes of speech events, the tone or manner of communication, the channel of communication employed (oral, written, telegraphic), nor all of the various parameters and components for the analysis of talk data that he has more recently advanced (Hymes 1967b; see figure 6A);

(S) SETTING or SCENE: time and place; also, psychological setting and cultural definition as a *type* of scene.

(P) PARTICIPANTS or PERSONNEL: e.g., addressor-addressee-audience

(E) ENDS: ends in view (goals, purposes) and ends as outcomes

(A) ART CHARACTERISTICS: the form *and* the content of what is said

(K) KEY: the tone, manner or spirit in which an act is done

(I) INSTRUMENTALITIES: channel (the choice of oral, written, telegraphic or other medium) and code (Spanish, English, etc.) or subcode (dialect, sociolect)

(N) NORMS OF INTERACTION and of INTERPRETATION: specific behaviors and properties that may accompany acts of speech, as well as shared rules for understanding what occurs in speech acts

(G) GENRES: categories or types of speech acts and speech events: e.g., conversation, curse, prayer, lecture, etc.

Figure 6a. Components of Speech Events:
A heuristic schema
(Hymes 1967b)

we have not discussed such social psychological parameters as the saliency of individual vs. collective needs (Herman 1961), nor the several functions of speech so revealingly discussed by Ervin-Tripp. Suffice it to say that there are several levels and approaches to sociolinguistic description and a host of linguistic, socio-psychological and societal constructs within each (see Figure 6b). One's choice from among them depends on the particular problem at hand (Ervin-Tripp 1964). This is necessarily so. The sociology of language is of interest to students of small societies as well as to students of national and international integration. It must help clarify the change from one face-to-face situation to another. It must also help clarify the different language-related beliefs and behaviors of ˙entire social sectors and classes. In some cases the variation between closely related varieties must be highlighted. In other cases the variation between obviously unrelated languages is of concern.

It would be foolhardy to claim that one and the same method of data collection and data analysis be utilized for such a variety of problems and purposes. It is one of the hallmarks of scientific social inquiry that methods are selected as a *result* of problem specifications rather

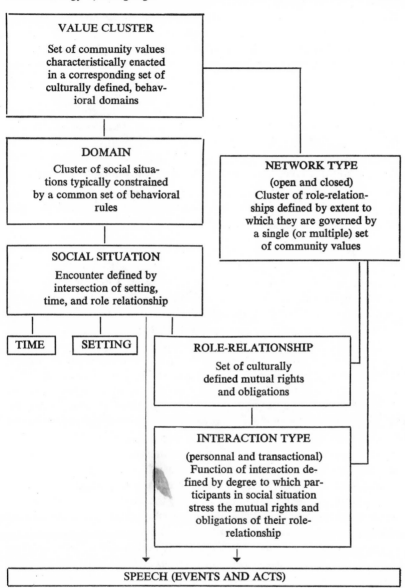

Figure 6b.
Relationships Among Some Constructs Employed in Sociolinguistic Analysis[1]

[1] From: Robert L. Cooper, "How can we measure the roles which a bilingual's languages play in his everyday behavior?" in L. G. Kelly (ed.), *The Description and Measurement of Bilingualism* (Toronto, Toronto University Press, 1969), p. 202.

than independently of them. The sociology of language is neither methodologically nor theoretically uniform. Nevertheless, it is gratifying to note that for those who seek such ties the links between micro- and macro-constructs and methods exist (as do a number of constructs and methods that have wide applicability through the entire range of the sociology of language). Just as there is no societally unencumbered verbal interaction so are there no large scale relationships between language and society that do not depend on individual interaction for their realization. Although there is no mechanical part-whole relationship between them microlevel and macrolevel sociology of language are both conceptually and methodologically complementary.

5.0 SOCIETAL DIFFERENTIATION AND REPERTOIRE RANGE

Speech communities – particularly those at the citywide, regional or national levels – obviously vary in the degrees and kinds of language diversity that they reveal. What do such differences imply with respect to the social differentiation and organization of the communities and networks to which they apply? If we examine the varieties of Javanese required by linguistic etiquette in the communities described by Geertz (1960), the varieties of Baghdadi Arabic described by Blanc (1964), the varieties of Hindi or Kannada described by Gumperz (1958) or McCormack (1960), and the varieties of Indonesian described by Tanner (1967) it is clear that these compose quite different kinds of repertoires than do the varieties of Norwegian described by Haugen (1961), or the varieties of American English described by Labov (1963, 1964, 1965), or by Levine and Crockett (1966). In addition, the types of speech communities in which these varieties are encountered also differ strikingly, as do the larger national or regional units in which the communities are imbedded. To put it very briefly, the speech communities in the first cluster seem to be much more stratified socially and to employ much more diversified repertoires linguistically than do those in the second. The documented co-occurrence of linguistic heterogeneity and societal heterogeneity – when both are examined in intra-group perspective – is a major contribution of the sociology of language to the study of social organization and social change.

5.1   The Significance of Pervasive Linguistic Discontinuity

Prior to the development of the sociology of language per se, area-dialectology had already clearly indicated that discontinuous populations (i.e., populations that lived at some distance from each other or that were impeded in their communication with each other by physical or political barriers) frequently revealed substantial phonological and morphological differences between their language systems (see, e.g., Herzog 1965 and Kandori 1968 for examples of such work today). Where such differences did not obtain despite the absence of communicational frequency and socio-cultural unity, recency of settlement from a single source or other similar unifying factors (conquest, religious conversion, etc.) were assumed and encountered. Indeed, if we view the entire world as a single geographic area we tend to find similar (i.e., genetically related) languages clustered contiguously or closely to each other ('language families' are normally clustered geographically, except for the confounding fact of colonization and distant migration). Some parts of the world, of course, are famous for their concentration of highly diversified languages found in close proximity to each other. However, these same areas are also noted for their mountains, jungles, deserts and rivers, i.e., for barriers that have limited travel, commerce and common endeavor.

More difficult to explain are those variations in language and behavior that are *co-territorial*. In such instances sheer physical distance cannot be invoked as either a causal or a maintenance variable for the variations encountered. In such cases cultural and social factors alone must be examined and they alone must be meaningfully related to the *degree* and *kind* of language differences noted. In reviewing co-territorial linguistic diversity throughout history it becomes clear that it can be maintained in an extremely stable manner. Throughout the world – but particularly throughout the ancient and traditional world – populations have lived side by side for centuries without learning each other's language(s) and without significantly modifying or giving up their distinctly discontinous repertoires. Except for the relatively few middlemen that connect them (merchants, translators, etc.) such populations represent distinct speech communities although they may be citizens of the same country, of the same city, and, indeed, of the same neighborhood. However, the maintenance of such well-nigh complete linguistic and socio-cultural cleavage – equal in degree and kind to that encountered between territorially discontinuous populations – is usually indicative of population relocation some time in the past that has subsequently been buttressed and maintained by socio-cultural (including ethnic and religious) differences. The *former* differences are responsible for the origin of the differences noted by Blanc (1964) between the Moslem Arabic, Christian Arabic and Jewish Arabic of Bagdad. The *latter* differences are responsible for the *maintenance* of these cleavages in as sharp a manner, or nearly so, as initially established.

While it may often be relatively difficult to overcome the cleavage between separate but co-territorial speech communities it is not impossible to do so. The forced conversion of various Jewish and Christian communities during certain periods of Islamic rule, the urban-industrial assimilation of hitherto rural or small town immigrants and their children in the United States (Nahirny and Fishman 1965, Fishman 1965a, 1965e, 1966c), the very similar assimilation of tribal populations moving to Wolof-speaking Dakar (Tabouret-Keller 1968), the Hellenization and Romanization of many 'barbarian' elites in ancient Rome and Alexandria, the convergence between illiterate speakers of Marathi and Kannada in India (Gumperz 1967) – these are all examples of the fusing into one of populations that originally functioned as largely separate though co-territorial speech communities. Conversely, the mutual alienation of populations that originally considered themselves to be united can create fargoing linguistic differences between them where none, or few, existed previously. In general, the more far-going the linguistics differences between any two co-territorial populations (i.e., the more the differences are basically grammatical-syntactic and morphological – rather than primarily phonological or lexical), the more linguistic repertoires are compartmentalized from each other so as to reveal little if any interference, and the more they reveal functionally different verbal repertoires in terms of the sociolinguistic parameters reviewed in Section 4, above – then the greater the interactional and socio-cultural gap between the speech communities involved.

Geertz's data (see Figures 7a, b and c) might well be examined in the light of the above generalization concerning the social significance of marked grammatical discontinuity between the repertoires of co-territorial speech communities. In Geertz's case we are dealing with co-territorial speech networks that differ greatly in verbal repertoires but that cannot be considered to be either of separate geographic origin or of separate cultural or religious self-definition. Here we find three different social classes or strata within Java each differing in repertoire range and each lacking entirely one or more speech varieties available to at least one of the others. While the intra-network variation shown by Geertz is probably less that which actually exists (thus, we may assume that metaphorical switching also occurs in Java and, if it does, level 2 (for example) may be employed on occasions which are normatively viewed and regulated as being more appropriate for level 1b or 1a) let us consider this to be merely an artifact of the data model that Geertz employs and ask ourselves (a) what *kind(s) of variations* does it reveal and (b) what *kind(s) of repertoire differences* does it reveal.

Geertz's data clearly indicate that social class differences exist (or existed at the time his field work was done) in Javanese verbal behavior. In addition, however, the data also indicate that contextual-situational variation also exists in Javanese verbal behavior. The very fact that both of these types of variation regularly co-occur is an indication that although stratificational differences involved are rigid and deep, nevertheless the strata constitute a single integrated speech community with shared normative expectations and regulations vis-a-vis intra-strata and inter-strata communication.

The fact that networks in each stratum lack at least one variety available to networks drawn from the other strata is a sign of far-going discontinuity also in their respective behavioral repertoires. Networks from certain strata are not expected to engage in certain role relationships and as a result, lack entirely certain morpho-syntactic co-occurrences available to networks from other strata. Thus, in these latter respects, the variation that occurs is *stratificational only* and not contextual at all. This stratificational discontinuity in morpho-syntactic co-occurrences is shown graphically in Figure 8 for the forms *apa, napa* and *menapa*. The strata that do possess these forms use them for identical contexts of interaction and with apparently equal frequency of realization. However, there is in each case also a stratum that lacks these forms. The graphic representation of social and verbal discontinuity should be kept in mind for comparison with other graphs presented further below (e.g. Figures 9a and 9b).

5.2 More Marginal but Systematic Linguistic Differences between Social Strata

However, most co-territorial populations that differ in verbal repertoire cannot be considered fully separate speech communities, even if the differences between them can be considered as basically geographic in origin. There are very many areas today, primarily urban in nature, where sub-populations that differ in social class, religion or ethnic affiliation, nevertheless view themselves as sharing many common norms and standards and where these sub-populations interact sufficiently (or are sufficiently exposed to common educational institutions and media) to be termed a single speech community. It is hardly surprising, therefore, that the linguistic differences between such socio-cultural sub-populations (or networks) within the same speech community are more linguistically marginal (i.e., lexical and, to a lesser degree, phonological) rather than syntactic and all-embracing. It is clear that the social class variation that exists in New York City English is of this kind rather than of the kind that develops between clearly separate, non-interacting and mutually

Level	are	you	going	to eat	rice	and	cassava	now	Complete sentence
3a	menapa	pandjenengan	badé	dahar	sekul	kalijan	kaspé	samenika	*Menapa pandjenengan badé dahar sekul kalijan kaspé samenika?*
3	menapa	sampéjan	badé	neḍa	sekul	kalijan	kaspé	samenika	*Menapa sampéjan badé neḍa sekul kalijan kaspé samenika?*
2	napa	sampéjan	adjeng	neḍa	sekul	lan	kaspé	saniki	*Napa sampéjan adjeng neḍa sekul lan kaspé saniki?*
1a	apa	sampéjan	arep	neḍa	sega	lan	kaspé	saiki	*Apa sampéjan arep neḍa sega lan kaspé saiki?*
1	apa	kowé	arep	mangan	sega	lan	kaspé	saiki	*Apa kowé arep mangan sega lan kaspé saiki?*

Figure 7a. Dialect of Non-Prijaji, Urbanized, Somewhat Educated Persons

SOCIAL CLASS DIFFERENCES IN JAVANESE LINGUISTIC REPERTOIRES (Geertz, 1960)

Level	are	you	going	to eat	rice	and	cassava	now	Complete sentence
2	napa	sampéjan	adjeng	neḍa	sekul	lan	kaspé	saniki	*Napa sampéjan adjeng neḍa sekul lan kaspé saniki?*
1a	apa	sampéjan	arep	neḍa	sega	lan	kaspé	saiki	*Apa sampéjan arep neḍa sega lan kaspé saiki?*
1	apa	kowé	arep	mangan	sega	lan	kaspé	saiki	*Apa kowé arep mangan sega lan kaspé saiki?*

Figure 7b. Dialects of Peasants and Uneducated Townspeople

Level	are	you	going	to eat	rice	and	cassava	now	Complete sentence
3a	menapa	pandjenengan	baḍé	ḍahar	sekul	kalijan	kaspé	samenika	*Menapa pandjenengan baḍé ḍahar sekul kalijan kaspé samenika?*
3	menapa	sampéjan	baḍé	neḍa	sekul	kalijan	kaspé	samenika	*Menapa sampéjan baḍé neḍa sekul kalijan kaspé samenika?*

Level	are	you	going	to eat	rice	and	cassava	now	Complete sentence
1b	apa	pandjenengan	arep	ḍahar	sega	lan	kaspé	saiki	*Apa pandjenengan arep ḍahar sega lan kaspé saiki?*
1a	apa	sampéjan	arep	neḍa	sega	lan	kaspé	saiki	*Apa sampéjan arep neḍa sega lan kaspé saiki?*
1	apa	kowé	arep	mangan	sega	lan	kaspé	saiki	*Apa kowé arep mangan sega lan kaspé saiki?*

Figure 7c. Dialect of the Prijajis

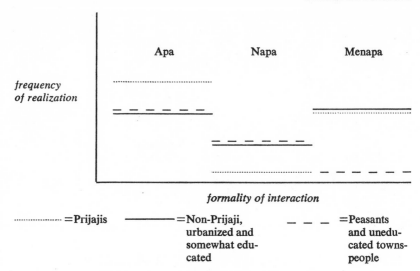

Figure 8. Verbal and Behavioral Discontinuity

alienated speech communities. One of the surest indications of this is the fact that (if we delete features attributable to Southern Negro, Puerto Rican and other recent, geographically derived differences) few of the characteristic phonological features of lower class speech in New York are entirely absent from the speech of other classes in New York City, just as few of the characteristic phonological features of its upper-class speech are entirely lacking from the lower class speech of that city. What does differentiate between the social classes in New York is the degree to which certain phonological *variabɩes* are realized in *certain ways* on *particular occaisions,* rather than their complete absence from the repertoire of any particular class.

Labov's studies of the phonological correlates of social stratification (1964, 1965, 1966a, 1966b, 1966c, 1968a, 1968b) illustrate this point. In one of his studies (1964) Labov gathered four different samples of speech (each by a different method calculated to elicit material approximating a different kind of speech situation) from four different social classes of informants. Studying such variables as *th* (as in thing, through), *eh* (the height of the vowel in bad, ask, half, dance), *r* (the presence or absence of final and preconsonantal /r/) and *oh* (the height of the vowel in off, chocolate, all, coffee) Labov found that *all* social classes yielded some values of each variable in nearly every speech situation (see figure 9). However, the differences between the social classes remained clear enough. Lower class speakers were less likely to pronounce the fricative form of the [Θ] when saying 'thing' or

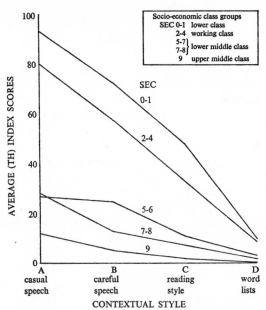

Figure 9a. *Class stratification diagram for (th)*
(Labov, 1964)

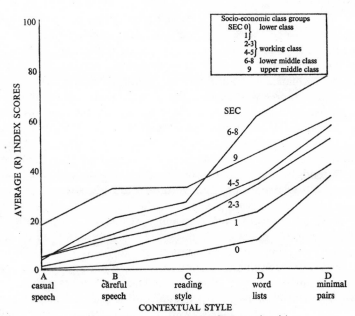

Fig. 9b. *Class stratification diagram for (r)*
(Labov, 1964)

'through' than were working class speakers; working class speakers less likely to pronounce it than lower middle class speakers; lower middle class speakers less likely to yield it than upper middle class speakers. Speakers of all classes were more likely to pronounce the standard fricative form (rather than the sub-standard affricate [tΘ] or lenis stop [t]) in reading word lists than they were when reading passages; more likely to pronounce it when reading passages than when being interviewed (= careful speech); more likely to pronounce it when being interviewed than when recounting "a situation where you thought you were in serious danger of being killed" (= casual speech).

This may be considered a hallmark of social class differences in speech where the classes as a whole share *continuous* experiences, goals and expectations, i.e., neither their role repertoires nor role access have been fully compartmentalized. As long as individuals in each class can differ in repertoire, depending on their personal opportunities and experiences with respect to interaction with various speech networks, there can be no complete discontinuity in repertoires, no complete freezing of social class position, and no overriding alienation into separate religious, ethnic or other relatively fixed and immutable speech communities.

Of course, not all variables yield such dramatic and clearcut social class differences as those found in connection with *th* in New York. With respect to *r*, *eh*, and *oh* Labov's data reveals much more *similarity* between the several social classes, although the differences between contexts and between classes remain quite clear. Labov's data also reveal a recurring *reversal* with respect to the lower middle class' performance on wordlists and passage reading. This reversal, dubbed *hypercorrection*, shows the lower middle class to be more 'correct' (more careful, more inclined to use the standard or cultured pronounciation) than is the upper middle class at its most correct or careful. Such a reversal may well indicate a variable that has become a stereotype rather than merely a marker of class position. As such it tends to be used (or overused) by those who are insecure about their social position, i.e., by those who are striving to create a more advantageous social position for themselves in a speech community in which upward social mobility seems to be possible. This explanation is not dissimilar from that which Labov utilized to explain observed differences in centralization of /ai/ and /au/ in Martha's Vineyard (1963). Such centralization was most common among minority group members (of Portuguese and Indian extraction) who sought to *stress their positive orientation to Martha's Vineyard*, rather than among the old Yankees whose feelings toward the Vineyard were more low-keyed and required no linguistic underscoring. Whether consciously employed or not the 'Pygmalion effect' in language is a striking indicator of reference group behavior and of social aspirations more generally (Ross 1956).

Similar results to Labov's (in the sense that the proportional realizations of particular variables were found to differ regularly and smoothly both between *social classes* and between *contexts*) have been reported by Lindenfeld 1969. Examining syntactic variation in French, Lindenfeld found that nominalization, relativization and sentence length

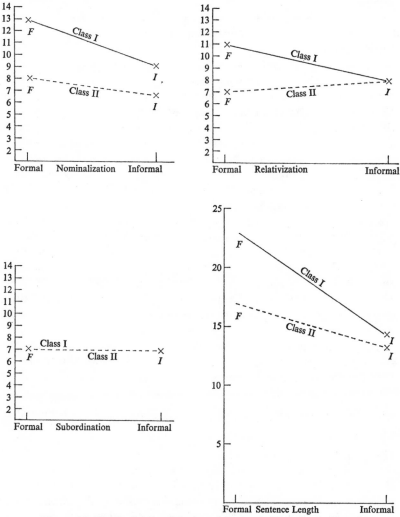

Figure 10. The Social Conditioning of Syntactic Variation in French
(Lindenfeld 1969)

(but not subordination) showed both types of variation, although upper middle class speakers were much more likely to reveal contextual variation than were lower class speakers (Figure 10). This may be taken as a sign that the socio-economically more favored subjects had more of a real repertoire range behaviorally so that the difference between formal and informal interactions was very real for them. For lower class speakers, on the other hand, this difference may be quite hypothetical in that it tends to have much less functional reality associated with it.

The demographic differentials observed in usage are as related to the societal allocation of codes as are the more directly contextual or functional differentials. The fact that an extensive cluster of phonological, lexical and grammatical realizations is more widely or characteristically employed by one particular social class than by another is commonly related to the fact that the social class in question is also more likely or characteristically engaged in particular pursuits or involved in particular situations. Demographic and contextual variations are particularly likely to be redundant in relatively closed societies in which role access is restricted and in which roles tend to be ascribed and compartmentalized However, the awareness of verbal and behavioral repertoires – a central awareness indeed in the sociology of language – should not keep us from realizing that even in relatively open societies there is often appreciable redundancy between demographic and contextual differentials in usage. Both Labov's and Lindenfield's data referred to previously reveal this redundancy when they show that for most levels of formality one social class is much more likely to yield a particular variant than are the others, even though repertoire continuity exists. This redundancy strengthens the normative sense of members of speech communities and, indeed, enables them to guide their own speech behavior more appropriately, as well as to comment upon it validly to one another and to outside investigators and to do so over and above the metaphorical variation that undoubtedly obtains round about them.

5.3 *The Implications of either Contextual-Situational or Demographic Variation*

The foregoing comparisons of social class differences and contextual-situational differences in language usage suffer in at least two ways. Neither Geertz nor Labov nor Lindenfeld have been able to indicate which of these two sources of language variation is the stronger for their data. In order to answer this question a more quantitative approach is needed to the study of social class or other demographic-group variation in usage. In addition, neither Geertz nor Labov nor Lindenfeld have asked the question "what could it mean – insofar as the overall societal organization of language behavior – if only *one or another* of these two sources of usage variation obtained?" In order to answer these two questions let us take another look at data obtained in the study of *Bilingualism in the Barrio* (Fishman, Cooper, Ma, et. al. 1968).

The data we will review was obtained as part of an interdisciplinary project on the measurement and description of widespread and relatively stable bilingualism in a Puerto Rican neighborhood in the Greater New York City area. The neighborhood studied by a team of linguists, psychologists, and sociologists included 431 Puerto Ricans (or individuals of Puerto Rican parentage) living in ninety households. All these individuals were covered in a language census that obtained the demographic data utilized for the purposes of this report at the same time that it obtained detailed self-reports on bilingual usage and ability (Fishman 1969d). The linguistic data utilized for this report was obtained in the course of two to four hour interviews and testing sessions with a random-stratified sample of those Puerto Ricans living in the study neighborhood who were over the age of 12.

Speech Contexts. The interviews and testing sessions were designed to elicit speech data in five different contexts that form a continuum from most formal or careful to most informal or casual as follows:

Contexts D: Word Reading. Subjects were asked to read two different lists of separate words, one in English and one in Spanish. The speech data obtained in this fashion was considered to be representative of the most careful pronunciation available to the subjects.

Context C: Paragraph Reading. Subjects were asked to read four different paragraphs, two in English and two in Spanish. The speech data obtained in this fashion was considered to be representative of (somewhat less) careful pronunciation.

Context WN: Word Naming. Subjects were asked to "name as many words as come to mind that have to do with (domain-locales)." This task was performed separately in English and in Spanish for each of the following domain-locales: home, neighborhood, school, work, church. The speech data obtained in this fashion was considered to be representative of intermediate pronunciation (neither markedly careful nor casual).

Context B: Careful Conversation. Subjects were asked factual questions concerning five taped 'playlets' to which they had just listened. Ideally, half of the questions were asked (and answered) in Spanish and half were asked and answered in English. The speech data obtained in this fashion was considered to be representative of somewhat (but not completely) casual pronunciation.

Context A: Casual Conversation. Subjects were asked their personal opinions and preferences with respect to the problems that figured in the 'playlets' to which they had just listened. The speech data obtained in this fashion was considered to be representative of the most informal pronunciation that could be elicited by an interviewer.

Only the last three contexts (WN, B, A) will be examined in the discussion that follows in view of the restricted corpuses obtained in the two reading contexts in the study population.

Linguistic Variables. The taped speech samples obtained for the above mentioned five contexts were independently scored by two linguists on seven Spanish and ten English variables. The reliability of scoring varied only slightly and irregularly from context to context and from one language to the other, the reliability coefficients obtained ranged from 0.73 to 0.94 with a median of 0.90. A full report on the contextual variation encountered for each variable as well as on the factorial relationship between all variables is available elsewhere (Ma and Herasimchuk 1968). The present discussion deals only with selected values on one Spanish and one English variable in order to illustrate a method of analysis hitherto not utilized in sociolinguistic research. The particular linguistic values selected for presentation in this study are further explained in the Results section below.

Demographic Variables. Four demographic factors (sex, age, education, and birthplace) are included in the analyses presented in this report. Social class, a variable frequently utilized in other sociolinguistic research on phonological variables, was not utilized in the present research due to the severe restriction in range that our overwhelmingly lower-class Puerto Rican subjects revealed in this connection. An extensive analysis of the demographic variation encountered in our study neighborhood is available elsewhere (Fishman 1968c). The reliability coefficients for the various items of obtained demographic information are all 0.90 or higher.

Sex has consistently proved to be a non-significant demographic variable in accounting for phonological variation in Puerto Rican Spanish. It was included in the present study merely in order to provide a comparison with prior studies.

Age was categorized in two separate ways. As a three-category variable the categories employed were <25, 25-34, >34. As a two-category variable the categories utilized were <25 and >25. By categorizing age in two different ways we will be able to tell whether one categorization is more related to linguistic variation than the other and, at the same time, sum both age categorizations into one age variable.

Education was categorized three different ways. As a four-category variable the categories were <7 years, all in Puerto Rico; 7 or more years, all in Puerto Rico; partially in Puerto Rico and partially in continental U.S.A.; all in continental U.S.A. As a two-category variable education was categorized in two different ways: first, all in Puerto Rico vs. all or part in continental U.S.A. and, second, all U.S.A. vs. all or part in Puerto Rico. Once again our analytic technique enabled us to sum these three different ways of categorizing education as well as to tell whether there is any difference between them in explaining linguistic variation.

Birthplace was categorized in two different ways. As a four-category variable the categories used were highland Puerto Rico, coastal Puerto Rico other than San Juan and suburbs, San Juan and suburbs, and continental U.S.A. As a two-category variable the categories utilized were highland Puerto Rico vs. all other birthplaces. As in the other two instances of multiple categorization of demographic variables, we will be able both to compare the effectiveness of these two categorizations of birthplace in explaining linguistic variation and to sum them into one birthplace variable.

Statistical Analysis. The statistical technique utilized in this report is that of analysis of variance via multiple regression analysis. Analysis of variance is a technique designed to answer questions concerning the separate significance as well as the interactional significance of several simultaneous effects. In the context of the present study, analyses of variance can tell us whether context, age, education, or birthplace are separately significant in explaining variation in the production of a particular linguistic variant or whether the interaction between any two of them, e.g., between context and birthplace, has explanatory significance. Multiple regression analysis is a technique designed to answer questions concerning the value of utilizing additional explanatory parameters beyond those already utilized at any given stage in the explanatory process (Bottenberg and Ward 1963; Cohen 1965, 1968a, 1968b). In the context of the present study multiple regression analysis can tell us whether or not certain explanatory parameters (e.g., context plus age) are already so powerful in explaining variation in the production of a particular linguistic variant that it is not necessary or productive to add other explanatory parameters even if the latter too are significantly related per se to the variation in question.

Hypotheses. Spanish Variables. Our general hypothesis regarding linguistic variation in Puerto Rican Spanish (PRS) in the speech community under study is that it will consist of contextual variation primarily and demographic variation only secondarily. Except for regionally related differences between speakers of highland origin and speakers of coastal origin we consider our subjects as constituting a single speech community. Our subjects have all learned the norms of Spanish communicative competence pretty much in the same way and at the same developmental period of their lives. These norms incorporate contextual variation. Too few of our subjects have had too little exposure to formal, educated Spanish to constitute an educated network of the speech community. Such a network might develop speech norms of its own that could significantly modify (i.e., raise or lower) the contextual variation norms that exist for the speech community as a whole.

Our general hypothesis is that beyond a highland-coastal difference in a few variables no significant demographic factors will be encountered in explaining any linguistic variation that may exist in Puerto Rican Spanish above and beyond contextual variation. This hypothesis will be tested here against one illustrative Spanish variant where a variant is described as one of the realizations that a variable can assume.

English Variables. With respect to linguistic variation in Puerto Rican English in the speech community under study our general hypothesis is that it will exist of demographic variation primarily and contextual variation secondarily (if at all). We do not view our subjects as constituting a unitary English speech community with its own contextual norms of communicative competence in that language. In general, the English-speaking horizons and experiences of most of our subjects are still too limited for contextual varieties of English to have developed (or to have been adopted) and to have been stabilized. On the other hand, there are within the speech community those whose English has been significantly modified by substantial influences stemming from outside the community, such as those that derive from American education in particular and increased time in the continental United States in general. We would expect their English to differ from those with other demographic characteristics who have not had these experiences. We expect these differences between demographic groups to be pervasive in their use of English rather than contextualized along a casualness-carefulness dimension for intra-group purposes. This hypothesis will be tested here against one illustrative English variant.

Results. Spanish Variant SpC-0. SpC-0 refers to the dropping of the plural marker *s* when the following word begins with a consonant. An example of this realization is *(los) muchacho comen* as opposed to the standard realization *(los) muchachos comen* (SpC-1) or the common PRS variation *(los) muchachoh comen* (SpC-2). This variable (SpC) had a very high number of occurrences, and the realization in question showed considerable contextual variation, accounting for just 17 percent of the cases of SpC in the most formal context but 62 percent in the least formal context (Ma and Herasimchuk 1968). *S* in this morphophonemic environment was realized quite differently from *s* in other environments. For instance, *s* before a consonant within a word showed zero realization only 11 percent of the time in the least formal context. Similarly, *s* marking a plural article preceding a word beginning with a consonant was realized as zero only 23 percent of the time in the least formal context. In these environments S-2 or [h] was the preferred realization 81 percent and 70 percent of all times respectively in style A. Thus SpC is definitly a favorable environment for zero realization of *s*, with the further advantage, for our present purposes, that there was substantial variation in the realization of SpC-0 across contexts. Under these circumstances, then, we decided to ask whether other parameters of a directly demographic nature might also be significantly related to differential production of SpC-0.

If we examine the first column in Table 3 (labeled r), we will note that only context, in each of its aspects, correlates significantly with differential use of SpC-0. The second aspect of context (that which differentiates between word naming and B + A) correlates with SpC-0 as well (0.423) as do both aspects taken together (column 3, R = 0.424).

The fact that only the two aspects of context correlate significantly with SpC-0 is corroborated in column 8, where only the two aspects of context yield significant F ratios. Thus we can safely conclude that in the speech community under study demographic differences are not significantly related to differential use of SpC-0, whereas contextual differences are so related. However, if we are to stop our prediction of SpC-0 with context alone, we will have accounted for only 18 percent of the casual variance (see column 6). If we add sex of speaker to the prediction of SpC-0, we can account for 24.4 percent of the casual variance. This increase is due to the fact that there is a slight tendency (column 1: r = -0.240) for males to use SpC-0 more frequently than females.

If we continue to add successive demographic variables, our multiple prediction of SpC-0 continues to rise (see column 5) and

TABLE 3

Analysis of Variance via Multiple Regression Analysis of Puerto Rican Spanish SpC-0 (n = 34)

Source	(1) r	(2) r^2	(3) R	(4) R^2	(5) Cum R	(6) Cum R^2	(7) $\triangle R^2$	(8) F_{r^2}	(9) F_{R^2}	(10) $F_{\triangle R^2}$
1. Context: WN vs. B vs. A	0.380[a]	0.144						5.4[a]		
2. Context: WN vs. all other	—0.423[a]	0.180	0.424	0.180	0.424	0.180		7.0[a]	3.0	
3. Sex	—0.240	0.058	0.240	0.058	0.494	0.244	0.064	2.0	2.0	2.5
4. Age: < 25 vs. 25–34 vs. > 34	—0.055	0.003						<1		
5. Age: < 25 vs. all other	—0.021	0.000	0.156	0.024	0.509	0.259	0.015	<1	<1	<1
6. Educ: < 7 yrs. PR vs. 7+ yrs. PR vs. PR and US vs. US only	—0.116	0.013						<1		
7. Educ: all PR vs. other	0.111	0.012						<1		
8. Educ: all USA vs. other	—0.022	0.001	0.193	0.037	0.535	0.286	0.037	<1	<1	<1
9. Birthplace: Highland vs. Coastal vs. San Juan vs. USA	0.063	0.004						<1		
10. Birthplace: Highland vs. all other	—0.163	0.027	0.216	0.047	0.585	0.342	0.056	<1	<1	<1
11. Context×Birthplace	0.239	0.057	0.239		0.602	0.362	0.020	2.0	2.0	<1

[a] Significant at 0.05 level.

finally reaches the appreciable figure of 0.602. A multiple correlation of this magnitude accounts for 36.2 percent of the causal variance in SpC-0, a substantial increase beyond that accounted for by context alone.

Although none of the demographic variables is significantly related to differential use of SpC-0, sex of speaker approaches such significance. This, however, is due to the fact that in the speech community under study more women than men are of highland origin in Puerto Rico. The context by birthplace interaction, therefore, also approaches significance, which indicates that some birthplace groups show more contextual variation than do others.

Table 4 reveals the mean number of occurrences of SpC-0 in the three different contexts for our sample as a whole and for two different birthplace subsamples. This table confirms that the effective contextual difference comes between WN and the two conversational styles. Table 4 also confirms the greater contextual sensitivity of Highland born subjects for whom we find greater average contextual differences than those found for other subjects.

TABLE 4

Contextual Differences in Mean Number of Occurrences of SpC-0, for Total Sample and for Birthplace Groups

Birthplace groups	Contexts			Total
	WN	*B*	*A*	
Highland	27.13	57.27	66.58	49.17
Other	30.38	53.29	57.05	56.09
Total	29.13	54.17	59.87	54.39

English Variant EH-2. EH-2 represents the Standard American English sound [æ], as in cat, bad, ham. Two other variants of this EH variable were recognized: EH-1, as in New York City [kɛðt, bɛðd, hɛðm], and EH-3, as in accented English cah'nt, bahd, hahm. EH-2 serves fairly effectively to differentiate accented from native English speakers, as the sound is not available in Spanish phonology. Mastery of this phone seems to imply mastery of a number of other typically English sounds not available in Spanish.

Use of the three variants of EH changed but slightly and irregularly with context (Ma and Herasimchuk 1968), which support the hypothesis of more or less fixed usage of one sound by any given speaker. EH-2 showed an overall higher incidence of occurrence and, for this reason, was chosen over EH-1 for testing. It is also less ambiguously American; EH-1 can be approximately by the Spanish [ɛ] or [e], so a score of EH-1 does not clearly isolate the sound as English but rather marks some form or other of dialect-realization. For reasons both of numerical frequency and of phonological exclusiveness, then, EH-2 is a very good variant for the statistical testing of relationships between differential use of sounds and the characteristics of their users.

Table 5 reveals quite a different picture from that shown in Table 3. The values in column 1 indicate that neither of the two aspects of context are significantly related to differential use of EH-2. Indeed even when both aspects of context are taken together, it is still the least important multiple predictor of EH-2 except for sex of speaker (column 3). If we utilize context alone, we are able to account for only 3.6 percent of the causal variance pertaining to differential use of EH-2 (column 6). If we add sex of speaker to context, our prediction rises only to 5.8 percent. However, as soon as we consider such demographic variables as age, education, and birthplace the picture changes radically.

Of the three major demographic variables related to differential use of EH-2, the most important is clearly education (column 1). If we combine all three aspects of education, we obtain a multiple correlation of 0.753 (column 3), which itself accounts for 56.7 percent of the causal variance (column 4).

Those of our subjects who were partly or entirely educated in the United States are more likely to utilize EH-2 than those entirely educated in Puerto Rico (note minus correlations in column 1). This relationship between differential use of EH-2 and education is further clarified in Table 6 which reveals it to be consistent for each speech context.

If education is now combined with the variables that precede it in Table 5 (context, sex of speaker, and age), then the resulting cumulative multiple correlation with EH-2 rises to 0.785 (column 5), and we have accounted for 61.6 percent of the causal variance in differential use of EH-2 (column 6).

Although neither age nor birthplace are as strongly related to EH-2 as is education, their independent correlations with EH-2 are clearly significant (columns 1 and 8). When all three of them are added to context and sex of speaker, we arrive at a cummulative correlation of 0.810 (column 5), which indicates that we have accounted for 65.6 percent of the causal variance in differential use of EH-2 (column 6).

TABLE 5

Analysis of Variance via Multiple Regression Analysis of Puerto Rican English EH-2 (n = 26)

Source	(1) r	(2) r^2	(3) R	(4) R^2	(5) Cum R	(6) Cum R^2	(7) $\triangle R^2$	(8) F_{r^2}	(9) F_{r^2}	(10) $F\triangle R^2$
1. Context: WN vs. B vs. A	0.174	0.030						<1		
2. Context: WN vs. all other	−0.112	0.013	0.189	0.036	0.189	0.036		<1		
3. Sex	−0.136	0.018	0.136		0.241	0.058	0.022	<1	<1	<1
4. Age: < 25 vs. 25-34 vs. > 34	−0.524	0.275						9.1[b]		
5. Age: < 25 vs. all other	0.555	0.308	0.556	0.309	0.582	0.338	0.280	10.7[b]	5.17[a]	4.2[a]
6. Educ: < 7 yrs. PR vs. 7+ yrs. PR vs. PR and US vs. US only	−0.717	0.514						25.2[a]		
7. Educ: all PR vs. other	−0.722	0.521						26.1[b]		
8. Educ: all USA vs. other	0.589	0.347	0.753	0.567	0.785	0.616	0.278	12.8[b]	9.45[b]	4.1[a]
9. Birthplace: Highladn vs. Coastal vs. San Juan vs. USA	0.446	0.199						6.0[a]		
10. Birthplace: Highland vs. all other	−0.309	0.095	0.491	0.241	0.810	0.656	0.040	2.5	3.67	<1
11. Context×Birthplace	0.428	0.183	0.428	0.183	0.815	0.664	0.008	5.4[a]	5.4[a]	<1

[a] Significant at 0.01 level. [b] Significant at 0.05 level.

TABLE 6

Contextual Differences in Mean Number of Occurrences of EH-2 for
Total Sample and for Educational Groups

Educational groups	Contexts			Total
	WN	B	A	
Educated entirely in Puerto Rico	15.75	16.43	19.40	16.46
Educated partially or entirely in USA	60.71	64.43	65.17	63.35
Total	35.79	38.57	57.71	40.20

Although context itself is not significantly related to differential
use of EH-2, the interaction between context and birthplace is significantly related to such use. This implies that certain birthplace groups
show more contextual variation than do others. Whereas our sample
as a whole increasingly uses EH-2 as it proceeds from WN (35.79)
to B (38.57) to A (51.71), this variation occurs primarily between
B and A for our highland-born subjects and between WN and B
for other subjects, with the latter using EH-2 more frequently in all
contexts.

Incremental Prediction of EH-2. Not only are age and education
significant variables in accounting for differential use of EH-2 but
they are also incrementally significant in this respect. Column 10 of
Table 5 reveals that it pays to add age as a predictor of differential
use of EH-2 when one has previously used only context and sex of
speaker in this connection. Another way of saying this is that 0.338
(column 6), the cumulative prediction of EH-2 based on three variables
(context, sex of speaker, and age), is significantly better than the
cumulative prediction based on only the first two (0.058). Similarly,
Table 5 indicates that it pays to add Education as well to our prediction
of differential use of EH-2, even after context, sex of speaker, and
age have been used cumulatively in this connection. The cumulative
prediction of EH-2 based upon these four variables (0.616) is
significantly greater than that based on the first three (0.338).

The same cannot be said, however, with respect to birthplace or
the interaction between birthplace and context. Although it is true
that their cumulative addition to the prediction of differential use
of EH-2 (after context, sex of speaker, age, and education have been

cumulatively utilized for this purpose) does increase the multiple prediction of EH-2 from 0.616 to 0.656 to 0.664, these increases, though welcome, are not statistically significant. Thus, if birthplace were an expensive or difficult measure to obtain, we would be justified in deciding to forego it because it does not produce a significant increment in our efforts to account for differential use of EH-2.

There have recently been several other studies of the importance of demographic factors in accounting for the variability of usage (see, e.g., Ellis 1967, Huffine 1966, Jernudd 1968, McCormack 1968). The study just reported gains considerably from the fact that it sought to compare demographic with contextual variation, and to do so in quantitative terms, as well as to do so separately for each of the languages used in a functioning community (rather than by a random sample of speakers).

Conclusions. The foregoing analysis of SpC-0 shows that its variable realization was primarily attributable to contextual-situational variation along a continuum of formality-informality. Whereas demographic factors (not social class in this case since our subjects were so uniformly of the lower class) added to the overall prediction of this variable – as did the interaction between demographic factors and speech context – it is clear that these are of lesser importance than the speech-community-wide norms relating SpC-0 to informality rather than to formality. Scores of other Spanish phonological variables behave in this same way in the Puerto Rican neighborhood under study. As a result we may consider it a single, relatively homogeneous speech network as far as Spanish phonology is concerned, i.e., one in which experiential differences have not resulted in the formation of significantly different groups within the population with substantially unique speech norms of their own. Our Puerto Rican subjects are behaving more like Labov's Lower East Siders than like Geertz's Javanese in this respect.

Just the opposite seems to be true vis-a-vis variability in the realization of English phonology. In connection with EH-2 – and scores of other English variables – no neighborhood-wide contextual-situational variation has as yet developed. Those individuals who have spent larger proportions of their lives in the USA and who have obtained more formal education in the USA have a different English phonology than do their more recently arrived and less American-educated neighbors. Instead of a single set of speech community norms with respect to English phonology there are several different demographic subgroups (social classes if you like) each with their own substantially different English phonologies used consistently in all contexts (by and large). Our Puerto Rican subjects are behaving more like Geertz's Javanese than like Labov's Lower East Siders in this respect. Without common contextual norms vis-a-vis English phonology they are fragmented into more and less advantaged discontinuous strata insofar as English phonology is concerned.

More generally stated in conclusion, the existence of societally shared contextual variation is a sure indication of the existence of a speech community or speech network. Societally shared contextual variation is indicative of social interaction governed by common normative regulations. On the other hand, demographic variation alone is not necessarily indicative of the existence of a speech community or speech network. Indeed, demographic variation in usage is, in and of itself, ambiguous in this very respect. On the one hand, it may be merely indicative of separate experiential groups (e.g., separate castes, social classes, regional origin groups, etc.) that are required to interact in marginal or limited ways. On the other hand, demographic variation may be indicative of relatively pervasive, inflexible and compartmentalized role-relationships within a speech community, such that members of network X always utilize variety x, members of network Y always utilize variety y, etc. Sorenson 1967 has described multilingual speech communities of this kind in the Northwest Amazon region.

The co-occurrences of contextual and demographic variations must not, therefore, be considered a necessary feature of speech communities. It reflects a degree of interaction, a degree of complexity of stratification, and a degree of shared open-network access and repertoire fluidity that are by no means encountered everywhere.

5.4   Non-proletarians of All Regions, Unite!

In a relatively open and fluid society there will be few characteristics of lower class speech that are not also present (albeit to a lesser extent) in the speech of the working and lower middle classes. Whether we look to phonological features such as those examined by Labov or to morphological units such as those reported by Fischer (1958) (Fischer studied the variation between *-in'* and *-ing* for the present participle ending, i.e., runnin' vs. running – and found that the former realization was more common when children were talking to each other than when they were talking to him, more common among boys than among girls and more common among 'typical boys' than among 'model boys'), we find not a clearcut cleavage between the social classes but a difference in rate of realization of particular variants of particular variables for particular contexts. Even the widely publicized distinction between the 'restricted code' of lower class speakers and the 'elaborated code' of middle class speakers (Bernstein 1964, 1966) is of this type, since Bernstein includes the cocktail party and the religious service among the social situations in which restricted codes are realized. Thus, even in the somewhat more stratified British setting the middle class is found to share some of the features of what is considered to be 'typically' lower class speech. Obviously then, 'typicality', if it has any meaning at all in relatively open societies, must refer largely to repertoire *range* rather than primarily to unique features of the repertoire.

This is the most suitable point at which to observe that between Bernstein's view that lower class speech is typically more restricted and Labov's view that lower class speech is typically more informal there is an implied contradiction, if "restricted" is defined as *more* predictable and "informal" as *less* predictable. Actually, the contradiction is more apparent than real. In terms of speech repertoire range both investigators would agree that the range of the lower class is typically narrower than that of the middle and upper middle classes. This is what Bernstein is reacting to when he considers lower class speech more restricted and, therefore, more predictable. On the other hand both investigators would certainly agree that the phonological, lexical or grammatical markers of lower class speech more commonly resemble those of informal usage within the larger speech community. However, as far as redundancy of speech is concerned, one must distinguish between predictability *between* varieties and predictability *within* any of them. Lower class usage may well be more predictable or redundant when *between*-variety variation is considered, as Bernstein claims, and yet be more eliptical and incomplete than middle or upper middle class usage when *within*-variety variation is considered. When Joos and others point to the greater redundancy (ritualization, predictability) of frozen and other more formal styles they are reacting to within-variety rather than between-variety variation. Thus, rather than being in conflict, Bernstein and Labov, taken together, sensitize us additionally to two different but equally important types of variation in the speech behavior of socially variegated speech communities.

Those speech networks with the widest range of experiences, interactions and interests are also those that have the greatest linguistic repertoire range. In many speech communities these networks are likely to be in one or another of the middle classes since some networks within these classes are most likely to maintain direct contact with the lower and working classes below them (in employer-employee, teacher-pupil and other role-relationships), as well as with the upper class above them (in educational, recreational and cultural interactions). However, whereas the repertoire ranges of the upper and lower classes are likely to be equally discontinuous (even if not equally restricted) there is likely to be a very major distinction between them if the larger speech community (the region, the country) is considered. Lower classes tend to be regionally and occupationally separated from each other to a far greater extent than do upper and middle classes (Gumperz 1958). Thus, there may well be several different lower class varieties in a country (depending on regional and on occupational or other specializations), while at the same time upper and upper-middle class speech may attain greater uniformity and greater regional neutrality. The more advantaged classes travel more frequently, engage in joint enterprises more frequently, control the agencies of language uniformation (schools, media, language planning agencies and government per se). They more quickly arrive at a common standard, at least for formal occasions, than do the lower classes who remain fragmented and parochial. Differences

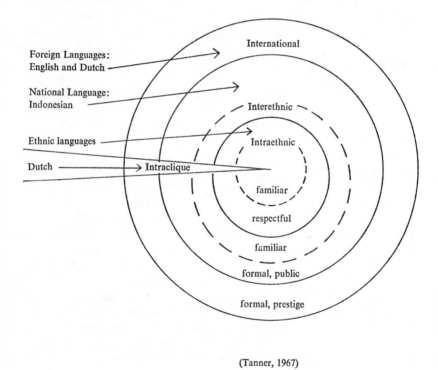

(Tanner, 1967)

Figure 11. Functional Specialization of Codes in Indonesia
and Among the Case Study Group (Tanner, 1967)

such as these are illustrated in Nancy Tanner's case study of an Indonesian elite group (1967; see Figure 11). Whereas the lower classes speak only their local ethnic language, the middle and upper classes also speak several varieties of Indonesian (including a regionally neutral variety that is least influenced by local characteristics) and the elites speak English and Dutch as well. One can predict that as these elites lose their local ties and affiliations and assume Pan-Indonesian roles, establishing speech communities of their own in Djakarta and in a few other large cities, their need for local languages and for locally influenced and informal Indonesian will lessen and their stylistic variation will proceed, as it has with elites in England, France, Germany, Russia and elsewhere in the world, via contrasts with foreign tongues.

Another way of arriving at the conclusions indicated above concerning the greater discontinuity between the lower class varieties than between upper or middle class varieties in most relatively open societies is to consider the differences referred to in Figure 12. Here

NETWORKS DRAWN FROM DIVERSE[a]	Lexical Differences	Phono-logical Differences	Grammatical Differences
EXTRA-REGIONAL-Origin Groups	++	++	++
RACIAL Groups	++	++	++
Ethnic Groups	++	+	+
OCCUPATIONAL Groups	++	+	+
Religious Groups	+	+	+
AGE Groups	++	—	—
SEX Groups	++	—	—

Legend: ++ =Substantial differences are judged to exist between categories (e.g., between different age groups) on the diversity parameter in question.

Legend: + =Moderate differences are judged to exist between categories on the diversity parameter in question.

Legend: — =Negligible or no differences are judged to exist between categories on the diversity parameter in question.

[a] Categories are compared on the assumption that all other bases of group-functioning are held constant when networks are selected at the level of any given diversity parameter. Thus, when considering networks drawn from diverse occupational groups judges were asked to assume that racial, ethnic, religious and other diversity parameters were held constant.

Figure 12. Extent of Linguistic Differences and Extent of Socio-Cultural Differences Within Various Kinds of Speech Networks (as judged by Stanford students native to the Lower Peninsula)

we note that when all other factors are held constant co-territorial groups of diverse regional origin may frequently be expected to differ most profoundly linguistically. The lower classes are exactly those whose regional origins are most diversified in most cities the world over. Indeed, the lower classes are likely to be more heterogeneous than the upper classes in exactly those factors – whether they be diversity of origin or diversity of experience – that are associated with more than peripheral lexical differences between co-territorial populations. They are far more likely to be regionally, socially, culturally, occupationally and religiously diverse than are the upper classes whose self-uniformizing tendencies and capacities have already been mentioned. Indeed, it is only in connection with sex and age variationability that the lower classes are often more homogeneous than the upper but these generally tend to be associated only with the more marginal linguistic differences.

As a result of the differential experiences and opportunities vis-a-vis uniformation to which they are exposed, social class differences in relatively open societies have commonly arrived at the following state of affairs: (a) the middle and upper middle classes have larger repertoires in language and in social behavior than do the lower classes; (b) the lower classes tend to remain more diverse – regionally, ethnically, religiously, racially, etc. – than the upper classes and, therefore, there are preserved more and more discontinuous varieties of lower class speech than of upper class speech. These two tendencies are not in conflict with each other, except as social conflict itself may exist and, therefore, come to disturb whatever societal and usage patterns have been stabilized. They are both due to societal differentials in normal social class role ranges and in exposure to the uniformizing institutions of the larger polity.

5.5 Diversification vs. Massification

One further consideration deserves at least brief attention in our review of societal differentiation and language variation; namely, the common view that there is a trend toward overall uniformation, in language and in other social behavior, as industrialization progresses (Bell 1961; Boulding 1963; Hertzler 1965; Hodges 1964). It is undeniable that life in urbanized and industrial countries is in some ways more uniform than is the case in countries where local and regional particularisms remain relatively untouched. Nevertheless, it seems to be erroneous to think of preindustrial rural heterogeneity and industrial urban homogeneity as either accurate or mutually exclusive designations. Both stages of development seem to foster as well as to inhibit certain kinds of uniformation and differentiation in language as well as in other aspects of behavior.

Certainly, the preindustrial rural society is not as internally heterogeneous as is the urban society with its variety of classes, religions, ethnic groups, and interest groups. Thus, the supposedly uniformizing effect of urbanization and industrialization must pertain to inter-regional or inter-urban comparisons rather than to intra-urban or intra-local ones. Nevertheless, the best available evidence indicates that no trend toward inter-regional homogeneity in religion, politics or other generalized behaviors is apparent in the United States (Glenn 1966, 1967a, 1967b), nor are such trends apparent in other countries, such as England, France, Holland or Belgium that have been industrialized or urbanized for the greatest length of time. There the differences in values, tastes, social and political orientations between manual and nonmanual workers seem to be as great or greater than they are today in the United States (Hamilton 1965; Bonjean 1966; Schnore 1966; Broom and Glenn 1966, etc.).

At the language level both uniformation and differentiation are found to go on simultaneously, indicative of the fact that the traditional and the modern are frequently *combined* into new constellations rather than *displaced* one by the other. Uniformation pressures seem to be strongest in conjunction with only certain varieties within a speech community's verbal repertoire as well as in conjunction with only some of the interaction networks of that community. The language variety associated with school, government and industry tends to be adopted differentially, the degree of its adoption varying with the degree of interaction in these domains. Not only need such adoption not be displacive (particularly when populations remain in their former places of residence) but – even though the adoption may be quite uniform and official for an entire country – it may remain an entirely passive rather than active component in the repertoire of many interaction networks. Thus, even though television viewing and radio listening are most frequent and prolonged among the lower classes their overt repertoires seem to be little influenced by such viewing or listening.

Finally, it should be recognized that urbanization may also foster certain kinds of differentiation. Whereas the number of different ethnic groups (and, therefore, the number of mutually exclusive language groups) may decline, new social differentiations and new occupational and interest groups normally follow in the wake of industrialization. These latter commonly develop sociolects and specialized usages of their own, thus expanding the repertoires of many speakers. Even the rise of languages of wider communication frequently results in differentiation rather than in uniformation. The spread of English as a second

language in the past 50 years has resulted in there being more varieties
of English today (including Indian English, East African English, Fran-
glais, Spanglish and others) rather than less. It is, of course, true that
certain languages, now as in the past, are in danger of dying out.
Nevertheless, others frequently regarded as 'mere varieties' rather than
as full-fledged languages, are constantly being 'born' in terms of differentiating themselves within the linguistic repertoires of certain interaction networks, and, at times, of entire speech communities. Modernization is a complex phenomenon. While it depresses the status and
decreases the number of speakers of certain varieties (e.g., in recent
years: Frisian, Romansch, Landsmal, Yiddish) it raises the status and
increases the speakers of others (Macedonian, Neo-Melanesian, Indonesian, Swahili, etc.).

Our own American environment is an atypical example. It reveals
the uniformation that results from the rapid urbanization and industrialization of *dislocated* populations. We must not confuse the American
experience with that of the rest of the world (Greenberg 1965). In addition, we must come to recognize that American uniformation, whether
in speech or in diet, is at times a surface phenomenon. It is an added
variety to the repertoires that are still there and that are still substantial
if we will but scratch a little deeper (Fishman 1967a).

6.0 SOCIETAL BILINGUALISM: STABLE AND TRANSITIONAL

Societal bilingualism has been referred to so many times in the previous
pages that it is time that we paused to consider it in its own right
rather than as a means of illustrating more general sociolinguistic
phenomena. The psychological literature on bilingualism is so much
more extensive than its sociological counterpart that workers in the
former field have often failed to establish contact with those in the
latter. It is the purpose of this section to relate these two research
traditions to each other by tracing the interaction between their two
major constructs: bilingualism (on the part of psychologists and psycholinguists) and diglossia (on the part of sociologists and sociolinguists).

6.1 Diglossia

In the few years that have elapsed since Ferguson (1959a) first advanced it, the term diglossia has not only become widely accepted by
sociolinguists and sociologists of language, but it has been further extended and refined. Initially it was used in connection with a *society*
that recognized two (or more) languages or varieties for intrasocietal

communication. The use within a single society of several separate codes (and their stable maintenance rather than the displacement of one by the other over time) was found to be dependent on each code's serving functions distinct from those considered appropriate for the other code. Whereas one set of behaviors, attitudes and values supported, and was expressed in, one language, another set of behaviors, attitudes and values supported and was expressed in the other. Both sets of behaviors, attitudes and values were fully accepted as culturally legitimate and complementary (i.e., non-conflictual) and indeed, little if any conflict between them was possible in view of the functional separation between them. This separation was most often along the lines of a H(igh) language, on the one hand, utilized in conjunction with religion, education and other aspects of High Culture, and an L(ow) language, on the other hand, utilized in conjunction with everyday pursuits of hearth, home and lower work sphere. Ferguson spoke of H as "superposed" because it is normally learned later and in a more formal setting than L and is, thereby, superposed upon it.

To this original edifice others have added several significant considerations. Gumperz (1961, 1962, 1964a, 1964b, 1966) is primarily responsible for our greater awareness that diglossia exists not only in multilingual societies which officially recognize several 'languages', and not only in societies that utilize vernacular and classical varieties but, also, in societies which employ separate dialects, registers, or *functionally differentiated language varieties of whatever kind*. He has also done the lion's share of the work in providing the conceptual apparatus by means of which investigators of multilingual speech communities seek to discern the societal patterns that govern the use of one variety rather than another, particularly at the leven of small group interaction. Fishman (1964, 1965a, 1965c, 1965d, 1965e, 1966a, 1968c), on the other hand, has attempted to trace the maintenance of diglossia as well as its disruption at the national or societal level. In addition he has attempted to relate diglossia to psychologically pertinent considerations such as compound and coordinate bilingualism (1965b). Finally, Kaye (1970) has indicated that diglossia is often a far more flexible, changeable and even ill-defined status, particularly in its linguistic aspects, than has often been presumed. The present section represents an extension and integration of these several previous attempts.

For purposes of simplicity it seems best to represent the possible relationships between bilingualism and diglossia by means of a four-fold table such as shown in Figure 13.

6.2 Speech Communities Characterized by both Diglossia and Bilingualism

The first quadrant of Figure 13 refers to those speech communities in which both diglossia and bilingualism are widespread. At times such

DIGLOSSIA

+   —

BILINGUALISM

+	1. Both diglossia and bilingualism	2. Bilingualism without diglossia
—	3. Diglossia without bilingualism	4. Neither diglossia nor bilingualism

Figure 13. The Relationships between Bilingualism and Diglossia

communities comprise an entire nation, but of course this requires extremely widespread (if not all-pervasive) bilingualism and, as a result, there are really few nations that are fully bilingual and diglossic. An approximation to such a nation is Paraguay, where more than half of the population speaks both Spanish and Guarani (Rubin 1962, 1968). A substantial proportion of the formerly monolingual rural population has added Spanish to its linguistic repertoire in connection with matters of education, religion, government, and High Culture (although in the rural areas social distance or status stressing more generally may still be expressed in Guarani). On the other hand, the vast majority of city dwellers (being relatively new from the country) maintain Guarani for matters of intimacy and primary group solidarity, even in the midst of their more newly acquired Spanish urbanity (See Figure 14). Note that Guarani is not an 'official' language (i.e., recognized and utilized for purposes of government, formal education, the courts, etc.) in Paraguay, although it was finally recognized as a "national language" at the 1967 constitutional convention. It is not uncommon for the H variety alone to be recognized as 'official' in diglossic settings without this fact threatening the acceptance or the stability of the L variety within the speech community. However, the existence of a particular 'official' or 'main' language should not divert the investigator from recognizing the fact of widespread and stable multilingualism at the levels of societal and interpersonal functioning (see Table 7).

Below the level of nationwide functioning there are many more examples of stable diglossia co-occurring with widespread bilingualism. The Swiss-German cantons may be mentioned since their entire popu-

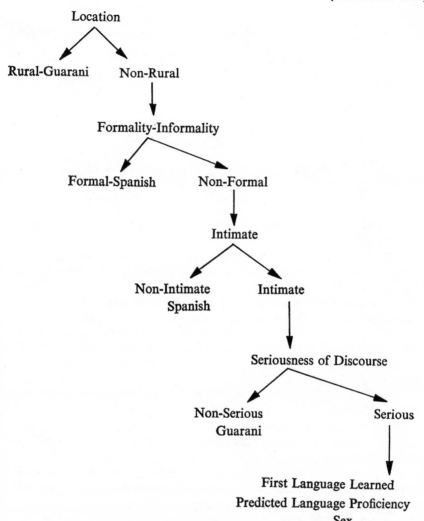

(Joan Rubin 1968)

Location

Rural-Guarani   Non-Rural

Formality-Informality

Formal-Spanish   Non-Formal

Intimate

Non-Intimate   Intimate
Spanish

Seriousness of Discourse

Non-Serious   Serious
Guarani

First Language Learned
Predicted Language Proficiency
Sex

Figure 14. National Bilingualism in Paraguay:
Ordered Dimensions in the Choice of Language in a Diglossic Society
(Joan Rubin, 1968)

lation of school age and older alternates between High German (H) and Swiss German (L), each with its own firmly established and highly valued functions (Ferguson 1959a; Weinreich, U. 1951, 1953a). Hughes (1970) has demonstrated how English (H) and French (L) diglossia-and-bilingualism are peripheral and external in many Montreal agencies

TABLE 7
Linguistic Unity and Diversity, by World Region

No. of Countries by Percent of Population Speaking Main Language

	90-100	80-89	70-79	60-69	50-59	40-49	30-39	20-29	10-14	Total 10-100%
Europe	17	4	2	2	2	—	—	—	—	27
East and South Asia	5	3	4	3	1	4	—	1	—	21
Oceania[a]	2	—	—	—	—	—	—	—	—	2
Middle East and Northern Africa	8	6	2	3	1	2	—	—	—	22
Tropical and Southern Africa	3	—	—	2	5	8	7	5	3	33
The Americas	15	6	—	—	2	2	1	—	—	26
World Total	50	19	8	10	11	16	8	6	3	131

Source: Table 1 (D. Rustow, 1967)
[a] Not including New Guinea, for which no breakdown by individual languages was available.

and businesses in which clients (or customers) and management (or owners) must interact although coming from different origins. On the other hand, in plants (where no customers/clients are present) the communication between workers and management reveals bilingualism-and-diglossia of a hierarchical and internal nature. Traditional (pre-World War I) Eastern European Jewish males communicated with each other in Hebrew (H) and Yiddish (L). In more recent days many of their descendants have continued to do so in various countries of resettlement, even while adding to their repertoire a Western language (notably English) in certain domains of *intragroup* communication as well as for broader *intergroup* contacts (Fishman 1965a, 1965e; Weinreich, U. 1953a; Weinreich, M. 1953). This development differs significantly from the traditional Eastern European Jewish pattern in which males whose occupational activities brought them into regular contact with various strata of the non-Jewish coterritorial population utilized one or more coterritorial languages (which involved H and L varieties of their own, such as Russian, German or Polish on the one hand, and Ukrainian, Byelorussian or 'Baltic' varieties, on the other), but did so primarily for *intergroup* purposes. A similar example is that of upper and upper middle class males throughout the Arabic world who use classical (Koranic) Arabic for traditional Islamic studies, vernacular (Egyptian, Syrian, Lebanese, Iraqui, etc.) Arabic for informal conversation, and, not infrequently, also a Western language (French or English, most usually) for purposes of *intragroup* scientific or technological communication (Blanc 1964; Ferguson 1959a; Nader 1962).

All of the foregoing examples have in common the existence of a

Percentage Bilingual, by Age and Sex, Montreal Area, 1931-61 (Lieberson 1965)

	Males					Females				
	Montreal-Verdun		Montreal-Outremont-Verdun			Montreal-Verdun		Montreal-Outremont-Verdun		
Age	1931 (1)	1941 (2)	1941 (3)	1951 (4)	1961 (5)	1931 (6)	1941 (7)	1941 (8)	1951 (9)	1961 (10)
0- 4 . . .	4.1	5.7	5.7	3.3	2.5	4.0	5.6	5.7	3.4	2.5
5- 9 . . .	18.2	11.3	11.5	9.7	9.9	18.0	11.5	11.8	9.7	9.6
10-14 . . .	43.4	22.2	22.6	20.5	22.4	41.4	21.9	22.3	20.1	21.9
15-19 . . .	62.4	51.4	51.7	50.6	49.6	54.7	43.1	43.5	44.5	46.7
20-24 . . .	67.2	67.1	67.2	64.9	59.4	53.3	51.5	51.7	48.2	44.4
25-34 . . .	61.9	68.8	68.8	63.8	59.7	49.0	47.8	48.1	47.8	41.1
35-44 . . .	62.2	63.6	63.7	68.1	65.3	44.5	40.9	41.2	45.2	45.5
45-54 . . .	59.3	60.3	60.3	62.7	63.6	41.6	35.6	36.0	37.4	42.6
55-64 . . .	57.4	53.7	53.8	57.3	57.2	37.1	31.2	31.6	30.8	34.5
65-69 . . .	56.4	49.4	49.6	49.7	52.0	34.3	28.0	28.5	26.5	28.5
70+	51.2	42.9	43.3	42.2	44.0	31.2	24.4	24.7	23.5	24.5

Socio-economic class groups
SEC 0-1 lower class
2-4 working class
5-7] lower middle class
7-8] upper middle class
9 upper middle class

Socio-economic class groups
SEC 0] lower class
1]
2-3] working class
4-5]
6-8] lower middle class
9 upper middle class

fairly large and complex speech community such that its members have available to them both a range of *compartmentalized* roles as well as ready *access* to these roles. If the *role repertoires* of these speech communities were of lesser range, then their *linguistic repertoires* would also be(come) more restricted in range, with the result that one or more separate languages or varieties would be(come) superfluous. In addition, were the roles not compartmentalized, i.e., were they not *kept separate* by dint of association with quite separate (though complementary) values, domains of activity and everyday situations, one language (or variety) would displace the other as role and value distinctions merged and became blurred. Finally, were widespread access not available to the range of compartmentalized roles (and compartmentalized languages or varieties) then the bilingual population would be a small, privileged caste or class (as it is or was throughout most of traditional India or China) rather than a broadly based population segment.

These observations must lead us to the conclusion that many modern speech communities that are normally thought of as monolingual are, rather, marked by both diglossia and bilingualism, if their several registers are viewed as separate varieties or languages in the same sense as the examples listed above. Wherever speech communities exist whose speakers engage in a considerable range of roles (and this is coming to be the case for all but the extremely upper and lower levels of complex societies), wherever the access to several roles is encouraged or facilitated by powerful social institutions and processes, and finally, wherever the roles are clearly differentiated (in terms of when, where and with whom they are felt to be appropriate), both diglossia and bilingualism may be said to exist. The benefit of this approach to the topic at hand is that it provides a single theoretical framework for viewing bilingual speech communities and speech communities whose linguistic diversity is realized through varieties not (yet) recognized as constituting separate 'languages'. Thus, rather than becoming fewer in modern times, the number of speech communities characterized by diglossia and the widespread command of diversified linguistic repertoires has increased greatly as a consequence of modernization and growing social complexity (Fishman 1966b). In such communities each generation begins anew on a monolingual or restricted repertoire base of hearth and home and must be rendered bilingual or provided with a fuller repertoire by the formal institutions of education, religion, government or work sphere. In diglossic-bilingual speech communities children do *not* attain their full repertoires at home or in their neighborhood playgroups. Indeed, those who most commonly remain at home or in the home neighborhood (the pre-school young and the post-work old) are most likely to be functionally monolingual, as

Lieberson's tables on French-English bilingualism in Montreal amply reveal (see Table 8). Once established, and in the absence of rapid and extensive social change, bilingualism under circumstances of diglossia becomes an ingredient in the situational and metaphorical switching patterns available for the purposes of intra-communal communicative appropriateness. Many conversations and utterances demonstrably 'mean something else', depending on the language in which they are expressed (Table 9) even when all other factors are kept constant (Kimple et al. 1969).

6.3 Diglossia without Bilingualism

Departing from the co-occurrence of bilingualism and diglossia we come first to polities in which diglossia obtains whereas bilingualism is generally absent (quadrant 3). Here we find two or more speech communities united politically, religiously and/or economically into a single functioning unit notwithstanding the socio-cultural cleavages that separate them. At the level of this larger (but not always voluntary) unity, two or more languages or varieties must be recognized as obtaining. However one (or both) of the speech communities involved is (are) marked by relatively impermeable group boundaries such that for 'outsiders' (and this may well mean those not born into the speech community, i.e., an emphasis on ascribed rather than on achieved status) role access and linguistic access are severely restricted. At the same time linguistic repertoires in one or both groups are limited due to role specialization.

Examples of such situations are not hard to find (see, e.g., the many instances listed by Kloss 1966a). Pre-World War I European elites often stood in this relationship with their countrymen, the elites speaking French or some other fashionable H tongue for their *intra-group* purposes (at various times and in various places: Danish, Salish, Provencal, Russian, etc.) and the masses speaking another, not necessarily linguistically related, language for their intra-group purposes. Since the majority of elites and the majority of the masses never interacted with one another they *did not form a single speech community* (i.e., their linguistic repertoires were discontinuous) and their inter-communications were via translators or interpreters (a certain sign of *intra-group* monolingualism). Since the majority of the elites and the majority of the masses led lives characterized by extremely narrow role repertoires their linguistic repertoirès too were too narrow to permit widespread societal bilingualism to develop. Nevertheless, the body politic in all of its economic and national manifestations tied these two groups together into a 'unity' that revealed an upper and a lower class, each with a language

TABLES 9 and 9b

The Interpretation of Language Switching (English-Spanish) given both Bilingualism and Diglossia (Kimple et al., 1969)

Analysis of variance for items requiring subjective judgement:
Conversation 1: boy calls girl for date

Item no.	Source	df	MS	F
10 (length of family's residence in N.Y.)	Treatments Within	3 45	4.13 1.18	3.50a
11 (length of boy's residence in N.Y.)	Treatments Within	3 45	11.70 1.75	6.69b
12 (kind of job held by girl's father)	Treatments Within	3 45	2.46 .62	3.97a
13	Treatments Within	3 45	.17 .73	.23
14	Treatments Within	3 45	.18 .35	.51
15	Treatments Within	3 45	.32 .42	.76
16 (naturalness of conversation between boy and girl)	Treatments Within	3 45	2.32 .33	7.03b
17 (naturalness of conversation between mother and girl)	Treatments Within	3 45	2.19 .56	3.91a
18	Treatments Within	3 45	.67 .46	1.45

a = p < 05   b = p < 01

Analysis of variance for items requiring subjective judgement:
Conversation 2: Invitation to stay for dinner

Item no.	Source	df	MS	F
9	Treatments Within	3 45	.37 .51	.73
10	Treatments Within	3 45	3.33 2.58	1.29
11	Treatments Within	3 45	1.42 .75	1.89
12	Treatments Within	3 45	.06 .93	.65
13 (naturalness of conversation between mother and guest)	Treatments Within	3 45	2.97 .51	5.82b
14 (naturalness of conversation between boy and guest)	Treatments Within	3 45	3.96 .48	8.25b

appropriate to its own restricted concerns. Some have suggested that the modicum of direct interaction that does occur between servants and masters who differ in mother tongue contributes to bringing into being the marginal languages (pidgins) for which such settings are known (Grimshaw, in press).

Thus, the existence of national diglossia does *not* imply widespread bilingualism amongst rural or recently urbanized African groups (as distinguished from somewhat more Westernized populations in those settings); nor amongst most lower caste Hindus, as distinguished from their more fortunate compatriots the Brahmins, nor amongst most lower class French-Canadians, as distinguished from their upper and upper middle class city cousins, etc. In general, this pattern is characteristic of polities that are economically underdeveloped and unmobilized, combining groups that are locked into opposite extremes of the social spectrum and, therefore, groups that operate within extremely restricted and discontinuous linguistic repertoires (Friederich 1962, Fishman 1969a, Pool 1969). Obviously such polities are bound to experience language problems as their social patterns alter as a result of industrialization, widespread literacy and education, democratization, and modernization more generally. Since few polities that exhibit diglossia without bilingualism developed out of prior socio-cultural consensus or unity, rapid educational, political or economic development experienced by their disadvantaged groups or classes is very likely to lead to demands for secessionism or for equality for their submerged language(s). The linguistic states of Eastern Europe and India, and the language problems of Wales and Belgium stem from origins such as these. This is the pattern of development that may yet convulse many African and Asian nations if their de-ethnicized and Westernized elites continue to fail to foster widespread and stable bilingual speech communities that incorporate the masses and that recognize both the official language(s) of wider communication and the local languages of hearth and home (Figure 15).

6.4 Bilingualism without Diglossia

We turn next to those situations in which bilingualism obtains whereas diglossia is generally absent (quadrant 2). Here we see more clearly than before that bilingualism is essentially a charcterization of *individual* linguistic versatility whereas *diglossia is a characterization of the social allocation of functions* to different languages or varieties. Under what circumstances do bilinguals function without the benefit of a well understood and widely accepted social consensus as to *which* languages is to be used between which interlocutors, for communication concerning

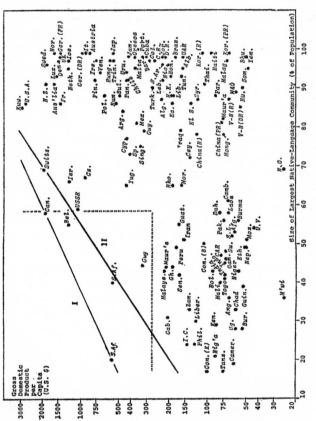

Figure 15. Gross Domestic Product per Capita (US $) and Size of Largest
Language Community (% of Population), c. 1962 (Pool 1969)

what topics or for *what* purposes? Under what circumstances do the varieties or languages involved lack well defined or protected separate functions? Briefly put, these are circumstances of rapid social change, of great social unrest, of widespread abandonment of prior norms before the consolidation of new ones. Children typically become bilingual at a very early age, when they are still largely confined to home and neighborhood, since their elders (both adult and school age) carry into the domains of intimacy a language learned outside its confines. Formal institutions tend to render individuals increasingly monolingual in a language other than that of hearth and home. Ultimately, the language of school and government replaces the language of home and neighborhood, precisely because it comes to provide status in the latter domain as well as in the former, due to the extensive social change to which home and neighborhood have been exposed (See section 7, below).

Many studies of bilingualism and intelligence or of bilingualism and school achievement have been conducted within the context of bilingualism without diglossia (for a review see Macnamara 1966), often without sufficient understanding on the part of the investigators that this was but one of several possible contexts for the study of bilingualism (Corpas 1969, Metraux 1965). As a result many of the purported 'disadvantages' of bilingualism have been falsely generalized to the phenomenon at large rather than related to the absence or presence of social patterns that reach substantially beyond bilingualism (Fishman 1965b, 1966a).

The history of industrialization in the Western world (as well as in those parts of Africa and Asia which have experienced industrialization under Western 'auspices') is such that the means (capital, plant, organization) of production have often been controlled by one speech community while the productive manpower was drawn from another (Deutsch 1966). Initially, both speech communities may have maintained their separate diglossia-with-bilingualism patterns or, alternatively, that of an overarching diglossia without bilingualism. In either case, the needs as well as the consequences of rapid and massive industrialization and urbanization were frequently such that members of the speech community providing productive manpower rapidly abandoned their traditional socio-cultural patterns and learned (or were taught) the language associated with the means of production much earlier than their absorption into the socio-cultural patterns and privileges to which that language pertained. In response to this imbalance some react(ed) by further stressing the advantages of the newly gained language of education and industry while others react(ed) by seeking to replace the latter by an elaborated version of their own largely pre-industrial, pre-urban, pre-mobilization tongue (Fishman 1968c).

Under circumstances such as these no well established, socially recognized and protected functional differentiation of language obtains in
many speech communities of the lower and lower middle classes. Dislocated immigrants and their children (for whom a separate 'political
solution' is seldom possible) are particularly inclined to use their mother
tongue and other tongue for intra-group communication in *seemingly*
random fashion (Fishman, Cooper and Ma 1968; Nahirny and Fishman
1965; Herman 1961). Since the formerly separate roles of the home
domain, the school domain and the work domain are all disturbed by
the massive dislocation of values and norms that result from simultaneous immigration and industrialization, the language of work (and of
the school) comes to be used at home. As role compartmentalization
and value complementarity decrease under the impact of foreign models
and massive change the linguistic repertoire also becomes less compartmentalized. Languages and varieties formerly kept apart come to influence each other phonetically, lexically, semantically and even grammatically much more than before. Instead of two (or more) carefully
separated languages each under the eye of caretaker groups of teachers,
preachers and writers, several intervening varieties may obtain differing
in degree of interpenetration. Under these circumstances the languages
of immigrants may come to be ridiculed as 'debased' and 'broken'
while at the same time their standard varieties are given no language
maintenance support.

Thus, bilingualism without diglossia tends to be transitional both in
terms of the linguistic repertoires of speech communities as well as in
terms of the speech varieties involved per se. Without separate though
complementary norms and values to establish and maintain functional
separation of the speech varieties, that language or variety which is
fortunate enough to be associated with the predominant drift of social
forces tends to displace the other(s). Furthermore, pidginization (the
crystallization of new fusion languages or varieties) is likely to set in
when members of the 'work force' are so dislocated as not to be able
to maintain or develop significantly compartmentalized, limited access
roles (in which they might be able to safeguard a stable mother tongue
variety), on the one hand, and when social change stops short of permitting them to interact sufficiently with those members of the 'power
class' who might serve as standard other-tongue models, on the other
hand.

6.5 Neither Diglossia nor Bilingualism

Only very small, isolated and undifferentiated speech communities may
be said to reveal neither diglossia nor bilingualism (Gumperz 1962;

Fishman 1965c). Given little role differentiation or compartmentalization and frequent face-to-face interaction between all members of the speech community, no fully differentiated registers or varieties may establish themselves. Given self-sufficiency, no regular or significant contact with other speech communities may be maintained. Nevertheless, such groups – be they bands or class – are easier to hypothesize than to find (Owens 1965; Sorensen 1967). All speech communities seem to have certain ceremonies or pursuits to which access is limited, if only on an age basis. Thus, all linguistic repertoires contain certain terms that are unknown to certain members of the speech community, and certain terms that are used differently by different sub-sets of speakers. In addition, metaphorical switching for purposes of emphasis, humor, satire or criticism must be available in some form even in relatively undifferentiated communities. Finally, such factors as exogamy, warfare, expansion of population, economic growth and contact with others all lead to internal diversification and, consequently, to repertoire diversification. Such diversification is the beginning of bilingualism. Its societal normification is the hallmark of diglossia. Quadrant four tends to be self-liquidating.

Many efforts are now underway to bring to pass a rapprochement between psychological, linguistic and sociological work on bilingualism (Fishman and Terry 1969). The student of bilingualism, most particularly the student of bilingualism in the context of social issues and social change, should benefit from an awareness of the various possible relationships between individual bilingualism and societal diglossia illustrated in this section. One of the fruits of such awareness will be that problems of transition and dislocation will not be mistaken for the entire gamut of societal bilingualism.

7.0 LANGUAGE MAINTENANCE AND LANGUAGE SHIFT

Modern history reveals at least five major instances of language shift, i.e., where huge populations adopted a new language or variety into their repertoires, whether or not at the same time they also gave up a language or variety that they had previously used. The instances referred to are (a) the vernacularization of European governmental, technical, educational, cultural activity, (b) the Anglification/Hispanization of the populations of North/South America respectively (Table 10), (c) the adoption of English and French as languages of elite for wider communication throughout much of the world, but particularly so in Africa and Asia, (d) the Russification of Soviet-controlled populations, and most recently (e) the growing displacement of imported languages of wider communication and the parallel vernacularization of govern-

300   Joshua A. Fishman

TABLE 10
1940–1960 Totals for 23 Non-English Mother Tongues in the USA
(Fishman 1966c)

Language	1940 Total	1960 Total	Total Change n	Total Change %
Norwegian	658,220	321,774	—336,446	—51.1%
Swedish	830,900	415,597	—415,303	—50.0%
Danish	226,740	147,619	—79,121	—65.1%
Dutch/Flemish	289,580	321,613	+32,033	+11.1%
French	1,412,060	1,043,220	—368,840	—26.1%
German	4,949,780	3,145,772	—1,804,008	—36.4%
Polish	2,416,320	2,184,936	—231,384	—9.6%
Czech	520,440	217,771	—302,669	—58.2%
Slovak	484,360	260,000	—224,360	—46.3%
Hungarian	453,000	404,114	—48,886	—10.8%
Serbo-Croatian	153,080	184,094	+31,014	+20.3%
Slovenian	178,640	67,108	—111,532	—62.4%
Russian	585,080	460,834	—124,246	—21.2%
Ukrainian	83,600	252,974	+169,374	+202.6%
Lithuanian	272,680	206,043	—66,637	—24.4%
Finnish	230,420	110,168	—120,252	—52.2%
Rumanian	65,520	58,019	—7,501	—11.4%
Yiddish	1,751,100	964,605	—786,495	—44.9%
Greek	273,520	292,031	+18,511	+6.8%
Italian	3,766,820	3,673,141	—93,679	—2.5%
Spanish	1,861,400	3,335,961	+1,474,561	+79.2%
Portuguese	215,660	181,109	—34,551	—16.0%
Arabic	107,420	103,908	—3,512	—3.3%
Total	21,786,540	18,352,351	—3,434,189	—15.8%

In 1940 the numerically strongest mother tongues in the United States
were German, Italian, Polish, Spanish, Yiddish, and French, in that order. Each
of these languages was claimed by approximately a million and a half or more
individuals. In 1960 these same languages remain the 'big six' although their
order had changed to Italian, Spanish, German, Polish, French, and Yiddish.
Among them, only Spanish registered gains (and substantial gains at that) in this
20-year interval. The losses among the 'big six' varied from a low of 2.5% for
Italian to a high of 44.9% for Yiddish. The only other languages to gain in
overall number of claimants during this period (disregarding the generational
distribution of such gains) were Ukrainian, Serbo-Croatian, 'Dutch'/Flemish, and
Greek. The greatest gain of all was that of Ukrainian (202.6%!). Most mother
tongues, including five of the 'big six', suffered substantial losses during this
period, the sharpest being that of Danish (65.1%). All in all, the 23 non-English
mother tongues for which a 1940-1960 comparison is possible, lost approximately
one-sixth of their claimants during this interval. Yet the total number of claimants of non-English mother tongues in the United States is still quite substantial,
encompassing nearly 11% of the total 1960 population (and an appreciably
higher proportion of the white population).[a]

[a] The 1940 and 160 totals shown in Table 10 must not be taken as the totals
for all non-English mother tongue claimants in those years. Figures for Armenian

mental, technical, educational and cultural efforts in many parts of Africa and Asia. Having previously noted (section 5) that divergence and differentiation of the verbal repertoire are reflections of societal distance and segmentation, we must now point out that the socio-cultural changes that carry with them changes in verbal repertoires are themselves differentially associated with the various speech communities and speech networks of any polity. As a result, not only are the verbal repertoires of communities and networks that experience the greatest socio-cultural change the most likely to be altered, but the repertoires of those who gain most in economic, political or other socio-cultural status are the most likely to be adopted or copied by others who see opportunities for desirable changes in their own status by so doing.

The study of language maintenance and language shift focuses upon cell 2 of Figure 13 above and is basically concerned with the relationship between degree of change (or degree of stability) in language usage patterns, on the one hand, and ongoing psychological, cultural or social processes, on the other hand, in populations that utilize more than one speech variety for intra-group or for inter-group purposes. That languages (or language varieties) *sometimes* displace each other, among *some* speakers, particularly in *certain* interpersonal or system-wide interactions, has long aroused curiosity and comment. However, it is only in quite recent years that this topic has been recognized as a field of systematic inquiry among professional students of language behavior. It is suggested here that the three major topical subdivisions of this field are: (a) habitual language use at more than one point in time or space; (b) antecedent, concurrent or consequent psychological, social and cultural processes and their relationship to stability or change in habitual language use; and (c) behavior toward language, including directed maintenance or shift efforts. It is the purpose of this section to discuss each of these three topical subdivision briefly, to indicate their current stage of development, and to offer suggestions for their further development.

7.1 Habitual Language Use at More Than One Point in Time

The basic datum of the study of language maintenance and language shift is that some demonstrable change has occurred in the pattern of

---

were reported in 1940 but not in 1960. Figures for Chinese and Japanese were reported in 1960 but not in 1940. Total figures for "All other" languages were reported in both years. None of these inconsistent or non-specific listings are included in Table 10. Adding in these figures, as well as the neccessary generational estimates based upon them, the two totals would become 1940: 22,036,240; 1960: 19,381,786.

habitual language use. The consequences that are of *primary* concern to the student of language maintenance and language shift are *not* interference phenomena per se but, rather, degrees of maintenance or displacement in conjunction with several sources and domains of variance in language behavior. Thus, the very first requirement of inquiry in this field is a conceptualization of variance in language behavior whereby language maintenance and language displacement can be accurately and appropriately ascertained. In the course of their labors linguists, psychologists, anthropologists and other specialists have developed a large number of quantitative and qualitative characterizations of variance in language behavior. By choosing from among them and adding to them judiciously, it may be possible to arrive at provocative insights into more sociolinguistic concerns as well. Whether those aspects of variance in language behavior that have, in the past, been conceived of as *qualitative*, can be rendered ultimately commensurable with those that have more frequently been considered *quantitative* is a topic to which we will return, after first considering the two aspects separately.

7.11   Degree of Bilingualism

For the student of language maintenance and language shift the *quantification* of habitual language use is related to the much older question of ascertaining *degree of bilingualism*. This question, in turn, has been tackled by a great number of investigators from different disciplines, each being concerned with a somewhat different nuance. Linguists have been most concerned with the analysis of bilingualism from the point of view of *switching or interference*. The measures that they have proposed from their disciplinary point of departure distinguish between phonetic, lexical and grammatical proficiency and intactness (Mackey 1962). At the other extreme stand educators who are concerned with bilingualism in terms of *total performance contrasts* in very complex contexts such as the school or even the society (Manuel 1963). Psychologists have usually studied degrees of bilingualism in terms of speed, automaticity, or habit strength (Macnamara 1966). Sociologists have relied upon relative frequencies of use in *different settings* (Hayden 1964, Hofman 1966a, 1966b, Nahirny and Fishman 1966). Thus, since a great number of different kinds of bilingualism scores or quotients are already available, the sociolinguistically oriented student of language maintenance and language shift must decide which, if any, are appropriate to his own concerns. Since the study of this topic cannot be reduced to or equated with the concerns of any particular discipline it seems highly likely that a *combination or organization of approaches* to the measurement and description of bilingualism will uniquely characterize the study of language maintenance and language shift.

7.12 The Need for a Combination of Interrelated Measures

It would seem that the linguist's interest in itemizing examples of interference and switching introduces an outside criterion into the study of language maintenance and language shift which may not at all correspond to that utilized by speech communities or speech networks under study. The linguist's distinction between what is English and what is French and the distinction made by English-French bilinguals may differ so widely that the linguist's *conclusions* about the drift of shift, based upon interference and switch data, may be seriously in error.

However, even where a linguist is obviously interested only in a carefully delimited question about the relative frequency of a particular instance or class of interferences or shifts, it is clear that it may be far easier to answer this question in some cases than in others (e.g., it may be easier to answer in connection with encoding than in connection with inner speech; it may be easier to answer in connection with writing than in connection with speaking; it may be easier to answer in connection with formal and technical communication than in connection with intimate communication), for the 'density', stability and clarity of interference and switching varies for the same individual from occasion to occasion and from situation to situation. Although interference and switching are lawful behaviors, there are advanced cases of language shift in which even linguists will be hard pressed to determine the answer to "which language is being used?", particularly if a single supra-level answer is required.

Similarly, concern with relative proficiency, relative ease and automaticity, and relative frequency of language use in a contact setting are also not necessarily indicative of overall language maintenance or shift. Conclusions based on such measures may be particularly far off the mark in bilingualism-plus-diglossia settings in which most speakers use both languages equally well (correctly), effortlessly and frequently but differ *primarily* in connection with the topics, persons, and places (or, more generally, the *situations* and situation types or domains) in which these language are used. Thus, in conclusion, the contribution that the student of language maintenance and language shift can make to the measurement of bilingualism, is precisely his awareness (a) that *various* measures are needed if the social realities of multilingual settings are to be reflected and (b) that the measures *can be organized* in terms of relatively *general variance considerations*. Of the many approaches to variance in language use that have been suggested the following is both simple enough for easy presentation as well as sufficiently involved to imply that even greater complexity exists not too far below the surface.

7.13 Media Variance: Written, Read and Spoken Language

Degree of maintenance and shift may be quite different in these very different media. Where literacy has been attained prior to interaction with an 'other tongue', reading and writing in the mother tongue may resist shift longer than speaking. Where literacy is attained subsequent to (or as a result of) such interaction the reverse may hold true (Fishman 1965e). More generally, the linguist's disinclination to be concerned with the written language is a luxury that cannot be afforded in the study of language maintenance and language shift, where the contrasts involved are so frequently between languages that vary greatly in the extent to which they have literacy or other 'higher' functions for the speech networks under study.

7.14 Overtness Variance

Degree of maintenance and shift may be quite different in connection with *inner speech* (in which ego is both source and target), *comprehension* (decoding, in which ego is target), and *production* (encoding, in which ego is the source). Where language shift is unconscious or resisted, inner speech may be most resistant to interference, switching and disuse of the mother tongue. Where language shift is conscious and desired, this may less frequently be the case (Fishman 1965f).

Location of Bilingualism: The Domains of Language Behavior. The *qualitative* aspects of bilingualism are most easily illustrated in connection with the *location* of language maintenance and language shift in terms of *domains* of language behavior. What is of concern to us here is the most parsimonious and fruitful designation of the societally or institutionally clusterable occasions in which one language (variant, dialect, style, etc.) is habitually employed and normatively expected rather than (or in addition to) another.

7.141 The Domains of Language Behavior and the Compound-Coordinate Distinction. If the concept of *domains of language behavior* proves to be as fruitful and as manageable a one as seems to be likely on the basis of recent empirical evidence it may also yield beneficial results in connection with other areas of research on bilingualism, e.g., in connection with the distinction between *coordinate* and *compound* bilingualism (Ervin and Osgood 1954, p. 140). The latter distinction arose out of an awareness (mentioned by several investigators over the years) that there are "at least two major types of bilingual functioning", one (the compound type) being "characteristic of bilingualism acquired by a child who grows up in a home where two languages are spoken more or less interchangeably by the same people and in the same situations" and the other (the coordinate) being "typical of the 'true' bilingual, who has learned to speak one language with his parents, for example, and the other language in school and at work. The total situations, both external and emotional, and the total behaviors occurring when one language is being used will differ from those occurring with the other." From our previous discussion of domains of language behavior it is clear these two types of bilingual functioning (more accurately put, two extremes of a continuum of psycho-neurological organization) have been distinguished on the bases of some awareness, however rudimentary, that *bilinguals vary with respect to the number and overlap of domains in which they habitually employ each of their languages.* However, this is true not only initially, in the acquisition of bilingualism (with which the compound-coordinate distinction is primarily concerned) but also subsequently, *throughout* life. Initially coordinate bilinguals may become exposed to widespread bilingualism in which both languages are used rather freely over a larger set of overlapping domains. Similarly, compound bilinguals may become exposed to a more restrictive or dichotomized environment in which each language is assigned to very specific and non-overlapping domains.

Going one step further it appears that the domain concept may facilitate a number of worthwhile contributions to the understanding of the compound-coordinate distinction in conjunction with language maintenance and language shift per se. Thus, domain analysis may help organize and clarify the previously unstructured awareness that language maintenance and language shift proceed quite unevenly across the several sources and domains of variance in habitual language use. Certain domains may well appear to be more maintenance-prone than others (e.g., the family domain in comparison to the occupational domain) across all multilingual settings charecterized by urbanization and economic development, regardless of whether immigrant-host or co-indigeneous populations are involved. Under the impact of these same socio-cultural processes other domains (e.g., religion) may be found to be strongly maintenance oriented during the early stages of interaction and strongly shift oriented once an authoritative decision is reached that their organizational base can be better secured via shift. Certain interactions between domains and other sources of variance may remain protective of contextually 'disadvantaged' languages (e.g., family domain: internal speech, husband-wife role relations), even when language shift has advanced so far that a given domain as such has been engulfed. On the other hand, if a strict domain separation becoms institutionalized such that each language is associated with a number of important but distinct domains, bilingualism may well become both universal and stabilized even though an entire population consists of bilinguals interacting with other bilinguals. Finally, in conjunction with language maintenance and language shift among American immigrant groups, the interaction between domain analysis and the compound-coordinate distinction may prove to be particularly edifying.

As suggested by Figure 16, most late 19th and early 20th century immigrants to America from Eastern and Southern Europe began as compound bilinguals, with English assigned to quite specific and restricted domains. With the passage of time (involving increased interaction

BILINGUAL FUNCTIONING TYPE	DOMAIN OVERLAP TYPE	
	Overlapping Domains	Non-Overlapping Domains
Compound ('Interdependent' or fused)	2. Second Stage: More immigrants know more English and therefore can speak to each other either in mother tongue or in English (still mediated by the mother tongue) in several domains of behavior. Increased interference.	1. Initial Stage: The immigrant learns English via his mother tongue. English is used only in those few domains (work sphere, governmental sphere) in which mother tongue cannot be used. Minimal interference. Only a few immigrants know a little English.
Coordinate ('Independent')	3. Third Stage: The languages function independently of each other. The number of bilinguals is at its maximum. Domain overlap it at its maximum. The second generation during childhood. Stabilized interference.	4. Fourth Stage: English has displaced the mother tongue from all but the most private or restricted domains. Interference declines. In most cases both languages function independently; in others the mother tongue is mediated by English (reverse direction of Stage 1, but same type).

Figure 16. Type of Billingual Functioning and Domain Overlap
During Successive Stages of Immigrant Acculturation

with English-speaking Americans, social mobility, and acculturation with respect to other-than-language behaviors as well) their bilingualism became characterized, first, by far greater domain overlap (and by far greater interference) and then by progressively greater coordinate functioning. Finally, language displacement advanced so far that the mother tongue remained only in a few restricted and non-overlapping domains. Indeed, in some cases, compound bilingualism once more became the rule, except that the ethnic mother tongue came to be utilized via English (rather than vice-versa, as was the case in early immigrant days). Thus the domain concept may help place the compound-coordinate distinction in socio-cultural perspective, in much the same way as it may well serve the entire area of language maintenance and language shift.

7.142 The Dominance Configuration. Section 7.141 above clearly indicates the need for basic tools of a complex and sophisticated sort. Precise measurement of *degree of maintenance or displacement* will be possible only when more diversified measures of degree of bilingualism (including attention to media and overtness variance) are at hand. Precise measurement of *domains of maintenance or displacement* will be possible only after concerted attention is given to the construction of instruments that are based upon a careful consideration of the various domains of language behavior (and the role-relations, topics and locales – these being the three components of situational variation) mentioned in a scattered international literature. The availability of such instruments will also facilitate work in several related fields of study, such as the success of intensive second-language learning programs, accurate current language facility censuses, applied 'language reinforcement' efforts, etc. Given such instruments, the inter-correlations between the several components of variance in degree of bilingualism will become amenable to study, as will the variation of such inter-correlations with age or with varying degrees of language ability, opportunity and motivation. The relationship between maintenance or displacement in the various domains of language will also become subject to scrutiny. Speculation concerning the relationship between shifts in degree and direction of bilingualism and shifts in the domains of bilingualism will finally become subject to investigation. Finally, out of all the foregoing, it will become possible to speak much more meaningfully about the *dominance configurations* of bilinguals and of changes in these configurations in language maintenance – language shift contexts.

7.143 Some Preliminary Suggestions. Figures 17 and 18 are primarily intended to serve as possible presentation formats for dominance configurations based upon several *domains* and *sources of variance* in language behavior mentioned earlier in this discussion. The types of language use data favored by linguists, psychologists and educators have been set aside temporarily in favor of grosser 'frequency use' data.

Source of Variance					
Media	Overtness	Family role-rels. 1 2 3	Neighb. role-rels. 1 2	Work role-rels. 1 2 3	Jew. Rel/Cult role-rels. 1 2
Speaking	Production Comprehension Inner				
Reading	Production Comprehension				
Writing	Production Comprehension				

Figure 17. Intragroup Yiddish-English Maintenance and Shift in the United States: 1940-1970 Summary Comparisons for Immigrant Generation 'Secularists' Arriving Prior to World War I ('Dummy Table' for Dominance Configuration).

Media	Overtness	Domains	Role-Relations	Summary-Ratings 1940	1970
Speaking	Production	Family	Husband-Wife	Y	Y
			Parent-Child	Y	E
			Grandparent-Grandchild	–	E
			Other: same generation	Y	Y
			Other: younger generation	E	E
		Neighborhood	Friends	Y	E
			Acquaintances	Y	E
		Work	Employer-Employer	E	E
			Employer-Employee	E	E
			Employee-Employee	E	E
		Jewish Rel./Cult	Supporter-Writer, Teacher, etc.	Y	Y
			Supporter-Supporter	Y	Y

Figure 18. Part of 'Dummy Table' in Greater Detail

However, of primary interest at this time are the suggested parameters rather than the rough data presented. An inspection of these figures reveals several general characteristics of the dominance configuration:

(a) the dominance configuration summarizes multilingual language use data for a particular population studied at two points in time and space; (b) a complete cross-tabulation of all theoretically possible sources and domains of variance in language behavior do not actually obtain. In some instances, logical difficulties arise. In others, occurrences are logically possible but either necessarily rare or rare for the particular populations under study; (c) each cell in the dominance configuration summarizes detailed process data pertaining to the particular role-relations (parent-child, teacher-pupil, etc.) pertinent to it and the situations, network types (open and closed) and/or transaction types (interactional and personal) encountered; (d) some of the domains utilized do not correspond to those listed in section 7.2 above, nor are all of the domains previously listed utilized here. This should sensitize us further to the probability that no invariant set of domains can prove to be maximally revealing, notwithstanding the efforts expended in pursuit of such a set (Dohrenwend and Smith 1962, Jones and Lambert 1959, Mackey 1962, Schermerhorn 1964); (e) an exhaustive analysis of the data of dominance configurations may well require sophisticated pattern analysis or other mathematical techniques which do not necessarily assume equal weight and simple additivity for each entry in each cell; (f) a much more refined presentation of language maintenance or language shift becomes possible than that which is provided by means of mother tongue census statistics (Kloss 1929, Nelson 1947). Word naming scores, self-ratings of frequency of usage, observed occurrences of various phonological, lexical, or gramatical realizations, all of these and many other types of scores or indices can be utilized for dominance configuration analysis of speech communities or networks. The need to *summarize* and *group* language usage data necessarily leads to some loss of refinement when proceeding from specific instances of actual speech in face to face interaction to grouped or categorized data. However, such summarization or simplification is an inevitable aspect of the scientific process of discovering meaning in continuous multivariate data by attending to differential relationships, central tendencies, relative variabilities and other similar characterizations. Moreover, the ultimate 'summary' nature of the dominance configuration and the further possibilities of collapsing domains according to higher order psychological or sociological similarities (e.g., 'public' vs. 'private' language use) obviates the proliferation of atomized findings.

All in all, the dominance configuration represents a great and difficult challenge to students of bilingualism and of language maintenance or language shift. It is possible that once this challenge is recognized, serious problems of configurational analysis will also arise, as they have in other substantive areas requiring attention to *patterns* of quantitative or qualitative measures. However, it is unnecessary to prejudge this matter. It does seem fitting to conclude that the dominance configuration – if it is to have maximal analytic value – might best be limited to those aspects of *degree of bilingualism* and of *location of bilingualism* which further inquiry may reveal to be of greatest relative *importance* and *independence*. Focused attention on the study of spoken production (as initially suggested by Table 11) has amply demonstrated the rich yield that a self-imposed limitation of this kind can produce in appropriately selected speech communities (Fishman, Cooper, Ma et al. 1968).

7.2 Psychological, Social and Cultural Processes Related to Stability or Change in Habitual Language Use

The second major topical subdivision of the study of language maintenance and language shift deals with the psychological, social and cultural processes associated with habitual language use. Under certain conditions of interaction the relative incidence and configuration of bilingualism stabilizes and remains fairly constant over time within various bilingual-diglossic speech communities. However, under other circumstances one variety or another may continue to gain speakers to the end that bilingualism initially increases and then decreases as the variety in question becomes the predominant language of the old and the mother tongue of the young. The second subdivision of the study of language maintenance and language shift seeks to determine the processes that distinguish between such obviously different conditions of interaction as well as processes whereby the one condition is transformed into the other. The processes pertaining to this topical subdivision may be conceived of either as antecedent, concurrent (contextual), or consequent variables, depending on the design of particular studies. Their major common characteristic is that they are primarily *outside* of language per se.

7.21 The Paucity of Cross-Cultural and Diachronic Regularities.
Just as an understanding of social-behavior-through-language must depend upon a general theory of society so the understanding of language maintenance or language shift must depend on a theory of socio-culture contact and socio-cultural change. Furthermore, it would seem that since we are concerned with the possibility of stability or change in language behavior on the one hand, we must be equally concerned with all of the forces contributing to stability or to change in societal behavior more generally, on the other. Thus the selection of psychological, social and cultural variables for the study of language maintenance and language shift may well be guided not only by impressions of what seem

TABLE 11

Claimed Frequency of Mother Tongue Use in Conversations by Oldest and Youngest Children of Four Ethnic Backgrounds[a] (Fishman, 1966c)

In Conversation with:	German			Jewish			Polish			Ukrainian		
	Almost Always N %	Fre-quently N %	Almost Never N %	Almost Always N %	Fre-quently N %	Almost Never N %	Almost Always N %	Fre-quently N %	Almost Never N %	Almost Always N %	Fre-quently N %	Almost Never N %
Grandparents	6 26.1	6 26.1	11 47.8	6 20.0	9 30.0	15 50.0	15 57.6	5 19.2	6 23.2	26 96.3	– –	1 3.7
Father	7 18.4	10 26.4	21 55.2	5 15.0	23 34.3	34 50.7	22 38.3	17 26.7	21 35.0	42 84.0	6 12.0	2 4.0
Mother	5 16.1	4 12.9	22 71.0	5 9.8	19 37.4	27 52.9	16 29.1	14 25.4	25 45.5	41 89.1	5 10.9	– –
Brothers and Sisters	2 8.7	2 8.7	19 82.6	– –	7 18.9	30 81.1	7 19.4	5 13.8	24 66.7	20 50.0	18 45.0	2 5.0
Friends	3 10.0	7 22.3	20 66.7	– –	10 22.7	34 77.3	4 9.8	9 21.9	28 68.3	15 27.3	20 36.4	20 36.4
Husband and Wife	2 11.1	1 5.6	15 83.3	– –	1 4.5	21 95.5	3 15.0	– –	17 85.0	4 36.4	3 27.3	4 36.4
Own Child	1 5.6	3 16.7	14 77.8	– –	1 5.3	18 94.7	3 20.0	– –	12 80.0	4 50.0	3 37.5	1 12.5

[a] Data reported by parents. The German and Polish parents studied were primarily second generation individuals. The Jewish and Ukrainian parents studied were primarily first generation individuals. All parents were ethnic cultural or organizational 'leaders'.

to be the most relevant processes in a particular contact situation but also by more general theories of personal, social, and cultural change. This is not to imply that all forces leading to *change* in other-than-language behaviors *necessarily* also lead to language *shift*. Indeed, whether or not this is the case (or, put more precisely, a determination of the circumstances under which language and non-language behaviors change concurrently, consecutively or independently) constitutes one of the major intellectual challenges currently facing this field of inquiry. If this challenge is to be met, it will be necessary for the study of language maintenance and language shift to be conducted within the context of studies of intergroup contacts that attend to important other-than-language processes as well: urbanization (ruralization), industrialization (or its abandonment), nationalism (or de-ethnization), nativism (or cosmopolitanization), religious revitalization (or secularization), etc.

Our current state of generalizeable knowledge in the area of language maintenance and language shift is insufficient for the positing of relationships of cross-cultural or diachronic validity. Indeed, many of the most popularly cited factors purportedly influencing maintenance and shift have actually been found to 'cut both ways' in different contexts or to have no general significance when viewed in broader perspective. Thus, Kloss illustrates that no uniform consequences for language maintenance or language shift are derivable from (a) absence or presence of higher education in the mother tongue, (b) larger or smaller numbers of speakers, (c) greater or lesser between-group similarity, and (d) positive or hostile attitudes of the majority toward the minority (Kloss 1966b, pp. 9-13). The presence of so many ambivalent factors is a clear indication that complex interactions between partially contributory factors (rather than a single overpowering factor) must frequently be involved and that a typology of *contact situations* (as well as a theory of socio-cultural change) may be required before greater regularity among such factors can be recognized.

Although debunking represents a rather primitive level of scientific development it may be a necessary stage on the path to greater maturity. Although we *cannot* currently formulate universally applicable regularities in our area of inquiry we *can* indicate that several attempts along these lines fall somewhat short of their mark:

7.211 *A Few Questionable Generalizations.*

7.2111 *Language Maintenance is a Function of Intactness of Group Membership or Group Loyalty, Particularly of Such Ideologized Expressions of Group Loyalty as Nationalism.* Among the evidence pointing to the need for refining or justifying this view is that which reveals that the Guayqueries of Venezuela preserved their groupness by preserving their property relations while giving up their language and religion (Hohenthal and McCorkle 1955), that lower caste groups in India pursue Sanskritization (emulation) rather than solidarity as a means of *group* mobility, that "the Raetoromans, like the Italian Swiss, cultivate the fullest possible loyalty to their language without aspiring to such nationalistic goals as political independence" (Weinreich 1953a, p. 100), that the 'Yiddishist' movement in Eastern Europe before and after World War I similarly concentrated on a language program rather than on political organization (Weinreich 1953, p. 100), that second and third generation Americans frequently maintain "cultural (refinement) bilingualism" after ethnic group loyalty disappears at any functional level and, vice versa, that vestiges of behavioral ethnicity often remain generations after language facility has been lost (Fishman and Nahirny 1964); that many Auslandsdeutsche maintained their self identification as Germans in the midst of Polish or Ukrainian majorities, long after completely giving up their German mother tongue (Kuhn 1930, 1934); that Language loyalty is low in many newly developing and highly nationalistic African states (Brosnahan 1963b, Spencer 1963), etc. Thus, it would seem, on the one hand, that language maintenance has continued under various and highly different forms of group membership, some of which have involved significant changes in traditional social relationships and in pre-established role-relations. On the other hand, it appears that group loyalty can be similarly (if not more) ubiquitous, continuing both with and without language maintenance. The American readiness to use language as an index of acculturation may, in itself, be quite culture bound (Samora and Dean 1956). Hymes' observation that "some languages do not enjoy the status of a symbol crucial to group identity" (Hymes 1962, p. 30) and Weinreich's observation that "the connection (between language maintenance and group maintenance) is thus at least flexible and cannot be taken entirely for granted" (Weinreich 1953, p. 100) really represent important intellectual challenges for the study of language maintenance and language shift. We very much need a more refined understanding of the circumstances under which behaviors toward language and behaviors toward the group are related to each other in particular ways. We can recognize today that the pre-World War II views of many German students of language maintenance and language shift (as to whether language and language consciousness create – or are derived from – race, peoplehood and consciousness of kind) were too simplified and too colored by then current political considerations. However, the fact remains that the relationship between language-saliency and group-saliency is almost as speculative today as it was at that time, although it seems clear that a language undergoing massive displacement may be retained most fully by increasingly atypical and self-consciously mobilized populations as displacement progresses. Nevertheless, it is also clear that ideologies normally mobilize only a relatively younger, more active and, perhaps, more alienated or dislocated segment of any large population. Language maintenance may depend *most* on nationalist ideologies in populations whose lives have otherwise been *greatly dislocated* and it may also depend *least* on such ideologies in those populations that have best preserved their total social context against the winds of change (Fishman, 1969d).

The nationalism of several African and Asian countries seems to be much more characterized by *nationism* than by the nationalistic elaboration of ethnicity per se. It is much more concerned with the instrumental political and economic conditions of *nationhood* than with the socio-cultural content of *peoplehood*. The political and administrative limits of new nations are now usually defined in advance of their formation rather than in the process of their formation. The new nations are less frequently formed as the result of the 'painful but glorious' unification of hitherto particularistics who have groped to define the language, the history, the customs, and the missions that unite them and set them apart from others. They are formed along supra-ethnic lines that normally follow colonial demarcations which depended on the fortunes of conquest and the skills of treaty-making. Political and economic self-determination are much more prominent considerations in the new nations than is cultural self-determination of the European pre- and post-World War I variety. Political leadership is much more evident than cultural leadership. The Western experience has typically been that industrialization preceded urbanization and (particularly in Eastern Europe) that nationalism preceded nationism and that the first set of phenomena preceded the second. In the new nations, the reverse sequences seem to be more common, and these may be among the major socio-cultural determinants de-emphasizing language issues in connection with local or regional languages, on the one hand, and which favor continued use of supra-regional and colonial languages on the other. Indeed, it may be that language concerns are most noticeable today where we find socio-cultural distinctions remaining (even after the attainment of considerably more politico-operational integration than has currently been attained in most new nations), particularly when hitherto backward, exploited or disadvantaged groups begin to experience great and rapid economic and cultural development in their own areas of primary population concentration (as, e.g., the French-Canadians, Flemings, Jura-regionists, etc.). The displacement of Western languages of wider communication in Africa and Asia is coming – particularly in connection with mass education and governmental operations and services – and it is coming on socio-cultural integrative grounds,

but it is still just coming, rather than having arrived together with independence.

*7.2112   Urban Dwellers are More Inclined to Shift; Rural Dwellers
(More Conversative and More Isolated) are Less Inclined to Shift.* This
is one of the most reasonable and best documented generalizations in
the study of language maintenance and language shift. Nevertheless, it
runs counter to the first mentioned generalization, above, in that
consciousness of ethnicity and the *espousal* of nationalism have been
primarily urban phenomena. Language revival movements, language
loyalty movements, and organized language maintenance efforts have
commonly originated and had their greatest impact in the cities. Intelli-
gentsia and middle class elements, both of which are almost exclusively
urban, have frequently been the prime movers of language maintenance
in those societies which possess both rural and urban populations.
Indeed, urban groups have been 'prime movers', organizers or mobi-
lizers more generally, that is in connection with other than language
matters as well as in connection with language behavior and behavior
toward language. Thus, whereas small rural groups may have been
more successful in establishing relatively selfcontained traditional interaction patterns and social structures, urban groups, exposed to interaction in more fragmented and specialized networks, may reveal more
conscious, organized and novel attempts to preserve or revive or change
their traditional language. The urban environment does facilitate
change. However, the *direction of such change* has not always favored
language shift at the expense of language maintenance. *When* it has
favored the one and *when* the other (and when urban-inspired language shift has actually signified a return to a languishing ancestral
language), represents a further challenge to this field of study.

   Discussions of rurality-urbanness in relation to language maintenance
have often unwittingly combined two related but importantly separate
factors: separation and concentration. Thus, rurality is often not so
much significant for language maintenance because of a higher relative
concentration of own-mother-tongue population as because rural populations can isolate themselves consciously – or are more isolated even
without particularly wanting to be – from differently speaking populations. Data from several countries illustrate this aspect of rurality. In
the United States in 1940 the 'second generation foreign white stock'
(that is native born individuals of foreign born parents) was regularly
more retentive of its ethnic mother tongues – regardless of whether this
stock was derived from less retentive old-immigrant (Scandinavian and
German) or from more retentive new-immigrant (Southern and Eastern
European) groups – if living in rural than if living in urban areas
(Haugen 1953, Table 12). Seemingly, at that time, it was more possible

TABLE 12
Mother Tongue of Second Generation Foreign White Stock for Urban and Rural Population in U.S. and Selected States (1940) (Haugen, 1953)

		Norway	Sweden	Denmark	Neth.	Germany	Austria	Poland	Finland	Italy
U.S. Urban	Stock	312,980	538,500	164,480	143,100	2,570,740	596,360	1,608,600	85,000	2,612,740
	Language	127,160	222,860	44,600	48,120	1,397,260		1,176,580	54,480	1,832,000
	Retention	40.7	41.4	27.1	33.6	42.6ᵃ		73.3	64.0	70.2
U.S. Rural Non-farm	Stock	134,660	148,360	64,380	48,020	651,360	125,680	186,000	35,140	283,100
	Language	72,080	63,100	19,120	18,320	412,380		151,420	24,420	193,300
	Retention	53.5	42.4	29.7	38.2	50.5		81.4	69.8	68.3
U.S. Rural	Stock	214,960	169,460	76,780	70,100	776,740	59,300	117,780	46,940	75,360
	Language	145,000	88,080	31,740	36,900	626,060		100,820	39,560	55,380
	Retention	67.5	52.5	41.3	52.6	70.7		85.6	84.3	73.6
Wis. Urban	Stock	30,600	14,680	12,820	8,520	214,080	17,040	60,980	2,460	18,260
	Language	14,900	6,260	5,100	3,480	145,120		53,600	1,460	13,800
	Retention	48.6	42.7	39.7	40.9	61.3		83.2	59.3	75.7
Wis. Rural Non-farm	Stock	17,980	6,920	4,860	2,840	63,640	4,200	7,740	1,480	2,440
	Language	11,500	3,020	1,620	1,700	46,220		7,200	1,180	1,820
	Retention	64.0	43.7	33.4	59.9	64.5		93.5	79.8	74.6
Wis. Rural	Stock	33,820	12,360	6,800	6,140	103,100	6,400	18,080	3,780	1,380
	Language	24,660	6,540	2,960	3,840	81,880		17,660	2,980	960
	Retention	72.9	52.9	43.5	62.6	70.7		97.8	79.8	69.6

Table 12 (continued)

		Norway	Sweden	Denmark	Neth.	Germany	Austria	Poland	Finland	Italy
Minn. Urban	Stock....	73,720	87,880	13,380	2,920	91,340	10,880	19,180	12,540	8,760
	Language	37,320	44,000	4,380	760	58,840		13,840	9,240	5,460
	Retention	50.7	50.2	32.7	26.0	55.7		72.3	73.6	62.4
Minn.Rural Non-farm.	Stock....	33,980	24,260	5,320	2,340	42,820	1,920	2,540	5,680	1,720
	Language	22,640	13,260	2,120	960	32,380		2,420	4,300	1,240
	Retention	66.8	54.6	39.2	41.0	70.7		95.3	75.8	72.2
Minn.Rural	Stock....	69,240	49,820	10,860	7,760	90,500	3,560	6,920	15,880	380
	Language	52,660	32,020	4,580	4,440	69,560		7,400	14,300	200
	Retention	76.2	64.4	42.2	57.2	72.4		?	90.2	—
N.Y.Urban	Stock....	27,700	44,380	12,160	12,380	433,180	207,960	365,220	7,500	952,440
	Language	9,620	17,260	2,000	2,440	210,780		196,580	3,500	664,760
	Retention	34.8	38.9	16.4	19.7	32.1		53.8	46.7	69.8
N.Y.Rural Non-farm.	Stock....	3,280	7,980	2,660	4,000	62,320	10,280	27,420	1,240	52,140
	Language	660	2,560	500	1,200	25,180		21,440	520	33,340
	Retention	20.1	32.1	18.8	30.0	33.4		78.3	41.9	63.8
N.Y. Rural	Stock....	680	2,560	900	3,430	22,620	3,880	14.920	880	8,240
	Language	160	1,180	200	1,680	12,100		13,260	640	5,720
	Retention	—	46.2	—	49.0	42.5		88.9	—	69.6

ᵃ Figures for Switzerland have everywhere been added to the German stock.

to hand on more traditional ways of life, including the traditional mother tongue, in rural areas, particularly in those that were populated largely by others of the same language background. Such separation no longer made much difference in the United States in 1960 (Fishman 1966c).

Similarly, non-rurality in India (as well as a more advanced level of education which accompanies non-rurality) is positively related to claiming English as a subsidiary language in contemporary India (Table 13), but it is negatively related to the claiming of Hindi as a subsidiary

TABLE 13

The Best Predictors of District Variation in English Claiming
(N = 129 districts)
(Das Gupta and Fishman, 1971)

Cumulative Predictor	r	CumR	CumR²	△R²	F△R²
% Male Pri + Jr	−.336b	.336	.113	—	—
% Male Matric +	.176a	.497	.247	.134	22.3c
Rural pop/Total pop	−.054	.649	.421	.174	37.8c
% Immigrants	.038	.659	.434	.013	2.8
% Female Matric	.057	.670	.448	.014	3.1
Crude Literacy	−.067	.672	.452	.004	< 1
% Female Pri + Jr	−.146	.678	.459	.007	1.6
Agricult/% Rural	−.122	.679	.461	.002	< 1
Workers in retail	.039	.679	.462	.001	< 1
Persons/sq. mile	.056	.680	.463	.001	< 1
Workers in manuf.	−.005	.681	.463	.000	0.0
Scheduled caste	.021	.681	.464	.001	< 1

a = significant at .05 level
b = significant at .01 level
c = significant at .001 level

language (Table 14). Seemingly, the acquisition of English depends on institutions, higher schools, government bureaus, organizations and media (newspapers, motion pictures) not readily available in the rural areas. However, the acquisition of Hindi (in non-Hindi mother tongue areas) depends more on lower schools, on radio broadcasts and on federal governmental agricultural demonstration and assistance programs and these *are* available in rural areas. Thus, rurality in India means well nigh full separation from English acquisition opportunities and, therefore, a relative intensification of Hindi acquisition opportunities. Language shift is occurring in both settings, but in different directions as a result of the differential separations that rurality represents

TABLE 14

The Best Predictors of District Variation in Hindi Claiming
(N = 75 districts) (Das Gupta and Fishman, 1971)

Cumulative Predictor	r	CumR	CumR^2	$\triangle$R^2	F$\triangle$R^2
% Male Pri + Jr.	.425[a]	.425	.181	—	—
Crude Literacy	−.167	.619	.384	.203	23.6[c]
% Female Matric +	−.019	.635	.403	.019	2.2
% Male Matric +	−.163	.680	.462	.059	7.7[b]
Agricult/% Rural	.303[b]	.719	.518	.056	8.0[b]
% Immigrants	−.086	.736	.542	.024	3.6
% Female Pri + Jr.	.055	.744	.553	.011	1.6
Rural Pop/Total Pop	.030	.746	.556	.003	< 1
Persons/Sq.Mile	−.120	.747	.558	.002	< 1
Scheduled caste	.046	.748	.559	.001	< 1
Workers in Manuf.	−.051	.752	.565	.006	< 1
Workers in Retail	−.142	.753	.566	.001	< 1

[a] = significant at .05 level
[b] = significant at .01 level
[c] = significant at .001 level

for English and for Hindi (Das Gupta and Fishman, in press). Of course, separation need not depend on rurality and can occur – although less readily – in urban areas as well. Lieberson (in press) has shown that "separating occupations" can serve language maintenance quite as well as does the separation factor in rurality (Table 15).

The impact of population concentration, i.e., the proportion that speakers of language X are of the total co-territorial population of a particular administrative unit, is quite another matter from rurality per se. Of course, rurality *is* related to population concentration in general but as we have used it here, concentration is a proportional matter rather than merely an absolute one. Once again, there is much evidence that population concentration is important in language maintenance, but this is true in urban rather than in rural settings. Thus, Lieberson (in press) has shown that in cities in which the proportions of non-English-speaking immigrants were higher in 1900 the proportion of second generation Americans unable to speak English was also higher (Table 16). Sixty years later, those non-English mother tongues that were numerically in the strongest position in the United States were exactly those that constituted the highest relative proportions of the total populations of the states in which their claimants were concentrated (Table 17). Seemingly, a relatively large community of speakers is necessary,

TABLE 15
*Foreign Born White Males Unable to Speak English,
By Occupation, 1890* (Lieberson, 1971)

Occupation	Per Cent Unable to
All	23
Agricultural Laborers	28
Miners (coal)	55
Stock Raisers, Herders	52
Professional Service	8
Dentists	4
Lawyers	2
Bartenders	6
Launderers	30
Auctioneers	4
Clerks and Copyists	6
Salesmen	5
Artificial Flower Makers	30
Brick and Tile Makers	46
Harness and Saddle Makers	10
Iron and Steel Workers	33
Printers, Lithographers	8
Tailors	29
Tobacco and Cigar Factory Operatives	44

Note: Persons born in England, Ireland, Scotland, and Canada (English) are excluded since it is assumed that virtually all could speak English prior to migration.

in many immigrant settings at least, in order for language maintenance to be most useful as well as most likely in the increasingly urban context with which it is faced. Under circumstances of high relative concentration non-English schools, publications, broadcasting, organization activity, and, above all, non-English family patterns can more readily be maintained in interactional American urban environments. Thus, not only is an inter-group diglossia fostered in urban centers with a high relative concentration on non-English speakers, but in addition, intra-group diglossia, in terms of the separate societal allocation of functions, becomes more of a possibility. Soviet developments during the past few decades also seem to reveal similar processes with respect to the co-existence of Russian and the languages of at least the major Soviet minorities (Table 18).

TABLE 16

Proportion Unable to Speak English in Cities,
Second Generation Cross-Tabulated by Foreign Born, 1900
(Lieberson, 1971)

Cities Classified by Propor'tion of Foreign Born Unable to Speak English	Mean Proportion Unable to Speak English Among	
	Foreign Born	Second Generation
.10+	.1957	.0065
.05 to .09	.0682	.0005
.04 or less	.0267	.0003

Data based on 20% sample of cities with 25,000 or more population. 'Foreign born' refers to Foreign Born Whites; 'Second Generation' refers to Native Whites of Foreign Parentage.

7.2113 The More Prestigeful Language Displaces the Less Prestigeful Language. Our earlier discussions of *sources of variance* and *domains of language behavior* may have prepared us for the realization that language prestige is not a unit trait or tag that can be associated with a given language under all circumstances. Indeed, our earlier discussions were necessary precisely *because* the prestige of languages can vary noticeably from one context to another for the same interlocutors, as well as from one speech network to another within the same speech community. It is for this very reason that Weinreich recommends that "as a technical term . . . 'prestige' had better be restricted to a language's value in social advance" (Weinreich 1953a, p. 79). However, even this limitation does not make the concept 'prestige' any more useful for research purposes since social advance itself is relative to various reference groups. Advance in family and neighborhood standing may require a different language than advance in occupational or governmental standing. The fact that an overall hierarchy of reference groups may exist does not mean that the top-most reference group will be dominant in each face-to-face situation.

It may be precisely because 'prestige' obscures so many different considerations and has been used with so many different connotations that the relationship between prestige data and language maintenance or language shift data has been more uneven than might otherwise be expected. Thus, whereas Hall claims that "it is hard to think of any modern instance in which an entire speech community is under pressure to learn a sub-standard variety of a second language" (Hall 1952, p.

TABLE 17

English Concentration (in Selected States), Internal Concentration and Urbanness (in the United States) of Foreign Born Claimants of 23 Non-English Mother Tongues (Fishman 1966a)

Composite Ranking of overall strength 1960	Foreign Born Claimants in selected States[a] 1960	Total Population in selected States[a] 1960	'External' Concentration	Rank	% Urban	Rank	'Internal' Concentration No. of States
1 Spanish	467,147	25,296,881	.01846	2	.848	12	2
2 German	694,824	53,900,032	.01196	3	.837	13	4
3 Italian	692,155	34,168,452	.02026	1	.932	5	3
4 French	173,775	40,183,320	.00432	6	.836	14	4
5 Polish	340,347	46,006,022	.00739	5	.905	8	4
6 Dutch/Flemish	72,823	46,389,484	.00157	15	.787	20	4
7 Hungarian	110,170	32,555,483	.00338	8	.900	9	3
8 Yiddish	295,308	16,782,304	.00760	4	.982	1	1
9 Ukrainian	58,678	34,168,452	.00172	14	.910	7	3
10 Russian	157,917	43,818,874	.00360	7	.927	6	3
11 Greek	89,429	47,729,244	.00185	13	.944	2	4
12 Norwegian	76,492	38,766,586	.00197	11	.765	21	4
13 Swedish	109,102	45,994,530	.00237	10	.806	17	4
14 Slovak	85,925	43,874,849	.00196	12	.831	16	4
15 Slovenian	16,692	31,106,921	.00054	21	.825	18	3
16 Serbo-Croatian	47,577	33,246,795	.00102	17	.880	11	4
17 Lithuanian	60,203	46,824,125	.00139	16	.899	10	4
18 Portuguese	56,257	43,331,406	.00270	9	.834	15	2
19 Czech	45,376	20,865,782	.00087	18	.803	19	4
20 Arabic	26,630	52,287,063	.00048	22	.937	4	5
21 Danish	37,415	55,177,677	.00083	19	.764	22	4
22 Rumanian	12,946	45,338,203	.00039	23	.739	3	3
23 Finnish	32,242	48,838,144	.00066	20	.669	23	5
		U.S.A.			.699		

a 'Selected states' = Least number of states required order tot include 50% of claimants.

TABLE 18

Proportions of Russians in populations of Union Republics in 1926
and 1959, and percentage of migrant and non-migrant populations
using Russian as native language

(Lewis, 1971)

Republic	% of Russians in population			% using Russian 1959	
	1926	1959		non-migrant	migrant
		Total	Urban		
Russia	78	83.0	87.2	—	—
Ukraine	9	16.9	29.9	12.0	23.0
Belorussia	8	8.2	19.4	15.0	28.0
Uzbekistan	6	13.5	33.4	0.3	12.6
Kazakhistan	20	42.7	57.6	1.2	4.3
Azerbaidjhan	10	13.6	24.9	1.2	9.3
Armenia	2	3.2	4.5	8.0	15.0
Georgia	4	10.1	18.8	0.4	8.0
Lithuania	–	8.5	17.0	0.1	3.5
Moldavia	9	10.2	30.8	3.0	15.0
Latvia	–	26.6	34.5	1.4	25.0
Tadzhikstan	5	13.3	35.3	0.5	18.0
Turkmenia	8	17.5	35.4	0.6	6.7
Estonia	–	20.1	30.8	0.5	25.0
Kirgisia	12	30.1	51.8	0.3	16.0

Sources — (a) Figures for 1926 and 1959 are drawn from the respective Census returns. (b) Volova, N.G. Voprosy Dvuyazychaya na Severnom Kaukaza, *Sovetskaya Etnografiya* 1967, No. 1, 27-40.

19), it is really not very hard to do so: A Low German dialect displaced Lithuanian in East Prussia before World War I, although many Lithuanians there were highly conversant with Standard German (Gerullis 1932). Unstandardized Schwyzertutsch is replacing Romansh, although several generations of Raetoromans have known Standard German as well (Weinreich 1951, pp. 284–286). Standard German completely displaced Danish in a trilingual area of Schleswig, but it was itself then increasingly displaced by the local Low German dialect (Selk 1937). Obviously, Schwyzertutsch maintains itself quite successfully in competition with Standard German; Landsmaal achieved considerable success (into the 1930's, at the very least) in competition with Dano-Norwegian; Yiddish won speakers and adherents among Russified, Polonized and Germanized Jewish elites in Eastern Europe before and after World War I; Castillian speaking workers settling in more industrialized Catalonia tend to shift to Catalan, etc. Indeed, the entire process whereby a few classical languages were displaced by 'lowly' vernaculars and whereby some of the latter, in turn, were later displaced by still other.and even 'less prestigeful' vernaculars (Deutsch 1942; the latter varieties are still referred to as 'dialects' in many popular [as well as in all too many socio-linguistically insensitive though scholarly] publications, e.g., Yiddish, Ukrainian, Byelo-Russian, Flemish, Afrikaans, Macedonian, to mention only European derivatives) indicates that the prestige notion is easily discredited unless serious qualifications and contextual redefinitions are attempted. This too may be an appropriate task for the study of language maintenance and language shift.

Quite clearly it is not some mystically invariant prestige of a language or variety that need concern us, but, rather the highly variant fates and fortunes of its speakers. The triumphs of English, Spanish (and Portuguese) in the New World is a triumph of physical might, of economic control and of ideological power. None of these are language factors *per se,* but languages that happen to be associated with such powerful forces and developments can open up advantages to their speakers far beyond those available to non-speakers of these languages. Under circumstances in which desired socio-cultural change follows from verbal repertoire change schools and media and organizations and programs have no difficulty facilitating shift (as e.g. in Israel, See Figure 19). Without such circumstances – and they are usually differentially available to various population segments – neither better pedagogic approaches nor more intense exhortation can have major impact on language shift.

7.22   Toward More General Theory and a More Inclusive Comparative Approach.

7.221   When bilingual speech networks are in touch with each other on the one hand, as well as with monolingual speech networks on the other, they are *differentially* involved in the crucial socio-cultural processes that influence or regulate their interaction. These processes serve to increase or decrease interaction between populations or sub-populations in question, to either detach them from or to confirm them in their accustomed sources of authority, to either lead them to influence others or to be particularly receptive to influence from others, to either emphasize or minimize their own groupness and its various manifestations, to either rise or fall in relative power or control over their own and each other's welfare, to either view with positiveness or negativeness the drift of the interaction between them and to react toward this drift on the basis of such views. We must look to these engulfing socio-cultural processes and, particularly, to indices of individual and group involvement in them, in our efforts to explain the direction or rate of language maintenance and language shift.

Index of Hebrew Speaking in the Jewish Population (Aged 2 and over), by age at
Immigration and Year of Immigration.

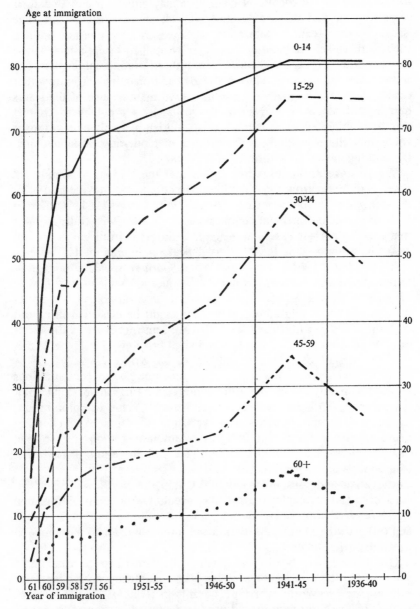

Figure 19. Population and Housing, Census, 1961; Government of Israel,
Jerusalem.

7.222   However, after having appropriately selected and specified one or more variables from among the endless subtleties that make up the 'process' of socio-cultural change, it may still be found that their cross-cultural and diachronic study reveals inconsistent results. The 'same' process (e.g., 'urbanization', as measured by constant indices such as those selected and cross-culturally applied by Reissman 1964) may result in language shift *away* from hitherto traditional languages in some cases, in language shift *back* to traditional languages in other cases, while revealing significantly unaltered maintenance of the status quo in still others. Under such circumstances a typology of contact situations might serve to control or regularize a number of group or contextual characteristics, in the manner of moderator variables, and, by so doing, reveal greater order in the data.

We all have an intuitive impression that the "American immigrant case" is different from the "Brazilian immigrant case" (Willems 1943); that the "Spanish conquest case" (Bright 1960; Dozier 1951) is different from the "Anglo-American conquest case" (Cook 1943; Gulick 1958); that the "immigrant case", in general, is different from the "conquest case" in general; that the "Yiddish speaking immigrant to America case" (Fishman 1965f) is different from "German speaking immigrant to America case" (Kloss 1966b), etc. The question remains how best to systematize these intuitive impressions, i.e., what variables or attributes to utilize in order that contact situations might be classified in accord with the differences between them that we sense to exist. In the terms of R.A. Schermerhorn's recently formulated typology (1964) the "American immigrant case" immediately prior to World War I would be characterized as revealing (i) sharply unequal power configurations between non-English speaking immigrants and English-speaking "old-Americans"; (ii) incorporation (rather than extrusion or colonization) as the *type of control* exercised by American core society over the immigrants; (iii) marked plurality and recent immigration (rather than duality, intermediate plurality without recent immigration, or any other of a continuum of patterns) as the *plurality pattern*; (iv) intermediate stratification and substantial mobility within the *stratification pattern*; (v) widespread mutual legitimization of acculturation and de-ethnization as the *interpretation of contact* in philosophical or group image terms; and (vi) growing industrialization, mass culture and social participation as *major social forces*.

Given the above typological framework, it has proved possible to summarize the current status of language maintenance and language shift among pre-World War I immigrants in terms of a very few *pre-contact factors, host factors,* and *product factors.* Unfortunately, Schermerhorn's typology for intergroup contacts is so recent that it has not yet been widely *tested* on either practical or theoretical grounds, whether in conjunction with language maintenance-language shift or in conjunction with other topics in the area of intergroup relations. While it may be expected that any typology based upon six parameters, each with several subdivisions, is likely to be somewhat unwieldy and require simplification, it is clear that Schermerhorn's system has at least heuristic value for the sociology of language from Verdoodt's efforts to put it to use in such fashion (in press).

At the opposite extreme of complexity from Schermerhorn's typology is one which is derivable from an intensive review of the extensive literature on Auslandsdeutschtum (Kuhn 1934). One of the major differentiations among the German settlers seems to have been the *original legitimization and concentration of their settlements.* A three-way break is recognizable here: *Stammsiedlungen* (settlements founded as a result of official invitation and assistance from non-German governments), *Tochtersiedlungen* (settlements founded by those who left the earlier *Stammsiedlungen* and who settled elsewhere as *groups,* but without governmental invitation or assistance), and *Einsiedlungen* (the inmigration of German individuals or of small occupationally homogeneous groups into non-German communities). Another related distinction is that between the relative 'cultural development' of the settlers and their hosts. During the decade before the Second World War the two most frequently recognized co-occurrences were (a) *Einsiedlungen* of 'culturally more mature' Germans living in the midst of a 'culturally less developed' population, as opposed to (b) *Stamm- and Tochtersiedlungen* of 'culturally younger' Germans surrounded by a 'more mature, nation-oriented' population. Thus, although only two diagonal cells of a theoretically complete two-by-two typology are extensively discussed it is possible to find examples of the remaining cells as well. Even when limited to the two co-occurrences mentioned above very interesting and consistent differences appear both in rate and in stages of language shift and acculturation. The implications of this rough typology and of the regularities that it has suggested deserve consideration in connection with quite different intergroup contact settings.

7.223   Although the study of language maintenance or language shift *need* not be completely limited to the comparison of separate cases it is nevertheless undeniably true that the comparative method is quite central to inquiry within this topic area. Certainly the comparative method is indispensable in our pursuit of cross-cultural and diachronic regularities. Assuming that a relatively uniform set of appropriate sociocultural process-measures could be selected and applied and assuming that a recognizably superior typology of contact situations were available it would then become possible to study:

TABLE 19a

Proportions of Types of Publication, 1930 and 1960 (Fishman 1966c)

Number

Ethnic Groups	1930 Mother Tongue n	%	1930 Mixed n	%	1930 English n	%	1930 Total n	1960 Mother Tongue n	%	1960 Mixed n	%	1960 English n	%	1960 Total n
French	28	80	6	17	1	3	35	13	76	3	18	1	6	17
Spanish	61	81	9	12	5	7	75	31	65	13	27	4	8	48
German	146	59	22	9	78	32	246	41	37	9	8	60	55	110
Jewish	20	21	13	14	62	65	95	15	14	4	4	85	82	104
Hungarian	35	90	4	10	0	0	39	32	94	1	3	1	3	34
Ukrainian	6	86	1	14	0	0	7	14	74	3	16	2	10	19
Italian	85	68	38	30	2	2	125	21	16	20	43	5	11	45
Polish	84	95	2	2	2	2	88	37	86	2	5	4	9	43
Greek	15	71	4	19	2	10	21	9	47	5	26	5	26	19
Czech	44	98	1	2	0	0	45	19	83	4	17	0	0	23
Other Slavic	53	79	14	21	0	0	67	46	68	19	28	3	4	68
Scandinavian	62	63	17	17	19	19	98	20	43	5	11	21	46	46
Other Germanic	13	56	5	22	5	22	23	1	8	2	15	10	77	13
Other Romance	15	94	1	6	0	0	16	7	88	1	12	0	0	8
Near Eastern	8	89	0	0	1	11	9	10	63	1	6	5	31	16
Far Eastern	18	67	6	22	3	11	27	12	57	8	38	1	5	21
All Others	44	86	6	12	1	2	51	49	78	7	11	7	11	63
Total	737	69	149	14	181	17	1067	377	54	107	15	214	31	698

TABLE 19b

Proportions of Types of Publications, 1930 and 1960 (Fishman 1966c)

Circulation

Ethnic Groups	1930 Mother Tongue		1930 Mixed		1930 English		1930 Total	1960 Mother Tongue		1960 Mixed		1960 English		1960 Total
	n	%	n	%	n	%	n	n	%	n	%	n	%	n
French	151a	94	10	6	—	—	161	118a	96	5	4	—	—	123
Spanish	298	98	3	1	—	—	304	268	81	54	16	7	2	329
German	1354	67	65	3	598	30	2017	281	10	146	5	2274	84	2701
Jewish	775	72	34	3	264	25	1073	179	9	63	3	1826	88	2068
Hungarian	238	96	9	4	0	0	247	198	95	4	2	6	3	208
Ukrainian	51	100	—	—	0	0	51	47	62	27	36	2	2	76
Italian	613	83	114	15	16	2	743	270	56	164	34	47	10	481
Polish	999	96	23	2	15	1	1037	690	96	9	1	18	2	717
Greek	74	77	12	12	10	10	96	65	62	15	14	24	23	104
Czech	513	100	—	—	0	—	513	274	94	17	6	0	0	291
Other Slavic	730	74	167	17	93	9	990	216	45	243	51	17	4	476
Scandinavian	580	85	82	12	21	3	683	120	26	40	9	303	65	463
Other Germanic	22	58	16	42	—	—	38	4	2	15	6	216	92	235
Other Romance	130	100	—	—	0	0	130	25	86	4	4	0	0	29
Near Eastern	38	100	0	0	—	—	38	37	69	6	11	11	20	54
Far Eastern	346	87	52	13	—	—	398	67	57	45	38	6	5	118
All Others	296	98	7	2	—	—	303	253	85	26	9	20	7	299
Total	7216	82	591	7	1023	12	8830	3118	35	889	10	4784	54	8791

(i) The same language group in two separate interaction contexts that are judged to be highly similar (with respect to primary socio-cultural process[es] and contact type), e.g., two separate German *Stammsiedlungen* in rural Poland.

(ii) The same language group in two separate interaction contexts judged to be quite dissimilar (with respect to major socio-cultural process[es] and contact type), e.g., one German-Swiss community in contact with Swiss Raetoromans and another German-Swiss community in Cincinnati, Ohio.

(iii) Different language groups in two separate interaction contexts judged to be highly similar (with respect to major socio-cultural process[es] and contact type), e.g., a Polish speaking and a Slovak speaking community, both of rural origin, in Cincinnati, Ohio.

(iv) Different language groups in two separate interaction contexts judged to be quite dissimilar (with respect to major socio-cultural process[es] and contact type), e.g., a German *Stammsiedlung* in rural Poland and a Slovak community in Cincinnati, Ohio.

Thus, by judiciously contrasting groups, socio-cultural processes and types of contact situations (*not* necessarily taken two at a time, if higher level interaction designs prove to be feasible) it should become possible to more meaningfully apportion the variance in language maintenance or language shift outcomes. Furthermore, the greater our insight with respect to socio-cultural processes and the more appropriate our typology of intergroup contact situations, the more possible it becomes to meaningfully assemble and analyze language maintenance and language shift files. Such files would permit both cross-cultural and diachronic analysis, of primary as well as of secondary data, based upon comparable data, collected and organized in accord with uniform sets of socio-cultural processes and contact categories. This state of affairs is still far off but it is the goal toward which we might attempt to move within this second topical subdivision of the study of language maintenance and language shift, once more basic methodological and conceptual questions reaching a somewhat more advanced level of clarification.

7.3 Behavior Toward Language

The third (and final) major topical subdivision of the study of language maintenance and language shift is concerned with behavior toward language (rather than with language behavior or behavior through language), particularly, with more focused and conscious behaviors on behalf on either maintenance or shift per se. Strictly speaking, this subdivision may be properly considered a subtopic under 7.2, above. However, it is of such central significance to this entire field of inquiry that it may appropriately receive separate recognition. Three major categories of behaviors toward language are discernible within this topical subdivision:

7.31   Attitudinal-Affective Behaviors.

We know all too little about language oriented attitudes and emotions (running the gamut from language loyalty — of which language nationalism is only one expression – to language antipathy – of which conscious language abandonment is only one expression) as distinguished from attitudes and emotions toward the 'typical' speakers of particular language variants. The features of language that are considered attractive or unattractive, proper or improper, distinctive or commonplace, have largely remained unstudied. However, in multilingual settings, particularly in those in which a variety of 'social types' are associated with each language that is in fairly widespread use, language *per se* (rather than merely the customs, values and cultural contributions of their model speakers) are reacted to as 'beautiful' or 'ugly', 'musical' or 'harsh', 'rich' or 'poor', etc. Generally speaking, these are language stereotypes (Fishman 1956). However, the absence or presence of a 'kernel of truth' (or of verifiability itself) is entirely unrelated to the mobilizing power of such views.

The manifold possible relationships between language attitudes and language use also remain largely unstudied at the present time. Although Lambert reports a positive relationship between success in school-based second language learning and favorable attitudes toward the second language and its speakers (Lambert et al 1963), this finding need not be paralleled in all natural multilingual contact settings. Thus, Ruth Johnston reports a very low correlation between subjective and objective (external) assimilation in the language area (1963b). Many older Polish immigrants in Australia identified strongly with English, although they hardly spoke or understood it several years after their resettlement. On the other hand, many young immigrants spoke English faultlessly and yet identified strongly with Polish, although they spoke it very poorly (1963a). Similarly, in summarizing his findings concerning current language maintenance among pre-World War I arrivals in the United States coming from rural Eastern and Southern European backgrounds, Fishman reported a long-term distinction between attitudes and use, namely, an increased esteem for non-English mother tongues concomitant with the increased relegation of these languages to fewer and narrower domains of language use (Fishman 1965f). In the latter case, the particular non-English mother tongues in question were now found to be viewed positively and nostalgically by older first and second generation individuals who had formerly characterized these tongues as ugly, corrupted and grammarless in pre-World War II days. Younger second and third generation individuals were found to view these mother tongues (almost always via translations) with less emotion but with even more positive valence. Instead of a "third generation return" (Hansen 1940) there seemed to be an "attitudinal halo-ization" within large segments of all generations, albeit unaccompanied by increased usage. This development (a negative relationship over time between *use rates* and *attitudinal positiveness*) was not predictable from most earlier studies of language maintenance or language shift in immigrant or non-immigrant settings. We are far from knowing whether its explanation in American contextual terms (i.e., in terms of the greater acceptability of marginal rather than either primordial or ideologized ethnicity) would also apply to other settings in which similar circumstances might obtain. Recent methodological clarification of the language-attitude area (Fishman and Agheyisi 1970) should now make it possible for workers to move ahead in this area along a broad front of little explored topics and approaches.

7.32 Overt Behavioral Implementation of Attitudes, Feelings and Beliefs.

Both language reinforcement ('language movements') and language planning may be subsumed under this heading. Language reinforcement may proceed along voluntary as well as along official routes and encompasses organizational protection, statutory protection, agitation and creative production. As for language planning, it has not always been recognized that much (if not most) of its activity (codification, regularization, simplification, purification, elaboration, and the implementation and evaluation of all of the foregoing) occurs in the context of language maintenance or language shift (Fishman 1966c, Ch. 21).

The possible relationships between language reinforcement (or language planning), on the one hand, and the waxing or waning of actual language use (or of other socio-cultural processes) are largely unknown at this time. Data from the American immigrant case imply that a number of unexpected relationships may obtain in that novel reinforcements may be introduced as actual language use diminishes. Thus, as even some of the more 'exotic' mother tongues (i.e., mother tongues not usually considered to be among the major carriers of European civilization and, therefore, hitherto usually associated only with foreign ethnicity in the minds of 'average Americans' (Hayden 1966)) have ceased to be primarily associated with immigrant disadvantages or with full-blown religio-ethnic distinctiveness among their own sometime-and-erstwhile-speakers, they have been increasingly introduced as languages of study at the university, college and public high school levels (Haugen

1953, Kloss 1966b). At the same time, massive displacement seems to have had greater inhibitory impact on language planning efforts in the American immigrant case than it has had on language reinforcement efforts. The latter are essentially conservative and seem to require less in the way of highly specialized leadership. The former are frequently innovative and dependent upon expert personnel working in concert with compliance producing or persuasive authority. To what extent this differential impact also holds true in other types of language shift settings is currently unknown but worthy of study.

Advocates of languages that are undergoing displacement are often much more exposed to (and identified with) the values and methods of . their linguistic competitors than were their less exposed (and less threatened) predecessors. As a result, they are more likely to adopt organized protective and publicity measures from more 'advantaged' co-territorial (other-tongue) models to serve language maintenance purposes (Fishman 1969a). The introduction of a few ethnically infused languages into the curricula of American high schools, colleges and universities represents just such a recent innovation on behalf of mother tongue maintenance – and an even more de-ethnicized one (Nahirny and Fishman 1965) one than was the innovative establishment of ethnic group newspapers, schools, cultural organizations and camps prior to World War I. In contrast, the normal processes of controlled *language change* and the more aroused processes of conscious *language planning* may require more than 'last ditch' ingenuity. However, to what extent reinforcement and planning are differently balanced given varying degrees of displacement or augmentation is currently unknown but worthy of study. In addition to its importance in its own right, the overall study of the relationship between language attitudes and language behaviors (Fishman 1969c) will also gain greatly from attention to topics such as this.

7.33 Cognitive Aspects of Language Response

Constantly flitting between the above two categories and overlapping partially with the one, with the other, or with both are such matters as: *consciousness* of mother tongue (or 'other tongue') as an entity separate from folkways more generally; *knowledge* of synchronic variants, language history and literature; and *perceptions of language as a component of 'groupness'*. We have little systematic information concerning the circumstances under which language consciousness, language knowledge and language-related groupness-perceptions do or do not enter into reference group behavior in contact situations. As a result, it is difficult to say at this time whether or when language maintenance and language shift are ideologically mediated as distinguished from their more obvious situational and instrumental determinants discussed thus far. We recognize very gross long-term contrasts in this connection, namely, that there were periods and regions when language "was in no way regarded as a political or cultural factor, still less as an object of political or cultural struggle" (Kohn 1945, p. 6); that there were other periods and regions marked by a sharp increase in such regard, so that language became a principle "in the name of which people ... (rallied) themselves and their fellow speakers consciously and explicitly to resist changes in either the functions of their language (as a result of language shift) or in the structure or vocabulary (as a consequence of interference)" (Weinreich 1953a, p. 99), and that there currently seems to be less of this than previously, particularly if we compare African with European nationbuilding. However, gross differentiations such as these are patently insufficient to enable us to clarify the conditions under which language becomes a prominent component in *perceptions* of 'own-groupness' and 'other-groupness'. This topic (language-related groupness-perception) is, of course, closely related to one previously mentioned, namely, the role of language in group membership and in group functioning (see section 7.2111, above). In the American immigrant case we have seen a growing dissocation between self-perceived ethnic identification and language maintenance. Far from being viewed as necessary components of groupness (whether in the sense of resultants or contributors) non-English mother tongues appear to be viewed increasingly in terms of non-ethnic *cultural* and non-ethnic *practical*

TABLES 20a and 20b

Attitudes and beliefs with respect to Spanish among Ordinary Puerto Ricans (OPR) and Intellectuals, Leaders and Artists (ILA) in the Greater New York Metropolitan Area (Fishman 1969e)

Response	OPR ($n = 32$)	ILA ($n = 20$)
No	20 (62%)	2 (10%)
Yes	12 (38%)	18 (90%)

TABLE 20b

Are there many "Nuyorquinos" who do not speak or understand Spanish?

Response	OPR ($n = 29$)	ILA ($n = 20$)
Yes (many do not understand)	2 (7%)	1 (5%)
Most understand little and speak poorly	3 (10%)	4 (20%)
Most understand well but speak poorly	3 (10%)	14 (70%)
Most speak and understand without real difficulty	21 (73%)	1 (5%)

considerations. At the same time, some form of ethnic self-identification is frequently still reported by many of those who no longer claim any facility at all in their ethnic mother tongues, implying that in several American immigrant-derived groups some kind of ethnicity usually appears to be a much more stable phenomenon than language maintenance. Indeed, some groups are able to maintain newspapers, schools and organization long after they have lost their non-ethnic mother tongues (Table 19a and Table 19b). Most immigrants became bilingual much before they embarked on de-ethnization or seriously contemplated the possibility of bi-culturism. However, there were obviously exceptions to this process, both in the United States and in other contact settings. We certainly do not seem to be in a position to indicate the underlying regularities in this subtle area of inquiry at the present time, except to point out that the segments of the population among which language consciousness, language interest, and language-related groupness-perceptions are likely to be in evidence are normally quite small and elitist in nature (Tables 20a and 20b).

We know very little about the interaction *among* the three components of behavior toward language or about the interaction *between* any of these components and the larger psychological, social and cultural processes discussed earlier. Rather than being a 'natural', omnipresent condition, either in monolingual or in multilingual settings, heightened and integrated behaviors toward language may be related to somewhat rare and advanced symbolic and ideological extensions of primordial ethnicity. Such extensions may well require a particular level of socio-cultural development and a particular group of custodians for their preservation and further elaboration. They almost certainly require a relatively advanced level of elitist concentration on intra-elitist concerns, often in advance of elitist concerns for communication within the masses. Nevertheless, none of these desiderata need have invariable consequences for behavior toward language. Even where heightened and integrated behaviors toward language are culturally present they will not be equally operative in all situations or among all population subgroups. Furthermore, even where they are culturally present they need not be uniformally related to other symbolically elaborated forms of behavior. Thus, this area remains the most unsystematized topical sub-division of the study of language maintenance and language shift. Perhaps it can be clarified in the future as a result of concomitant clarification and constant interrelation in connection with the two other major sub-divisions within this field of inquiry.

7.34   Interference and Switching.
Within the topical subdivision of behavior toward language we once

again meet the topic of interference and switching, first introduced in section 7.1, above. The absence or presence of interference and switching can have cognitive, affective and overt implementational implications for language maintenance and language shift. Certainly, both interference and switching are related to the domains and variance sources of bilingualism, on the one hand, and to socio-cultural processes and type of interaction, on the other hand. Moreover, within this topical subdivision it is appropriate to stress that where attitudes and awareness concerning purism obtain, interference is sometimes viewed as *an imperfection* – not in the speaker or in his productions but *in the language itself*. At the opposite pole, there are multilingual contact situations in which conscious, purposive interference obtains. In these instances speakers attempt to incorporate into their language usage as many elements or features as possible from another language including (in very advanced cases) interference in stress patterns, intonation, and *Denkformen*. In either case (i.e., when interference occurs although it is considered undesirable, or when interference occurs and is considered desirable) interference is not always considered to be all of one piece. Certain occurrences are considered to be more acceptable, excusable, permissible, necessary than others. In either case it can become a factor in hastening language shift, particularly since bilinguals tend to interpret interference in each of the languages known to them quite differently. Finally, at a point when language shift is appreciably advanced, certain sounds and forms of the language undergoing displacement may become so difficult for the average speaker (while errors in connection with them may become so stigmatized among purists) that this in itself may accelerate further shift. All in all, recognition of interference, attitudes toward interference, and the behavioral consequences of interference represent interesting and important topics within the field of language maintenance and language shift.

7.4 A Glance Back and a Glance Ahead

Various language maintenance and language shift phenomena have long been of interest to scholars and to laymen. Several sub-topics within this area have indisputed relevance to the daily concerns and joys of millions. Others, of more theoretical interest, are closely related to topics of recognized concern to linguists, anthropologists, sociologists, psychologists, political scientists, educators, etc. Culture contact and language contact will always be with us, and out of these contacts will come modifications in habitual behavior as well as attempts to restrain or channel such modifications. Whether (or when) language habits change more or less quickly than others, whether or when language loyalties are more or less powerful than others, indeed, whether (or when) men can live in a supraethnic tomorrow without strong links (linguistic or non-linguistic) to their ethnic yesterday and today – these are questions to which there are currently no definitive answers. However, interest in social-psychological aspects of language behavior is currently growing (whether under that name or under the name of sociolinguistics, anthropological linguistics, ethno-linguistics, the ethnography of speaking, the ethnography of communication, the sociology of language, or some other designation). In most instances, there is some recognition of *behavior toward language* as a crucial topic within the field of social behavior through language. This growing interest will undoubtedly contribute answers to many of the currently unanswerable questions within the field of language maintenance and language shift.

Three major subdivisions of the study of language maintenance and language shift have been suggested. The first deals with the precise establishment of habitual language use in a contact situation. This requires instruments just beginning to become available for the measurement of *degree of bilingualism* and of *location of bilingualism* along sociologically relevant dimensions. Degree of bilingualism, hitherto recognizable in terms of automaticity, proficiency, and code-intactness at the phonetic, lexical and grammatical levels, must also be investigated with respect to media variance and overtness variance. *Location of bilingualism* requires investigation with respect to functional diversification in appropriately designated domains of language, each domain being abstracted from patterned role-relations, topics, locales and/or other lower order phenomena. The complex relationships between the several components of degree of bilingualism and location of bilingualism may be represented by a *dominance configuration* which, in turn, may or may not be reducible to a single index of direction of bilingualism. The drift of language maintenance or language shift may be established by diachronic measures pertaining to some or all af the above factors.

The second major topical subdivision of the study of language maintenance and language shift deals with psychological, social and cultural processes that are associated with ascertained changes in habitual language use. No conceptual systematization of these processes is currently available although several preliminary typologies of "contact situations" exist and require further refinement in cross-cultural perspective. The greatest encouragement in this topical subdivision comes from the accelerating interdisciplinary work on socio-cultural and politico-operational change (including work on development and modernization).

To the extent that the study of language maintenance and language shift will become increasingly linked to ongoing theoretical and empirical refinements in the study of psycho-socio-cultural stability and change more generally the more rapidly will mutually rewarding progress occur.

The third (and final) major subdivision of the study of language maintenance and language shift pertains to behavior toward language, including (but not limited to) more focused and conscious behaviors on behalf of maintenance or shift. Three major sub-topics within this topic are recognizable: Attitudinal-affective behaviors (loyalty, antipathy, etc.), overt behavioral implementation (control or regulation of habitual language use via reinforcement, planning, prohibition, etc.), and (overlapping partially with each of the two foregoing sub-topics) cognitive behaviors (language consciousness, language knowledge, language-related group-perceptions, etc.).

Two socio-linguistic patterns, that of the urban American immigrant and that of the urban French-Canadian nationalist, have been repeated many times in the past century. The increasing use of Russian alone by Soviet minorities – particularly the smaller ones – whether they be immigrants to large urban centers in other regions or outnumbered by Russians and various other immigrants into their own regions, has followed the same path as the increasing use of English alone by immigrants to the United States, the increasing use of Spanish alone by indigenous Indian populations moving to urban centers throughout Latin America, or the increasing use of Wolof alone by the diverse Senegalese populations that began to move to Dakar more than a generation ago. Similarly, the increasing use of the mother tongue in the domains of education, industry and government (which had previously 'belonged', so to speak, to English), that has increasingly typified French-Canada, is not at all unlike the growing displacement of English or another Western language of wider communication in Puerto Rico, Tanzania, Kenya, India, Pakistan, Malaysia and the Philippines. The one group of cases illustrates the general inability of dislocated populations to maintain domain separation and, therefore, a sufficiently distinctive functional allocation of codes in their verbal repertoires, such as to render their mother tongues necessary for membership and status even within the home, neighborhood and other intra-group domains. The other group of cases illustrates the generally far greater ability of sedentary populations to withstand the onslaught of foreign-inspired political, educational, social and economic domination. If domain separation is maintained, at least between the L domains of home and neighborhood and the H domains of government, education and religion, a subsequent mobilization of the indigenous population around a new, nationalist proto-elite may yet lead to the introduction (or re-introduction) of the vernacular into those domains from which it has been barred or displaced.

In the urban American immigrant case – as in all instances in which severely dislocated populations have been presented with tangible op-portunities to share in new role-relationships and in vastly improved power- and status-networks – a new language initially entered the verbal repertoire of the speech community for marginal metaphorical purposes only. Situational *and* metaphorical switching *both* were pos-sible only with respect to several varieties of the ethnic mother tongue or its H + L matrix. However, with the passage of time *intra-group* power, status and even membership *per se*, all come to be granted on the basis of mastery of the new language. As a result, the ethnic mother tongue became increasingly relegated to metaphorical purposes (humor, contrast, tenderness) and, therefore, to oblivion as a third generation arose that had itself directly experienced none of the situations upon which the metaphorical functions of the ethnic mother tongue rested in the usage of 'old timers' and the second generation.

In the case of less dislocated populations – where the absence of widespread social mobility or of physical extirpation from established roles and networks helped preserve the distinction between intra-group and extra-group domains – the new language normally gained metapho-rical recognition *only* insofar as the majority of intra-group networks and role relations were concerned. As a result, it served primarily as an intergroup H for the few well-placed individuals with inter-group roles. Little wonder then that among the rank and file of such less dislocated populations – including the Alsatians discussed by Tabouret-Keller (1968) and by Verdoodt (1971) and the Swabians discussed by Fishman and Lueders (1971) – H varieties do not displace L varieties and indeed, are themselves easily displaced by yet newer H varieties resulting from the temporary intrusions of new political authorities.

The above sketch is still more suggested than demonstrated. It de-pends more on theoretical parsimony than on empirical data. The ex-haustive study of language maintenance and language shift ultimately requires not merely theory but also theory tested and revised in the light of hard data. Since the basic instruments and theory required for the establishment of degree and direction of language maintenance or language shift are now beginning to be available (certainly this is true relative to the situation five years ago) it would now seem to be most crucial to devote increasing amounts of theoretical and empirical atten-tion to comparative (cross-network, cross-speech community, cross-polity and cross-cultural) study of the psycho-socio-cultural antecedents and concomitants of language maintenance and language shift. The next few years will doubtlessly see the greatest progress precisely along these lines, i.e., along lines for which the social anthropologist, social psychologist and sociologist – rather than the linguist – must take primary responsibility.

8.0 SOCIO-CULTURAL ORGANIZATION:
LANGUAGE CONSTRAINTS AND LANGUAGE REFLECTIONS

One of the major lines of social and behavioral science interest in language during the past century has been that which has claimed that the radically differing structures of the languages of the world constrain the cognitive functioning of their speakers in different ways. It is only in relatively recent years – and partially as a result of the contributions of psycholinguists and sociolinguists – that this view (which we shall refer to as the linguistic relativity view) has come to be replaced by others: (a) that languages primarily reflect rather than create socio-cultural regularities in values and orientations and (b) that languages throughout the world share a far larger number of structural universals than has heretofore been recognized. While we cannot here examine the work related to language universals (Greenberg 1966; Osgood 1960), since it is both highly technical and hardly sociolinguistic in nature, we can pause to consider the linguistic relativity view itself as well as the linguistic reflection view which is increasingly coming to replace it in the interests and in the convictions of social scientists. It is quite clear why so much interest has been aroused by the question of language as restraint and language as reflection of socio-cultural organizations. Both of these views are undirectional. One posits that language structure and language usage are fundamental and 'given' and that all behavior is influenced thereby. The other claims that social organization and behavior are prior and language merely reflects these. A position on one side or another of this argument must be taken by those who are interested in changing or influencing the 'real world' of behavior.

8.1 Grammatical Structure Constrains Cognition

The strongest claim of the adherents of linguistic relativity – whether by Whorf (1940, 1941), Hoijer (1951, 1954), Trager (1959), Kluckhohn (1961), or by others – is that cognitive organization is directly constrained by linguistic structure. Some languages recognize far more tenses than do others. Some languages recognize gender of nouns (and, therefore, also require markers of gender in the verb and adjective systems) whereas others do not. Some languages build into the verb system recognition of certainty or uncertainty of past, present, or future action. Other languages build into the verb system a recognition of the size shape and color of nouns referred to. There are languages that signify affirmation and negation by different sets of pronouns just as there are languages that utilize different sets of pronouns in order to indicate tense and absence or presence of emphasis. Some languages utilize tone and vowel length in their phonological systems whereas English and most other modern European languages utilize neither. There are languages that utilize only twelve phonemes while others require more than fifty. A list of such striking structural differences between languages could go on and on – without in any way denying that each language is a perfectly adequate instrument (probably the *most* adequate instrument) for expressing the needs and interests of its speakers. That the societies using these very different languages differ one from the other in many ways is obvious to all. Is it not possible, therefore, that these socio-cultural differences – including ways of reasoning, perceiving, learning, distinguishing, remembering, etc. – are directly relatable to the structured differences between the languages themselves? The Whorfian hypothesis claims that this is indeed the case (Fishman 1960).

Intriguing though this claim may be it is necessary to admit that many years of intensive research have not succeeded in demonstrating is to be tenable. Although many have tried to do so no one has successfully predicted and demonstrated a cognitive difference between two populations on the basis of the grammatical or other structural differences between their languages alone. Speakers of tone languages and of vowel length languages and of many-voweled languages do *not* seem to hear better than do speakers of languages that lack all of these features. Speakers of languages that code for color, shape and size in the very verb form itself do not tend to categorize or classify a random set of items much differently than do speakers of languages whose verbs merely encode tense, person and number (Carroll and Casagrande 1958). Whorf's claims (namely, that ". . . the background linguistic system [in other words, the grammar] of each language is not merely a reproducing instrument for voicing ideas, but rather is itself the shaper of ideas, the program and guide for the individual's mental activity, for his analysis of impressions, for his synthesis of his mental stock in trade. Formulation of ideas is not an independent process, strictly rational in the old sense, but it is part of a particular grammar and differs, from slightly to greatly, between grammars" 1940) seem to be overstated and no one-to-one correspondence between grammatical structure and either cognitive or socio-cultural structure measured independently of language has ever been obtained. Several of the basic principles of sociolinguistic theory may help explain why this is so, although the psychological maxim that most men think about what they are talking about (i.e., that language structure is *always being struggled with via cognitive processes*) should also be kept in mind.

In contrast with the older anthropological-linguistic approach of Whorf, Sapir, Kluckhohn, Korzybski and others who pursued this problem during the first half of the twentieth century, sociolinguistics is less likely to think of *entire languages or entire societies* as categorizable or typable in an overall way. The very concepts of linguistic repertoire, role repertoire, repertoire range and repertoire compartmentalization argue against any such neat classification once functional realities are brought into consideration. Any reasonably complex speech community contains various speech networks that vary with respect to the nature and ranges of their speech repertoires. Structural features that may be present in the speech of certain interaction networks may be lacking (or marginally represented) in the speech of others. Structural features that may be present in certain varieties within the verbal repertoire of a particular interaction network may be absent (or marginally represented) in other varieties within that very same repertoire. Mother-tongue speakers of language X may be other-tongue speakers of language Y. These two languages may co-exist in a stable diglossic pattern throughout the speech community and yet be as structurally different as any two languages chosen at random.

Certainly, all that has been said above about the difficulty in setting up 'whole-language' typologies is equally true when we turn to the question of 'whole-society' typologies. Role repertoires vary from one interaction network to the next and roles themselves vary from one situation to the next within the same role-repertoire. Distinctions that are appropriately made in one setting are inappropriate in another and behaviors that occur within certain interaction networks do not occur in still others within the same culture. The existence of structured biculturism is as real as the existence of structured bilingualism and both of these phenomena tend to counteract any neat and simple linguistic relativity of the kind that Whorf had in mind.

Nevertheless, there are at least two large areas in which a limited degree of linguistic relativity *may* be said to obtain: (a) the structuring of verbal interaction and (b) the structuring of lexical components. The first area of concern points to the fact that the role of language (when to speak, to whom to speak, the importance of speaking per se relative to inactive silence or relative to other appropriate action) varies greatly from society to society (Hymes 1966). However, this type

	Data of (Cognitive) Behavior	
Data of Language Characteristics	Language data ('cultural themes')	Non-linguistic data
Lexical or 'semantic' characteristics	Level 1	Level 2
Grammatical characteristics	Level 3	Level 4

Figure 20. Schematic Systematization of the Whorfian Hypothesis (Fishman 1960)

Level 1 of the Whorfian ('linguistic relatively') hypothesis predicts that speakers of languages that make certain lexical distinctions are enabled thereby to talk about certain matters (for example, different kinds of snow among speakers of Eskimo and different kinds of horses among speakers of Arabic) that cannot as easily be discussed by speakers of languages that do not make these lexical distinctions. Similarly, Level 3 of the Whorfian hypothesis predicts that speakers of languages that possess particular grammatical features (absence of tense in the verb system, as in Hopi, or whether adjectives normally precede or follow the noun, as in English vs. French) predispose these speakers to certain cultural styles or emphases (timelessness; inductiveness vs. deductiveness). These two levels of the Whorfian hypothesis have often been criticized for their anecdotal nature as well as for their circularity in that they utilized verbal evidence for both their independent (causal) and dependent (consequential) variables. Level 2 of the Whorfian hypothesis predicts that the availability of certain lexical items or distinctions enables the speakers of these languages to remember, perceive, or learn non-linguistic tasks more rapidly or completely than can the speakers of languages that lack these particular lexical items or distinctions. This level of the Whorfian hypothesis has been demonstrated several times—most recently and forcefully in connection with the differing color terminologies of English and Zuni—but it is difficult to argue that the absence of lexical items or distinctions in a particular language is more a *cause* of behavioral differences than a *reflection* of the differing socio-cultural concerns or norms of its speakers. As soon as speakers of Zuni become interested in orange (color) they devise a term for it. Language relatively should be more stable and less manipulable than that! Level 4 of the Whorfian hypothesis is the most demanding of all. It predicts that grammatical characteristics of languages facilitate or render more difficult various non-linguistic behaviors on the part of their speakers. This level has yet to be successfully demonstrated via experimental studies of cognitive behavior.

of relativity has nothing to do with the *structure* of language per se in which Whorf was so interested. The second area of concern deals with lexical taxonomies and with their consequences in cognition and behavior. However, these border on being linguistic *reflections* of socio-cultural structure rather than being clearly and solely linguistic *constrains* that inevitably and interminably must bring about the particular behaviors to which they are supposedly related. It is to a consideration of these lexical taxonomies that we now turn.

8.2 Lexical Structure Constrains Cognition

For many years it was believed that the only tightly structured levels of language were the grammatical (morphological and syntactic), on the one hand, and the phonological, on the other. These two levels certainly received the brunt of linguistic attention and constituted the levels of analysis of which linguists were most proud in their interactions with other social and behavioral scientists. By contrast, the lexical level was considered to be unstructured and exposed to infinite expansion (as words were added to any language) and infinite interference (as words were borrowed from other languages). A small but hardy group of lexicographers (dictionary makers) and etymologists (students of word origins) continued to be enamoured of words per se but the majority of linguists acted as though the lexicon was the black sheep, rather than a bona fide member in good standing, of the linguistic family. The discover of structured parsimony in parts of the lexicon has done much to revive linguistic interest in the lexical level of analysis. The discovery as such is one in which psychologists, anthropologists and sociologists were every bit as active as were linguists themselves (if not more so). This may also explain why the interrelationship between lexical organization *and* behavioral organization has been so prominent in conjunction with the investigation of lexical structure.

The psychological contributions to this area of analysis take us back to one level of the Whorfian hypothesis (see level 2 in Figure 20). Psychologists had long before demonstrated that the availability of verbal labels was an asset in learning, perception and memory tasks (see, e.g., Carmichael et al. 1932; Lehmann 1889; Maier 1930). A new generation of psychologists has recently set out to determine whether this could be demonstrated both interlinguistically (i.e., by comparing different languages) as well as intralinguistically (i.e., within a given language) on a structured set of behaviors that corresponded *to a structured portion of lexicon.*

They chose the color spectrum to work with because it is a real continuum that tends to be environmentally present in all cultures. Nevertheless, the investigators hypothesized that language labels for the color spectrum are culturally idiosyncratic. These labels not only chop up the color continuum into purely conventional segments in every language community, but they probably do so differently in different language communities. By a series of ingenious experiments, Brown and Lenneberg (1954), Lenneberg (1953, 1957), Lantz and Stefflre (1964), and others have demonstrated that this was indeed true. They have demonstrated that those colors for which a language has readily available labels are more unhesitatingly named than are colors for which no such handy labels are available. They have shown that the colors for which a language has readily available labels (i.e., highly codable colors) are more readily recognized or remembered when they must be selected from among many colors after a delay subsequent to their initial presentation. They have demonstrated that somewhat different segments of the color spectrum are highly codable in different language communities. Finally, they have shown that the learning of nonsense-syllable associations for colors is predictably easier for highly codable colors than for less codable colors that require a phrase – often an individually formulated phrase – in order to be named.

All in all, this series of experiments has forcefully shown that the availability of a structured set of terms has both intralinguistic as well as interlinguistic consequences. However, in addition, it has underscored the equally important fact that every speech community has exactly such terms for those phenomena that are of concern to it. Certainly, artists, painters, and fashion-buyers have a structured color terminology that goes far beyond that available to ordinary speakers of English. The relative absence or presence of particular color terms in the lexicon of a given speech network is thus not a reflection of the state of that network's *code per se* as much as it is a reflection of the color interests, sensitivities and conventions of that network at a particular time in its history.

A color terminology is merely one kind of *folk-taxonomy,* i.e., it is an example of the many emic semantic grids that are contained in the lexicons of all speech communities. Other such examples are the kinship terminologies of speech communities, their disease or illness terminologies, their plant terminologies, their terms of address, etc. (Basso 1967; Conklin 1962; Frake 1961, 1962; Pospisil 1965; Friederich 1966; Metzger and Williams 1966; Price 1967; Wittermans 1967; etc.). In each of these instances the particular lexicons involved constitute "un systeme on tout se tient".

Each such system is considered by its users to be both literally exhaustive and objectively correct. Nevertheless, each system is socially particularistic, i.e., for all of its self-evident objectivity ("what other kind of kinship system could there *possibly* be?" – we can imagine the average member of each of the scores of such systems asking himself), it is a reflection of locally accepted conventions rather than a necessary reflection either of nature or of language per se. This last is particularly well demonstrated in the work of Friederich (on Russian kinship terms), Wittermans (on Javanese terms of address), and Basso (on Western Apache anatomical terms and their extension to auto parts; see Figure 21).

The Russian revolution brought with it such fargoing social change that the kinship terms in use in Czarist days had to be changed to some degree. In contrast with the refined stratificational distinctions that existed in Czarist days – distinctions that recognized gradations of

Figure 21. Lexical structure and social change (Basso, 1967)

ndε bi tsi ("man's body").															
									ni ("face")		εbiyɪ' ("entrails")				
ɬikɔ ("fat")	dɔ ("chin and jaw")	wos ("shoulder")	gən ("hand and arm")	kai ("thigh and buttock")	zε' ("mouth")	kε' ("foot")	ʔən ("back")	inda ("eye")	čį ("nose")	ta ("forehead")	tsǝs ("vein")	zɪk ("liver")	pɪt ("stomach")	či ("intestine")	ji ("heart")	jisolε ("lung")

Note: Black bars indicate position of additional (unextended) anatomical terms.
Figure 21a. Taxonomic Structure of Anatomical Set

Western Apache

naɬbil bɪ tsi ("automobile's body")															
									niᵃ		εbiyɪ' ("machinery under hood")				
ɬikɔ ("grease")	dɔ ("front bumper")	wos ("front fender")	gən ("front wheel")	kai ("rear fender")	zε' ("gas pipe opening")	kε' ("rear wheel")	ʔən ("bed of truck")	inda ("headlight")	čį ("hood")	ta ("front of cab," "top")	tsǝs ("electrical wiring")	zɪk ("battery")	pɪt ("gas tank")	či ("radiator hose")	ji ("distributor")	jisolε ("radiator")

ᵃ "Area extending from top of windshield to bumper"
Figure 21b. Taxonomic Structure of Extended Set

power, wealth and proximity within the universe of kin, not unlike those that were recognized in the larger universe of social and economic relationships – Soviet society stressed far fewer and broader distinctions. As a result, various kinship terms were abandoned entirely, others were merged and other were expanded. A very similar development transpired in Javanese with respect to its highly stratified system of terms

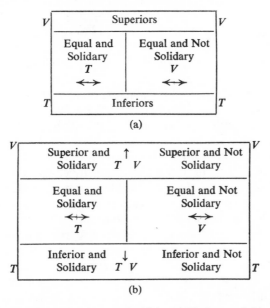

(a)

(b)

Figure 22. The two-dimensional semantic (a) in equilibrium and (b) under tension (Brown and Gilman, 1960)

Solidarity comes into the European pronouns as a means of differentiating address among power equals. It introduces a second dimension into the semantic system on the level of power equivalents. So long as solidarity was confined to this level, the two-dimensional system was in equilibrium (see Figure 22a), and it seems to have remained here for a considerable time in all our languages. It is from the long reign of the two-dimensional semantic that *T* derives its common definition as the pronoun of either condescension or intimacy and *V* its definition as the pronoun of reverence or formality. These definitions are still current but usage has, in fact, gone somewhat beyond them.

The dimension of solidarity is potentially applicable to all persons addressed. Power superiors may be solidary (parents, elder siblings) or not solidary (officials whom one seldom sees). Power inferiors, similarly, may be as solidary as the old family retainer and as remote as the waiter in a strange restaurant. Extension of the solidarity dimension along the dotted lines of Figure 22b creates six categories of persons defined by their relations to a speaker. Rules of address are in conflict for persons in the upper left and lower right categories. For the upper left, power indicates *V* and solidarity *T*. For the lower right, power indicates *T* and solidarity *V*.

Well into the nineteenth century the power semantic prevailed and waiters, common soldiers, and employees were called *T* while parents, masters, and elder brothers were called *V*. However, all our evidence consistently indicates that in the past century the solidarity semantic has gained supremacy. The abstract result is a simple one-dimensional system with the reciprocal *T* for the solidary and the reciprocal *V* for the nonsolidary.

of address. The impact of post-war independence, industrialization, urbanization and the resulting modification or abandonment of traditional role-relationships led to the discontinuation of certain terms of address and the broadening of others, particularly of those that implied relatively egalitarian status between interlocutors. Howell's review of changes in the pronouns of address in Japan (1967) also makes the same point, as did his earlier study of status markers in Korean (1965). Not only does he indicate how individuals change the pronouns that they use in referring to themselves and to each other, as their attitudes and roles vis-a-vis each other change, but he implies that widespread and cumulative changes of this kind have occurred in Japan since the war, to the end that certain pronouns have been practically replaced by others. Certainly the best known study of this kind is Brown and Gilman's review of widespread Western European social change with respect to the use of informal (T) vs. formal (V) pronouns and verb forms for the third person singular (1960). Feudalism, renaissance, reformation, the French Revolution, 19th century liberalism and 20th century democratization each had recognizable and cumulative impact. As a result, both T and V forms were retained in interclass communication (except in the case of English) but their differential use came to indicate differences primarily in *solidarity* or differences in *solidarity and in power* rather than differences in *power alone* as had been the case in the early middle ages (See Figure 22).

Note that the complexities of the pre-revolutionary kinship taxonomies in Russia did not keep Russians from thinking about or from engaging in revolution. Note also that the revolution did not entirely scrap the pre-existing kinship taxonomy. Similarly, the Apache anatomical taxonomy did not preclude (but rather assisted) taxonomic organization of automobile parts. Thus, while we are clearly indicating the untenability of any strong linguistic *relativity* position when we show that semantic taxonomies are subject to change, expansion and contraction as the socio-cultural realities of their users change, we are also demonstrating that their linguistic *reflection* of social reality is also likely to be both slow and partial. Nevertheless, as between the two, the taxonomic *reflection* of socio-cultural reality is more likely to have widespread heuristic utility at any given time, however much the existence of such taxonomies is likely to be *constraining* in the momentary cognitive behavior of individual members of socio-cultural systems.

The emic distinctions which underlie these taxonomies are differentially constraining for various interaction networks within any speech community. Some networks (e.g., the networks of quantitative scientists) can repeatedly rise above the cognitive constraints of the taxonomies current in their speech communities. These networks are likely to be the ones that are most actively engaged in social change and in taxonomic change as well. Other networks are unable to break out of the socio-cultural taxonomies that surround them. In such cases, as, e.g., in connection with Kantrowitz' race relations taxonomy among White and Negro prison inmates (1967; See Figure 23), or Price's botanical taxonomies among the Huichols (1967), these taxonomies may be taken not only as useful *reflections* of the cognitive world of the speech community from which they are derived but also as forceful *constraints* on the cognitive behavior of most, if not all, of the individual members of these networks.

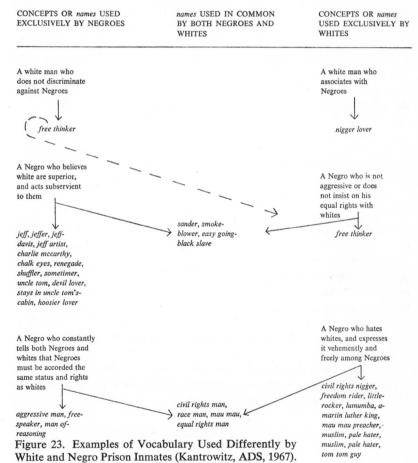

CONCEPTS OR *names* USED EXCLUSIVELY BY NEGROES	*names* USED IN COMMON BY BOTH NEGROES AND WHITES	CONCEPTS OR *names* USED EXCLUSIVELY BY WHITES

A white man who does not discriminate against Negroes

free thinker

A Negro who believes white are superior, and acts subservient to them

jeff, jeffer, jeff-davis, jeff artist, charlie mccarthy, chalk eyes, renegade, shuffler, sometimer, uncle tom, devil lover, stays in uncle tom's-cabin, hoosier lover

sander, smoke-blower, easy going-black slave

A white man who associates with Negroes

nigger lover

A Negro who is not aggressive or does not insist on his equal rights with whites

free thinker

A Negro who constantly tells both Negroes and whites that Negroes must be accorded the same status and rights as whites

aggressive man, free-speaker, man of-reasoning

civil rights man, race man, mau mau, equal rights man

A Negro who hates whites, and expresses it vehemently and freely among Negroes

civil rights nigger, freedom rider, little-rocker, lumumba, a-martin luther king, mau mau preacher, muslim, pale hater, muslim, pale hater, tom tom guy

Figure 23. Examples of Vocabulary Used Differently by White and Negro Prison Inmates (Kantrowitz, ADS, 1967).

8.3 Lexical Structure Reflects Social Organization

There are, however, more pervasive (and, therefore, seemingly less systematic) ways in which lexicons in particular and languages as a whole are reflective of the speech communities that employ them. In a very real sense a language variety is an inventory of the concerns and interests of those who employ it at any given time. If any portion of this inventory reveals features not present in other portions this may be indicative of particular stresses or influences in certain interaction networks within the speech community as a whole or in certain role-relationships within the community's total role-repertoire. Thus, Epstein's study of linguistic innovation on the Copperbelt of Northern Rhodesia (1959) revealed that the English and other Western influences on the local languages were largely limited to matters dealing with urban, industrial and generally non-traditional pursuits and relationships. Similarly, M. Weinreich's meticulous inquiry into the non-Germanic elements in Yiddish (1953) sheds much light on the dynamics of German-Jewish relations in the 11th Century Rhineland.

Like all other immigrants to differently-speaking milieus, Jews, learning a variety of medieval German in the 11th Century, brought to this language learning task sociolinguistic norms which incorporated their prior verbal repertoire. In this case the repertoire consisted of a vernacular (Loez, a variety of Romance) and a set of sacred languages (Hebrew-Aramaic). However, the pre-existing sociolinguistic norms did not impinge upon the newly acquired Germanic code in either a random fashion or on an equal-sampling basis. Quite the contrary. Both the Romance and the Hebraic-Aramaic elements in Yiddish were overwhelmingly retained to deal with a specific domain: traditional religious pursuits and concerns. The Christological overtones of many common German words, for example *lesen* (to read) and *segnen* (to bless), were strong enough to lead to the retention of more neutral words of Romance origin (*leyenen and bentshn*) in their stead. Similarly, Hebrew and Aramaic terms were retained not only for all traditional and sanctified objects and ceremonies but also in doublets with certain Germanic elements in order to provide contrastive emphases: *bukh* (book) vs. *seyfer* (religious book, scholarly book); *lerer* (teacher) vs. *melamed* or *rebi* (teacher of religious subjects), etc. Thus, Yiddish is a wonderful example of how *all* languages in contact borrow from each other selectively and of how this very selectivity is indicative of the primary interests and emphases of the borrowers and the donors alike (for examples pertaining to early Christianity see Knott 1956, Mohrman 1947, 1957). Indeed, M. Weinreich has conclusively demonstrated (1953, 1967, etc.) that a language not only reflects the society of its speakers but, conversely, that societal data per se is crucial if language usage and change are to be understood.

Findling's work too (1969) is interpretable in this fashion, demonstrating as it does that Spanish and English among Puerto Rican youngsters and adults in the Greater New York Metropolitan area reflect different psycho-social needs and conflicts. In word-association tasks Findling found his subjects mentioning humans more frequently in English than in Spanish and more frequently in the work and education domains than in the home and neighborhood domains (Table 21a and 21b). According to various previous studies in the area of personality theory, the prevalence of human terms in such unstructured tasks is indicative of 'need affiliation', that is, the need to be accepted into positive relationships with others. Findling therefore maintains that the language of Puerto Ricans in New York reveals this need to be stronger (because less gratified) in English interactions and in Anglo-controlled domains than in Spanish interactions and Puerto Rican controlled domains. Knowing, or suspecting, as we do from other sources, that Puerto Ricans in New York are struggling for acceptance in an Anglo-dominated world, Findling's interpretations seem reasonable and intriguing indeed.

TABLE 21a

Analysis of Variance of Human Ratio
(Need Affilation) Scores (Findling 1969)

Source of Variance	Sum of Squares	df	Mean Square	F	F_{95}	F_{99}
Between subjects	19,573.09	31				
Occupation (C)	110.73	1	110.73	.17	4.17	7.56
Error (b)	19,463.08	30	648.77			
Within subjects	65,904.10	288				
Language (A)	701.69	1	701.69	3.78[a]	4.17	7.56
Domain (B)	12,043.27	4	3,010.82	12.10[b]	2.44	3.47
AB	239.49	4	59.87	.48	2.44	3.47
AC	181.84	1	181.84	.98	4.17	7.56
BC	1,855.50	4	463.87	1.86	2.44	3.47
ABC	446.16	4	111.54	.89	2.44	3.47
Error (w)	50,436.15	270				
$Error_1$ (w)	5,571.17	30	185.71			
$Error_2$ (w)	29,851.83	120	248.77			
$Error_3$ (w)	15,013.15	120	125.11			
Total	85,477.19	319				

[a] $= p > .07$
[b] $= p > .01$

TABLE 21b
Mean Need Affilation Ratio Scores by Language and Domain

Language	Work	Education	Religion	Neighborhood	Home	Total
English	33	24	20	17	14	22
Spanish	28	23	17	13	14	19
Total	30	23	18	15	14	20

8.4 Language Behavior and Societal Behavior; a Circular Process of Mutual Creations

The difference between the language constraint view and the language reflection view is related to the difference between being interested in language as *langue* and language as *parole*. It is also related to the difference between being interested in inter-cultural variation and being interested in intra-societal variation. Obviously, the sociology of language is more fully at home with the latter level of analysis, in both cases, than with the former. However, the latter level too can be over-stated, particularly if it is claimed that not only is language behavior a *complete* index to social behavior, but, also, that it is nothing more than an index of such behavior. While indices are merely passive, language behavior is an active force as well as a reflective one. Language behavior feeds back upon the social reality that it reflects and helps to reinforce it (or to change it) in accord with the values and goals of particular interlocutors.

When Weinreich relates that Yiddish (then Judeo-German) came to be the vernacular of Rhineland Jewry because Jews and non-Jews on the eastern shore of the Rhine shared open networks and because higher status in these Jewish-Gentile networks also came to provide Jews with higher status in their own closed networks, he is saying much more than that language usage reflects social interaction. Of course, Judeo-German was a reflection of the fact that Jews and Gentiles participated in common open networks. However, Judeo-German also helped implement and reinforce these networks, and, thus, became a co-participant in creating or preserving the social reality that it reflected. Similarly, when Weinreich tells us that Judeo-German became increasingly more indigeneously normed (and therefore increasingly more Yiddish and less Judeo-German) he is referring to much more than a linguistic reflection of the primacy of its closed networks for this Jewish community. He is also telling us that the uniquely Jewish aspects of Yiddish (in phonology, lexicon and grammar) also helped foster the primacy of Jewish closed networks for its speakers. As a result, Yiddish not only reflected (as it does today) the cohesiveness and separateness of its speakers, but it helped to preserve and to augment these characteristics as well.

Thus, both unidirectional views are outgrowths of an artificial search for independent variables and original causes. The original cause of any societal behavior may well be of some interest but it is a historical interest rather than a dynamic one with respect to life as it continues round about us. If we can put aside the issue of 'what first caused what' we are left with the fascinating process of ongoing and intertwined conversation and interaction. In these processes language and societal behavior are equal partners rather than one or the other of them being 'boss' and 'giving orders' to the other.

9.0 APPLIED SOCIOLOGY OF LANGUAGE

On of the wisest maxims that Kurt Lewin bequeathed to social psychology is that which claims that "nothing is as practical as a good theory". In addition, social science theory is undoubtedly enriched by attempting to cope with the real problems of the workaday world. Thus, if social science theory is *really* any good (really powerful, really correct), it should have relevance for practitioners whose work brings them into contact with larger or smaller groups of human beings. Applied sociology of Language attempts both to enrich the sociology of language and to assist in the solution of societal language problems. The applied sociology of language is of particular interest whenever: (a) language varieties must be 'developed' in order to function in the vastly new settings, role-relationships or purposes in which certain important networks of their speakers come to be involved, or (b) whenever important networks of a speech community must be taught varieties (or varieties in particular media or uses) that they do not know well (or at all) so that these networks may function in the vastly new settings, role-relationships or purposes that might then become open (or more open) to them. In many instances (a) and (b) co-occur, that is, language varieties must be both developed and taught in order that important networks within a speech community may be fruitfully involved in the new settings, role-relationships and purposes that have become available to them. This is but another way of saying that planned language change and planned social change are highly interrelated activities and that the sociology of language is pertinent to their interaction.

Comments on the uses of sociology of language must keep in mind four separate categories of actual and potential users, namely, linguists and sociologists on the one hand, and the users of linguistics as well as the users of sociology on the other hand. The sociology of language as a hybrid or bridge-building specialization, is useful not *only* as it pertains to the front line of contact between science and society but *also* as it enables those in theoretical heartlands to understand their basic fields afresh and in refreshing ways. Application and applicability are themselves an endless array of concentric circles that surround all immediate problems in an ever-widening and interlocking flow. It is never wise to rigidly declare some knowledge 'useful' and other 'useless', for neither knowledge nor usefulness (nor even the very problems to which both are referred) hold still long enough for such judgments to be more than myopic indicators of how near or far we stand with respect to a particular and often fleeting goal. All knowledge is useful, and if at any point in time we nevertheless grope toward a consideration of the 'uses of X', it is merely because for some particular purposes at some particular time some knowledge may seem *more useful* than others.

This section proceeds by reviewing a few recognized topics within applied linguistics in order to illustrate and document a point of view with respect to the usefulness of the sociology of language. Its point of departure is Charles A. Ferguson's well known attempt to divide applied linguistics into its six most common American branches: the creation and revision of writing systems, literacy efforts, translation work, language teaching efforts, and language policy efforts (Ferguson 1959; for a German and a Soviet view see Kandler 1955 and Andreev and Zinder 1959). Although it will be impossible to give equally detailed attention to all five of these branches of applied linguistics here, it would seem that essentially similar questions must be addressed to each of them; namely, what has been accomplished *without* formal sociolinguistic awareness and sophistication? what has the sociology of language *contributed* to more recent applied linguistic efforts in these topical areas? finally, what more *could* the sociology of language contribute to these (and even to other) applied linguistic concerns if its practitioners were to really take *both* parts of this hybrid field with *equal seriousness* and with the deep technical and theoretical proficiency that they *both* require.

9.1   Creation of Writing Systems

The sophistication of phonological theory, both that of the early part of this century as well as that of very recent years, and the recent linguistic interest in theories of writing systems and in the relations between such systems and spoken language are, and have long been, powerful linguistic contributions to the worldwide efforts to create writing systems for pre-literate peoples. However, the very sophistication of the linguist's professional skills in code description and code creation merely intensified the separation trauma when it became obvious that it was necessary to go outside the code and to confront the real world if writing systems were not only to be devised (this being the only apparent concern of Pike 1947 or Ray 1963) but also *employed*. The first steps in this direction were moderate indeed. These consisted of Vachek's (1945/49 and 1948) and Bolinger's (1946) protests (among others) that the writing system must be viewed separately from the spoken code, i.e., that it could not properly be viewed as merely the phonetic transcription of the spoken code, and that it was basically a "visual system" (being not unlike the language interaction of the deaf in this respect) with regularities all its own.

The reverberations of these early protests are still with us. As Berry has pointed out (1958), new alphabets have clearly become less purely phonemic and more inclined to the "use of reason and expedience" (rather than to rely on phonemicization alone) in their pursuit of acceptance. Indeed, the latter concern, that of acceptance, has tended to replace the former, that of "reduction to writing", and, as a result, arguments pertaining to intra-(written) code phenomena have tended to recede evermore into the background. While "phonetic ambiguity" is still considered a "bad" thing and while it is generally agreed that "words pronounced differently should be kept graphically apart" (Bradley 1913/14) it is considered to be an even "worse thing" if alphabets of exquisite perfection remain unused or unaccepted. More and more work on the creation of writing systems has shown awareness of the fact that such nonacceptance is only to a relatively minor degree governed by intra-code ambiguities, inconsistencies or irrelevancies (all of these being rampant characteristics of the most widely used writing systems today and throughout history). Time and again in recent years the greater importance of extra-code phenomena has been hinted at (Gelb 1952, Bowers 1968), pointed to (Sjoberg 1964, 1966, Walker 1969) and, finally, even listed and catalogued (Nida 1954, Smalley 1964).

9.2 Desired Similarity and Dissimilarity

Perhaps because their attention is basically directed toward intra-code factors, linguists and applied linguists were quickest to notice those extra-code factors in the adoption or rejection of writing systems which indicated societal preferences or antipathies for writing conventions associated with some other language or languages. Thus, among the "practical limitations to a phonemic orthography" Nida (1954) discussed the fact that both the Otomi and the Qeuchua "suffer from cultural insecurity" and want their writing systems not only to "look like Spanish" but to operate with the same graphematic alternances as does Spanish, *whether these are needed or not* in terms of their own phonemic system. In a related but crucially different vein Hans Wolff recommended (1954) that Nigerian orthographies be created not only in terms of tried and true technically linguistic criteria (such as "accuracy, economy and consistency") but that "similarity to the orthographies of related languages" also be used as a guide. Of course, Wolff was merely following in the footsteps of the Westermann Script of the late 20's, which, in its fuller, more generally applicable form, became the All-Africa Script of the International African Institute (Anon. 1930). However, he was also following in the tradition that placed the linguist or other outside expert in the position of judging not only *which languages* were sufficiently related in order to deserve a common writing system, but that placed them in the position of deciding whether such similarity in writing systems was or was not a 'good thing' and whether it was or was not desired by the speech communities involved.

However, once having stepped outside of the charmingly closed circle of intra-code considerations, Pandora's box had been opened never again to be shut. In very recent days, to mention only such examples, Serdyuchenko has assured us that the Cyrillic alphabet is used as the model in "the creation of new written languages in the USSR" only because of the widespread and still growing interest in subsequently more easily learning Russian, just as Sjoberg (1966) mentions Tlingit insistence that their orthography "follow the rather chaotic orthographic patterns of English wherever possible in order to conform to the demands of the broader society (p. 217)", and the Institut Français d'Afrique Noire concludes that speakers of African vernaculars in Francophone countries want their orthographies to look as French as possible (Smalley 1964). Walker (1969), like Serdyuchenko before him (1962), is quite willing to champion such modeling at the explicit expense of maximal phonemic efficiency. Recently the Bamako Meeting on the Use of the Mother Tongue for Literacy (February 28 – March 5, 1966, UNESCO sponsored) went a step further. It not only recommended that new writing systems be similar to those of *unrelated but important languages for the learners* (Bowers 1968), but it also warned of "possible repercussions of a technical and economic nature" following upon the adoption of Non-European diacritics and special letters in the standard transcriptions of West African languages (Ferru

1966). Such letters and diacritics, it is pointed out, increase the cost of printing and typing, as well as the cost of manufacturing printing and typing equipment, and do so at the time when the per capita cost of printed or typed material is already likely to be troublesomely high in view of the limited number of consumers available for them in newly literate societies. On these same grounds the Institut d'Afrique Noire insisted as far back as 1959 that "when symbols have to be made up they should be typable on a standard French typewriter" (Smalley 1959).

The obverse case has been less fully documented, namely, that in which newly literate communities have desired a more *distinctive* writing system, one that they could call *their own* or one that would more effectively differentiate their language from others with respect to which they sought not similarity but rather *dissimilarity*. Dickens' (1953) discussion of the Ashante rejection of the Akuapem-based writing system for standard Twi (in the late 30's and early 40's) is one such case. Another is Ferguson's brief reference to the fact that St. Stefan of Perm (14th century) purposely created a separate alphabet for the Komi (giving "some of the letters an appearance suggestive of the Tamga signs in use among the Komi as property markers and decorations" 1967, p. 259) "so that the Komi could regard the writing system as distinctively theirs and not an alphabet used for another language." There must be many examples of this kind, e.g., St. Mesrop's creation of the Armenian alphabet in the fifth century, utilizing in part characters like those of far-distant brother-Menophysite Christians in Ethiopia with whom contact had probably been made (according to Olderogge) as a result of the presence of both Armenian and Ethiopian churches in Jerusalem. Another such example is Sequoyah's syllabary which was "not associated with aliens but developed within the Cherokee language community itself" (Walker 1969, p. 149; also see White 1962). Finally, to the above cases there must be added the few preliminary studies of indigenous African and Asian scripts of relatively small communities that weathered competitive pressures precisely because of their real or assumed local origins (e.g., Dalby 1967, 1968, Hair 1963, Stern 1968, Stewart 1967). Perhaps the relative reluctance to document such cases is not unrelated to the more general reluctance of those who practice applied linguistics upon others to recognize the frequent desires of non-literate peoples to be themselves (albeit "in a modern way"), rather than merely to be imitative copies of *ourselves* (whether we be Chinese, Russian, Arab, French, British, American, Spanish, or Portuguese).

9.3 'A Little More Complicated Than That'

If economics answers all questions with 'supply and demand', psychology with 'stimulus and response' and education with 'it all depends', then the first contribution of the sociology of language to applied linguistics is doubtlessly to stress the fact that the relations and interpenetrations between language and society are 'a little more complicated than that', whatever *that* may be. Indeed, although it is nearly half a century since Radin first implied that the adoption (actually, the borrowing) of an alphabet by an aboriginal people was a fascinatingly complex and internally differentiated chain of social processes, we have not to this very day seriously followed up this seeming complexity, let alone tried to reduce it to some underlying set of basic dimensions. Our technical expertise and theoretical sophistication lead us more readily to agree with Burns' (1953) early conclusion, based on sad experience with the failure of "linguistics without sociology" in Haiti, that the choice of an orthography has widespread social and political implications. They also lead us to continually admire Garvin's accounts (1954, also see 1959) of his attempts to achieve consumer consensus and participation in the creation of a standard orthography for Ponape, and to share his disappointment that even this was not enough to assure the use of that orthography. Beyond such agreement and admiration, however, we can only suggest that the process of gaining acceptance for technically sound writing systems is even 'a little more complicated than that'. In spelling out this complexity applied sociology of language uniquely stresses that it is crucial to systematically look *outside* of the linguistic system itself if one is to locate the reasons for the differential acceptance or rejection of programs of linguistic change. Modern sociology of language can contribute most by linking this particular topic of applied linguistics with the body of theory and practice that has grown up in connection with the acceptance of other systematic innovations, the planning of social change more generally, and the amelioration of the inevitable dislocations that follow upon the introduction of innumerable innovations and changes of which new writing systems are merely symptomatic.

The creation of writing systems is itself necessarily an outgrowth of culture contact, if not of political and economic domination from outside. Thus, the creation of a writing system is singularly unlikely to be viewed dispassionately and its propagation and acceptance by indigenous networks are necessarily viewed as having implications for group loyalty and group identity. Latinization, Arabization, Cyrillization or Sinoization are not merely fargoing indications of desired (and frequently of subsidized or directed) social change and cognitive-emotional reorganization, but they have immediate consequences for the relevance of traditional elitist skills and implications for the distribution of new skills and statuses related to literacy and to the philosophy or ideology which is the carrier of literacy.

The creation of writing systems is significant only insofar as it leads to the acceptance and implementation of writing systems. The latter are broadly revolutionary rather than narrowly technical acts. They succeed or fail far less on the basis of the adequacy of their intra-code phonological systems or on the basis of their fidelity to model systems, than on the basis of the success of the larger revolutions with which they are associated; revolutions in the production and consumption of economic goods (leading to new rural-urban population distributions, new jobs, new training programs, new avocations, new pastimes, and new purposive social groups) and revolutions in the distributions of power and influence. All of these both lead to and depend upon an increasing number of new texts and new written records. Thus, when sociolinguistic attention is finally directed to the creation of writing systems it will be focused upon the organization, functioning and disorganization of an increasingly literate society. This is potentially a very useful addition to the linguist's disciplinary focus because even more than writing changes speech (via 'spelling pronunciations') literacy changes speakers and societies. It is this perspective on the creation of writing systems – as always, a perspective which is outside of the linguistic system alone – that is part of the programmatic promise of the sociology of writing systems.

How will such attention improve or alter the creation of writing systems? Precisely by relating the problem of creation to the problem of acceptance, of impact, of possible dislocation, of possible manipulation, of possible exploitation, of possible redistribution of power and, in general, of the dependency of the very best writing system on revolutionary processes at their most pragmatic as well as at their most symbolic.

9.4 Orthographic Reform

To some extent such liberation and immersion are more advanced with respect to the study and planning of orthographic *reforms*, perhaps because the truly vast amount of technical linguistic effort invested in these reforms has yielded such meager results. Even though orthographic reform may be so sweeping as to involve the complete replacement of one writing system by another (and, in that sense, it may be viewed as a subcategory of the topic just reviewed), it deals with already literate networks and as a result, more clearly reveals the societal ramifications and reverberations of seemingly technical linguistic adjustments.

If the introduction of a newly created writing system easily threatens to change established lines of relative advantage and disadvantage, practical and symbolic, the revision of traditional orthographies most often obviously *attempts* to do so. Orthographic change represents departure from an established written tradition and, as such, it *must* cope with the gatekeepers of that written tradition, the poets, priests, principals and professors, and the institutions and symbols that they create and serve, or be destined to oblivion. Indeed, the greater and grander the tradition of literacy, literature and liturgy in an orthographic community, the less likely that even minor systematic orthographic change will be freely accepted and the less likely that any orthographic change will be considered minor.

In this connection we have a larger number of rather detailed and, to some extent, *sociolinguistically oriented* descriptions, than is the case for the creation of writing systems, but, as yet we have no sociological analyses or hypotheses per se. The soci-culturally contextualized descriptions of orthographic reforms in the USSR (Kolarz 1967, Orenstein 1959b, Quelquejay and Bennigsen 1961, Serdyuchenko 1965, Weinreich 1953, Winner 1952), Turkey (Rossi 1927, 1929, 1935, 1942, 1953, Heyd 1954, Ozmen 1967, Gallagher 1967 and 1969), Norway (Haugen 1966a, which contains an exhaustive bibliography of other studies) and Vietnam (Haudricourt 1943, Nguyen dinh Hoa 1960, Thompson 1965) again point to the literally revolutionary nature of the societal processes that have often accompanied system-wide orthographic change. On the other hand, the available descriptions of far less successful attempts to bring about orthographic change under less dramatic circumstances, e.g., in Japan (DeFrancis 1947, Holton 1947, Meyenburg 1934, Scharshmidt 1924, Toshio 1967), Haiti (Valdman 1968, Burns 1953) and Israel (Rabin 1969), or to bring about the orthographic unification of closely related languages in the absence of accompanying societal unification, e.g., in India (Anon 1963, Jones 1942, Ray 1963), Africa (Dickens 1953, Ward 1945) and Indonesia-Malaysia (Alisjahbana 1969 and in press), all indicate the difficulties encountered and the failures experienced thus far.

However, there is no justification for interpreting the above cited investigations as implying 'revolutionary success and non-revolutionary failure' as the proper summation of experience with orthographic reform. In earlier centuries a great deal of orthographic reform seems to have been accomplished both quietly and successfully without the involvement of mobilized populations or, indeed, of any other population segments than 'the authorities' whose business it was to make wise decisions for the community. The initial orthographic distinctions between Serbian and Croatian, or between Ruthenian (Ukrainian) and Polish, were decided upon by representatives of God and/or Caesar who sought to cultivate differences between speech communities that were otherwise 'in danger' of religious, political and linguistic unification. Indeed, the Ausbau languages (in Kloss' sense, 1952) are all instances of the success of applied linguistics and should be carefully studied as such. The restoration of written Czech (and Slovak) in Latin script was engineered by Count Sedlnitzsky, the administrative director of the Austro-Hungarian police and one of the most influential officials under the Emperor Francis (early 19th century), by subsidizing the publication of the Orthodox prayer book in Latin letters as "an important device to fight the political danger of the Pro-Russian Pan-Slav movement (Fischel 1919, p. 57). The Roumanian shift from Cyrillic to Latin script in 1863 was accomplished by a painless edict which sought to further that nation's self-defined Latinizing and Christianizing role in the heathen 'Slavo-Moslem' Balkans (Kolarz 1946). In more recent days Irish orthography has been changed without arousing unusual interest or opposition (Macnamara 1969), as was the type font (from an 'Irish looking' font to an ordinary roman font). Indeed, the relative ease with which these changes were made may be a reflection of the lack of widespread Irish interest or concern for the Language Revival.

Not only *has* there been much successful orthographic reform without revolutionary change (particularly where mass mobilization along language-related lines was absent for one reason or another) but there has also been a good bit of unsuccessful orthographic reform even when these have been accompanied by revolutionary social changes. Thus, the Soviet 'rationalization' of Yiddish orthography (Szajkowski 1966) initially aimed at both the *phonetization* of words of Hebrew-Aramaic origin, as well as at the *discontinuation* of the socalled final letters of the traditional Hebrew alphabet. However, twenty five years after the October revolution, the names of the grandfathers of Modern Yiddish literature were neither spelled מענדעלע מויכער ספֿאָרים, ייצכאָק

לייבוש פּערעצ און שאָלעמ אַלייכעמ

(as they *had* been throughout the 20's and 30's), nor were they spelled

מענדעלע מוכר ספרים· יצחק לייבוש פרץ או שלום עליכם

(as they *had* been before the Revolution and continued to be everywhere outside of the Soviet Union), but, rather, in an attempt to reach a compromise that would maximize the propaganda value of the few permitted Yiddish publications primarily distributed to and published for

362   Joshua A. Fishman

readers outside of the USSR: מענדעלע מויכער ספֿאָרים, ייצכאָק
לייבוש פּערעץ און שאָלעם אַלייכעם

However, even in its heyday the Soviet revolution in Yiddish orthography could not overcome the visual traditions of the orthographic
community. The initial silent aleph at the beginning of words that would
otherwise begin with the vowels ' and ' was *never* dropped, regardless
of its phonemic uselessness, perhaps because the initial silent aleph in
such cases was considered to be too strong a visual convention to be
tampered with (Hebrew writing itself – i.e., the visual precursor to
written Yiddish – never beginning words with vocalic ' or ').

A far more widely renowned revolutionary attempt at orthographic
reform which has failed (certainly thus far) is the once promised phonetization of (Northern Mandarin) Chinese. While the basic sources
available to us in English (DeFrancis 1950 and 1968, Mills 1956 and
Hsia 1956) all agree that the Latinized New Writing was abandoned
sometime late in the fifties, the reason for this abandonment can
still only be surmised.

By 1956 it had become necessary to defend the "Han (Chinese)
language phonetization draft plan" as being concerned with an alphabet
(Latin) which was truly progressive and international rather than necessarily related to any anti-proletarian class (Chinese Writers Language
Reform Committee 1956, Wu Yu-Chang 1956). By 1959 Chou En-
lai had officially demoted phonetization from its original goal of immediate "liberation and development of the whole Chinese language from
the shackles of the monosyllabic Chinese characters" (Ni Hai-shu 1949,
cited by DeFrancis 1968) to third place and the indefinite future, after
both simplification of the traditional characters and adoption of a
spoken standard for "Common Speech" had been attained (Chou En-
lai 1965). While work on the first two tasks is constantly going on
in a very direct fashion (see, e.g., Wu Yu-Chang 1965) work on the
latter is primarily nominal (that is, phonetization is kept alive as a
distant goal but is not substantively advanced) and indirect (i.e.,
phonetization is utilized for subsidiary purposes, such as annotating
novel or complex Chinese characters in technical texts, furthering
instruction in the Common Speech among speakers of other regional
languages, or creating "initial alphabetic scripts" for illiterate non-
Chinese speaking minorities). Indeed, while phonetization has recently
been reported to be superior for such special purposes as telegraphic
communication (Wu Yu-Chang 1964) and minority group initial literacy
(Li Hui 1960) the traditional characters have again been proclaimed
as superior in connection with general education for the bulk of the
population among whom these characters are viewed as symbolic of

education and the standard pronunciation (Serruys 1962)! The goal of phonetization is, seemingly, still a long way off and may or may not be reached any more rapidly than the withering away of the state (See several references to this effect in Kwan-wai Chiu 1970).

From the foregoing examples it is clear that if we but dichotomize both 'success' (acceptance) and 'revolutionary social change' we have examples of all four possible types of co-occurrences: successful orthographic revision with and without revolutionary social change and revolutionary social change with and without successful follow-through of planned orthographic revision. The discussions of revolutionary social change thus far encountered in studies of either the creation of writing systems or the revision of orthographies is still far too crude to be considered as more than rough labeling. As sociolinguistic description it is regrettably out of touch with the sizable modernization literature in economics, political science, sociology and anthropology. It lacks both the concepts and the technical data collection methods and data analysis skills needed to inquire into the intensity, extensity or continuity of the change forces and processes or the counter-change forces and processes that underly the gross labels so frequently encountered.

It is also unfortunate that there are *so few* localized case studies of *variation in sub-group reactions* to new writing systems or to revised orthographies and, conversely, proportionally *so many* commentaries, studies, evaluations, and recommendations that deal with entire countries, continents, and even the world at large. The result is an imbalance with respect to the usual mutual stimulation between micro-analysis and its emphases on process and function concerns, on the one hand, and macro-analysis and its emphases on structure, quantification, compositing and weighing of parameters on the other hand. Either type of study, when pursued too long without correction from the other, becomes myopic and, therefore dangerous for theory as well as (or even more so) for application. However, whereas both macro and micro-studies are equally necessary for the growth of general sociolinguistic theory, the future of *applied* sociology of language is particularly tied to *within-context* studies (within nation X, within region Y, within district Z) and, therefore, to ever more detailed studies of differential acceptance processes, rather than to studies of large-scale between-context variation (the latter not having as immediate applied significance for any particular within-context problem).

9.5 Language Planning

Perhaps the area of applied linguistics which most clearly illustrates the full complexity of societal phenomena which the sociology of language

Les grandes enquêtes de l'Office du Vocabulaire français de Paris

Depuis quelques années, l'opinion publique est alertée sur les dangers que court la langue française, et divers organismes, tant officiels que privés, ont été créés pour assurer la défense d'un idiome parlé par la communauté sans cesse grandissante des francophones: 90 millions aujourd'hui, ils seront 200 millions avant l'an 2000. Mais comment obtenir que la langue française, ciment de cette francophonie dont on parle tant, ne s'altère pas, ne dégénère pas, ne devienne pas un jargon à la syntaxe désordonnée et au vocabulaire truffé de néologismes mal assimilés?

Les règles du bon langage, on peut les connaître. Les atteintes au bon langage, tout le monde les connaît également, ou peut les connaître à la lecture de maints ouvrages ou articles de presse. Ce que l'on connaît mal, c'est le moyen d'obtenir que les règles soient mieux respectées et l'invasion des néologismes contenue. L'opinion sait que l'usage est à corriger selon les principes d'une norme raisonnable. Mais elle ignore comment la norme, une fois établie, peut descendre jusqu'à l'usage, c'est-à-dire comment l'usage peut être *orienté*, sinon *dirigé* par la norme de manière efficace.

Précisément, la troisième Biennale de la langue française a inscrit à l'ordre du jour de ses prochains travaux une formule significative d'enquête: *De la norme à l'usage.*

L'Office du Vocabulaire français, qui, on le sait, est à l'origine des Biennales, entend participer à cette recherche et fournir aux orateurs de la Biennale qui désireront s'informer sur l'opinion du grand public éclairé une riche documentation. Celle-ci sera puisée à la meilleure source qui soit: le groupe que constituent les membres consultants de l'Office du Vocabulaire français.

C'est pourquoi nous vous demandons de bien vouloir répondre au questionnaire que voici:

1. Pensez-vous, d'une manière très générale, qu'il soit possible d'agir sur les habitudes de langage d'une grande communauté humaine?
   N.B. — A cette première question, les membres de l'Office du Vocabulaire français répondront, de toute évidence, par un « oui ». Mais toute personne qui répondra « non » devra développer ses raisons, qui pourront être constructives.
2. Pensez-vous que l'Enseignement soit le seul dispensateur de la norme et que nulle action sur l'usage ne soit concevable hors de l'école?
3. Croyez-vous que les adultes puissent recevoir un enseignement prolongé de la langue française, de la même manière qu'ils reçoivent, par les publications spécialisées, par les revues de vulgarisation scientifique ou technique, un enseignement prolongé en histoire, en physique, en histoire naturelle, en géographie . . . et même en àstronautique?

Nous vous serions reconnaissants de bien vouloir répondre à ces questions, en portant en tête de votre lettre vos nom et prénom, profession, adresse. Vous voudrez bien ajouter, également en tête de votre réponse, selon votre choix:
J'accepte que mon nom figure dans un compte rendu de synthèse (signature);
Je désire garder l'anonymat (id.).

Les réponses devront être adressées au secrétariat de

l'Office du Vocabulaire français, 17, rue de Montparnasse, Paris-VIe, France

Figure 24. From *Le Travailleur* (Worchester, Mass.), June 7, 1969

may someday enable us to understand is that which is concerned with language planning. Just as sociolinguistic inquiry into the creation of writing systems and into the revision of orthographies permits us to first recognize and to then refine our appreciation of the magnitudes of social change and social planning (if not social dislocation) with which such activities are commonly associated, so the systematic sociolinguistic study of language *planning* as a whole (incorporating the creation of writing systems and the revision of orthographies, but going beyond them to conscious governmental efforts to manipulate both the structure and the functional allocation of codes within a polity) enables us to appreciate the societal complexity impinging on the determination, implementation and evaluation of language *policy* as a whole. The study of language planning is the study of organized efforts to find solutions to societal language problems (Jernudd and Das Gupta 1969). As such, it is necessarily most dependent – of all the fields of applied language concerns – on the sociology of language and on the social sciences as a whole in order to move from theory to informed practice (Figure 24).

Of the language planning studies recently completed or currently underway a few have dealt with the cost-benefit analysis of alternative or hypothetically alternative decisions between which governmental or other bodies must choose (Jernudd 1969, Thurburn 1969). Others have discussed the pressure functions focused upon decision making/decision implementing bodies in the language field (whether the latter be legislative-executive within government or political-religious-literary-academic outside of government) from a variety of special interest groups running the gamut from professional associations of educators, to manufacturers of typewriters and publishers of textbooks, to spokesmen for literary, journalistic and ideological groupings, etc. (Das Gupta 1969). There are now several theoretical models (happily commensurable) of the interaction of sentimental and instrumental integrative and disintegrative forces in the language planning process (Kelmann 1969, Fishman 1971). There are recent critiques and integrations of the literature on the evaluation of planned change in education, industry, agriculture and other areas of conscious societal planning, in an effort to suggest evaluative methods that might be most fruitfully adopted for the evaluation of success or failure in language planning (Macnamara 1971, Rubin 1971). A four-country study has recently gotten underway (involving linguists, anthropologists, political scientists, sociologists, psychologists and educationists) in order to obtain roughly comparable data concerning the processes of language planning *per se* in each of the above context (decision making, pressure functions, national integration, implementation and evaluation). Obviously, the study of language planning is rapidly moving away from intra-code efficiency considerations alone (the latter being the primary emphasis of Tauli 1968) and moving steadily into ever-richer contextual concerns. Hopefully, as language planning and social planning agencies become more aware of the possible contributions of applied sociology of language they may become more inclined to involve sociolinguists and other language specialists in *guiding* the decision making *process* itself rather than merely in *implementing* decisions *already reached*. Several signs already point in this direction. Thus, the several nations of East Africa are interested in the current "Survey of Language Use and Language Teaching" (Prator 1967) in order to adopt (or revise) language operations in schools, mass media, public services, etc., on the basis of more precise information as to the age, number, location and interactions of the speakers of various local languages. Similarly, the Philippine government has long followed a policy of evaluating language policy in the area of education via research projects dealing with such matters as the advisability of initiating education in the local mother tongues and introducing the national language (Filipino) only in some optimal subsequent year (Ramos et al. 1967). The Irish government has sponsored "motivation research" and opinion polls in order to determine how its citizens view the Irish language and how they react to the government's efforts to "restore" it to wider functions (Anon. 1968). One of the most widely cited guides to governmental language policies and their educational implications is an applied sociolinguistic report issued by Unesco and dealing with "The Use of the Vernacular in Education" (Anon. 1953). Once a policy is adopted it is then necessary to implement it. Such implementation not only takes the obvious route of requiring and/or encouraging the functional re-allocation of varieties but also their phonological, lexical and grammatical realization along prescribed lines. Language agencies, institutes, academies or boards are commonly authorized to develop or plan the variety selected by policymakers. Such agencies are increasingly likely to seek feedback concerning the effectiveness or the acceptability of the 'products' (orthographies, dictionaries, grammars, spellers, textbooks, translation series, subsidized literary works, etc.) that they have produced. Sociologists of language have already produced many studies which language agencies are likely to find extremely useful in terms of their implications for the work that such agencies conduct.

The difficulties encountered and the lessons learned in planned lexical expansion to cope with the terminology of modern technology, education, government and daily life are recounted by Alisjahbana (1962, 1965, 1971), Bacon (1966), Morag (1959), Passin (1963) and Tietze (1962) in their accounts of language planning in Indonesia,

Central Asia, Japan, Israel and Turkey, respectively. The problems of planned language standardization have been illuminated by Ferguson (1968), Garvin (1959), Guxman (1960), Ray (1963), U. Weinreich (1953b), Havranek (1964), Valdman (1968) and Twaddell (1959) in sufficiently general terms to be of interest in any speech community where this process needs to be set in motion.

Even the very process of government involvement in language issues has begun to be documented. In this connection one must mention the reports of the Irish government on its efforts to restore the Irish language (Anon. 1965); Goodman's review of Soviet efforts to provide – as well as deny – indigenous *standard* languages to the peoples under their control (Goodman 1960); Haugen's many insightful reports of the Norwegian government's attempts to cope with language conflict by both protecting and limiting the linguistic divergence of its citizenry (Haugen 1961, 1966a, 1966b); Heyd's account of language reform in modern Turkey (Heyd 1954); Lunt's account of the studied efforts in Titoist Yugoslavia to separate Macedonian from Serbian and from Bulgarian (Lunt 1959) and Mayner's comments on the attempts to fuse Serbian and Croatian in that country (Mayner 1967); the contrasts between different parts of Africa noted by Mazrui (1967), Armstrong (1968), Polome (1968) and Whiteley (1968); Mills' report of how Communist China advanced and retreated in connection with the writing reform it so desperately needs (Mills 1956); Wurm's descriptions of the very beginnings of language policy in reference to Pidgin English ("Neomelanesian") in New Guinea (Wurm and Laycock 1961/62), and several others (e.g., Brosnahan 1963b; LePage 1964, Fishman 1968c) of more general or conceptual relevance.

One of the most necessary areas of applied sociology of language is that which deals with educational problems, related to language policy formulation or evaluation. In this connection there have been studies of the organization and operation of bilingual schools (Gaarder 1967); of the academic consequences of compulsory education via the weaker language for most learners (Macnamara 1966, 1967); of different approaches to teaching hitherto untaught mother tongues (Davis 1967); of varying South American and West Indian approaches of teaching both local and 'wider' languages (Burns 1968, LePage 1968, Rubin 1968); of difficulties in teaching English (as the compulsory school language for non-English speakers) encountered by teachers who are themselves non-native speakers of English (Lanham 1965); and, more specifically, of the problem of teaching standard English to speakers of very discrepant, non-standard varieties of that language (Stewart 1964, 1965). A more generalized interest in applied sociology of language is that shown by the recent Canadian Royal Commission on Bilingualism and Biculturism (Royal Commission 1965, 1967, 1968). It authorized studies not only on bilingual schooling but also on bilingualism in broadcasting, in industrial operations, in military operations and in the operation of various other societal enterprises.

Notwithstanding the obvious recent strengthening of applied sociology of language, several nations throughout the world are currently engaged in language planning without anything like the information available to them in other areas of planning. Sociolinguistic research on language planning must aim, first, to locate, then, to apportion the variation in behavior-toward-language which is to be observed in language planning contexts. It must seek detailed knowledge of how orthographic decisions (or script decisions, or national language decisions, or nomenclature decisions, etc.) are arrived at, how they are differentially reacted to or followed up by agencies inside and outside government, how they are differentially accepted or resisted by various population segments, how they are differentially evaluated and how subsequent policies and plans are differentially modified as a result of feedback from prior policy and planning. The sociology of language is just now beginning to describe the variation that constantly obtains in all of these connections. After this has been done sufficiently well and in sufficiently many contexts it should begin to successfully account for this variation and, at that point, be able to offer suggestions that are useful from the point of view of those seeking to influence, implement or evaluate language planning in the future.

9.6 Some Straws in the Wind

However, even in the absence of the amount of detail and sophistication that is needed before practical information becomes available, 'sociolinguistically motivated' changes in applied linguistics are clearly on the increase. Not only are such topics as the creation of writing systems, the reform of orthographies and language planning more generally marked (as we have seen) by a constantly increasing awareness of societal interpenetration and of the need for truly professional competence (which is more than simply being either critical or admiring) if one is to understand, let alone influence, the societal forces at work, but such awareness is growing in most other fields of applied linguistics as well.

The planning, implementation and evaluation of literacy campaigns increasingly ceased being merely applied linguistics plus education (pedagogy) plus ethnography as the period of immediate post World War II exuberance was left behind (Smith 1956). What is currently being developed in this field goes beyond advice on how to establish proper local contacts and obtain official cooperation (Young 1944, Russell 1948), important though such advice undoubtedly is. It goes beyond care to adapt programs to local needs (Jeffries 1958), to utilize a variety of methods on a variety of fronts (Ivanova and Voskresensky 1959), or to evaluate outcomes broadly enough to include health, economic and other pertinent indices (UNESCO 1951). Current efforts to advance literacy are increasingly based upon efforts to more fully understand the meaning and impact of literacy via small pilot studies which seek to recognize and weigh alternatives (Correa and Tinbergen 1962, Lewis 1961, McClusker 1963) and clarify the societal dimensions of literacy enterprises in different context (Goody 1963, Hayes 1965, Nida 1967, Schofield 1968, Wurm 1966).

A similar systematic intrusion of societal considerations has become noticeable in the field of *translation*. It is here, in particular, that sociolinguistic differentiation of language into varieties and of speech communities into situations is beginning to be felt, perhaps more so than in any other field of applied linguistics. One cannot read Catford's *Linguistic Theory of Translation* (1965) without being delighted by the fact it is far broader than 'immaculate linguistics' alone, and one cannot read Wonderly's *Bible Translations for Popular Use* (1968) without wishing that its sensitivity to social varieties and social occasions were part of the professional orientation of translation for far more worldly purposes as well. Certainly the deep concern with recognizing the significance of functional variation in language variety use, the sensitivity shown with respect to the *situational analysis* of repertoires of social and linguistic behavior – viewing Bible reading and listening as kinds of situations that may require particular kinds of language – and the repeated attention given to the contextual-functional differences between written and spoken language (and the multiple varieties of each) must sooner or later feed back into religious work on the creation of writing systems and on literacy more generally. This is, indeed, the beginning of technical sociolinguistic utility for an applied field. Having once embarked along the path or recognizing that all of the factors influencing communicative appropriateness in a particular speech community also influence the acceptability and the impact of translations in that community, the probability of mutual enrichment between application and theory for both fields of endeavor (translation and sociology of language) is indeed very great.

The same may yet be the case for the huge field of language teaching, where the contacts with the sociology of language are still far more tenous, if only because the contacts between an elephant and a sparrow must always be rather incomplete. Nevertheless, although the problems and prospects of language teaching could easily swallow up or trample underfoot not only all of the sociology of language but also all of sociology, psychology and linguistics *per se,* first linguistics and, more recently, the sociology of language *have* had some impact on the beast. A valuable introduction to sociology of language has been presented to language teachers generally by Halliday, McIntosh and Strevens (1964). In this introduction teachers are urged to recognize the different uses (and, therefore, the different varieties) of language that coexist within speech communities rather than, as has usually been the case thus far, to persist in the erroneous and deadening fiction that there is always *only one* (and always the *same* one) correct variety.

More recently we have witnessed a deluge of 'sociolinguistically oriented' interest in the language of disadvantaged speakers of non-standard English with Bernstein's work (e.g. 1964) being best known in England and Labov's (1965) or McDavid's (1958) in the U.S.A. Most of the products of this interest seek to contrastively highlight the basic structure of the speech of such communities so that teachers may be able to more successfully recognize and overcome the difficulties that learners will encounter when confronted with the phonological and grammatical structures of standard (school) English (e.g., Labov 1966d, 1968b, Wulfram 1969, Baratz and Shuy 1969). Nevertheless much (if not all) of what is currently offered to teachers in this connection is merely "sociolinguistically oriented" (in that it recognizes that minority group members often utilize varieties of English unfamiliar to others) rather than sociology of language proper (Fishman 1969b, Fishman and Lueders, in press). "Sociolinguistically oriented" advice is now also being directed toward teachers of bilinguals (Anderson 1969, Boyd 1968, Gaarder 1965). Such teachers are admonished that learners should be encouraged to maintain or acquire repertoires (incorporating several varieties) in each of their languages – rather than to displace all non-standard varieties in favor of one artificial standard version of each. Teachers of bilinguals are being urged to enable their students to select from each repertoire in accord with the norms for communicative appropriateness of the particular networks with which they (the pupils) seek mutually accepting interaction (Fishman and Lovas 1970, Mackey 1970). Nevertheless, the teachers of bilinguals (particularly in countries of mass immigration) have just begun to be shown how to influence the bilingual settings in which they and their students live and in which one or another of their languages may be roundly ignored, if not attacked, as soon as school is over (Andersson and Boyer 1970, John and Horner 1971).

Of course, the distance is still considerable between "sociolinguistically oriented" advice or sensitivity training for teachers and any more complete interrelationship between teaching methodology and sociology of language. Thus the education of bilinguals is still viewed primarily within the context of disadvantaged and dislocated minorities (whose lot in life will be far easier if only they learn English, French, Russian, etc.) rather than within the broader context of worldwide experience with bilingual education – whether in conjunction with elitist bilingualism, traditional bilingualism, or, more generally, widespread and stable (i.e., non-dislocated) bilingualism. As a result, the education of speakers of non-standard English is being pondered without awareness, for example, of the fact that most students entering German, French, Italian, and other schools during the past century have also been speakers of non-standard varieties of their respective languages. A true meeting of education and the sociology of language will enable *both* to discover why proportionally so many dialect speakers *do* and *did* seem to become readers and speakers of the standard language (and even of classical languages) in other parts of the world whereas so few seem to accomplish this in the U.S.A. today (Fishman and Lueders, in press). As with many other social science fields, a severe test of the power of the sociology of language will be its ability to be useful in the world of affairs. The education of non-literates, of bilinguals and of non-standard speakers are all fields about which the sociology of language must have more to say if it is really a discipline worth listening to at all.

APPENDIX

Linguistics: The Science of Code Description . . . and More

If one part of sociolinguistics comprises the 'study of the characteristics of language varieties' then we must turn to that science that has specialized in the systematic description of language: linguistics. To attempt to describe and analyze language data, in this day and age, without a knowledge of linguistic concepts and methods is to be as primitive as to try to describe and analyze human behavior more generally (or the functions of language varieties and the characteristics of their speakers) without knowledge of psychological and sociological concepts and methods.

It is no more possible to provide an adequate introduction to linguistics 'in one easy lesson' than to provide such for sociology or psychology. Nevertheless, it may be possible to briefly sketch some of the major concerns and methods of linguistics that bear upon sociolinguistics. The purpose of the next few pages, therefore, is to bring about 'linguistics appreciation', and of a very selective sort at that, rather than to present a full-fledged introduction to what is a very technical and complicated science which intersects the humanities, the social sciences and the natural sciences in its various subdivisions. The specialist knows full well that 'music appreciation' is not the same as music mastery. Similarly, 'linguistics appreciation' is not the same as linguistics mastery. Nevertheless, it is a beginning.

As a formal discipline, particularly insofar as the American academic scene is concerned, linguistics is a very recent field of specialization. The Linguistic Society of America was founded only in 1924. (The oldest linguistic society in the world, that of Paris, was founded in 1864.) Even today, when the number of linguists and linguistics programs in American universities is greater than ever before, there are only some two score graduate linguistics departments in the United States. Nevertheless, this discipline has not only come to be of prime interest to a growing band of dedicated scholars and practitioners within linguistics per se, but it has also in very recent years forcefully come to the attention of all other disciplines that recognize the centrality of verbal interaction in human affairs. Interdisciplinary contacts between linguistics and anthropology have been well established since the very appearance of linguistics in American universities. The anthropological linguist is a well recognized and highly regarded specialist among linguists and anthropologists alike. Indeed, linguistics is recognized as a 'branch' of anthropology in many textbooks and training programs. Of more recent vintage is psycholinguistics. Most recent of all is sociolinguistics, an interdisciplinary field which is just now beginning to train specialists that can bridge linguistics and sociology-social psychology in such a manner as to expand the horizons of both.

Descriptive Linguistics. The basic field in which most (if not all) linguists have been trained is that which is known as descriptive or synchronic linguistics. As its names imply, this field focuses upon the systematic description of a given language in a given time and place. It is not historical; it is not comparative; it is not prescriptive. Its emphasis is definitely on *spoken language,* the assumption being that written language is both derivative and different from natural language or speech.

It is common for the uninitiated to think of a language as being well represented by an unabridged dictionary. This view implies that the way to describe a language is to consider its components to be words. Any careful or consistent and exhaustive presentation and definition of the words of a language (which may be exactly what dictionaries attempt to do) would, therefore, from this point of view, be considered a description of that language. For most linguists, however, there are two other kinds of systematic presentations which are considered even more basic to their goal of describing language: the sound system of a language and the grammatical system of that language.

The branch of linguistics that is concerned with the systematic description of the sounds (phones) of a language is *phonology*. Some of the more general subspecialties within phonology are articulatory phonetics (how tongue, lips, teeth, vocal chords, velum, nasal passage and other speech organs produce the sounds of language) and acoustic phonetics (the physical properties of the sound waves or signals emitted by the speaker). Linguistics have devised for purposes of phonetic notation the International Phonetic Alphabet which is roughly adequate for the transcription of speech in all languages, although minor adjustments or additions to it are required in most individual cases.

On the foundation of these more general branches of phonology linguistics has been able to establish the study of *phonemics*, i.e., the study of those sounds that enter into meaningful contrasts or combinations in a given language, as compared to all of the physically differentiable sounds of a language (which are of interest in *phonetics*). A skilled phonetician differentiates far more fine shades of language sounds than do the native speakers of any particular language. Phonetic analysis is now sufficiently refined to demonstrate that no two speakers of a given language pronounce their words in exactly the same way. Indeed, the degree of refinement available to phonetic analysis has gone so far that it is possible to show that even an idiolect (the way of speaking that characterizes an individual) is not entirely consistent. The same individual does not pronounce the same word in the same way on all occasions of the same type. Into this endless series of successively refined analysis of language sound differences *phonemics* seeks to introduce the parsimony that derives from a knowledge of those sound-differences that are meaningfully distinctive (i.e., that serve to distinguish between linguistic signs and their meanings) for the native speakers of a particular language. The following brief example may illustrate the phonemic approach to demonstrable phonetic differences.

Let us consider the "b" sound in English, Arabic and Bengali. That each of these languages has some sound that the American man-in-the-street would unhesitatingly represent by the letter *b* is, for linguistics, a nonstructural comment and, therefore, one of no particular interest. It *is* of interest, however, to point out that in English *aba* and *apa* are differentiated, the voiced bilabial stop ("b) in the first being considered clearly different from the unvoiced bilabial stop ("p") in the second because the difference between *b* and *p* is crucial to recognizing the difference in meaning between "bit" and "pit", "bet" and "pet", and hundreds of other meaningful contrasts. In Arabic, on the other hand, no such meaningful substitutions of *b* and *p* are made. The native speaker of Arabic says only *aba* and uses a *p* sound only under special conditions, such as before *s* or *t*. More generally put, whatever sound differences exist in the *p-b* range in Arabic are not distinctive, i.e., they do not regularly signal meaning differences.

Thus, it is not enough to say that both English and Arabic have a *b* sound, for the sound functions far differently in the two languages. In English *b* and *p* function as phonemically different sounds (and, therefore, are notated /p/ and /b/); in Arabic they do not.

The absence or presence of a meaningful contrast between *b* and *p* takes on even greater linguistic significance if Bengali is examined. Not only are /b/ and /p/ differentiated by the ordinary native speaker of Bengali, but, in addition, an *unaspirated p* (as in the English *spin*) is differentiated from an *aspirated p* (as in the English *pin*). Similarly, an *unaspirated b* is regularly differentiated from an *aspirated b*.

Note, that while English recognizes a phonemic (meaning-related) difference between two sounds (one voiced and one unvoiced) that represent only a meaningless difference in Arabic, Bengali recognizes a further phonemic difference between two pairs of sounds (each with an aspirated and an unaspirated component) that represent only meaningless phonetic differences in English. Furthermore, as the English and Bengali languages change over time, changes in their "b" sounds will presumably be correlated with changes in their "p" sounds, precisely because these sounds are systematically related to each other.

It is in this last respect – i.e., in terms of systematic interrelationships – that descriptive linguistics is interested in the sounds of a language. This is also why descriptive linguistics is sometimes referred to as structural linguistics. It is not merely the sounds of a language that are of interest to linguistics, nor even the meaningfully different sounds, but, above all, the systematic links that exist between the meaningfully different sounds of a language. The phonemes of a language, like all other features of a language at a given point in time, are part of a system (a 'structure') that operates as a whole. Changes in one part of the structure affect the other parts; indeed, in true Gestalt fashion, any phonemic part can be truly appreciated only in terms of the phonological whole. A famous linguist of the first part of this century was the first to emphasize that language is a system in which every part has its (interlinked) place ("un systeme ou tout se tient"; de Saussure 1916) and this structural dictum has since then come to characterize not only descriptive linguistics but other branches of linguistics as well.

So basic is descriptive linguistics to linguistic science as a whole that another example of its concerns, this time at the level of grammatical analysis, is in order. Such an example is particularly desirable because the grammatical structure of language is so completely inter-woven with its sound structure, so much so that some linguists claim that phonological analysis depends on and must be part of an exhaustive grammatical analysis (although most linguists consider phon-ology, grammar, lexicon and semantics as quite separate *levels* of analysis).

Just as there is a minimal unit of meaningful sound (actually, of substitutionally meaningful sound, since the sounds in question are not meaningful per se), the phoneme, so is there a minimal unit of meaningful grammatical (i.e. of ordered or environmental) form, the *morpheme*. As a result, one branch of grammatical study is known as *morphology*. It studies the ordered relationships between small mean-ingful segments such as occur within words. (Syntax, on the other hand, studies the ordered relationships between units such as words in a phrase or utterance.) Thus, many English verbs form the past tense by adding a morpheme, which may be represented as $\{d\}$, to the present tense of the verb: I open – I opened. $\{d\}$ means past tense in English. Similarly, many English nouns form their plural by adding a morpheme, which may be represented as $\{z\}$, to their singular: car – cars. In both of these instances, however, the morphemes in question occur in several different forms that also differ somewhat as to their sound. Functionally equivalent alternatives of the same morpheme are referred to as *allomorphs*, precisely because there is no functional difference between them, however much they may differ in sound, just as sounds that revealed no functional difference were referred to earlier as *allophones*. The allomorphs of $\{d\}$ for the common, pro-ductive English verbs may sound like a *d* (as in opened), like a *t* (as in laughed), or like *ed* (as in mended). However, these allomorphs are not used at random. How would linguistics provide a rule to indicate when the native speaker of English employs which? What would such a rule be like?

To begin with, linguists would list as many verbs as possible that utilize each variant of the $\{d\}$ morpheme. Such a list might initially look like that shown in Table 1. After inspecting the array of final sounds in each of the columns of that table a linguist is able to do that which no ordinary native speaker of English can do: formulate a very few rules which summarize the systematic variation in the three allomorphs of $\{d\}$. Such rules might proceed as follows:

TABLE 1

Allomorphs of {d} in the past tense of some common, productive
English verbs

ed	t	d
mend	bank	open
lift	cook	use
boot	drop	save
raid	help	bomb
kid	walk	mail
tend	laugh	try
sift	shop	play
hoot	stamp	radio
shade	rank	hinge
hand	staff	rig

1. If the verb stem ends in /t/ or /d/ the past tense ends in *ed* (with the exception of a small number of verbs that retain the same form in past and present: cut, hit, put),
2. If the verb stem ends in a voiceless stop (other than /t/) or in a voiceless spirant, the past tense ends in *t*,
3. Otherwise, the past tense ends in *d*.

The above three brief rules pertain to the phonological conditioning of allomorphs. The allomorphs of {d} are realized according to their phonological environment. Thus, variations in grammatical form and variations in phonological form may and frequently do coincide. In general, linguistics has traditionally pursued two kinds of structured variation: variation relatable to change in meaning (such as the substitutional meaning that underlies phonemic analysis) and variation relatable to change in environment (such as the positional meaning that underlies morphemic analysis). Further synchronic variation in language, i.e., variation that cannot be identified either with change in meaning (i.e. change in referent) or with change in linguistic environment, when geographic area is held constant, has traditionally been thought of as 'free variation', i.e. as variation (not to say 'irregularity') due to factors outside of *langue* (the latent structure underlying speech) and, therefore, outside of the descriptive rules pertaining to *langue*. It is in some of the kinds of free variation – in variations which may co-occur with differences in a speaker's alertness or emotional state, with differences in topic, role relationship, communicational setting or interpersonal purpose – that sociolinguistics (and other interdisciplinary studies of language usage) attempts to discover additional regularity.

Linguistics has long been aware that 'free variation' might have a structure of its own. However, *that* structure (when and if it obtains) has usually been considered as being part of the structure of the speech event rather than part of the structure of the speech code per se. Although descriptive linguistics has emphasized the spoken language, the *speech act* itself was long considered to be outside of the domain of linguistics, for the speech act, just as the message content of speech, was considered to be part of 'communication' (long considered by linguists to be an outer or surface phenomenon) rather than part and parcel of *langue* per se (the heart of the matter). Many famous linguists have warned against confusing the two.

Thus, if it appeared that certain phonemic, morphological, syntactic or lexical regularities were not *always* as regular as one would hope (time and place remaining constant) this was attributed to the irregularity of *parole* (speaking, behavioral realization) as distinct from the systematic and abstract purity of *langue* (language, underlying structure) with which linguists should really be concerned. *Parole* is subject to many factors that produce variation (among those not previously mentioned: fatigue, anger, limitation in memory span, interruptions, etc.). These are all factors of 'degree', of 'more or less', of 'sometimes'. It was thought that the goal of linguistics was to cut through these psychological and sociological sources of 'static' and to concern itself with matters that were clearcut enough to be viewed as all or none phenomena: the basic code which, at any given time and place, might be considered to be one and the same for all who employed it. Thus, not only were linguists warned to distinguish sharply between *parole* and *langue* (de Saussure 1916), but they were also admonished to keep their distance from psychological or sociological data and theories which were viewed as inherently more concerned with the highly variable and seemingly irregular processes of verbal interaction and communication (and, therefore, with the messy data of *parole*) than with the pure code underlying these processes (Bloomfield 1933). It is only in more recent days, when the traditionally rigid distinction between *langue* and *parole* has come to be reexamined and when the varying interaction between them has come to be pursued that larger groups of linguists and of social scientists have found things to say to each other.

Other Branches of Linguistics. Other branches of linguistics – some of them older than descriptive linguistics (even though the latter has come to be so central to all linguistic pursuits) – have long been on friendlier terms with the social sciences. *Historical* (diachronic) *linguistics*, for example, in studying the changes that occur in a given code over time (sound changes, grammatical changes and word changes) has, of necessity, been interested in human migrations, intergroup contacts (conquest, trade), and whatever other diversification within a speech community that leads some of its members to interact with each other differentially (rather than equally or randomly), or that leads some of its members to interact with outsiders much more than do the rest. Historical linguistics (also known as *comparative linguistics*) focuses on tracing how one, earlier, parent ('proto') code subsequently divided into several related but separate ('sister' or 'daughter') codes or, alternatively, how several codes were derived from one pre-existing code. Although time is the crucial dimension in the development of *families of languages* between which *genetic relationship* can be shown to exist, as it is in the reconstruction of all common ancestries, nevertheless, historical linguists realize full well that the language changes that occurred were due to differential interaction and contact processes that transpired as time passed, rather than to the mere passing of time per se. As a result, historical linguistics has interacted fruitfully with history, archeology, anthropology and with other disciplines that can provide information concerning coterritorial influences between populations. In recent years, the fluctuating interaction between *langue* and *parole* (e.g., how one of the alternative systems of speaking available to a speech community spreads through the entire speech community and, increasingly displacing other alternatives, becomes an unvarying part of its basic code) has been studied by linguists working with social science concepts and methods of data collection and data analysis on what would once have been considered a 'purely' comparative problem (Labov 1963; Haugen 1961). The ties between comparative linguistics and the social sciences become stronger as the *dynamics* of language change come under increasing linguistic scrutiny, as distinct from the static, stepwise contrasts between the written records of one century and those of another that formerly dominated this field of study.

Another branch of linguistics that has frequently maintained close ties to the social sciences is *dialectology* (also known as *linguistic* or *dialect geography*). In comparison to historical linguistics this branch is concerned with variation in language on some dimension *other than time*. The achronic dimension with which dialectologists have most commonly been concerned has been geographic space or distance. Language that are employed over considerable expanses are often spoken somewhat differently (or even quite differently) in different parts of their speech areas. These differences may be phonological, such as President Kennedy's "Cuber" (for Cuba) and "vigah" (for vigor), where a Philadelphian would have said "Cubah" and "vigor" while many a Southerner would have said "Cubah" and "vigah". Dialect differences may also apply to the lexicon (milk shake vs. frappe; soda vs. pop) and even to parts of the grammatical system. Dialectologists have traditionally prepared *linguistic atlases* to show the geographic distribution of the linguistic features that have been of interest to them. Such atlases consist of maps on which are indicated the geographical limits within which certain usages are current. These limits are known as isoglosses (Weinreich, U. 1962; Herzog 1965).

However, dialectologists are well aware that the variations that are of interest to them are not due to geographical distance per se, but rather to the interactional consequences of geographic and other kinds of 'distance'. Phonological, lexical and grammatical uniformity may obtain over large geographic expanses when settlement is simultaneous and when verbal interaction as well as common identification are frequent. On the other hand, major language differences (sometimes referred to as 'social dialects' or 'sociolects') may arise and be maintained within relatively tiny geographic areas (e.g. in many cities) where the above conditions do not obtain. Considerations such as these have led many dialectologists, particularly those who have been interested in urban language situations, to be concerned with educational, occupational, religious, ethnic and other social groups and societal processes (although all or most of these groups may, in part, be traceable to originally diverse geographic origins) rather than with geographic distance per se. As a result, the ties between dialectologists and social scientists (not to mention sociolinguists) have been many and strong, particularly in recent years (Blanc 1964; Ferguson and Gumperz 1960), when the entire speech act – rather than merely the code rules abstracted from the speech act – has come to be of interest to an increasing number of dialectologists (Hymes 1962).

Of late, many linguists have taken to examining the structure of language – rather than the structure of particular languages – and to doing so in order to discover the nature of those fundamental human capacities which make for the competence of native speakers. Native speakers possess a rare gift which they themselves usually overlook: the ability to generate sentences that are recognized as structurally acceptable in their speech communities, and, what is more, to generate only such sentences. Many linguists now believe that a linguistic theory than can specify an adequate grammar (i.e. the rules that native speakers implicitly grasp and that constitute their native speaker competence) will also specify the language acquiring and language using nature of man. These linguists say that only an adequate theory of human capacity to acquire and use language will yield an adequate theory of what language itself is (Chomsky 1957, 1965).

Sociolinguistics may ultimately serve similarly basic purposes in the ongoing quest of the social sciences to understand communicative competence as a fundamental aspect of the social nature of man. The sociolinguistic theory that can specify adequate communicative competence (i.e. the rules that native members of speech communities implicitly grasp and that constitute their native member sociolinguistic behavior) will also specify the nature of social man as an acquirer and utilizer of a repertoire of verbal and behavioral skills. Man does not acquire or use his communicative competence in a single-code or single-norm community. Indeed, pervasively homogeneous communities with respect to communicative and other social behaviors do not exist except in the simplified worlds of some theorists and experimentors. Ultimately, sociolinguistics hopes to go beyond comfortably simple theory concerning the nature of communicative competence in the conviction that only an adequate theory of human capacity to acquire and to use a repertoire of interlocking language varieties and their related behaviors will yield an adequate theory of what communicative competence in social man really is.

Just as there are branches of linguistics that seek to study *langue* and *language* alone (indeed, to study language at its 'deepest', most abstract, and, therefore, at its socially most uninvolved) so are there branches of linguistics that have departed from a strict separation between *langue* and *parole* (since *parole* too has its very definite structure, since *parole* constantly influences *langue*, and since the individual's meaningful differentiation must be referred to, even though these are outside of *langue* per se, in order to establish a description of phonemic and other distinctions). Similarly, some branches of social psychology (and other social sciences as well) have moved closer to linguistics. Many sociologists and social psychologists now realize (whereas few did so a decade ago) that the norms that apply to and that may be thought of as generating human verbal interaction pertain not only to the communicative *content* and *context* of that interaction but to its linguistic *form* as well. As linguistics is developing outward – in the hopes of some: to become an all-encompassing science of language behavior – sociology and social psychology are developing toward increasing technical competence in connection with language description and analysis. The sociology of language is one of the byproducts of these two complementary developments and, as such, it must refer not only to the work of linguists but attend as well to those topics that are essentially sociological and social psychological and to which few linguists have, as yet, paid much attention.

SUGGESTED READINGS

I. *A Few Popular Introductions and Overviews*
   1. Hall, Robert A., Jr., *Linguistics and Your Language* (New York: Doubleday, 1960).
   2. Orenstein, Jacob, and Wm. W. Gage, *The ABC's of Language and Linguistics* (Phila. and New York: Chilton, 1964).
   3. Bolinger, Dwight, *Aspects of Language* (New York: Harcourt, Brace and World, 1967). •

II. *Some Traditional American Texts*
   1. Bloomfield, Leonard, *Language* (New York: Holt, Rinehart and Winston, 1933).
   2. Gleason, H. A., Jr., *An Introduction to Descriptive Linguistics* (revised) (New York: Holt, Rinehart and Winston, 1961).
   3. Hockett, Charles F., *A Course in Modern Linguistics* (revised) (New York: Macmillan, 1963).
   4. Sapir, Edward, *Language* (New York: Harcourt, Brace, 1921). (Paperback: New York: Harvest Books, 1955).

III. *One Classic and Three Recent Texts by European Authors*
   1. de Saussure, Ferdinand, *Course in General Linguistics* (translation of 1916 French Original by Wade Baskin) (New York: Philosophical Library, 1959).
   2. Martinet, Andre, *Elements of General Linguistics* (translation of 1960 French Original by Elisabeth Palmer) (Chicago: University of Chicago Press, 1964).
   3. Halliday, M. A. K., Angus McIntosh, and Peter Strevens, *The Linguistic Sciences and Language Teaching* (London: Longmans, Green, 1964).
   4. Robins, Robert H., *General Linguistics: An Introductory Survey* (Bloomington: Indiana University Press, 1966).

IV. *Examples of the Newer 'Transformationalist' Approach*
   1. Bach, Emmon W., *An Introduction to Transformational Grammars* (New York: Holt, Rinehart, Winston, 1964).
   2. Chomsky, Noam, *Aspects of the Theory of Syntax* (Cambridge: MIT Press, 1965).
   3. Langacker, Ronald W., *Language and its Structure* (New York: Harcourt, Brace and World, 1968).

V. *Journals to Glance At*
   1. *Language.*
   2. *Lingua.*
   3. *Linguistics.*
   4. *Linguistic Reporter.*
   5. *International Journal of American Linguistics.*
   6. *Language in Society.*

VI. *References*
   1. Rutherford, Phillip R., *A Bibliography of American Doctoral Dissertations in Linguistics, 1900-1964* (Washington: Center for Applied Linguistics, 1968).
   2. *Linguisticinformation* (Washington: Center for Applied Linguistics, 1965).

3. Cartter, Allan M., "Doctoral programs in linguistics", in his *An Assessment of Quality in Graduate Education* (Washington: American Council on Education, 1966).
4. Various articles on linguistic topics in the new *International Encyclopedia of the Social Sciences* (New York: Macmillan, 1968). (See the review of these topics in *Language*, 1969, 45, 458-463.)

10.0 BIBLIOGRAPHY

Alisjahbana, S. Takdir,
    1962 "The modernization of the Indonesian language in practice", in his *Indonesian Language and Literature: Two Essays* (New Haven, Yale University, Southeast Asia Studies), 1-22.
Alisjahbana, S. Takdir,
    1965 "New national languages: a problem modern linguistics has failed to solve", *Lingua, 15*, 515-530.
Alisjahbana, S. Takdir,
    1969 "Some planning processes in the development of the Indonesian/Malay language", *Consultative Meeting on Language Planning Processes.* (Honolulu, IAP); subsequently in (Rubin, Joan and Jernudd, Bjorn, (eds.), *Can Language be Planned?* (Honolulu, East-West Center Press) 1971.
Alisjahbana, S. Takdir (ed.),
    1971 *The Modernization of the Languages of Asia* (Kuala Lumpur, University of Malaysia Press).
Andersson, Theodore,
    1969 "Bilingual schooling: oasis or mirage?" *Hispania, 52*, 69-74.
Andersson, Theodore and Mildred Boyer (eds.),
    1970 *Bilingual Schooling in the United States*, 2 vols., Washington, D.C., USGPO.
Andreev, N. D. and L. R. Zinder,
    1959 Osnovnye problemy prikladnoj lingvistiki, *Voprosy Jazykoznaiya*, no. 4, 1-9.
Anon.,
    1930 *Practical Orthography of African Languages,* (International Institute of African Languages and Cultures, Memorandum 1) (Oxford, Oxford University Press) revised edition.
Anon.,
    1953 *The Use of Vernacular Languages in Education* (Paris, UNESCO).
Anon.,
    1963 *A Common Script for Indian Languages* (Delhi, Ministry of Scientific Research and Cultural Affairs).
Anon.,
    1965 *The Restoration of the Irish Language* (Dublin, The Stationery Office), Also note *Progress Report for the Period Ended 31 March, 1966* and *Progress Report for the Period Ended 31 March 1968.* (Dublin, The Stationery Office) 1966 and 1968.
Anon.,
    1968 *A Motivational Research Study for the Greater Use of the Irish Language*, 2 vols. (Croton-on-Hudson (N.Y.), Ernest Dichter International Institute for Motivational Research).

Armstrong, Robert,
1968 "Language policies and language practices in West Africa", in (Fishman, J. A., C. A. Ferguson and J. Das Gupta (eds.), *Language Problems of Developing Nations*. (New York, Wiley), 227-236.

Bacon, Elizabeth E.,
1966 "Russian influence on Central Asian languages", in her *Central Asians Under Russian Rule* (Ithaca, Cornell University Press).

Baratz, Joan and Roger W. Shuy,
1969 *Teaching Black Children to Read* (Washington, Center for Applied Linguistics).

Barker, George C.,
1947 "Social Functions of Language in A Mexican-American Community", *Acta Americana*, 5, 185-202.

Basso, Keith H.,
1967 "Semantic aspects of linguistic acculturation", *American Anthropologist* 69, 471-477.

Barker, George C.,
1947 "Social Functions of Language in A Mexican-American Community", *Acta Americana* 5, 185-202.

Basso, Keith H.,
1967 "Semantic aspects of linguistic acculturation", *American Anthropologist* 69, 471-477.

Bell, Daniel,
1961 *The End of Ideology* (New York: Collier).

Bernstein, Basil,
1964 "Elaborated and restricted codes: Their social origins and some consequences", *American Anthropologist* 66, No. 6, Part 2, 55-69.
1966 "Elaborated and restricted Codes: An Outline", *Sociological Inquiry* 36, 254-261.

Berry, Jack,
1958 "The making of alphabets", *Proceedings of the International Congress of Linguistics* (Oslo: Oslo University Press), 752-764; also reprinted in J. A. Fishman (ed.), *Readings in the Sociology of Language* (The Hague: Mouton, 1968), 737-753.

Blanc, Chaim,
1964 *Communal Dialects in Baghdad* (Cambridge: Harvard University Press).

Blom, Jan Peter, and John J. Gumperz,
In press "Some social determinants of verbal behavior", in John J. Gumperz and Dell Hymes (eds.), *The Ethnography of Communication: Directions in Sociolinguistics* (New York: Holt, Rinehart and Winston).

Bloomfield, Leonard,
1933 *Language* (New York: Holt).

Bock, Philip K.,
1964 "Social Structure and Language Structure", *Southwestern Journal of Anthropology* 20, 393-403; also in J. A. Fishman (ed.), *Readings in the Sociology of Language* (The Hague: Mouton, 1968), 212-222.

Bolinger, D. L.,
1946 "Visual morphemes", *Language* 22, 333-340.

Bonjean, Charles M.,
1966 "Mass, class and the industrial community: A comparative analysis of managers, businessmen and workers", *American Journal of Sociology* 72, 149-162.

Bottenberg, R. A., and K. H. Ward, Jr.,
  1963   *Applied Multiple Linear Regression* (Lackland, Tex.: Lackland AF
          Base PRL-TDR-63-6).
Boulding, Kenneth,
  1963   "The death of the city: A frightened look at postcivilization", in
          Oscar Handlin and John Burchard (eds.), *The Historian and the City*
          (Cambridge: MIT Press and Harvard University Press), 145.
Bowers, John,
  1968   "Language problems and literacy", in J. A. Fishman, C. A. Ferguson
          and J. Das Gupta (eds.), *Language Problems of Developing Nations*
          (New York: Wiley), 381-401.
Boyd, Dorothy L.,
  1968   "Bilingualism as an educational objective", *The Educational Forum* 32,
          309-313.
Bradley, Henry,
  1913/14 "On the relation between spoken and written language", *Proceed-
            ings of the British Academy* 6, 212-232.
Bright, William,
  1960   "Animals of acculturation in the California Indian languages", *Uni-
          versity of California Publications in Linguistics* 4, No. 4, 215-246.
Broom, Leonard, and D. Norval Glenn,
  1966   "Negro-White differences in reported attitudes and behavior", *Sociology
          and Social Research* 50, 187-200.
Brosnahan, L. F.,
  1963a "Some historical cases of language imposition", in Robert Spencer (ed.),
          Language in Africa (Cambridge, Eng.: Cambridge University Press),
          7-24.
  1963b "Some aspects of the linguistic situation in tropical Africa", *Lingua* 12,
          54-65.
Brown, Roger W., and Albert Gilman,
  1960   "The pronouns of power and solidarity", in Thomas A. Sebeok (ed.),
          Style in Language (Cambridge and New York: Technology Press of
          MIT and Wiley), 253-276; also in J. A. Fishman (ed.), *Readings in the
          Sociology of Language* (The Hague: Mouton, 1968), 252-275.
Brown, Roger W. and Eric H. Lenneberg,
  1954   "A study in language and cognition", *Journal of Abnormal and Social
          Psychology* 49, 454-462.
Burns, Donald,
  1953   "Social and political implications in the choice of an orthography",
          Fundamental and Adult Education 5(2), 80-85.
  1968   "Bilingual education in the Andes of Peru", in J. A. Fishman, C. A.
          Ferguson and J. Das Gupta (eds.), *Language Problems of the Develop-
          ing Nations* (New York: Wiley), 403-414.
Carmichael, L., H. P. Hogan, and A. A. Walter,
  1932   "An experimental study of the effect of language on the perception
          of visually perceived form", *Journal of Experimental Psychology* 15,
          73-86.
Carroll, John B., and J. B. Casagrande,
  1958   "The function of language classifications in behavior", in E. Maccoby,
          T. Newcomb and E. Hartley (eds.), *Readings in Social Psychology*
          (New York: Holt), 18-31.

Catford, J. C.,
1965   *A Linguistic Theory of Translation* (London: Oxford University Press).
Chinese Written Language Reform Committee,
1956   "Several points concerning the Han language phoneticization plan (draft) explained", *Current Background*, No. 380 (March 15), 4-13.
Chomsky, Noam,
1957   *Syntactic Structures* (The Hague: Mouton).
1965   *Aspects of the Theory of Syntax* (Cambridge: MIT Press).
Chou En-lai,
1965   "Current tasks of reforming the written language", in *Reform of the Chinese Written Language* (Peking: Foreign Language Press), 7-29.
Cohen, Jack,
1965   "Some statistical issues in psychological research", in B. B. Wolmand (ed.), *Handbook of Clinical Psychology* (New York: McGraw-Hill), 95-121.
1968a "Prognostic factors in functional psychosis: A study in multivariate methodology", invited address at the New York Academy of Sciences, March 18, mimeographed.
1968b "Multiple regression as a general data-analytic system", *Psychological Bulletin* 70, 426-443.
Conklin, Harold C.,
1962   "Lexicographic treatment of folk taxonomies", in Fred W. Householder and Sol Saporta (eds.), *Problems in Lexicography* (Bloomington: Indiana University Research Center in Anthropology, Folklore and Linguistics), Publication 21, 119-141.
Cook, S. F.,
1943   "The conflict between the California Indian and white civilization", *Ibero-Americana* 21, 1-194, 1-55; 23, 1-115; 24, 1-29.
Corpas, Jorge Pineros,
1969   "Inconvenientes de la enseñanza bilingüe a la luz de la fisiología cerebral", *Noticias Culturales* (Bogotá), No. 99, 1-4.
Correa, Hector, and Jan Tinbergen,
1962   "Quantitative adaptation of education to accelerated growth", *Kyklos* 15, 776-785.
Dalby, David,
1967   "A survey of the indigenous scripts of Liberia and Sierra Leone: Vai, Mende, Loma, Kpelle and Bassa", *African Languages Studies* 8, 1-51.
1968   "The indigenous scripts of West Africa and Surinam: Their inspiration and design", *African Languages Studies* 9, 156-197.
Das Gupta, Jyotirindra,
1969   "Religious loyalty, language conflict and political mobilization", *Consultative Meeting on Language Planning Processes* (Honolulu: EWC-IAC); subsequently in Joan Rubin and Bjorn Jernudd (eds.), *Can Language be Planned?* (Honolulu: East-West Center Press, 1971).
Das Gupta, Jyotirindra, and Joshua A. Fishman,
1971   "Interstate migration and subsidiary language-claiming; an analysis of selected Indian census data", *International Migration Review*, 5, no. 2
Davis, Frederick B.,
1967   *Philippine Language-Teaching Experiments* (Phillippine Center for Language Study, No. 5) (Quezon City: Alemar-Phoenix).
DeFrancis, John,
1947   "Japanese language reform: Politics and phonetics", *Far Eastern Survey*

16, No. 19, 217-220.

1950   *Nationalism and Language Reform in China* (Princeton: Princeton University Press).

1968   "Language and script reform (in China)", *Current Trends in Linguistics* (The Hague: Mouton), 130-150, also in J. A. Fishman (ed.), *Advances in the Sociology of Language* (The Hague: Mouton, 1971).

de Saussure, Ferdinand,

1959   *Course in General Linguistics* (translated by Wade Baskin) (New York: Philosophical Library). Original (French) publication: 1916.

Deutsch, Karl W.,

1942   "The trend of European nationalism – the language aspect", *American Political Science Review* 36, 533-541.

1966   *Nationalism and Social Communication* (Cambridge: MIT Press) (2nd edition).

Dickens, K. J.,

1953   "Unification: The Akan dialects of the Gold Coast", in *The Use of Vernacular Languages in Education* (Paris, UNESCO), 115-123.

Dohrenwend, Bruce P., and J. Robert Smith,

1962   "Toward a theory of acculturation", *Southwest Journal of Anthropology* 18, 30-39.

Dozier, Edward P.,

1951   'Resistance to acculturation and assimilation in an Indian pueblo", *American Anthropologist* 53, 56-66.

Edelman, Martin, Robert L. Cooper, and Joshua A. Fishman,

1968   "The contextualization of school children's bilingualism", *Irish Journal of Education* 2, 106-111.

Ellis, Dean S.,

1967   "Speech and social status in America", *Social Forces* 45, 431-437.

Epstein, A. L.,

1959   "Linguistic innovation and culture on the Copperbelt, Northern Rhodesia", *Southwestern Journal of Anthropology* 15, 235-253; also in J. A. Fishman (ed.), *Readings in the Sociology of Language* (The Hague: Mouton, 1968), 320-339.

Ervin, Susan M., and Charles E. Osgood,

1954   "Second language learning and bilingualism", *Journal of Abnormal and Social Psychology* 49, Supplement, 139-146.

Ervin-Tripp, Susan M.,

1964   "An analysis of the interaction of language, topic and listener", *American Anthropologist* 66, Part 2, 86-102; also in J. A. Fishman (ed.), *Readings in the Sociology of Language* (The Hague: Mouton, 1968), 192-211.

1969   "Sociolinguistics", in L. Berkowitz (ed.), *Advances in Experimental Social Psychology*, Vol. 4 (New York: Academic Press), 91-165; also in J. A. Fishman (ed.), *Advances in the Sociology of Language* (The Hague: Mouton, 1971).

Ferguson, Charles A.,

1959a   "Diglossia", *Word* 15, 325-340.

1959b   "Myths about Arabic" (= *Monograph Series on Languages and Linguistics*) (Georgetown University) 12, 75-82; also in J. A. Fishman (ed.), *Readings in the Sociology of Language* (The Hague: Mouton, 1968), 375-381.

1965 "Directions in sociolinguistics; Report on an interdisciplinary seminar", *SSRC Items* 19, No. 1, 1-4.
1967 "St. Stefan of Perm and applied linguistics", in *To Honor Roman Jakobson* (The Hague: Mouton); also in J. A. Fishman, C. A. Ferguson and J. Das Gupta (eds.), *Language Problems of Developing Nations* (New York: Wiley, 1968), 253-266.
1968 "Language development", in J. A. Fishman, C. A. Ferguson and J. Das Gupta (eds.), *Language Problems of Developing Nations* (New York: Wiley).

Ferguson, Charles A., and J. John Gumperz (eds.),
1960 "Linguistic diversity in South Asia: Studies in regional, social and functional variation", *International Journal of American Linguistics* 4, No. 1 (entire issue).

Ferguson, Charles A., and Raleigh Morgan, Jr.,
1959 "Selected Readings in applied linguistics", *Linguistic Reporter*, Supplement 2, 4 pp.

Ferru, Jean Louis,
1966 "Possible repercussions of a technical and economic nature of the particular letters for the standard transcription of West African languages", *Damako (Mali) Meeting on the Standardization of African Alphabets, Feb. 28-March 5, 1966*. UNESCO (CLT) Baling.

Findling, Joav,
1969 "Bilingual need affiliation and future orientation in extragroup and intragroup domains", *Modern Language Journal* 53, 227-231; also in J. A. Fishman (ed.), *Advances in the Sociology of Language* 2 (The Hague: Mouton, 1971).

Fischel, A.,
1919 *Der Panslawismus bis zum Weltkrieg* (Stuttgart/Berlin: Cotta).

Fischer, John L.,
1958 "Social influences in the choice of a linguistic variant", *Word* 14, 47-56.

Fishman, Joshua A.,
1956 "The process and function of social stereotyping", *Journal of Social Psychology* 43, 27-64.
1960 "A systematization of the Whorfian Hypothesis", *Behavioral Science* 8, 323-339.
1964 "Language maintenance and language shift as a field of inquiry", *Linguistics* 9, 32-70.
1965a *Yiddish in America* (Bloomington, Ind.: Indiana University Research Center in Anthropology, Folklore and Linguistics), Publication 36.
1965b "Bilingualism, intelligence and language learning", *Modern Language Journal* 49, 227-237.
1965c "Varieties of ethnicity and language consciousness", *Georgetown University Monograph Series on Languages and Linguistics* 18, 69-79.
1965d "Who speaks what language to whom and when?", *Linguistique*, No. 2, 67-88.
1965e "Language maintenance and language shift; The American immigrant case within a general theoretical perspective", *Sociologus* 16, 19-38.
1965f "Language maintenance and language shift in certain urban immigrant environments: The case .of Yiddish in the United States", *Europa Ethnica* 22, 146-158.
1966a "Bilingual sequence at the societal level", *On Teaching English to Speakers of Other Languages* 2, 139-144.

1966b "Some contrasts between linguistically homogeneous and linguistically heterogeneous polities", *Social Inquiry* 36, 146-158. Revised and expanded in J. A. Fishman, C. A. Ferguson and J. Das Gupta (eds.), *Language Problems of Developing Nations* (New York: Wiley, 1968), 53-68.

1966c *Language Loyalty in the United States* (The Hague: Mouton).

1966d "Planned reinforcement of language maintenance in the United States; Suggestions for the conservation of a neglected national resource", in J. A. Fishman, *Language Loyalty in the United States* (The Hague: Mouton), Chapter 21.

1967a "The breadth and depth of English in the United States", *University Quarterly*, March, 133-140.

1967b "A Sociology of Language (Review)", *Language* 43, 586-604.

1968a *Readings in the Sociology of Language* (The Hague: Mouton).

1968b "Sociolinguistic Perspective on the Study of Bilingualism", *Linguistics* 39, 21-50.

1968c "Sociolinguistics and the language problems of developing nations", *International Social Science Journal* 20, 211-225.

1968d "A sociolinguistic census of a bilingual neighborhood", in *Bilingualism in the Barrio*, J. A. Fishman, R. L. Cooper and Roxana Ma, et al. (New York: Yeshiva University). Final Report to Department of Health, Education, and Welfare under Contract No. OEC-1-7-062817-0297; also *American Journal of Sociology*, 1969d, 75, 323-339.

1969a "National language and languages of wider communication in the developing nations", *Anthropological Linguistics* 11, 111-135.

1969b "Literacy and the language barrier", *Science* 165, 1108-1109.

1969c "Bilingual attitudes and behaviors", *Language Sciences,* No. 5, 5-11; also in J. A. Fishman, R. L. Cooper and Roxana Ma et al., *Bilingualism in the Barrio* (New York: Yeshiva University, 1968). Final Report to DHEW under contract No. OEC-1-7-062817-0297, and Bloomington, Ind., *Language Sciences Series*, 1971.

1969d "The impact of nationalism on language planning: some comparisons between early 20th century Europe and subsequent developments in South and South-East Asia", *Consultative Meeting on Language Planning Processes* (Honolulu: East-West Center, Institute of Advanced Projects); also in *Can Languages be Planned?*, Joan Rubin and Bjorn Jernudd (eds.) (Honolulu: East-West Center Press), 1971.

1969e "Puerto Rican intellectuals in New York; Some intragroup and intergroup contrasts", *Canadian Journal of Behavioral Sciences* 1, 215-226.

In press "The links between micro- and macro-sociolinguistics in the study of who speaks what language to whom and when", in John J. Gumperz and Dell Hymes (eds.), *The Ethnography of Communication: Directions in Sociolinguistics* (New York: Holt, Rinehart and Winston); also in J. A. Fishman, R. L. Cooper and Roxana Ma et al., *Bilingualism in the Barrio* (Bloomington, Ind., *Language Science Series*, 1971).

Fishman, Joshua A., and Rebecca Agheyisi,
    1970 "Language attitude studies", *Anthropological Linguistics*, 12, 137-157.

Fishman, Joshua A., Robert C. Cooper, and Roxana Ma et al.,
    1968 *Bilingualism in the Barrio*. Final Report on Contract-OEC-1-7-062817-0297 to DHEW (New York: Yeshiva University); also Bloomington, Ind., *Language Sciences Series*, 1971.

Fishman, Joshua A., and Lawrence Greenfield,
1970   "Situational measures of normative language views in relation to person, place and topic among Puerto Rican bilinguals", *Anthropos* 65, 602-618; also in *Advances in the Sociology of Language*, Vol. 2, J. A. Fishman (ed.) (The Hague: Mouton, 1972).
Fishman, Joshua A., and Eleanor Herasimchuk,
1969   "The multiple prediction of phonological variables in a bilingual speech community", *American Anthropologist* 71, 648-657; also in J. A. Fishman (ed.), *Advances in the Sociology of Language*, Vol. 2 (The Hague: Mouton, 1972).
Fishman, Joshua A., and John C. Lovas,
1970   "Bilingual education in sociolinguistic perspective", *TESOL Quarterly*, 4, 215-222.
Fishman, Joshua A., and Erika Lueders,
1970   "What has the sociology of language to say to the teacher?" (On teaching the standard variety to speakers of dialectal or sociolectal varieties), in C. Cazden, V. John and D. Hymes (eds.), *The Functions of Language* (New York: Teachers College Press).
Fishman, Joshua A., and Vladimir C. Nahirny,
1966   "The ethnic group school in the United States", in J. A. Fishman et al., *Language Loyalty in the United States* (The Hague: Mouton), Chapter 6; also *Sociology of Education* (1964), 37, 306-317.
Fishman, Joshua A., and Charles Terry,
1969   "The validity of sensus data on bilingualism in a Puerto Rican neighborhood", *American Sociological Review* 34, 636-650.   ∗
Frake, Charles O.,
1961   "The diagnosis of disease among the Subanun of Mindanao", *American Anthropologist* 63, 113-132.
1962   "The ethnographic study of cognitive systems", in T. Gladwin and William C. Sturtevant (eds.), *Anthropology and Behavior* (Washington, D. C.: Anthropological Society of Washington), 77-85; also in J. A. Fishman (ed.), *Readings in the Sociology of Language* (The Hague: Mouton, 1968), 434-446.
Friederich, Paul,
1966   "The linguistic reflex of social change: From Tsarist to Soviet Russian kinship", *Sociological Inquiry* 36, 159-185.
1962   "Language and politics in India", *Daedalus*, Summer, 543-559.
Gaarder, A. Bruce,
1965   "Teaching the bilingual child: Research, development and policy", *The Modern Language Journal* 49, 165-175.
1967   "Organization of the bilingual school", *Journal of Social Issues* 23, 110-120.
Gallagher, Charles F.,
1967   "Language rationalization and scientific progress", Paper prepared for Conference on Science and Social Change, California Institute of Technology, October 18-20.
1969   "Language reform and social modernization in Turkey", *Consultative Meeting on Language Planning Processes* (Honolulu, EWS-IAP); subsequently in Joan Rubin and Bjorn Jernudd (eds.), *Can Language be Planned?* (Honolulu: East-West Center Press, 1971).
Garfinkel, Harold,
1967   *Studies in Ethnomethodology* (New York: Prentice Hall).

Garfinkel, Harold and H. Sacks (eds.),
  in press *Contribution in Ethnomethoaology* (Bloomington: Indiana University Press).
Garvin, Paul L.,
  1954 "Literacy as problem in language and culture", *Georgetown University Monograph Series on Languages and Linguistics* 7, 117-129.
  1959 "The standard language problem: Concepts and methods", *Anthropological Linguistics* 1, No. 2, 28-31.
Geertz, Clifford,
  1960 "Linguistic etiquette", in his *Religion of Java* (Glencoe: Free Press); also in J. A. Fishman (ed.), *Readings in the Sociology of Language* (The Hague: Mouton, 1968), 282-295.
Gelb, I. F.,
  1952 *A Study of Writing* (Chicago: University of Chicago Press).
Gerullis, Georg,
  1932 "Muttersprache und Zweisprachigkeit in einem preussisch-litauischen Dorf", *Studi Baltici* 2, 59-67.
Glenn, Norval D.,
  1966 "The trend in differences in attitudes and behavior by educational level", *Sociology of Education* 39, 255-275.
  1967 "Differentiation and massification: Some trend data from national surveys", *Social Forces* 46, 172-179.
Glenn, Norval D., and J. L. Simmons,
  1967 "Are regional cultural differences diminishing?", *Public Opinion Quarterly* 31, 176-193.
Goodenough, Ward H.,
  1965 "Rethinking 'status' and 'role': Toward a general model of the cultural organization of social relationships", in M. Banton (ed.), *The Relevance of Models for Social Anthropology* (New York: Praeger), 1-24.
Goodman, Elliot R.,
  1960 "World state and world language", in his *The Soviet Design for a World State* (New York: Columbia University Press), 264-284; also in J. A. Fishman (ed.), *Readings in the Sociology of Language* (The Hague: Mouton, 1968), 717-736.
Goody, Jack,
  1963 *Literacy in Traditional Societies* (London: Cambridge University Press),
Greenberg, Joseph R.,
  1965 "Urbanism, migration and language", in Hilda Kuper (ed.), *Urbanization and Migration in West Africa* (Los Angeles and Berkeley: University of California Press), 50-59.
  1966 *Universals of Language*, 2nd edition (Cambridge, Mass.: The MIT Press).
Greenfield, Lawrence,
  1968 "Situational measures of language use in relation to person, place and topic among Puerto Rican bilinguals", *Bilingualism in the Barrio*. Final Report to DHEW re Contract No. DEC-1-7-062817-0297 (New York: Yeshiva University).
Grimshaw, Allen D.,
  1969 "Sociolinguistics and the sociologist", *The American Sociologist* 4, 312-321.
  in press "Some social sources and some social functions of pidgin and creole languages", in D. Hymes (ed.), *Proceedings of the Social Science*

Research Council Conference on Creolization and Pidginization (Cambridge: Cambridge University Press).
Gulick, John,
1958 "Language and passive resistance among the eastern Cherokees", *Ethnohistory* 5, 60-81.
Gumperz, John J.,
1958 "Dialect differences and social stratification in a North Indian village", *American Anthropoligst* 60, 668-682.
1961 "Speech variation and the study of Indian civilization", *American Anthropologist* 63, 976-988.
1962 "Types of linguistic communities", *Anthropological Linguistics* 4, No. 1, 28-40; also in J. A. Fishman (ed.), *Readings in the Sociology of Language* (The Hague: Mouton, 1968), 460-476.
1964a "Linguistic and social interaction in two communities", *American Anthropologist* 66, No. 2, 37-53.
1964b "Hindi-Punjabi code switching in Delhi", in Morris Halle (ed.), *Proceedings of the International Congress of Linguistics* (The Hague: Mouton).
1966 "On the ethnology of linguistic change", in William Bright (ed.), *Sociolinguistics* (The Hague: Mouton), 27-38.
1967 "The linguistic markers of bilingualism", *Journal of Social Issues* 23, No. 2, 48-57.
Guxman, M. M.,
1960 "Some general regularities in the formation and development of national languages", in M. M. Guxman (ed.), *Voprosy Formirovanija Nacional'nyx Jazykov* (Moscow), 295-307; also in J. A. Fishman (ed.), *Readings in the Sociology of Language* (The Hague: Mouton, 1968), 766-779.
Hair, P. E. H.,
1963 "Notes on the discovery of the Vai script, with a bibliography", *Sierra Leone Language Review* 2, 36-49.
Hall, Robert A., Jr.,
1952 "Bilingualism and applied linguistics", *Zeitschrift für Phonetik und allgemeine Sprachwissenschaft* 6, 13-30.
Halliday, M. A. K., Angus MacIntosh, and Peter Strevens,
1964a *The Linguistic Sciences and Language Teaching* (London: Longmans).
1964b "The users and uses of language", in H. A. K. Halliday, A. MacIntosh and P. Strevens (eds.), *The Linguistic Sciences and Language Teaching* (London: Longmans, Green); also in J. A. Fishman (ed.), *Readings in the Sociology of Language* (The Hague: Mouton, 1968), 139-169.
Hamilton, Richard F.,
1965 "Affluence and the worker: The West German case", *American Journal of Sociology* 71, 144-152.
Hansen, Marcus L.,
1940 *The Immigrant in American History*, Arthur M. Schlesinger (ed.) (Cambrige: Harvard University Press).
Haudricourt, A. G.,
1943 "De l'origine des particularites de l'alphabet Vietnamien", *Dan Vietnam*, No. 3, 61-68.
Haugen, Einar,
1953 *The Norwegian Language in America; A Study in Bilingual Behavior* (Philadelphia: University of Pennsylvania Press), 2 volumes; 2nd ed.

(Bloomington: Indiana University Press, 1969).

1961   "Language planning in modern Norway", *Scandinavian Studies* 33, 68-
81; also in J. A. Fishman (ed.), *Readings in the Sociology of Language*
(The Hague: Mouton, 1968), 673-687.

1966a   *Language Planning and Language Conflict; The Case of Modern Nor-*
wegian (Cambridge: Harvard University Press).

1966b   "Linguistics and language planning", in Wm. Bright (ed.), *Sociolinguis-*
tics (The Hague: Mouton), 50-66.

1966c   "Dialect, Language, Nation", *American Anthropologist* 68, 922-935.

Havranek, Bohuslav,

1964   "The functional differentiation of the standard language", in Paul L.
Garvin (ed.), *A Prague School Reader on Esthetics, Literary Structure*
and Style (Washington, D. C.: Georgetown University Press), 1-18.

Hayden, Robert G., and Joshua A. Fishman,

1966   "The impact of exposure to ethnic mother tongues on foreign language
teachers in American high schools and colleges", in J. A. Fishman et
al., *Language Loyalty in the United States* (The Hague: Mouton), Chapter 13; also, *Modern Language Journal* (1964), 48, 262-274.

Hayes, Alfred S.,

1965   *Recommendations of the Work Conference on Literacy* (Washington:
Center for Applied Linguistics).

Herman, Simon N.,

1961   "Explorations in the social psychology of language choice", *Human*
Relations 14, 149-164; also in J. A. Fishman (eds.), *Readings in the*
Sociology of Language (The Hague: Mouton, 1968), 492-511.

Hertzler, Joyce O.,

1965   *The Sociology of Language* (New York: Random House).

Herzog, Marvin I.,

1965   *The Yiddish Language in Northern Poland: Its Geography and History*
(Bloomington, Ind.: Indiana University Research Center in Anthropology, Folklore and Linguistics), Publication 37.

Heyd, Uriel,

1954   *Language Reform in Modern Turkey* (Jerusalem: Israel Oriental Society).

Hodges, Harold M.,

1964   *Social Stratification: Class in America* (Cambridge: Schenkman).

Hofman, John E.,

1966a   "Mother tongue retentiveness in ethnic parishes", in Joshua A. Fishman et al., *Language Loyalty in the United States* (The Hague: Mouton).

1966b   "The language transition in some Lutheran denominations", in J. A.
Fishman et al., *Language Loyalty in the United States* (The Hague:
Mouton), Chapter 10; also in J. A. Fishman (ed.), *Readings in the*
Sociology of Language (The Hague: Mouton, 1966), 620-638.

Hofman, John E. and Haya Fisherman,

1971   "Language Shift and Maintenance in Israel", *International Migration*
Review, 5, no. 2, 204-226; also in J. A. Fishman (ed.), *Advances in the*
Sociology of Language, Vol. 2 (The Hague: Mouton, 1972).

Hohenthal, W. D., and T. McCorkle,

1955   "The problem of aboriginal persistence", *Southwestern Journal of*
Anthropology 11, 288-300.

Hoijer, H.,

1951   "Cultural implications of the Navaho linguistic categories", *Language*

27, 111-120.

1954 "The Sapir-Whorf hypothesis", in H. Hoijer (ed.), *Language in Culture* (= *American Anthropological Association*, Memoir No. 79) (Chicago: University of Chicago Press), 92-104.

Holton, Daniel C.,
1947 "Ideographs and Ideas", *Far Eastern Survey* 16, No. 19, 220-223.

Howell, Richard W.,
1965 "Linguistic status markers in Korean", *Kroeber Anthropological Society Papers* 55, 91-97.
1967 "Terms of address as indices of social change", paper presented at American Sociological Association Meeting, San Francisco, Sept. 1967.

Huffine, Carol L.,
1966 "Inter-Socio-Economic Clan Language Differences: A Research Report", *Sociology and Social Research* 50, 3, 351-355.

Hughes, Everett C.,
1970 "The linguistic division of labor in industrial and urban societies", *Georgetown University Monograph Series on Languages and Linguistics*, in press; also in J. A. Fishman (ed.), *Advances in the Sociology of Language*, Vol. 2 (The Hague: Mouton, 1972).

Hsia, Tao-tai,
1956 *China's Language Reforms* (New Haven: Yale University Press).

Hymes, Dell H.,
1962 "The ethnography of speaking", in T. Gladwin and W. C. Sturtevant (eds.), *Anthropology and Human Behavior* (Washington, D. C.: Anthropology Society of Washington), 13-53; also in J. A. Fishman (ed.), *Readings in the Sociology of Language* (The Hague: Mouton, 1968), 99-138.
1966 "Two types of linguistic relativity", in Wm. Bright (ed.), *Sociolinguistics* (The Hague: Mouton), 114-157.
1967a "Why Linguistics Needs the Sociologist", *Social Research* 34, 7, 632-647.
1967b "Models of interaction of language and social setting", *Journal of Social Issues* 23, No. 2, 8-28.

Ivanova, A. M., and V. D. Voskresensky,
1959 "Abolition of adult illiteracy in USSR, 1917-1940", *Fundamental and Adult Education* 11, 3, 131-186.

Jeffries, W. F.,
1958 "The literacy campaign in Northern Nigeria", *Funding and Adult Education* 10, 1, 2-6.

Jernudd, Bjorn,
1969 "Notes on economic analysis and language planning", *Consultative Meeting on Language Planning Processes* (Honolulu: EWC-IAP); subsequently, in Joan Rubin and Bjorn Jernudd (eds.), *Can Language be Planned?* (Honolulu: East West Center Press, 1971).

Jernudd, Bjorn, and Jyotirindra Das Gupta,
1969 "Towards a theory of language planning", *Consultative Meeting on Language Planning Processes* (Honolulu: EWC-IAP); subsequently, in Joan Rubin and Bjorn Jernudd (eds.), *Can Language be Planned?* (Honolulu: East-West Center Press, 1971).

Jernudd, Bjorn H., and Tommy Willingsson,
1968 "A sociolectal study of the Stockholm region", *Svenska Landsmal och Svenskt Folkliv* 289, 140-147.

John, Vera, and Vivian Horner,
  1971 *Early Childhood Bilingual Education* (New York: Modern Language Association).
Johnston, Ruth,
  1963a "Factors in the Assimilation of Selected Groups of Polish Post-War Immigrants in Western Australia", Unpublished Ph.D. Dissertation, University of Western Australia (Perth); subsequently: *Immigrant Assimilation; A Study of Polish People in Western Australia* (Perth: Paterson Brokensha, 1965).
  1963b "A new approach to the meaning of assimilation", *Human Relations* 16, 295-298.
Jones, D.,
  1942 *Problems of a National Script for India* (Hartford: Hartford Seminary Foundation).
Jones, Frank E., and Wallace E. Lambert,
  1959 "Attitudes toward immigrants in a Canadian community", *Public Opinion Quarterly* 23, 538-546.
Joos, Martin,
  1950 "Description of language design", *Journal of the Acoustical Society of America* 22, 701-708. Reprinted in his *Readings in Linguistics* (Washington, D. C.: American Council of Learned Societies, 1958), 349-356.
  1959 "The isolation of styles", *Georgetown University Monograph Series on Languages and Linguistics* 12, 107-113; also in J. A. Fishman (ed.), *Readings in the Sociology of Language* (The Hague: Mouton, 1968), 185-191.
Kandler, C.,
  1955 "Zum Aufbau der angewandten Sprachwissenschaft", *Sprachforum* 1, 3-9.
Kandori, Takehiko,
  1968 "Study of dialects in Japan", *Orbis* 17, 47-56.
Kantrowitz, Nathan,
  1967 "The vocabulary of race relations in a prison", Paper presented at American Dialect Society Meeting, Chicago, December, 1967.
Kaye, Alan S.,
  1970 "Modern standard Arabic and the colloquials", *Lingua* 24, 374-391.
Kelman, Herbert C.,
  1969 "Language as aid and barrier to involvement in the national system", *Consultative Meeting on Language Planning Processes* (Honolulu: EWC-IAP); subsequently, in Joan Rubin and Bjorn Jernudd (eds.), *Can Language be Planned?* (Honolulu: East-West Center Press, 1971); also in J. A. Fishman (ed.), *Advances in the Sociology of Language* 2 (The Hague: Mouton, 1972).
Kimple, James, Jr., Robert L. Cooper, and Joshua A. Fishman,
  1969 "Language switching in the interpretation of conversations", *Lingua* 23, 127-134.
Kloss, Heinz,
  1929 "Sprachtabellen als Grundlage für Sprachstatistik, Sprachenkarten und für eine allgemaine Soziologie der Sprachgemeinschaften", *Vierteljahrsschrift für Politik und Geschichte* 1(7), 103-117.
  1952 *Die Entwicklung Neuer Germanischer Kultursprachen* (Munich, Pohl).
  1966a "Types of multilingual communities: A discussion of ten variables",

Sociological Inquiry 36, 135-145.
1966b "German-American language maintenance efforts", in J. A. Fishman et al., *Language Loyalty in the United States* (The Hague: Mouton), Chapter 15.
1967 " 'Abstand' languages and 'Ausbau' languages", *Anthropological Linguistics* 9, No. 7, 29-41.

Kluckhohn, Clyde,
1961 "Notes on some anthropological aspects of communication", *American Anthropologist* 63, 895-910.

Knott, Betty I.,
1956 "The Christian 'special language' in the inscriptions", *Vigiliae Christianae* 10, 65-79.

Kohn, Hans,
1945 *The Idea of Nationalism: A Study of its Origin and Background* (New York: Macmillan).

Kolarz, Walter,
1946 *Myths and Realities in Eastern Europe* (London: Lindsay Drummond).
1967 *Russia and her Colonies* (Hamden, Conn.: Archon Books) (originally published in 1952).
1969 *The Peoples of the Soviet Far East* (Hamden, Conn.: Archon Books) (originally: 1954).

Kuhn, Walter,
1930 *Die jungen deutschen Sprachinseln in Galizien: ein Beitrag zur Methode der Sprachinselforschung* (Münster: Aschendorffsche Verlagsbuchhandlung).
1934 *Deutsche Sprachinselforschung* (Plauen: Gunther Wolff).

Kwan-Wai Chiu, Rosaline,
1970 *Language Contact and Language Planning in China (1900-1967); A Selected Bibliography* (Quebec: Les Presses de l'Université Laval).

Labov, William,
1963 "The social motivation of a sound change", *Word* 19, 273-309.
1964 "Phonological correlates of social stratification", *American Anthropologist* 66, No. 2, 164-176.
1965 "On the mechanism of linguistic change", *Georgetown University Monograph Series in Language and Linguistics* 18, 91-114.
1966a "The effect of social mobility on linguistic behavior", *Sociological Inquiry* 36, 186-203.
1966b "Hypercorrection by the lower middle class as a factor in linguistic change", in Wm. Bright (ed.), *Sociolinguistics* (The Hague: Mouton), 84-101.
1966c *The Social Stratification of English in New York City* (Washington: Center for Applied Linguistics).
1966d "Stages in the acquisition of standard English", in Roger W. Shuy (ed.), *Social Dialects and Language Learning* (Champaign: NCTE).
1968 "The reflection of social processes in linguistic structures", in J. A. Fishman (ed.), *Readings in the Sociology of Language* (The Hague: Mouton), 240-251.

Labov, William, Paul Cohen, Clarence Robins, and John Lewis,
1968 *A Study of the Non-Standard English of Negro and Puerto Rican Speakers in New York City*. Final Report, Cooperative Research Project No. 3288 (New York: Columbia University), 2 vols.

Lambert, Wallace E., R. C. Gardner, H. C. Barick, and K. Tunstall,

1963   "Attitudinal and cognitive aspects of intense study of a second language", *Journal of Abnormal and Social Psychology* 66, 358-368.
Lanham, L. W.,
1965   "Teaching English to Africans: A crisis in education", *Optima* 15, December, 197-204.
Lantz, De lee, and Volney Stefflre,
1964   "Language and cognition revisited", *Journal of Abnormal and Social Psychology* 49, 454-462.
Lehmann, A.,
1889   "Uber Wiedererkennen", *Philos. Stud.* 5, 96-156.
Lenneberg, Eric H.,
1953   "Cognition in ethnolinguistics", *Language* 29, 463-471.
1957   "A probabilistic approach to language learning", *Behavioral Science* 2, 1-12.
LePage, Robert,
1964   *The National Language Question* (London: Oxford University Press).
1968   "Problems to be faced in the use of English as the medium of education in four West Indian territories", in J. A. Fishman, C. A. Ferguson and J. Das Gupta (eds.), *Language Problems of Developing Nations* (New York: Wiley), 431-441.
Levine, William L., and H. J. Crockett,
1966   "Speech variation in a Piedmont community: Postvocalic r", *Sociological Inquiry* 36, 204-226.
Lewis, E. Glynn,
1971   "Migration and language in the USSR", *International Migration Review*, 5, no. 2, 147-179; also in J. A. Fishman (ed.), *Advances in the Sociology of Language*, Vol. 2 (The Hague: Mouton, 1972).
Lewis, W. Arthur,
1961   "Education and economic development", *Social and Economic Studies* 10, No. 2, 113-127.
Li Hui,
1960   "The phonetic alphabet – short cut to literacy", *Peking Review* 13, No. 28 (July 12).
Lieberson, Stanley,
1965   "Bilingualism in Montreal: A demographic analysis", *American Journal of Sociology* 71, 10-25; also in J. A. Fishman (ed.), *Advances in the Sociology of Language*, Vol. 2 (The Hague: Mouton, 1972).
1971   "Language shift in the United States: some demographic clues", *International Migration Review* 5, no. 2.
Lind, Andrew W.,
1969   "Race relations in New Guinea", *Current Affairs Bulletin* (Sydney: Australia) 44, No. 3, 34-48.
Lindenfeld, Jacqueline,
1969   "The social conditioning of syntactic variation in French", *American Anthropologist* 71, 890-898; also in J. A. Fishman (ed.), *Advances in the Sociology of Language*, Vol. 2 (The Hague: Mouton, 1972).
Lunt, Horace G.,
1959   "The creation of Standard Macedonian: Some facts and attitudes", *Anthropological Linguistics* 1, No. 5, 19-26.
Ma, Roxana, and Eleanor Herasimchuk,
1968   "The linguistic dimensions of a bilingual neighborhood", in J. A. Fishman, R. L. Cooper and Roxana Ma et al., *Bilingualism in the Barrio*

(New York, Yeshiva University). Final Report to Department of Health, Education and Welfare under Contract No. OEC-1-7-062817-0297; also in J. A. Fishman (ed.), *Advances in the Sociology of Language*, Vol. 2 (The Hague: Mouton, 1972).

Mackey, William F.,
1962 "The description of bilingualism", *Canadian Journal of Linguistics* 7, 51-85.
1970 "A typology of bilingual education", *The Foreign Language Annals* 3, 596-608; also in J. A. Fishman (ed.), *Advances in the Sociology of Language*, Vol. 2 (The Hague: Mouton, 1972).

Macnamara, John,
1966 *Bilingualism in Primary Education* (Edinburgh, Edinburgh University Press).
1967 "The effects of instruction in a weaker language", *Journal of Social Issues* 23, 121-135.
1969 "Successes and failures in the movement for the restoration of Irish", *Consultative Meeting on Language Planning Processes* (Honolulu: EWC-IAP), subsequently in Joan Rubin and Bjorn Jernudd (eds.), *Can Language be Planned?* (Honolulu: East-West Center Press, 1971).

Maier, Norman R. F.,
1930 "Reasoning in humans, I. On direction", *Journal of Comparative Psychology* 10, 115-143.

Manuel, Herschel T.,
1963 *The Preparation and Evaluation of Interlanguage Testing Materials* (Austin: University of Texas). Mimeographed report, Cooperative Research Project Number 681.

Mayner, Thomas F.,
1967 "Language and nationalism in Yugoslavia", *Canadian Slavic Studies* 1, 333-347.

Mazrui, Ali A.,
1967 "The national language question in East Africa", *East Africa Journal*, No. 3, 12-19.

McClusker, Henry F., Jr.,
1963 *An Approach for Educational Planning in the Developing Countries* (Menlo Park: Stanford Research Institute).

McCormack, William,
1960 "Social dialects in Dharwar Kannada", In C. A. Ferguson and J. J. Gumperz (eds.), "Linguistic Diversity in South Asia", *IJAL* 4, No. 1, 79-91.
1968 "Occupation and residence in relation to Dharwar dialects", in M. Singer and B. S. Cohn (eds.), *Social Structure and Social Change in India* (New York: Viking Fund), 475-486.

McDavid, Raven I.,
1958 "The dialects of American English", in W. N. Francis (ed.), *The Structure of American English* (New York: Ronald).

Metraux, Ruth W.,
1965 "A study of bilingualism among children of U.S.-French parents", *French Review* 38, 650-655.

Metzger, Duane, and Gerald E. Williams,
1966 "Some procedures and results in the study of native categories: *Tzeltal* 'firewood' ", *American Anthropologist* 68, 389-407.

Meyenburg, Erwin,
1934   "Der heutige Stand der Romazi-Bewegung in Japan", *Forschungen und Fortschritte* 10, No. 23-24.
Mills, H. C.,
1956   "Language reform in China", *Far Eastern Quarterly* 15, 517-540.
Mohrmann, Christine,
1947   "Le latin commun et le latin des Chretiens", *Vigiliae Christiannae* 1, 1-12.
1957   "Linguistic problems in the Early Christian Church", *Vigiliae Christiannae* 11, 11-36.
Morag, Shelomo,
1959   "Planned and unplanned development in modern Hebrew", *Lingua* 87, 247-263.
Nader, Laura,
1962   "A note on attitudes and the use of language", *Anthropological Linguistics* 4, No. 6, 24-29; also in J. A. Fishman (ed.), *Readings in the Sociology of Language* (The Hague: Mouton, 1968), 276-281.
Nahirny, Vladimir C., and Joshua A. Fishman,
1965   "American immigrant groups: ethnic identification and the problem of generations", *Sociological Review* 13, 311-326.
Nelson, Lowry,
1947   "Speaking of tongues", *American Journal of Sociology* 54, 202-210.
Nguyen dinh Hoa,
1960   *The Vietnamese Language* (Saigon: Department of National Education) (= *Vietnam Culture Series*, No. 2).
Nida, Eugene A.,
1954   "Practical limitations to a phonemic orthography", *Bible Translator* 5, 35-39 and 58-62.
1967   "Sociological dimensions of literacy and literature"; Chapter 11 of Floyd Shacklock et al. (eds.), *World Literacy Manual* (New York: Committee on Literacy and Christian Literature).
Orenstein, Jacob,
1959   "Soviet language policy: Theory and practice", *Slavic and East European Journal* 17, 1-24.
Osgood, Charles E.,
1960   "The cross-cultural generality of visual-verbal-synesthetic tendencies", *Behavioral Science* 5, 146-149.
Owens, Roger C.,
1965   "The patrilocal band: A linguistically and culturally hybrid social unit", *American Anthropologist* 67, 675-690.
Özmen, Yücel,
"A Sociolinguistic Analysis of Language Reform in Turkey 1932-1967, with Special Reference to the Activities of the Turk Dil Kurumu", MS Thesis, Georgetown University, 1967 (unpublished).
Passin, Herbert,
1963   "Writer and journalist in the transitional society", in Lucian W. Pye (ed.), *Communication and Political Development* (Princeton: Princeton University Press), 82-123; also in J. A. Fishman, C. A. Ferguson and J. Das Gupta (eds.), *Language Problems of Developing Nations* (New York: Wiley, 1968), 442-458.
Pike, Kenneth L.,
1947   *Phonemics: A Technique for Reducing Languages to Writing* (Ann

Arbor: University of Michigan Press).

Polome, Edgar,
1968 "The choice of official languages in the Democratic Republic of the Congo", in J. A. Fishman, C. A. Ferguson and J. Das Gupta (eds.), *Language Problems of Developing Countries* (New York: Wiley), 295-312.

Pool, Jonathan,
1969 "National development and language diversity", *La Monda Lingvo-Problemo* 1, 129-192; also in J. A. Fishman (ed.), *Advances in the Sociology of Language*, Vol. 2 (The Hague: Mouton, 1972).

Pospisil, Leopold,
1965 "A formal semantic analysis of substantive law: Kapauka Papuan laws of land tenure", *American Anthropologist* 67, Part 2, 186-214.

Prator, Clifford H.,
1967 "The Survey of Language Use and Language Teaching in Eastern Africa", *Linguistic Reporter* 9, No. 8.

Price, P. David,
1967 "Two types of taxonomy: A Huichol ethnobotanical example", *Anthropological Linguistics* 9, No. 7, 1-28.

Quelquejay, C., and A. Bennigsen,
1961 *The Evolution of the Muslim Nationalities of the USSR and Their Linguistic Problems* (London: Central Asian Research Center).

Rabin, Chaim,
1969 "Spelling reform: Israel, 1968", *Consultative Meeting on Language Planning Processes* (Honolulu: EWC-IAP); subsequently in Joan Rubin, Bjorn Jernudd (eds.), *Can Language be Planned?* (East-West Center Press, 1971).

Radin, Paul,
1924 "The adoptation of an alphabet by an aboriginal people", *Cambridge University Reporter* (Proceedings of the Cambridge Philological Society), Nov. 25, 27-34.

Ramos, Maximo, Jose V. Aguiler and Bonifacio P. Sibayan, *The Determination and Implementation of Language Policy* (= *Philippine Center for Language Study, Monograph 2*) (Quezon City: Alemar-Phoenix).

Ray, Punya Sloka,
1963 *Language Standardization* (Chapter 9: Comparative description and evaluation of writing systems, 106-120) (The Hague: Mouton).

Read, Allen Walker,
1967 "The splitting and coalescing of widespread languages", *Proceedings of the Ninth International Congress of Linguistics*, 1129-1134.

Reissman, Leonard,
1964 *The Urban Process: Cities in Industrial Societies* (New York: Free Press).

Ross, Allan S. C.,
1956 "U and non-U; An essay in sociological linguistics", in N. Mitford (ed.), *Noblesse Oblige* (London, Hamish Hamilton), 11-38.

Rossi, Ettore,
1927 "La questione dell' alfabeto per le lingue turche", *Oriente Moderno* 7, 295-310.
1929 "Il nuovo alfabeto latino introdotto in Turchia", *Oriente Moderno* 9, 32-48.
1935 "La riforma linguistica in Turchia", *Oriente Moderno* 15, 45-57.

1942   "Un decennio di riforma linguistica in Turchia", *Oriente Moderno* 22, 466-477.
1953   "Venticinque anni di rivoluzione dell'alfabeto e venti di riforma linguistica in Turchia", *Oriente Moderno* 33, 378-384.
Royal Commission on Bilingualism and Biculturism,
1965   *A Preliminary Report* (Ottawa, Queen's Printer).
1967   *Book I: General Introduction, The Official Languages* (Ottawa: Queen's Printer).
1968   *Book II: Education* (Ottawa: Queen's Printer).
Rubin, Joan,
1962   "Bilingualism in Paraguay", *Anthropological Linguistics* 4, No. 1, 52-58.
1968   "Language and education ino Paraguay", in J. A. Fishman, C. A. Ferguson and J. Das Gupta (eds.), *Language Problems in Developing Nations* (New York: Wiley), 477-488.
1969   "Education and language planning", *Consultative Meeting on Language Planning Processes* (Honolulu: EWC-IAP), subsequently in Joan Rubin and Bjorn Jernudd (eds.), *Can Language be Planned?* (Honolulu: East-West Center Press, 1971); also in J. A. Fishman (ed.), *Advances in the Sociology of Language*, Vol. 2 (The Hague: Mouton, 1972).
Russell, J. K., "Starting a literacy campaign", *Books for Africa* 18, No. 2, 17-20.
Rustow, Dankwart A.,
1967   *A World of Nations: Problems of Political Modernization* (Washington: Brookings Institution); also, adapted as "Language, modernization and nationhood – an attempt at typology", in J. A. Fishman, C. A. Ferguson and J. Das Gupta (eds.), *Language Problems of Developing Nations* (New York: Wiley, 1968), 87-106.
Samora, Julian, and Wm. N. Deane,
1956   "Language usage as a possible index of acculturation", *Sociology and Social Research* 40, 307-311.
Scharshmidt, Clemens,
1924   "Schriftreform in Japan: Ein Kulturproblem", *Mitteilungen des Seminars für Orientalische Sprachen* 26/27, No. 1, 183-186.
Schegloff, Emanuel A.,
1968   "Sequencing in conversational openings", *American Anthropologist* 70, 1075-1095; also in J. A. Fishman (ed.), *Advances in the Sociology of Language* (The Hague: Mouton, 1971).
Schermerhorn, Richard A.,
1964   "Toward a general theory of minority groups", *Phylon* 25, 238-246.
Schofield, R. S.,
1968   "The Measurement of Literacy in Pre-Industrial England", in Jock Goody (ed.), *Literacy in Traditional Societies* (London: Cambridge University Press).
Shnore, Leo,
1966   "The rural-urban variable: An urbanite's perspective", *Rural Sociology* 21, 137.
Selk, Paul,
1937   *Die sprachlichen Verhaltnisse im deutsch-dänischen Sprachgebiet südlich der Grenze* (Flensburg: Verlag Heimat und Erbe) (Erganzungsband, 1940).
Serdyuchenko, G. P.,
1962   "The eradication of illiteracy and the creation of new written languages

in the USSR", *International Journal of Adult and Youth Education* 14, 1, 23-29.

1965   *Elimination of illiteracy among the people who had no Alphabets* (Moscow, USSR: Commission for UNESCO, Ministry of Education, RSFSR), 16 pp.

Serruys, Paul L. M.,

1962   *Survey of the Chinese Language Reform and the Anti-Illiteracy Movement in Communist China* (= *Studies in Communist Chinese Terminology*, No. 8) (Berkeley: Center for Chinese Studies, UC-B).

Shuy, Roger W. (ed.),

1966   *Social Dialects and Language Learning* (Champaign: NCTE).

Sjoberg, Andree F.,

1964   "Writing, speech and society: Some changing interrelationships", in *Proceedings of the Ninth International Congress of Linguists* (The Hague: Mouton), 892-897.

1966   "Socio-cultural and linguistic factors in the development of writing systems for preliterate peoples", in Wm. Bright (ed.), *Sociolinguistics* (The Hague: Mouton), 260-276.

Smalley, William A.,

1964   *Orthography Studies: Articles on New Writing Systems* (London: United Bible Societies) (Help for Translators, Vol. 6).

Smith, Alfred G.,

"Literacy Promotion in an Underdeveloped Area", Madison, University of Wisconsin, Unpublished Ph.D. thesis, 1956.

Sorensen, Arthur P., Jr.,

1967   "Multilingualism in the Northwest Amazon", *American Anthropologist* 69, 670-684.

Spencer, John (ed.),

1963   *Language in Africa* (Cambridge: Cambridge University Press).

Stern, Theodore,

1968   "Three Pwo Karen scripts: A study of alphabet formation", *Anthropological Linguistics* 10, No. 1, 1-39.

Stewart, Gail,

1967   "Present-day usage of the Vai script in Liberia", *African Language Review* 7, 71-74.

Stewart, Wm. A.,

1964   *Non-Standard Speech and the Teaching of English* (Washington: Center for Applied Linguistics).

1965   "Sociolinguistic factors affecting English teaching", in Roger W. Shuy (ed.), *Social Dialects and Language Learning* (Champaign: NCTE), 10-18.

1968   "A sociolinguistics typology for describing national multilingualism", in J. A. Fishman (ed.), *Readings in the Sociology of Language* (The Hague: Mouton), 531-545.

Szajkowski, Zosa,

1966   *Catalogue of the exhibition on the history of Yiddish orthography from the spelling rules of the early sixteenth century to the standardized orthography of 1936* (New York: Yivo Institute for Jewish Research).

Tabouret-Keller, Andree,

1968   "Sociological factors of language maintenance and language shift: A methodological approach based on European and African examples", in J. A. Fishman, C. A. Ferguson and J. Das Gupta (eds.), *Language Problems of Developing Nations* (New York: Wiley), 107-118.

Tanner, Nancy,
1967 "Speech and society among the Indonesian elite: A case study of a multilingual community", *Anthropological Linguistics* 9, No. 3, 15-40.

Tauli, Valter,
1968 *Introduction to a Theory of Language Planning* (Uppsala: Acta Universitatis Upsaliensis (= *Studia Philologiae Scandinavicae Upsaliensia*).

Thompson, Laurence C.,
1965 *A Vietnamese Grammar* (Seattle: University of Washington Press).

Thorburn, Thomas,
1969 "Cost-benefit analysis in language planning", *Consultative Meeting on Language Planning Processes* (Honolulu: EWC-IAP); subsequently in Joan Rubin and Bjorn Jernudd (eds.), *Can Language be Planned?* (Honolulu: East West Center Press, 1971); also in J. A. Fishman (ed.), *Advances in the Sociology of Language* (The Hague: Mouton, 1972).

Tietze, Andreas,
1962 "Problems of Turkish lexicography", *IJAL* 28, no. 2, part 4, 263-272 (= Publication no. 21 of Indiana Univ. Center of Anthropology, Folklore and Linguistics).

Toshio, Yamada,
1967 "The writing system: Historical research and modern development", *Current Trends in Linguistics* 2, 693-731.

Trager, George L.,
1959 "The systematization of the Whorf hypothesis", *Anthropological Linguistics* 1, No. 1, 31-35.

Twadell, W. I.,
1959 "Standard German", *Anthropological Linguistics* 1, No. 3, 1-7.

UNESCO,
1951 *The Haiti Pilot Project* (Paris: UNESCO).

Vachek, Joseph,
1945-1949 "Some remarks on writing and phonetic transcription", *Acta Linguistica* (Copenhagen), 5, 86-93.
1948 "Written language and printed language", *Recueil Linguistique de Bratislava* 1, 67-75. Reprinted in J. Vachek (ed.), *A Prague School Reader in Linguistics* (Bloomington: Indiana University Press, 1964), 453-560.

Valdman, Albert,
1968 "Language standardization in a diglossia situation: Haiti", in J. A. Fishman, C. A. Ferguson and J. Das Gupta (eds.), *Language Problems of Developing Nations* (New York: Wiley), 313-326.

Verdoodt, Albert,
1971 "The differential impact of immigrant French speakers on indigenous German speakers: A case study in the light of two theories", *International Migration Review*, 5, no. 2, 138-146; also in J. A. Fishman (ed.), *Advances in the Sociology of Language*, Vol. 2 (The Hague: Mouton, 1972).

Walker, Willard,
1969 "Notes on native writing systems and the design of native literacy programs", *Anthropological Linguistics* 11, No. 5, 148-166.

Ward, Ida C.,
1945 *Report of an Investigation of some Gold Coast Language Problems* (London: Crown Agents for the Colonies).

Weinreich, Max,
 1953 "Yidishkayt and Yiddish: On the impact of religion on language in Ashkenazic Jewry", in *Mordecai M. Kaplan Jubilee Volume* (New York: Jewish Theological Seminary of America); also in J. A. Fishman (ed.), *Readings in the Sociology of Language* (The Hague: Mouton, 1968), 382-413.
 1967 "The reality of Jewishness versus the ghetto myth: The sociolinguistic roots of Yiddish", in *To Honor Roman Jacobson* (The Hague: Mouton), 2199-2211.

Weinreich, Uriel,
 1951 "Research problems in bilingualism, with special reference to Switzerland". Unpublished Ph.D. dissertation. Columbia University.
 1953a *Languages in Contact* (New York: Linguistic Circle of New York).
 1953b "The Russification of Soviet Minority Languages", *Problems of Communism* 2(6), 46-57.
 1962 "Multilingual Dialectology and the New Yiddish Atlas", *Anthropological Linguistics* 4, No. 1, 6-22.

White, John K.,
 1962 "On the revival of printing in the Cherokee language", *Current Anthropology* 3, 511-514.

Whiteley, W. H.,
 1968 "Ideal and reality in national language policy: A case study from Tanzania", in J. A. Fishman, C. A. Ferguson and J. Das Gupta (eds.), *Language Problems of Developing Nations* (New York: Wiley), 327-344.

Whorf, Benjamin L.,
 1940 "Science and linguistics", *Technology Review* 44, 229-231, 247-248.
 1941 "The relation of habitual thought to behavior and to language", in L. Speier (ed.), *Language, Culture and Personality* (Menasha, Wisc.: Sapir Memorial Publication Fund), 75-93.

Willems, Emilio,
 1943 "Linguistic changes in German-Brazilian communities", *Acta Americana* 1, 448-463.

Winner, T. G.,
 1952 "Problems of Alphabetic Reform among the Turkic Peoples of Soviet Central Asia", *Slavonic and East European Review*, 132-147.

Wittermans, Elizabeth P.,
 1967 "Indonesian terms of address in a situation of rapid social change", *Social Forces* 46, 48-52.

Wolff, Hans,
 1954 *Nigerian Orthography* (Zaria: Gaskiya Corp.).

Wolfram, Walter A.,
 1969 *A Sociolinguistic Description of Detroit Negro Speech* (Washington: Center for Applied Linguistics).

Wonderly, William L.,
 1968 *Bible Translation for Popular Use* (London: United Bible Societies).

Wu Yu-Chang,
 1956 "Concerning the (draft) Han Language Phonetization Plan", *Current Background*, No. 380 (March 15), 4-20.
 1964 "Widening the use of the phonetic script", *China Reconstructs* 13, No. 6, 29-31.
 1965 "Report of the current tasks of reforming the written language and the

draft scheme for a Chinese phonetic alphabet", in *Reform of the Chinese Written Language* (Peking: Foreign Language Press).

Wurm, S. A.,
1966   "Language and literacy", in E. K. Fisk (ed.), *New Guinea on the Threshold* (Canberra: Australian National University), 135-148.

Wurm, S. A., and D. C. Laycock,
1961/62   "The question of language and dialect in New Guinea", *Oceania* 32, 128-143.

Young, R. R.,
1944   "An adult literacy campaign in Sierra Leone", *Oversea Education* 15, No. 3, 97-100.

SUBJECT INDEX

Abstand, 229
Address
  deferential address, 39
Address forms
  American English, 17-24
  Bisayan, 23, 24
  English, 22, 23
  Korean, 23
  Puerto Rican, 26, 27f
  Russian, 24, 25f
  variant, 58
  Yiddish, 24, 25f, 26
Address systems, 17-29
  two-choice, 24-29
  learning of, 28
Address terms, 118, 345, 346-348
  Russian, 119
  Japanese, 119
  Korean, 119
African scripts, 356-357
African vernaculars and French orthography, 356-357
Allomorphs, 375
American
  German, 39
  Greek, 39
  standard, 233
Anglification, 299
Anglo-Irish, 193
Arabic
  bipolar kin terms in, 58, 259

  classical, 290
  colloquial, 51
  vernacular, 290
Arabization, 358
Armenian alphabet, 357
Ascription, 236
Asian scripts, 357
Assimilation, 102, 111
Attitudes
  towards language, 228-232
  language attitudes vs. language use, 330
  social attitudes towards speech, 206
  towards speech diversity, 230-231
Ausbau, 230
Autonomy, 229, 231f

Behavior
  attitudinal-affective, 331-332
  toward language, 330-331
  normative, 200
Behavioral implementation, 332-333
Bilingualism, 45, 61, 94, 103-106, 298, 299
  coordinate vs. compound, 304-305
  degree of, 302-303, 337
  vs. diglossia, 295, 297, 298
  without diglossia, 295-298
  as group phenomenon, 104
  and intelligence, 297
  interference in, 302, 304

NAME INDEX

ADVANCES IN THE SOCIOLOGY OF LANGUAGE

Volume II: Selected Studies and Applications

Edited by Joshua A. Fishman

CONTENTS

Preface by Joshua A. Fishman

CONTENTS OF VOLUME II
(continued)

Section III: Bilingual and Diglossia

Section IV: Language Maintenance and Language Shift

Section V: Applied Sociology of Language: Policy, Planning and Practice

1972 – 534 pages – ISBN: 90-279-2302-7 (paperback)
'Contributions to the Sociology of Language', Vol. 2

MOUTON PUBLISHERS · THE HAGUE · PARIS